To my wonderful family,
Sonje, Todd, April, Chris, Ben and Dusty

Coal Tipple, Sunshine *(drawing by Julia McMillan)*

Acknowledgements

Thanks goes to LaVonne Ewing for her cover and book design. Many thanks goes to the patient staff at the Colorado Historical Society and the Denver Public Library. In addition, thanks goes to my readers Sandy Perlic, Mary Edelmaier, Mike and Sylvia Arnold, Phyllis Tegtman, Sonje Jessen and Christine Skellett. For her fine illustrations, I would also like to thank Julia McMillan.

About The Author

This is Kenneth Jessen's tenth book; other works include *Railroads of Northern Colorado, Thompson Valley Tales, Eccentric Colorado, Colorado Gunsmoke, Bizarre Colorado, Estes Park - A Quick History, Georgetown - A Quick History, An Ear in His Pocket* and *Ghost Towns, Colorado Style Volume One.* Ken is also author of well over 550 published articles plus several booklets. His column on Colorado ghost towns has been featured in the Loveland *Reporter-Herald* for two years. He is a life member of the Colorado Railroad Museum, a long time member of the Rocky Mountain Railroad Club, a member of the Colorado Historical Society and one of the founders of the Western Outlaw-Lawman History Association. He also belongs to the San Luis Valley Historical Society. Ken owns and operates J. V. Publications.

Ken spent thirty-three years as an engineer for Hewlett-Packard. Now retired, Ken continues to work part-time as a system design engineer.

Sonje Jessen, Ken's wife, was a major contributor to this book and acted as editorial consultant. She was also instrumental in locating and photographing many of the ghost towns on various field trips.

Ken and Sonje live in Loveland, Colorado.

GHOST TOWNS

Colorado Style

VOLUME TWO
CENTRAL REGION

KENNETH JESSEN

J. V. Publications

2212 Flora Ct.
Loveland, Colorado 80537

Ghost Towns, Colorado Style
Volume Two - Central Region
Copyright © 1999 by Kenneth Jessen

Published by J. V. Publications, 2212 Flora Ct., Loveland, CO 80537

First Edition

2 3 4 5 6 7 8 9

Library of Congress Catalog Card Number: 98-66536
ISBN 0-9611662-9-0 (pbk.)

Printed in the United States of America

Book designed by LaVonne Ewing; produced by LaVonne Ewing and Candace Harron. Front and Back Cover Photographs of St. Elmo by Greg Beam. Illustrations by Julia McMillan and Kenneth Jessen. Maps drawn by Kenneth Jessen. Contemporary photography by Kenneth Jessen, Sonje Jessen and Greg Beam. Photographic processing and printing by Gerards; digital imaging by Superior One Hour Photo.

THE AREAS OF

GHOST TOWNS
Colorado Style

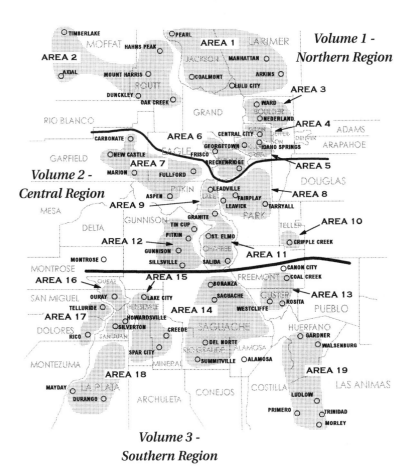

Volume 1 -
Northern Region

Volume 2 -
Central Region

Volume 3 -
Southern Region

The Three Volumes Of

GHOST TOWNS

Colorado Style

Volume One - Northern Region
ISBN: 0-9611662-8-2

Includes the following counties:
Boulder, Clear Creek, Gilpin, Grand, Jackson, Larimer,
Moffat, Routt and Summit

Volume Two - Central Region
ISBN: 0-9611662-9-0

Includes the following counties:
Chaffee, Eagle, Garfield, Gunnison, Lake, Park, Pitkin and Teller

Volume Three - Southern Region
ISBN: 0-9611662-4-x

Includes the following counties:
Conejos, Costilla, Custer, Dolores, Fremont, Hindsdale,
Huerfano, Las Animas, La Plata, Mineral, Ouray, Rio Grande,
Saguache, San Juan and San Miguel

VOLUME TWO - CENTRAL REGION

Table of Contents

vii

Organization Of This Book

This three-volume book is broken into areas, an area being similar to a chapter. In most cases, an area is a single Colorado County. In this volume, an area consists of twenty to sixty ghost towns, abandoned mining camps plus some occupied towns. Most of the sites within an area can be visited in one or two days. Contemporary and historic photographs are combined to provide a perspective of how a given town once appeared and how it looks today.

An overall map plus a table of contents is presented at the beginning of an area. Each area has its own introduction with short stories about people and events that shaped that area's history. After the introduction, the story of each town is presented in alphabetical order.

Each town history starts with a summary of its general location, accessibility, and if any of its historic structures are still standing. Within the text are facts on how the town was named, when it was founded, and if it had its own post office. The text may also include the peak population along with an estimate of the number of structures, and a general description of the businesses and schools. For a town that has vanished, a chronology of its disappearance may be included, based on the observations of other historians. For towns that are difficult to locate, maps are included to guide the adventurous.

For some readers, it is important to know where the information on an individual town came from, and endnotes present the source material for each story.

Research For This Project

Every possible reliable source of information, which added to the knowledge about a particular town, was consulted. Some sources, where the research was not performed well, were intentionally ignored, while others were used to distill the history of a particular site. In some cases, newspaper articles were used, however, reliable secondary sources of information dominate the material. To provide some insight as to which sites remain physically, the author and his wife visited most of the sites included in this work.

The basis for the maps are field trips combined with United States Geological Survey topographic maps. In some cases, Trails West maps and the Colorado Atlas & Gazetteer were consulted to verify road locations and numbers.

INTRODUCTION

This book, presented in three volumes, concentrates on towns and mining camps in the Colorado mountains. The first volume covers the northern region, this volume covers the central region, and the third volume covers the southern region of the state. The emphasis is placed on towns that are completely or partially abandoned, but other towns, important to the region's history, are also included.

What's A Ghost Town?

Just the mention of a ghost town seems to peak the interest of many people. It is among the most romantic historical topics Colorado has to offer. How could a once thriving boomtown be abandoned and fall to ruin? Many have disappeared leaving hardly a trace. What happened to the tens of thousands of people? Some towns were abandoned only to be re-populated, then abandoned again. There are well over 400 ghost town sites in the Colorado mountains, most associated with the mining industry. Their varied and interesting history is covered in these volumes.

The term "ghost town" is applied liberally to describe practically any mountain town, mining camp or even random collection of shanties which, at some point in time, was abandoned. Even the use of the word "town" is misleading since many of these places did not have the structure normally associated with a town such as a post office, stores, hotels, schools and some type of government. A ghost town could also be a town that was a ghost of its former self. Some ghost towns could better be referred to as camps, since they were never anything more than a collection of cabins and tents scattered near a mine. Despite arguments over definitions, there are interesting stories behind these locations.

Many towns and camps were never officially surveyed or registered, much less incorporated. Their existence may yet be verified. "New" ghost towns have been found during recent years in some of the more remote areas of the state. Real estate developers have been around for a long time, and there are sites that were surveyed, promoted, given names and even presented on maps, although not a single structure was ever built. In many cases, a group of nameless cabins high on a mountainside will remain anonymous. Some smaller, less important camp will appear in numerous ghost town books because it had a name.

Changes in the mountain economy, especially after World War II, have drastically altered the fate of many abandoned towns. Breckenridge, Frisco and Keystone, with brand new buildings and fully occupied, hardly seem like former ghost towns. At one time, however, they were nearly abandoned. For example, the old cabins in Gold Hill, Whitepine and Platoro have been restored and meet the demand for mountain property. This book deals with traditional ghost towns as well as those rejuvenated by changes in the economy.

Most town sites were withdrawn from public lands long ago. This is called "preemption," meaning that the right to purchase a specific piece of government land is given ahead of others. Where a plat or drawing for a town was filed, the preemption took effect. Title to individual lots were sold, and through generations of owners, most remain private property. Within the information on a given town, this book delineates from those accessible by the public from those where access is limited by private property.

Most mining towns and camps are directly associated with the recovery of gold and silver. There were also important Colorado towns that were based on mining coal, uranium, copper, iron, molybdenum, gypsum, stone and other minerals. There are other towns which acted as supply points to the mining towns where freighting was important to the economy. Although not covered in this book, there is a whole category of ghost towns based on failed attempts at agricultural colonies.

The mental picture of a ghost town is a group of ram-shackled abandoned cabins set in a deep, forested valley high in the mountains where the only noise is the wind. There are certainly picturesque places like this, but one disappointment is that few traces remain of most of Colorado's true ghost towns. Some were destroyed by fire never to be rebuilt, others were built in an avalanche track and were eventually leveled, and still others fell victim to vandals. Wooden buildings are biodegradable, and a century of high winds and heavy snow claimed the majority of structures. Large trees have grown in the middle of many an old cabin, and the forest has hidden others from view. There are several cases where buildings from one town were simply moved a short distance to form a new town. Even heavy two-story log buildings were skidded to other sites.

At the rate structures are vanishing, precious little will be left of Colorado's ghost towns for the next generation, and it is a case of ashes to ashes and dust to dust. Where once destructive mining practices stripped the land barren of vegetation, the natural healing process is restoring the land. After the passage of another century, the land will again look like it did prior to human invasion.

A simplification of the early demographic history of Colorado goes something like this: gold or silver was discovered, thousands of prospectors poured into the area, towns were established and gained instant population. When the ore was exhausted, the prospectors moved on, abandoning the town just like in the musical Paint Your Wagon. If a new strike was made, the once abandoned town would be repopulated. Sometimes the mines closed because of the difficulty processing the ore. If a new smelting process was introduced, then a once abandoned site may again flourish. Colorado society during the 1860s through the 1880s was very mobile, and the majority of people were willing to pick up and move on a moment's notice. There was little loyalty to a particular town.

Surprising reversals of fortune include the town of

Nevadaville, which was at one time larger than Denver or its neighbor, Central City. Nevadaville is almost a ghost town today, and a very small fraction of its original buildings are left standing. It is a challenge to find any remains, dilapidated or not, of Parkville. At one time, it was the Summit County Seat and the largest town in the region. It had three theaters and its own mint for gold coins. There is little left of the Garfield County Seat of Carbonate, located on a high plateau north of Glenwood Springs. Oro City, the forerunner to Leadville, had a population of 10,000, yet hardly a stick of wood remains. A single rusted metal sign marks its location. Dayton was the Lake County Seat, and when the ore was exhausted in the area mines, it was abandoned. Dayton was discovered by tourists wanting a peaceful place to relax and was reborn as Twin Lakes. The town sites of Ruedi, Montgomery and old Dillon are under reservoirs. Victims of avalanches, Masontown, Tomichi and Woodstock, were never rebuilt.

Unusual names are pervasive among Colorado's ghost towns, such as Sky City and Spook City near Del Norte or Royal Flush, northeast of Hahns Peak. Near Hahns Peak, a town nicknamed "Bugtown" was founded. West of Boulder there was a camp called Puzzler, and not too far away in Gilpin County, Wideawake was named by alert miners. Mosquito got its name when the flattened remains of that insect were found on the blank line where the name of the town was to have been filled in by its settlers. Orient was located in the northeast corner of the San Luis Valley, and Bachelor City sat in a flat above Creede. The remains of Pieplant are located northeast of the Taylor Reservoir. Stringtown, located near Leadville, still shows up on contemporary maps. It was located between Jacktown and Bucktown, but well below Stumptown.

It is the sincere hope of the author that you find this book entertaining and yet informative.

Kenneth Jessen
2212 Flora Court
Loveland, CO 80537

AREA SEVEN

Eagle, Garfield and Pitkin Counties

continued

AREA 7: Eagle, Garfield and Pitkin Counties
Selected Towns

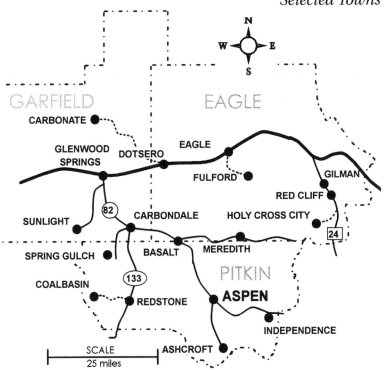

Introduction to Eagle, Garfield and Pitkin Counties

This area is composed of a wide variety of towns founded for different reasons. Along the Frying Pan River, for example, the towns were closely associated with the construction of the Colorado Midland Railway. Many of these towns were based on quarry operations for limestone, gypsum or sandstone. At the upper end of the Frying Pan was the ghost town of Sellar, where workers cut trees and made charcoal for use in the smelters.

The Jerome Park area west of Carbondale was the location of several coal mining towns, among them Spring Gulch and

Marion. Another town, Sunlight, was in the Fourmile Creek drainage directly over a low ridge from Jerome Park. Cardiff, immediately south of Glenwood Springs, was supported by the coke industry using coal hauled down from Jerome Park. North of Grand Junction, far removed from the Jerome Park coal deposits is the ghost town of Carpenter. Another coal mining area was near Redstone and included Placita and Coalbasin. Coal was hauled by rail to Redstone for conversion to coke. Redstone survived the end of the coal mining era, and there are a couple of buildings at Placita. Coalbasin is devoid of structures, yet this small valley was once filled with homes, a store and mine buildings.

Aspen's silver mines supported great wealth. Even after the United States abandoned the silver standard in 1893 and the price of silver fell, Aspen's mines continued to produce millions of dollars. Satellite towns included Ashcroft, Highland, Ruby, Independence, Lenado and others.

Fulford, in Eagle County, was an isolated case of mineralization. The town now serves a seasonal population. Many of its original buildings have been restored. Upper Fulford, a short distance from Fulford, was a community of cabins. Little is left to see except the remains of cabins a few logs high.

Carbonate, high in the Flat Tops, was an isolated case of mineralization and didn't last long. Its primary claim to fame was that it became the Garfield County seat. In just a few months, Glenwood Springs took the title and the records were moved.

The best preserved ghost towns in this area are Ashcroft, Ruby and Independence. The buildings in Ashcroft and Independence have been stabilized, while some of the structures in Ruby are privately owned and have been restored for seasonal use. Fulford is also worth visiting, but access to its structures is limited by private property. Most of the area's coal mining towns, such as Spring Gulch, Sunlight and Marion, are true ghost towns. Even though Cardiff is occupied, the schoolhouse appears to be the only original structure. Along the Frying Pan River there were a number of towns and some still have their original buildings.

B. Clark Wheeler

If ever there was a wheeler-dealer, it was B. Clark Wheeler. He was a professional boomer, and his career was marginal at best. After receiving a degree at the University of Pennsylvania, he became a teacher, then a high school principal. He switched to the study of law, and when he came West, he became a self-proclaimed mining engineer. His final title was that of "professor." A promoter of endless energy, he dressed as an explorer or prospector and exclaimed in a loud voice, cigar in hand, how great Aspen's mineral wealth was to anyone who would listen. He spent a great deal of time in the eastern part of the United States raising investor's hopes.

When he came to the Aspen area from Leadville over Hunter's Pass on snowshoes during the winter of 1879-1880, he had with him from the Surveyor General of Colorado an official document to survey a town site along the Roaring Fork. He represented Cincinnati investors who apparently had already plunked down a substantial amount of money on mining property and now wanted to see what they had gotten in return.

An informal mining camp called Ute City already existed, but Wheeler ignored its existence and went ahead in five feet of snow and staked out a new town. He wrote across the sketch "Aspen" for the many aspen trees that surrounded the location.

Wheeler returned to Leadville and reported back to the investors he represented. The Aspen Town & Land Company was formed using the new plat officially on file at the state offices. When the spring of 1880 arrived, the town was ready to move from the primitive mining camp of Ute City to the full-fledged town of Aspen. Aspen was destined to become the largest, richest and most important town in Pitkin County.

B. Clark Wheeler was not always popular and tried to sell the water from Ute Springs which had previously been set aside as a public water supply. He diverted its output into his own ditch. Aspen had grown to 3,800 people and needed a reliable supply of domestic water. Wheeler claimed a monopoly on all water by virtue of his ownership of the Aspen Ice and Water Company. Aspen was able to work around these problems and develop an independent water supply.

There are also stories of Wheeler's generosity. At one time, he purchased all of the candy in town. He had it put into bags, hired a wagon and distributed it to Aspen's children. When he was interested in seeing a particular candidate win an election, or when he was running for office, he went from saloon to saloon. He tossed a twenty dollar gold piece on the counter to buy all of the patrons drinks and without waiting for change, walked to the next establishment. Aspen's saloons were so numerous that such an act required enough gold to break a bank.

Wheeler also owned the *Aspen Times*, perfect for the kind of promotions he practiced.

B. Clark Wheeler set out to gain control over one of the area's best mines, the Little Annie. He already owned a few shares of stock, but not nearly the 51% needed to gain control. Shortly before the stockholders meeting, he ran an ad in his *Aspen Times* offering to purchase shares at more than the market value. When the number of sellers fell short of the amount he needed, he ran another ad at a higher price.

Mine management laughed their heads off at this frantic effort. When the stockholders meeting took place, they were no longer laughing. Wheeler gained controlling interest and replaced all of the management with people he selected. He named himself as president. He then moved all of the company files, plus the safe, to his newspaper office.

The going wage for a miner was $3.00 a day. Wheeler managed to pay his miners $1.50 a day with the addition of eight shares of stock in the Little Annie valued at a quarter each. To the miners, it looked liked they made $3.50 a day.

In the 1892 election, Wheeler ran on the Populist ticket. This party believed in the unlimited coinage of silver by the United State government. He won the office of state senator.

John Cleveland and Alma Regina Osgood

Much has been written about the Osgoods, but this section will be confined to their life at Redstone. The couple developed a keen interest in the miners and their families. The Osgoods were wealthy beyond all means, and John was head of Colorado Fuel & Iron, the largest industry in Colorado. He controlled a steel mill, several railroads and thirty mining towns, and had 15,000 employees.

He and his wife settled in Redstone after it became a C. F. & I. town. Mrs. Osgood organized lavish Christmas parties for the children of the workers. She encouraged the children to write Santa. The letters were delivered

The life of John C. Osgood was intertwined with the Colorado Fuel & Iron Company. Osgood, its president, was possibly the most powerful industrialist in Colorado during the early years of this century. *(Denver Public Library, Western History Department F16607)*

to Mrs. Osgood who made many a child's dream come true by traveling each year to New York City and purchasing gifts.

She traveled among the people who lived in Redstone and was quite approachable. Any time she detected that a family needed help, she saw to it that they received what they needed. This was especially true for health-related problems. She became known locally as "Lady Bountiful." Another side to this woman was her riding ability and the fact that she was a crack shot. Many of the trophies displayed at the Osgood mansion, Cleveholm, were hers.

John C. Osgood set up a Sociological Department within C. F. & I. under the direction of Dr. Richard Corwin. The areas included in its charter were education, social training, industrial training, housing and communication. Kindergartens were introduced to the C. F. & I. mining towns, and each town had a grade school. The company also owned stores in these towns which accepted the scrip the miners were paid.

Redstone was to be a model for all the rest of the camps. Each Redstone worker received a new home of a standard design. The architectural styles were varied and pastel paint colors were changed from home to home to provide variety and to eliminate the look of a typical company town. The homes included lawns, a garden and white picket fence. Running water and electricity was supplied to each home. Redstone miners enjoyed what was probably the highest standard of living among Colorado's working class. Company homes built in other C. F. & I. towns were not as elaborate.

The Redstone Club, described in more detail in "Redstone and its Club," was grand in all respects. It provided the miner the finest

Alma Regina Osgood, John C. Osgood's second wife, took an interest in the families of the workers who lived in Redstone. For her generosity, she was known as "Lady Bountiful." *(Denver Public Library, Western History Department F18723)*

facility in which to shower, then relax after a hard day. Redstone also had a well-stocked library with books donated by the Osgoods.

Although some consider this style of management social manipulation, Osgood, never the less, brought a previously unheard of level of comfort and security to his workers. Other Colorado coal towns not under C. F. & I. control could better be described as shanty towns lacking even sanitation.

Despite these efforts, C. F. & I. miners walked off their jobs in 1903 demanding recognition for the United Mine Workers Union. The social experiment ended.

After stepping down as head of C. F. & I., Osgood went on to other ventures including the development of marble quarries south of Redstone. He left Redstone and his mansion for 12 years to return in 1925 with his third wife, Lucille. She was just twenty-five, and he was in his seventies. He was very ill with cancer and died in 1926, leaving his entire estate to her.

Sylvia Ruland, *The Lion of Redstone*, Johnson Books, Boulder, Colorado, 1981, pp. 27, 29, 34, 43, 50-55, 106-108.

Frank L. Wentworth, *Aspen on the Roaring Fork*, Francis B. Rizzari (publisher), 1950, pp. 22-33.

Malcolm J. Rohrbough, *Aspen*, Oxford University Press, New York, 1986, pp. 20-22, 30-31, 77, 217.

ASHCROFT
Worth a Visit

- *Pitkin County, Castle Creek drainage*
- *Accessible by paved road*
- *Town had a post office; many abandoned structures still standing*

The old hotel in Ashcroft, as it looked in 1935, has since been stabilized and remains standing. *(Denver Public Library, Western History Department X-5347)*

One of the best-preserved ghost towns in Colorado is Ashcroft. Many of its original buildings sit along its main street as a reminder of things past. A parking lot and trail through the town constructed by the Forest Service provide easy access. Interpretive signs allow visitors to learn about Ashcroft's past.

In 1879, a group of prospectors from Crested Butte came over Pearl Pass into the headwaters of Castle Creek and found rich pockets of native gold. The following year, Amos Kindt and Charles Culver traveled down to the confluence of Express Creek and Castle Creek and spent the winter. They started a town called

Castle Forks City. Another source credits the establishment of Castle Forks City to a Leadville prospector named William Coxhead. Coxhead presumably filed a placer claim and then struck a vein of rich ore at a place he named the Highland Mary. He lost interest in the town and sold out to T. E. Ashcraft.

Ashcraft and his associates took over the town site in 1881 and began to promote the sale of lots. They didn't like the name Castle Forks City and changed it to Ashcroft. (It is not known why it wasn't spelled "Ashcraft.") About 200 people settled in the new town during that year, and the population increased to 500 the following year. By some accounts, Ashcroft's population reached 2,000 in 1883, and in 1885, it topped out at 3,500. Both of these population estimates seem high relative to the town's physical size.

Like Coxhead, Ashcraft lost interest in the town and left to concentrate on prospecting and mining. In August, 1880, Ashcroft got its own post office, and its name was changed to Chloride a year later. Then it was changed back to Ashcroft and remained active until 1912.

The *Rocky Mountain News* reported in 1882 that fifteen men were at work clearing and grading the new street. At this time, hotels were being constructed. Rich silver ore was found in the nearby drainages which boosted the camp's development. Trails were constructed for long pack trains to bring supplies to the high mines and ore down with the return trip. The Tam O'Shanter-Montezuma claim was the richest southwest of Ashcroft. Several men leased the claim, and converted into today's terms, some two million dollars were removed before the lease expired.

Ashcroft once rivaled Aspen in size and importance. Frank Hall wrote, "Ashcroft, fourteen miles from Aspen, is a mining district that one day will prove a valuable auxiliary to the main center of mineral production. Its inaccessibility has prevented extended development, though its veins are large..."

Access to Ashcroft was via Taylor Pass where wagons had to be disassembled and lowered over a cliff. Independence Pass, because of its altitude and lingering snow, was not much better.

In 1882, a wagon road was constructed over Pearl Pass to the railroad at Crested Butte. Using this pass, stage service to Ashcroft started this same year.

Town lots in Ashcroft sold for $50 each. According to the *Aspen Times*, a half dozen new homes were built, and the town had four stores, four saloons, a meat market, real estate office, surveyor's office, two assay offices, shoe shop, hotel, bakery, plus a number of tents. Judge Waite and his son constructed a log newspaper office for the *Ashcroft Journal.* Its first issue was June 2, 1881.

The final hope for Ashcroft as a major economic center faded in 1887 when the Denver & Rio Grande Railroad built into Aspen. No plans were announced to extend the railroad up Castle Creek to Ashcroft, and the town began to lose population. Some log homes were skidded down the dozen miles along Castle Creek to Aspen. Newspaper reports indicate, however, that Ashcroft didn't die and held a Fourth of July celebration in 1888.

The mines around Ashcroft produced a silver-lead ore. As the depth of the mines increased, the ore became more complex and was mixed with zinc, making milling expensive. This factor would spell the end for Ashcroft.

One of Colorado's most famous mining men was H. A. W. Tabor. His luck ran out at the Tam O'Shanter-Montezuma claim above Ashcroft. The mine did have some good returns during the 1890s, but fell far short of the estimated twelve million Tabor poured into the property. Pack trains were still hauling ore from this mine in 1895, and the property was finally sold in 1906.

At a camp called Kellogg, south of Ashcroft, a smelter was constructed to process ore. Another smelter was constructed in Ashcroft which was later purchased by Tabor and his associates. But these smelters were not enough to keep the economy of the area going.

H. A. W. Tabor made frequent trips to Ashcroft and, in 1883, arrived with his new wife, Baby Doe. For this particular trip, a celebration was staged for Tabor complete with a banquet followed by a ball. Part of the ghost town legend was that Tabor bought drinks for everyone in all of Ashcroft's thirteen saloons.

By 1890, Ashcroft was in decline, and most businesses had already closed except for Felix Kinney's grocery store. A restaurant also remained open. In 1912 the post office closed, and only Dan's Bar, owned by Daniel McArthur, remained in business. Daniel became the town's last resident, and when he passed away in 1939, Ashcroft became a ghost town.

As to its state of preservation, Muriel Sibell Wolle wrote during the late 1940s in *Stampede to Timberline*, "It has stood lonely and unspoiled for years, the grass growing high in the main street and the deer flies feasting gluttonously on any chance visitor ... Store after store lines the principal street, each in a different state of disintegration. The roof of one is caved in; the false front of another is striped of its cornice and presents a bare upthrust palisade of boards; a third has shuttered windows, through whose cracks the interior with its counters and shelves can be seen; and a fourth has succumbed to wind and snow, and lies a pile of jumbled lumber."

Despite the loss of many of its buildings, Ashcroft is one of the best preserved ghost towns in Colorado and is well worth a visit. This is a false front log store, one of many which used to line the main street. *(Kenneth Jessen 092B7)*

Many of these structures are gone now, but a row of substantial log buildings remains along the main street with the ghostly old hotel at the far end. Ashcroft is near the end of FR102, a paved road leaving Aspen.

For a map showing Ashcroft in relationship to Kellogg and Cooper's Camp, see "Cooper's Camp."

These wonderful log buildings are among a number of original structures which remain standing in the ghost town of Ashcroft, south of Aspen and accessible via a paved road. *(Kenneth Jessen 092B5)*

"Ashcroft," *Rocky Mountain News*, June 5, 1882.

Frank Hall, *History of Colorado*, Vol. IV. The Blakely Printing Company, Chicago, 1895, pp. 279-280.

Frank L. Wentworth, *Aspen on the Roaring Fork*, Francis B. Rizzari (publisher), 1950, pp. 183-184, 190, 196, 198.

Len Shoemaker, *Roaring Fork Valley*, Sage Books, Denver, 1958, pp. 27, 40, 66-68, 87, 153-155.

Muriel Sibell Wolle, *Stampede to Timberline*, Sage Books, Chicago, 1949, 1974, pp. 228-230.

William H. Bauer, James L. Ozment, John H. Willard, *Colorado Post Offices*, Colorado Railroad Museum, Golden, Colorado, 1990, pp. 15, 33.

ASPEN

Once Called Ute City

- *Pitkin County, Roaring Fork drainage*
- *Accessible by paved road*
- *Town has a post office; many original structures remain*

Aspen's main street in 1887. *(Denver Public Library, Western History Department X6171)*

A spen never became a ghost town, and its history is unique among Colorado silver mining towns. When the United States abandoned the silver standard in 1893, virtually every silver mine stopped production. The price of silver fell to nearly half of its previous value. Nearly all of the silver mining camps were deserted, but Aspen was the exception. Due in part to the value of its ore, many mines reopened. Aspen was not exempt, however, from many lean years. Many of its fine Victorian homes sat abandoned. Summer fishing and ski touring sustained Aspen. The real change in its economy, however, came with the construction of a ski lift as Aspen evolved into a year round resort. During the last two decades, many celebrities purchased lots and built homes in the Aspen area.

Stepping back in time, Aspen's early beginning was very much like any other mining town. In June, 1879, a group of three prospectors came over Hunters Pass (Independence Pass), by-passed the newly formed camp at Independence, and continued down the Roaring Fork. They pitched camp at a spring situated in a meadow surrounded by aspen trees. The site would later become the town of Aspen. Rich deposits of silver ore were dis-covered. In July, a second group of four prospectors arrived, and these men had read Dr. Hayden's report which mentioned rich ore deposits in the Roaring Fork Valley. They were surprised to find that they were not the first into the area, and the two groups joined forces. The number of prospectors swelled to twenty-three, and they set out to spend the winter. The Meeker Massacre at the White River Indian Agency changed their minds, however. Governor Frederick Pitkin sent out a courier to the Roaring Fork

Aspen had many Victorian homes such as the Gillespie House shown in this 1941 pho-tograph. *(Denver Public Library, Western History Department X-4901)*

Valley to warn any settlers that the Ute Indians might be on the war path. All but two left, and when no Indians were seen, the prospectors began returning to the camp.

Henry Gillespie suggested that the camp be given some sort of name, to which Phil Pratt suggested Ute City. The miners voted unanimously on the name, and a rough survey was made. Each man present was allowed two lots.

B. Clark Wheeler purchased a claim and was anxious to see just what he had bought. He and others crossed the Continental Divide over Hunters Pass and went down the Roaring Fork to Ute City. He was authorized by the Surveyor General of Colorado to survey a proposed town site. This survey was done in February, 1880, then filed at the Gunnison county clerk's office. Gunnison County included the Roaring Fork area at this time.

Walter Clark, a member of the Wheeler group, suggested the town be named Aspen because of the surrounding aspen forest. Other sources say that B. Clark Wheeler gave the town its name. Whichever the case, the Ute City name was ignored.

The town of Aspen started slowly with a single cabin in the summer of 1879. This cabin was one story made of unhewn logs and had two doors and a single window of four panes. The roof was covered with brush and dirt. It was used as a law office, and Pitkin County records were kept in the structure at one time.

A second cabin was erected the following year. The Aspen Town & Land Company was formed and during the next few years. Thousands of men arrived staking hundreds of mining claims. Many town lots sold, and in 1880, fifty log cabins and over 100 tents marked the spot. A store was constructed and supplies began to flow into the area. The Delmonico Restaurant opened, and construction began on the Claredon Hotel.

This same year, a rival town was formed called Roaring Fork City, located between Castle and Maroon Creeks. A town plat was filed and many lots sold. The town company promoting the site constructed one "token" cabin on the site. This cabin became the location for the area's first post office, which was soon moved to

Aspen. Roaring Fork City folded, and the cabin was the former town's only building.

In 1880-1881, thirty-five people stayed through the winter. As the mines were developed, it became widely known that the ore was very rich. Aspen began to grow, and the population soared to 2,000 in 1881, then to 3,000 in 1886. Before the close of 1887, it hit an estimated 5,000. By 1893, Aspen was a substantial town of 10,000.

Fabulous amounts of silver were removed from Aspen's leading mines. The most famous were the Mollie Gibson and the Smuggler. The Mollie Gibson had some selecte ore containing 3,300 ounces of silver per ton. With silver content well over a dollar an ounce, the wealth produced for its owners was sizeable. In 1894, the Smuggler yielded a one-ton nugget which was 93% pure silver.

Economic prosperity was solidified with the arrival of the Denver & Rio Grande Railroad in 1887, followed the next year by the standard gauge Colorado Midland. Ore could be shipped economically to distant smelters while the local smelters were being perfected. People could travel freely between towns. Supplies and machinery could be shipped into Aspen economically.

By 1893, more than 3,000 men were working in the mines alone. The Sherman Act was repealed in November, relieving the U. S. Government of its obligation to purchase a fixed amount of silver per year. The price of silver was no longer tied to the price of gold. Silver fell to almost half of its previous price, and within months, 30,000 Colorado silver miners were out of work. By the end of the year, eighty percent of the businesses in Aspen went bankrupt. It was the end of an era, and the roads leading out of Aspen were filled with families leaving to seek work elsewhere. Most of the mines closed forever.

In some mines, however, the underground wealth was staggering and the best mines continued to operate. At reduced wages, 350 Aspen miners went back to work in 1894. Lumber mills, the brewery and ranches continued to provide employment.

Deep-sea divers were brought in to clear the pumps at the Smuggler and allow the mine to be fully drained. For twenty-five more years, the great mines around Aspen continued to operate. When the cost of pumping exceeded the profit from the sale of ore, the mines closed.

It was Aspen's powder snow that would eventually spawn a revival. The first ski run was cleared in 1937, and a primitive ski lift took skiers up Aspen Mountain. In 1939, Aspen hosted its first sanctioned ski race. World War II slowed the development of skiing, but after the end of the war, there was rapid growth converting Aspen from mining to recreation.

The Mollie Gibson Mine near Aspen represented the height of the town's silver mining era. *(drawing by Julia McMillan)*

Len Shoemaker, *Roaring Fork Valley*, Sage Books, Denver, 1958, pp. 23-25, 33-36.

Frank L. Wentworth, *Aspen on the Roaring Fork*, Francis B. Rizzari (publisher), 1950, pp. 37-39, 44-45.

Muriel Sibell Wolle, *Stampede to Timberline*, Sage Books, Chicago, 1949, 1974, pp. 234-235.

Sally Barlow-Perez, *A History of Aspen*, Who Press, Aspen, Colorado, 1991, pp. 21-25.

CARBONATE

Garfield County Seat

- *Garfield County, Grizzly Creek drainage*
- *Accessible via graded dirt road*
- *Town was a county seat and had a post office; two standing structures remain on private property*

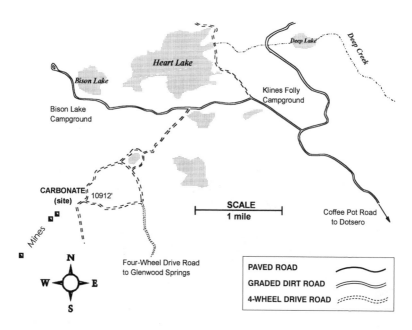

Carbonate can be reached via the Deep Creek Road (17R) about two miles north of Dotsero off of 301RD (Colorado River Road). The road is passable by passenger car, but it is a very long drive.

A t an elevation of nearly 11,000 feet in the Flat Tops north of Glenwood Springs is a ghost town site called Carbonate. It occupied 640 acres, a square mile, and was ambitious in its scope. Several thousand prospectors came to this town looking for silver ore, and since it was the only population center in the newly formed Garfield County, it became its county seat in 1883. The ore, however, turned out to be low grade, and because of the winter snow depth, only seasonal occupation was possible. In addition, there wasn't any way to economically transport the ore to a smelter. Carbonate's history was short.

The story of Carbonate began when prospectors Bell, John Blake and "Frenchy" Cleiopfar traveled from Leadville searching for silver ore in 1878. Near the point where the Eagle River joins the Grand (now the Colorado) River at Dotsero, they followed a Ute Indian trail which climbed into the Flat Tops. This trip led them above timberline to an unusual area where the carbonate ore was fully exposed, much like paving. The carbonate was primarily lead with some silver content. The prospectors thought they had discovered an entire mountain of ore and envisioned a new bonanza similar to Leadville.

The men returned to Leadville, and the following spring a hoard of prospectors showed up at Dotsero waiting for the snow to melt on the Flat Tops.

The name of the camp, Dotsero, has its own unique history. Presumably, it got its name from the surveyor's symbol, a dot inside a zero known as a "dot-zero." While waiting, miners drew up rules for the new camp and defined the size of a claim. Frank Belding came to Dotsero with a load of supplies in hopes of setting up a store in Carbonate. A wagon load of liquor was waiting to stock a new saloon, and a young girl hired a freight outfit to bring in supplies for a restaurant. All of them had to wait so long that they opened up their own establishments at Dotsero and never moved on. It got its own post office in 1883. (Other books lead the reader to another story about the naming of Dotsero contending that it was named in 1935 when the Denver, Rio Grande &

Western constructed a cutoff between its main line and the Denver & Salt Lake Railroad. The cutoff began at Orestod, on the Denver & Salt Lake Railroad, ending at Dotsero which is Orestod spelled backward.)

In her booklet, *Cold Snows of Carbonate*, Lena Urquahart points out that Carbonate was located within the boundary of the Ute reservation, formed by the Treaty of 1868. The white settlers were clearly trespassing without any opposition by the U.S. Government. Chief Ouray had given orders to his braves to protect their land. The prospectors were aware of this and constructed a primitive fort called Fort Defiance.

Hundreds of claims were staked out in the Flat Tops at the headwaters of Grizzly and No-Name creeks. Reports vary as to how many men swarmed over the area, with estimates ranging from 2,000 to 5,000.

The cost of supplies at Carbonate was prohibitive. Only a crude wagon road had been constructed along the Ute Indian trail via Coffee Pot Springs. In 1883, a toll road was graded from Glenwood Springs directly to Carbonate, helping to alleviate its isolation.

Mining was performed on a very limited scale with most activity amounting to nothing more than prospect holes. The most ambitious development work was George Ryan's one-hundred-foot shaft. Ryan also built the first cabin and made news by killing a large bear. The creek at that location was named Grizzly Creek.

The town of Carbonate was above timberline and sat on solid rock, making it difficult to construct cabins without hauling lumber some distance. A saw mill was opened up about two miles east of the town. Lots in Carbonate were sold for $50 to $100 each, and a number of cabins were constructed. Most of Carbonate's "buildings," however, were tents.

The claims were typically sold many times. The first sale was by the unsuccessful prospector who wanted to leave the area as fast as possible. Outside mining companies, based solely on speculation, eventually purchased most claims at inflated prices.

When Garfield County was formed in 1883, Carbonate was the only substantial population center in the area and immediately became the county seat. The winters were so severe that Carbonate was, for all purposes, a seasonal town. In October, the county records were brought down to Glenwood Springs. It was clear to the commissioners that Carbonate was not a good location, assuming that year round access was important! In November, Glenwood Springs was voted the permanent county seat. Carbonate was the county seat for just four months.

Lena Urquahart quoted from an account published in 1929, written by O. W. Daggett, of just what the county seat at Carbonate looked like in September, 1883. It consisted of a tent measuring 16 by 24 feet with a ridge pole ten feet from the ground. There were a few scrub jack pines on one side that were used to support the canvas "county building" and also for hanging game to cure. The tent sat on native rock, which for all the world looked like paving stone. This meant that there wasn't any green lawn, trees or landscaping in front of the Garfield County offices.

Nailed on a board near the top of the tent, a sign read "Garfield County," lest a visitor mistake the place for the home of a prospector. A second sign over the tent flaps noted the clerk and recorder. The county records were piled in the center of the tent on a long kitchen table. The tent flaps were tied open, and the records could be seen from the road leading into Carbonate. At the rear of the tent was the kitchen complete with a cook stove. Blocks of wood cut to varying heights served as stools for those working in the county offices.

Daggett brought up a load of supplies and sold them out of his wagon. He said that only after four feet of snow had accumulated in Carbonate were the county records packed up and moved down to Glenwood Springs. It took three days for the pack train with the records to reach its destination.

The post office in Carbonate opened in 1883 only to close in 1886. This leads to one of the greatest legends in Colorado ghost town history. E. E. Winslow won the contract to haul the mail from Glenwood Springs to Carbonate. It was a tough forty miles starting at an elevation of 5,800 feet and climbing to 10,912 feet. To add to the difficulty, Winslow unwisely signed up for daily service. When Winslow arrived on his first visit, he discovered that Carbonate contained but one resident, an old miner. Winslow did not want to repeat the trip and asked the man how much it would take to have him leave. The old miner came up with the figure of one hundred dollars. This was a price Winslow gladly paid, and after the miner left, Carbonate was a ghost town and did not require daily mail service.

Muriel Sibell Wolle, in her book *Stampede to Timberline*, reported that Carbonate had fifteen log homes, a store and a post office. It was a ghost town by 1884.

On her trip to Carbonate in 1947, a good Forest Service road took her within six miles of the town site. From there, only two ruts extended across meadows and around bogs. Within a quarter of a mile, a stone wall made further progress impossible. At the site, only the broken-down frames of several cabins remained along with a marker indicating that this was the Carbonate site.

Today, the Carbonate site is on private property, and there isn't any public access. The owner has restored two of the original cabins.

Colorado, *A Guide to the Highest State*, Hastings House, New York, 1970, p. 232.

Lena Urquahart, *Cold Snows of Carbonate*, The Golden Bell Press, Denver, 1967, pp. 1-18.

Muriel Sibell Wolle, *Stampede to Timberline*, Sage Books, Chicago, 1949, 1974, pp. 260-263.

Perry Eberhart, *Guide to the Colorado Ghost Towns and Mining Camps*, Sage Books, Chicago, 1959, pp. 182-183.

William H. Bauer, James L. Ozment, John H. Willard, *Colorado Post Offices*, Colorado Railroad Museum, Golden, Colorado, 1990, pp. 28, 46.

CARBONDALE

And Its Marriage Bet

- *Garfield County, Roaring Fork River drainage*
- *Accessible by paved road*
- *Town has a post office; several original structures remain; occupied site*

Carbondale is anything but a ghost town, and its history is included in this section for completeness. A group of town promoters founded the Carbondale Town & Land Company and named the new town for their Carbondale, Pennsylvania home town. The town company filed the necessary papers in August, 1887, and requested incorporation the following year.

Lots were purchased early in Carbondale's history, and several stores were constructed. A restaurant and hotel were built, and the small community gained a millinery shop, livery stable and a saloon. The original post office had been moved to Moffat, about a mile to the northwest. Carbondale was successful in getting its own post office in January, 1887. It closed the following month, but reopened in May and is still an active post office. The town also built a school and hired a teacher.

Originally, the Denver & Rio Grande Railroad was going to locate its depot at Moffat. Apparently the railroad's management changed their mind and not only constructed a railroad depot at Carbondale, but a section house as well. The Aspen & Western Railroad, also a narrow gauge railroad, began building a branch line west from Carbondale to service a coal mine on Thompson Creek.

The Advance, Carbondale's first newspaper, began publication in 1887, and its name was changed by the subsequent owner to the *Carbondale Avalanche*. Carbondale gained two doctors and a number of fraternal organizations during its first few years.

Len Shoemaker, author of *Roaring Fork Valley*, tells of an interesting bet made between two young men, Jake and Alec. Jake bet Alec $5 that a certain candidate would be elected. Alec counter-offered half interest in his store if the candidate lost. Jake could not afford to match this bet. Alec suggested that if Jake lost, he would marry a certain local young lady of generous proportions. Jake agreed, provided of course, the young lady was willing.

Alec secretly approached the young woman and explained the nature of the bet and asked for her cooperation. If Alec won, she agreed to pretend to go along with the plan to marry Jake. As it turned out, Alec won and Jake tried desperately to get out of his marital obligation. In the meantime, the young woman acted more than willing and even anxious to marry Jake.

The day of the wedding a crowd gathered to enjoy the day's festivities and see Jake "pay" his debt. The minister stood by while everyone waited for the bride to appear. As time passed, Jake's anxiety level raised. After a half-hour or so with no bride, Alec conceded and released Jake from his obligation. This was provided that Jake purchased two twenty-pound buckets of candy and hand them to the crowd. In Jake's mind, this was a considerable relief. The buckets were opened and the crowd passed by to take handfuls. The prospective bride eventually showed up and appeared to be very distressed and emotionally shaken when she learned that the bet to marry her had been called off. She grabbed Jake, hugged and kissed him, then paraded him around, much to the delight of the crowd. Everyone, with the possible exception of Jake, seemed to enjoy the moment.

Carbondale continued to grow, and even a devastating fire in 1891 hardly slowed the town down. New buildings replaced the old ones, and the town gained a barber ship, meat market and a paper hanger. It now relies on the tourist business and is also home to many individuals working in Aspen.

William H. Bauer, James L. Ozment, John H. Willard, *Colorado Post Offices*, Colorado Railroad Museum, Golden, Colorado, 1990, p. 30.

Len Shoemaker, *Roaring Fork Valley*, Sage Books, Denver, 1958, pp. 125-128, 172.

CARDIFF

Named for Town in Wales

- *Garfield County, Roaring Fork River drainage*
- *Accessible by paved road*
- *Town had a post office; one standing structure remains; occupied site*

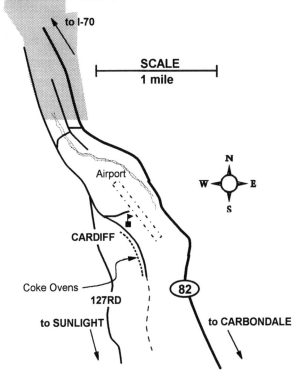

Cardiff is located immediately south of Glenwood Springs on the road leading to the airport. The schoolhouse still stands, but a trailer court occupies most of the site.

Immediately south of Glenwood Springs on the west side of the
Roaring Fork River near the Glenwood Springs Municipal
Airport is the old mining town of Cardiff. Its economy was based
on the manufacture of coke for use in smelters and steel mills.
Today, Cardiff is filled with trailers, but its old schoolhouse stands
in a grove of trees opposite the long row of crumbling coke ovens.
The Colorado Midland Railway constructed a railroad spur up
Fourmile Creek from Cardiff to bring coal down from the mines at
Sunset, Marion and Spring Gulch. This was known as the Jerome
Park Branch.

The coal was dumped directly from railroad cars into large
bins from an elevated track. Small bottom-dump mine cars were
loaded at the bottom of the bins. A track (called a Larry track) ran
from the bins along the top of the coke ovens. Each oven, when
empty, was filled first with a layer of dried cord wood, then the
coal was dumped through the top of the oven. From a door in the
bottom, the lower layer of cord wood was ignited. Once the wood
ignited the coal, the door was shut. The coking process is one
where coal is burned in a confined area such that the carbon

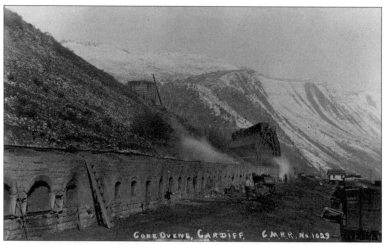

This is what Cardiff was all about; its coke ovens. Coal was brought down by the
Colorado Midland from the Jerome Park mines and converted into coke for use in the
steel industry. *(Colorado Historical Society F12394)*

remains and the volatile portion is burned away. When only the porous coke remains, the door is opened and water is immediately used to extinguish the fire. The coke is then racked out and loaded into railroad cars for shipment.

The Cardiff school is about all that is left of this once thriving town. The site is now dominated by a trailer court. *(Kenneth Jessen 106B1)*

Cardiff's origins began when the Grand River Coal & Coke Company selected the area. The Colorado Midland arrived in December, 1887, at the time the town of Cardiff was laid out. The town's name was selected because it was hoped that the quality of coke would only be exceeded by the coke from Cardiff, Wales, in the United Kingdom.

The railroad constructed a station and roundhouse as well as other servicing facilities. The Colorado Midland made Cardiff a division point where train crews were changed. A row of fifty bee-hive style coke ovens was constructed immediately and were first fired in January, 1888. The men who kept the ovens operating, as well as railroad workers, moved to Cardiff, and by 1890, the town had grown to 150. Several hotels, including the Railroad Inn and the Hotel DeCardiff, were constructed along with several stores. The Cardiff post office opened in 1899.

In 1892, the Colorado Fuel & Iron Company took over the operations, and Cardiff became a company town. A company-owned Colorado Supply Company store was built, and it accepted the script payed to employees of C. F. & I.

Another 197 coke ovens of the rectangular Belgium type were added, bringing the total number of ovens to 249. As a result, Cardiff became one of the top coke producers in Colorado, and under C. F. & I. ownership, most of the product was shipped to the steel mill in Pueblo. The air pollution was awful and filled the valley, obscuring visibility.

As the demand for coke fell, the coke ovens at Cardiff were shut down, and by 1910, no coke was being produced. The Colorado Midland moved its railroad facilities to Basalt, and in 1918, the Cardiff post office closed. The Jerome Park Branch was abandoned, and by 1920, Cardiff stood deserted.

Cardiff can be reached by heading south from Glenwood Springs on Colorado 82 (Grand Avenue). At the southern edge of Glenwood Springs, a road to the right crosses a bridge over the Roaring Fork River. A sign marks the way to the Sunlight Ski Area. This road heads south and parallels 82, but on the west side of the river. Beyond the turnoff up Fourmile Canyon is the Cardiff site. It is adjacent to the airport, and only the school and the coke ovens remain.

The Colorado Supply Company Store and post office at Cardiff. *(from Camp and Plant CP030)*

Anna Johnson and Kathleen Yajko, *The Elusive Dream*, Gran Furnum Printing & Publishing Company, Glenwood Springs, Colorado, 1983, pp. 34-35, 63.

Edward M. McFarland, *A Colorado Midland Guide and Data Book*, Colorado Railroad Museum, Golden, Colorado, 1980, pp. 225-229, 279-282.

Len Shoemaker, *Roaring Fork Valley*, Sage Books, Denver, 1958, pp. 136-137, 170-171.

William H. Bauer, James L. Ozment, John H. Willard, *Colorado Post Offices*, Colorado Railroad Museum, Golden, Colorado, 1990, p. 30.

CAREY'S CAMP

- *Pitkin County, Conundrum Creek drainage*
- *Accessible by foot trail*
- *Town had a post office; no standing structures remain*

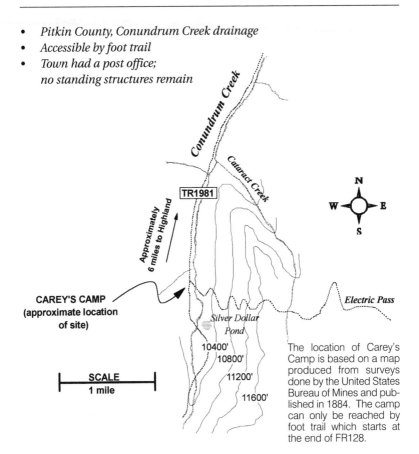

The location of Carey's Camp is based on a map produced from surveys done by the United States Bureau of Mines and published in 1884. The camp can only be reached by foot trail which starts at the end of FR128.

Carey's Camp is most noted for how life at the camp ended rather than how it began. On March 10, 1884, the entire camp was buried in an avalanche, and all five of its human occupants died. The men had been sitting around a table in one of the cabins. Members of a rescue party reached the location thirty-three days later and discovered that a dog, buried under twenty-five feet of snow, was the sole survivor of the avalanche. The dog was named "Bruiser" and recovered in Aspen to become a local hero. The dog was presented with a silver collar with an inscription that provided all the details of this story.

The earliest settler along Conundrum Creek was Abe Lee who constructed a cabin and tended a flock of sheep. Captain Carey located some placer claims in 1882 at a point seven miles south of Highland. The source for the gold found in the creek was the object of an intense search, and its location was never discovered. One prospector remarked, "It sure is a conundrum," and that is how the creek got its name.

About a dozen cabins were built at Carey's Camp, and the place gained its own post office in 1883. A primitive wagon road was constructed to the camp. Very little mineral wealth was discovered, however, and the post office closed in 1884, just prior to the avalanche.

Captain Carey returned to the site and continued mining. A tunnel was opened up about a half-mile below (north) the camp. Since the mine was vulnerable to snow slides, its boiler and machinery were housed in a large underground room.

Beyond the town site was a hot spring. Long after Carey's Camp had been demolished by the avalanche, a bath house was erected over the spring. The spring was never developed commercially, but still attracts avid nature lovers. Located at 11,200 feet, the spring is a hard nine-mile walk from the trail head three miles south of Highland. There are two pools of reasonable size.

Frank L. Wentworth, *Aspen on the Roaring Fork*, Francis B. Rizzari (publisher), 1950, p. 155.

Len Shoemaker, *Roaring Fork Valley*, Sage Books, Denver, 1958, pp. 77-78.

Perry Eberhart, *Guide to the Colorado Ghost Towns and Mining Camps*, Sage Books, Chicago, 1959, pp. 245-246.

Rick Cahill, *Colorado Hot Springs Guide*, Pruett Publishing Company, Boulder, Colorado, 1983, pp. 140-145.

William H. Bauer, James L. Ozment, John H. Willard, *Colorado Post Offices*, Colorado Railroad Museum, Golden, Colorado, 1990, p. 30.

CARPENTER
Coal Camp

- *Mesa County, Leach Creek drainage*
- *Accessible via graded dirt road*
- *No standing structures remain*

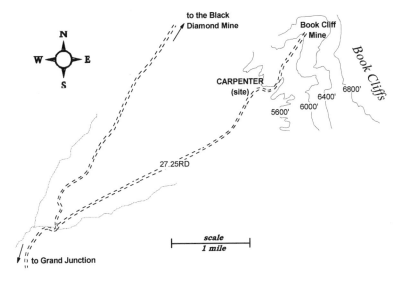

Carpenter is located at the end of a graded dirt road, 27.25 RD, originating in Grand Junction and running on the west side of the airport.

The Book Cliff mine was located north of Grand Junction. A local banker, W. T. Carpenter, decided to develop the mine by constructing an eleven mile narrow gauge railroad to the site. Construction began in 1890 and was finished the following year, and the mining camp of Carpenter was developed at the end of the track.

45

The mine was located high above the town, and a long gravity tram brought small pit cars to a mule tram track. The gravity tram used cables to lower load cars down a 700 foot trestle. That same cable wound over a drum at the top, and it pulled empty cars up to the mine opening. The mule tram track wound its way around the base of the cliff to the tipple at Carpenter. The mules were used to slow loaded cars and to pull the empty cars back to the base of the gravity tram. Later, the narrow gauge railroad was extended to the base of the gravity tram and replaced the tram track.

The Carpenter post office opened in June, 1890, prior to the completion of the railroad, and closed the following year. Access by rail to the Grand Junction post office may have been the reason for the closure.

Carpenter just before the turn of the century. Nothing remains today at this site. *(Museum of Western Colorado Collection)*

In May, 1891, the *Grand Valley Star* described Carpenter as having a boarding house and bath house with hot and cold water. There was also a blacksmith shop and commissary. Several cabins had been built at that time. In January of 1893, the *Grand Junction News* described Carpenter as a village of six or eight houses, an eating house, store, and bunk houses for the miners and their families. Historic photographs taken after the turn of the century show Carpenter as having about a dozen cottages plus various mine buildings. Its population was around fifty.

The railroad expanded its business from hauling coal to also hauling people on excursions. It claimed to have taken 4,000 people from Grand Junction to Carpenter in 1892. It was a lot cooler at Carpenter than in the Grand Valley, and excursions gave residents of Grand Junction a chance to escape from the heat. A pavilion was constructed, and the place was generally referred to as Poland Springs for its mineral water spring high above the town. W. T. Carpenter installed a pipe line from the spring down to the town and tried to make a business out of selling the water.

In 1924, an underground fire forced the owners to seal the Book Cliff Mine, which was subsequently abandoned. The following year, the railroad was dismantled. Time and vandals took care of the town of Carpenter, and nothing remains today except for foundations and root cellars. The site can be reached by 27.25 RD. From Grand Junction, 1st N becomes 27 RD but several turns are necessary in the vicinity of the airport to reach the correct dirt road leading to the site.

Grand Valley Star, May 30, 1891.

Grand Junction News, January 7, 1893.

Lyndon L. Lampert and Robert W. McLeod, *Little Book Cliff Railway*, Pruett Publishing Company, Boulder, Colorado, 1984, pp. 23, 37, 36-39, 140, 153-156.

Robert Ormes, *Tracking Ghost Railroads in Colorado*, Century One Press, Colorado Springs, Colorado, 1975, p. 145.

William H. Bauer, James L. Ozment, John H. Willard, *Colorado Post Offices*, Colorado Railroad Museum, Golden, Colorado, 1990, p. 30.

COALBASIN

Gets a Clubhouse

- *Pitkin County, Coal Creek drainage*
- *Access may be limited by private property*
- *Town had a post office; no standing structures remain*

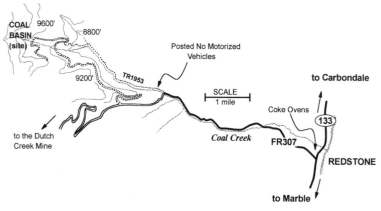

The Coalbasin site is approximately twelve miles west of Redstone via a dirt road that is graded to the Dutch Creek-Coal Creek confluence. A foot trail gives access to Coal Basin.

Coalbasin (also spelled Coal Basin) was located a dozen miles west of Redstone and was served by a narrow gauge railroad. The standard gauge Crystal River Railroad was completed from Carbondale to Redstone in 1898. A narrow gauge branch was constructed in 1900 from Redstone, a dozen miles up to Coalbasin and was dubbed the "Columbine Road." The altitude gain required a 4.4% grade with extremely sharp curves, and in the entire length of the line, there was only one piece of straight track. The output from the mine within Coalbasin was shipped down the railroad, which dropped 2,242 feet, to the coke ovens at Redstone.

In 1882, a prospector named William Batt filed the first claim in Coalbasin. Other claims followed, and the coal deposits were eventually sold to become part of the Colorado Fuel & Iron Company holdings. The primary coal seams were located high on the mountainside, and a 1,200 foot tunnel was necessary to reach the four coal seams which totalled twenty to thirty feet in thickness. Work began in 1892, and the mine closed the following year because of a recession in the mining industry. Work resumed in 1898, and by 1902, the mine's output was 800 tons a day with plans by C. F. & I. to further expand operations. The coal was ideal for coke with a low percentage of ash and few impurities. It was highly valued for precious metal smelters.

The consumption of alcohol by its miners was a chronic problem for the Colorado Fuel & Iron Company in Coalbasin. In the summer of 1901, the Fourth of July celebration got a little out of hand when four kegs of whiskey, eight barrels of beer and a great deal of wine were smuggled in for the event. The aftermath was that all work in the mine had to be suspended for several days to allow the miners to dry out.

Not wanting a repeat of this incident, C. F. & I. president John C. Osgood tested a new method to curb the consumption to

Coalbasin was not a very inviting looking place during the winter. The small valley was filled with company homes with alternating roof styles. *(Camp and Plant CP064)*

The Coalbasin Club, the first of many C. F. & I. clubhouses, was composed of two standard company houses joined by an interconnecting structure. *(Camp and Plant CP063)*

a reasonable level. This involved the construction of the comfortable Coalbasin Club. He instituted this club," ... primarily to do away with promiscuous and intemperate drinking." As put by a C. F. & I. publication, *Camp and Plant*, "The bar room is neatly, though plainly, furnished and equipped, and is purposely made not so attractive as other parts of the club." Any kind of beverage could be ordered, but the consumption of "wholesome lemonade" was encouraged.

The clubhouse, constructed in 1902, had a billiard room, card room, reading room and the bar. The manager lived on the premises. Under the structure was a cellar for the cold storage of liquor and wine. Beer was piped up from a keg in the cellar. Large additions were made the following year to the clubhouse to add an additional billiard room and card room, plus indoor plumbing.

There were a dozen strict rules imposed on the miners. Closing time was 10 p.m. on weekdays and 11 p.m. on Saturday. No one could buy a drink for someone else, in other words, "no treating." Miners could not enter wearing their working clothes. No women or children were allowed inside with the exception of Rule 6 which stated that "Strangers, including women and children, will be permitted to visit the Club Rooms for the purpose of inspection between 9 am and 5 p.m...." Some interpretation is required for Rule 6. It might have been used to find missing husbands/fathers hiding from their families.

The notion of the clubhouse was extended to Redstone, only there, a far more elaborate structure was built. It had a second-story theater.

At the town of Coalbasin, historic photographs taken from different angles reveal seventy cottages. They were of a standard C. F. & I. design with a choice of three, four or six rooms. Styles alternated between two roof types so that the rows of cottages didn't all look alike. William Batt's original cabin was kept as sort of a historical landmark.

At Coalbasin, 265 workers at the mine included native-born Americans, Austrians, and Italians. Coalbasin got its own post office which remained open until 1909. The Colorado Supply Company constructed a company store made of logs in 1901, then built a handsome frame store the following year. The town also had a water system that supplied each home and also connected to fire hydrants. Spread out throughout the town were hose boxes which could reach any hydrant and supply water under pressure to any home. The town also had its own school, and the circulating library had fifty books.

The need for coke by precious metal smelters declined, and C. F. & I. determined that it was too expensive to supply coke from Redstone to its steel mill in Pueblo. Around 1910, the mine closed and Coalbasin was abandoned. C. F. & I. sold the buildings in place to be razed for their scrap lumber value.

A mountain property development is taking over the lower portion of the road up Coal Creek, and the first three and a half miles are paved. The road is open to the public. At the end of the pavement at the confluence of Dutch Creek

Colorado Supply Company Store No. 26 was a handsome building in a beautiful location, however, an avalanche knocked the structure off its foundation and over the railroad tracks. The manager was carried off with the building, but survived the experience. *(Camp and Plant)*

and Coal Creek are gates. One gate marks the closure of the road up Dutch Creek because of reclamation work on a large mine. The other gate is across the road that follows Coal Creek. This road is in good shape and passable by automobile, but for some reason, is closed to motorized vehicles. It is, however, open to foot traffic and is designated as TR1953. After about a half mile, this road joins the old railroad grade to Coalbasin. The distance to the Coalbasin site from the gate is about three miles.

An inclined tram was used to lower mining cars loaded with coal from the mine entrance to the tipple at Coalbasin *(Camp and Plant CP060)*

"Coalbasin, Colorado," *Camp and Plant*, September 13, 1902, pp. 249-259.

Dell McCoy and Russ Collman, *The Crystal River Pictorial*, Sundance, Denver, Colorado, 1972, pp. 30, 32, 88-95.

H. Lee Scamehorn, *Pioneer Steelmaker in the West*, Pruett, Boulder, Colorado, 1976, pp. 20, 73, 84, 86. 89-90, 119-125, 153-154.

Sylvia Ruland, *The Lion of Redstone*, Johnson Books, Boulder, Colorado, 1981, pp. 9, 28, 53, 55.

Tivis Wilkins, *Colorado Railroads*, Pruett Publishing Company, Boulder, Colorado, 1974, pp. 117, 129.

William H. Bauer, James L. Ozment, John H. Willard, *Colorado Post Offices*, Colorado Railroad Museum, Golden, Colorado, 1990, p. 35.

COOPER'S CAMP

- *Pitkin County, Cooper Creek drainage*
- *Town did not have a post office; no structures remain*

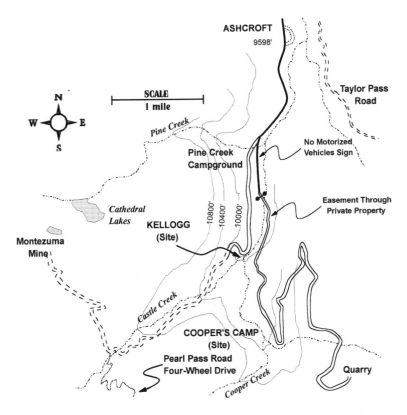

This map, showing the location of Kellogg and Cooper's Camp, was derived from an 1884 map produced by the United States Bureau of Mines and held at the Denver Public Library, Western History Department.

There is little information on this obscure mining camp located on Cooper Creek about two miles south of Ashcroft. An extensive iron mine was worked at Cooper's Camp beginning with its discovery in 1880. In 1886, Colorado Coal & Fuel Company purchased the deposit, and thousands of tons of iron ore were sent to Aspen, some fourteen miles to the north. The iron ore was used by precious metal smelters as a flux to separate the metallic portion of the area's silver ore from waste rock. Once the railroads arrived in Aspen, it was cheaper to ship the silver ore to distant smelters, and the demand for iron ore from Cooper's Camp came to a halt.

Muriel Sibell Wolle tried to find Cooper's Camp during the late 1940s for her book, *Stampede to Timberline.* The road beyond Ashcroft was good for a mile, but then became nothing more than a trail. She found, at the edge of a grove of aspens, the frames of a few log cabins and some stone foundations of one or two other buildings. She continued beyond this site, finding nothing. She never knew for certain if she had found Cooper's Camp.

Ore wagons were once a common means of bringing ore down from the more remote mountain towns to smelters. *(drawing by Kenneth Jessen KJ002)*

Well after *Stampede to Timberline* was published, she received a letter from a person running a guide service. This individual talked to an old timer, a Mr. Fitzpatrick, who said that Cooper's Camp was farther south and that the ruins Wolle found were the remains of a town called Kellogg.

Today, part of the Kellogg site is blocked by private property, but all of the area can be seen from a public road. There are no standing structures on the site dating back to the origins of the town. A sign at the Pine Creek Campground prohibits motorized vehicles on the very end of the paved road. A gate at Cooper Creek restricts passage on the quarry road (see map) to an easement through the private property. The site of Cooper's Camp, therefore, cannot be reached by motorized vehicle. In addition, dense undergrowth along the creek restricts even a clear view of the site.

The Pearl Pass Road, however, parallels the paved road for about a half-mile before it begins climbing away from the area. This road is open to traffic, but requires four-wheel drive.

H. Lee Scamehorn, *Pioneer Steelmaker in the West*, Pruett, Boulder, Colorado, 1976, pp. 20, 65, 103, 105.

Muriel Sibell Wolle, *Stampede to Timberline*, Sage Books, Chicago, 1949, 1974, pp. 230-231.

Muriel Sibell Wolle, *Timberline Tailings*, Sage Books, Chicago, 1977, p. 186.

Perry Eberhart, *Guide to the Colorado Ghost Towns and Mining Camps*, Sage Books, Chicago, 1959, p. 245.

EMMA

- *Pitkin County, Roaring Fork River drainage*
- *Accessible by paved road*
- *Town had a post office; several abandoned structures remain; some of the site occupied by modern homes*

Sitting along Colorado 82 between Glenwood Springs and Aspen are two abandoned stores and behind them, an old abandoned school. This was downtown Emma, a small community located about a mile and a half west of Basalt. Despite the dilapidated buildings, there are a number of newer homes in the residential part of Emma.

These abandoned stores sit along Colorado 82 as a reminder of better days in Emma.
(Kenneth Jessen 092A10)

Emma began as a station along the Aspen Branch of the Denver & Rio Grande. The railroad constructed a water tower, section house and a few other buildings. A store was constructed, then in 1888, a post office was opened. The town got its name from the first postmistress, Emma D. Garrison. (Postal records in *Colorado Post Offices* lists the Emma post office as having opened in 1883, four years before the railroad arrived.)

Charles Mather became the postmaster in 1889; he also opened a general merchandise store. He put the post office in the store, a common practice in small Colorado towns. He also constructed a large brick home near his store.

The mining industry in Aspen tapered off and the coke ovens at Cardiff closed. By the 1920s, Emma was on a downward slide. Its post office closed as people left the area.

In subsequent years, as the focus shifted away from mining and toward the recreation industry, Emma was populated once again. The stores, however, were abandoned and residents purchase their groceries in nearby Basalt.

Len Shoemaker, *Roaring Fork Valley*, Sage Books, Denver, 1958, pp. 128-129.

Sandra Dallas, *Colorado Ghost Towns and Mining Camps*, University of Oklahoma Press, Norman, Oklahoma, 1985, p. 71.

William H. Bauer, James L. Ozment, John H. Willard, *Colorado Post Offices*, Colorado Railroad Museum, Golden, Colorado, 1990, p. 51.

FULFORD

Tragic History

- *Eagle County, Brush Creek drainage*
- *Accessible via graded dirt road; private property*
- *Town had a post office; lower town contains homes occupied seasonally; standing structures remain*

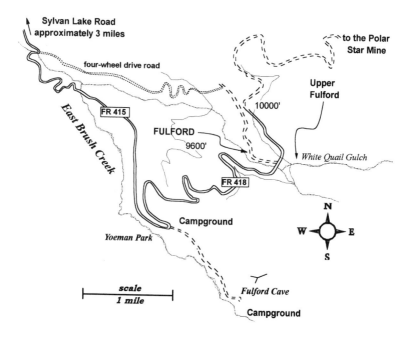

F ulford was originally called Nolan's Camp and received its name for an early prospector who discovered rich ore in 1887. That same year, William Nolan was crossing Brush Creek on a log with a loaded gun in one hand. The gun was carried straight up and the trigger accidentally caught on something. The discharge cut off Nolan's tongue. He was alone and bled to death. This particular branch of Brush Creek was renamed Nolan Creek.

Arthur H. Fulford had a ranch on Brush Creek below Nolan's Camp. Fulford served as town marshal for Red Cliff before settling on Brush Creek. His ranch became the stage stop called the Halfway House on the road between Eagle and Nolan's Camp. During the summer of 1890, a rich strike was made by Dick Morgan on Nolan Creek. Morgan and Arthur Fulford laid out the town of Fulford at or near the Noland's Camp site.

Muriel Sibell Wolle, in her books *Stampede to Timberline* and *Timberline Tailings*, goes into a rather long series of events surrounding the history of Fulford involving a prospector named Buck Rogers. There are inconsistencies between the two books, however. Exactly how true these stories are is hard to verify.

In 1849, well before the first gold discoveries in Colorado, Buck Rogers organized a party of thirty men in Illinois to go to California. On their way to California, they discovered gold nuggets in a surface deposit somewhere in Colorado. The rich ore was collected and stored in the mine. When their provisions ran low, they selected Buck Rogers to go to the nearest camp, some one hundred and fifty miles away near Pikes Peak, for supplies.

There were a number of cabins still standing in the upper part of Fulford in 1942. Only the crumbling walls of a couple of these cabins remain today. *(Denver Public Library, Western History Department X-3258)*

A nicely restored cabin in Fulford, one of the better preserved mining towns. *(Kenneth Jessen 104A7)*

Buck Rogers was given gold dust with which to purchase supplies. Instead, he went on a drinking spree. After six weeks, Rodgers returned to locate his companions. At the spot where the mine was situated, he found it had been swept clean by an avalanche. Only the smooth, polished bed rock composed of slate remained. In 1881, he told a tale about the lost treasure.

In 1891, Fulford met a prospector who was searching for the lost treasure using Rogers' notebook. Based on the description in the notebook, the prospector claimed he had located the exposed slate face where the slide occurred with a pile of debris at its base where presumably the treasure was hidden. The prospector told Fulford he dug into the mound and recovered human bones, tools and the gold nuggets. Skeptical, Fulford would not believe the story until he saw the gold.

The prospector was killed in a brawl in a Red Cliff saloon. Using the prospector's description of where the mine was located, Fulford found the prospector's cabin which was near the mine. Inside, Fulford recovered notes as to where the treasure was located. In September, 1891, Fulford set out with provisions for a long trip and began searching for the hidden gold. In January, he was killed in a snow slide on New York Mountain. This story of lost treasure is one of many in Colorado history.

The town of Fulford got its own post office in 1892 which remained open until 1910, when mining activity declined.

When Muriel Sibell Wolle traveled to Fulford during the late 1940s, it was a difficult trip over a narrow shelf road. The road ran through private property, which required stopping and opening gates, then closing them. Fulford had not yet been opened to summer home development. She noted that its log houses were in good condition, but that the town was almost deserted. A woman and her elderly mother were its only occupants, and they lived in an old hotel. Also standing was a store, complete with a wooden sidewalk, along with many abandoned cabins. Significant was Wolle's discovery of a second town referred to as Upper Fulford. A foot trail leads to the upper town higher and about a half-mile away from lower Fulford. Upper Fulford had its own hotel, some boarding houses, saloons, a livery stable, store and assay office. Wolle reported that the hotel still contained a pool table and piano.

A newer, graded dirt road (FR 415 then FR 418) now makes the trip to Fulford possible without the use of four-wheel drive. The road branches off of the Brush Creek Road (FR 400) south of Eagle to the left. (The easiest way to locate the Brush Creek Road is to look for signs pointing to Sylvan Lake.) The trip to Fulford should only be made in dry weather. The road is composed of red clay which becomes extremely slippery when wet, causing loss of vehicle control. Under these conditions, the trip can become very exciting on the more exposed sections of this road. The original wagon road following Nolan Creek is also kept open from Brush Creek to Fulford. It is marked as a four-wheel drive road and passes through the Fulford cemetery.

The main portion of Fulford is below FR 418. A trail sign marks the route to the upper town which uses an old mining road not passable by vehicle. The walk to Upper Fulford is about a quarter of a mile and gains about one hundred feet in elevation. The old road goes through the town site with the remains of cabins both above and below the road. In all, a half-dozen foundations and partially standing structures can be located including what appeared to be a spring house.

In the lower portion of Fulford, there are many summer cabins spread out over a large meadow. Among the newer cabins

There are few abandoned structures in Fulford. Most have been converted into season-al residences. *(Kenneth Jessen 104C8)*

and mountain homes are a few original structures. It is difficult to determine just how many structures there were in the original town, since access is limited by private property. Fulford is locat-ed in a beautiful place, situated in a lush meadow surrounded by mature trees.

Beyond Fulford, the graded road continues up New York Mountain using a series of switchbacks. The road ends near the Polar Star Mine at timberline. At one time, there were cabins in this area referred to as New York Cabins, but today their location is difficult to determine.

Frank Hall, *History of Colorado*, Vol. III. The Blakely Printing Company, Chicago, 1895, pp. 125-126.

Muriel Sibell Wolle, *Stampede to Timberline*, Sage Books, Chicago, 1949, 1974, pp. 255-260.

Muriel Sibell Wolle, *Timberline Tailings*, Sage Books, Chicago, 1977, pp. 198-202.

William H. Bauer, James L. Ozment, John H. Willard, *Colorado Post Offices*, Colorado Railroad Museum, Golden, Colorado, 1990, p. 59.

GILMAN

A Cliff Hanger

- *Eagle County, Eagle River drainage*
- *Accessible by paved road; site on private property*
- *Town had a post office; many standing structures remain*

This is the Iron Mask Hotel in 1890, and it may have been Gilman's finest hostelry. It was destroyed in the fire of 1899. *(Colorado Historical Society F43184)*

If ever a town was a cliff hanger, it is Gilman. Situated between Red Cliff and Minturn just off of U.S. 24, the town sits at the edge of a bench on Battle Mountain. There is a sheer 1,200-foot drop to the Eagle River. The mill and one of the mines was down by the river, and workers commuted on a funicular railroad. The small cars were lowered by wire rope to the canyon floor.

The camp started out as Rock Creek, which became Battle Mountain, then Clinton. It was formally founded by Henry M. Gilman in 1886.

The location of one of the mines and a large mill, owned by the Eagle Mining & Milling Company, was below the town. When the Denver & Rio Grande constructed its line through Eagle Canyon in 1887, the railroad siding along the Eagle River was called Beldon.

A variety of ore was found in the area, including silver, gold, zinc and copper. This is what sustained the population of Gilman for a century, one of the longest runs for a Colorado town based entirely on mining.

The Gilman post office was established in 1886, the same year the town was officially established. The post office was closed a century later.

Obediah M. Warner, a state legislator, came from Gilman and, in 1890, was accused of obtaining $500 under false pretenses. The Eagle County sheriff had to travel to Denver to bring back Mr. Warner for trial. The two men got on the Rio Grande night train to Red Cliff. The sheriff had known Warner for some time and did not insist on handcuffs. The two men settled down into their respective berths. Warner managed to get up during the night, got dressed and went out onto the car's platform. When the train stopped at a siding, Warner stepped off and was never seen again.

The town of Gilman grew and gained stores, a school and the Iron Mask Hotel. Half of Gilman was destroyed by fire in 1899, including the hotel. That same year its population was estimated at 300.

New Jersey Zinc Company acquired the mines and the town in 1915. They recovered enormous quantities of various metals. For example, in 1950, seven million dollars in metals were

The Gilman school sits empty in this ghost town, and the only sound is swings creaking in the wind. *(Kenneth Jessen 102C6)*

shipped. The following year, the amount rose to twelve million dollars, then in 1952, the output cooled off to five million dollars. In 1981, with its ore reserves exhausted, the mine closed. A Cañon City businessman purchased the town and mines. Mining resumed briefly. The next owner was the Battle Mountain Corporation who took title to Gilman in 1984. It was determined that the water system was inadequate, and in 1985, the sixty remaining residents were asked to leave. The town was put up for sale for $2.75 million and was advertised as having forty-five homes, a bowling alley, commercial space, a post office and was serviced by a natural gas line. Not much activity has taken place to sell Gilman, and the town remains abandoned.

Gilman is perched at the edge of a cliff on Battle Mountain more than a thousand feet above the Eagle River. *(Kenneth Jessen 102C5)*

John K. Aldrich, *Ghosts of Northern Colorado*, Centennial Graphics, Lakewood, Colorado, 1987, pp. 18-22.

Muriel Sibell Wolle, *Stampede to Timberline*, Sage Books, Chicago, 1949, 1974, pp. 254-255.

Robert A. LeMassena, "Tennessee Pass," *Colorado Rail Annual No. 17*, Golden, Colorado, 1987, p. 193.

Robert L. Brown, *Colorado Ghost Towns - Past and Present*, Caxton Printers, Caldwell, Idaho, 1977, pp. 109-112.

William H. Bauer, James L. Ozment, John H. Willard, *Colorado Post Offices*, Colorado Railroad Museum, Golden, Colorado, 1990, p. 61.

GOLD PARK

- *Eagle County; Homestake Creek drainage*
- *Access limited by private property*
- *Town had a post office; two standing structures remaining*

Closely associated with Holy Cross City was Gold Park. During its boom years, the mill at Gold Park processed the ore from Holy Cross City using a forty-stamp mill. Ore was received via a two-and-a-half mile iron flume bypassing the steep wagon road up to Holy Cross City. The Gold Park Mining and Milling Company also constructed a mill at Holy Cross City, and it is not known how the two mills were deployed. It is likely that the mill at Holy Cross City replaced the milling process at Gold Park. There was also some placer mining along Homestead Creek. The gravel was laced with gold that, over tens of thousands of years, had washed down from the lode at Holy Cross City.

John H. Bailey founded Gold Park and developed the mines in the area based on assay values from claims along Homestake Creek. He made his money from mines throughout Colorado as well as the Black Hills of South Dakota. By the latter part of 1880, Gold Park, elevation 9294 feet, was home to about four hundred people. Winter snows drove most of them to lower elevation, but they returned in the spring. In the meantime, Bailey traveled to the East to raise money and in the process, founded the Gold Park Mining and Milling Company with 100,000 shares of stock.

In the spring of 1881, substantial structures began to appear in Gold Park using lumber from a local mill. The town included four saloons, but as families were attracted to the area, the town gained a church and school. Gold Park had its own post office and daily stagecoach service from Leadville. The town also had a drug store, blacksmith shop and a store which carried boots and shoes. A transfer company was located in Gold Park as well as two general stores, two hotels and mining offices.

Holy Cross City was located at 11,335 feet, and during the winter months, seven feet of snow could accumulate. It certainly was more comfortable for the miners and their families to live in Gold Park at the modest elevation of 9,359 feet. Miners and their families may have wintered in Gold Park.

Most of the time, life in a mining town was quiet. Gold Park, however, had an incident in December, 1881. The foreman of the Gold Park Mining and Milling Company, H. Weston, was shot and killed by a man named Bagley. Bagley had been dis-charged as the blacksmith. To get even, he killed Weston and made an attempt to kill the superintendent. He fled to his cabin, then fortified himself. An angry mob surrounded the cabin and placed a liberal amount of blasting powder at the front of the door. It blew the cabin into small pieces. Bagley was already dead with a self-inflicted bullet through his heart.

When Muriel Sibell Wolle returned to Gold Park in 1972 after her first visit in the 1940s, one particular large house had van-ished. At the time of her first visit, this house was in excellent shape and looked out of place in a remote mining camp. The house was torn down during World War II by the U.S. Army to cre-ate a machine gun range on the gravel flats.

Gold Park did not last long and lost its post office in 1883. Many historians believe that this was also the time Holy Cross City was abandoned. There are two original structures remaining, but they are within a fenced, posted area. *For a map showing Gold Park's location, see "Holy Cross City."*

Muriel Sibell Wolle, *Stampede to Timberline*, Sage Books, Chicago, 1949, 1974, pp. 246-251.

Muriel Sibell Wolle, *Timberline Tailings*, Sage Books, Chicago, 1977, p. 197.

Robert L. Brown, *Holy Cross: The Mountain and the City*, Caxton Printers, 1970, pp. 116-122.

Robert L. Brown, *Jeep Trails to Colorado Ghost Towns*, Caxton Printers, Caldwell, Idaho, 1973, pp. 100-102.

William H. Bauer, James L. Ozment, John H. Willard, *Colorado Post Offices*, Colorado Railroad Museum, Golden, Colorado, 1990, p. 63.

HIGHLAND

County's First Ghost Town

- *Pitkin County, Castle Creek drainage*
- *Access limited by private property*
- *Town did not have a post office; no original structures remaining*

A group of town promoters, including T. E. Ashcraft, followed the prospectors in 1879 and laid out a town site which they called Highland. It was located just east of the junction with Conundrum Creek and Castle Creek. This placed the new town between Ashcroft and Aspen. The town was located within Ute territory by treaty with the U. S. government.

Merchandise was packed in from Buena Vista, and an open-air tent store sold supplies to the area's prospectors. A number of mining claims were filed in the area, but it was A. W. Zern who located the first ore of any value. Soon, Highland was a "three-street" town with thirty cabins and three stores housed in tents. Mail came three times a week, but apparently, Highland never had the population sufficient to get its own post office. The president of the town company, by the way, was T. E. Ashcraft.

The prospects did not yield any rich ore, and Highland became a deserted village. As covered in the *Aspen Times*, December, 1881, "Soon we reached the mushroom camp of Highland. It well deserves the name applied to it — the deserted village. But one house is inhabited. The structures, numbering hundreds, are falling down and look distressed. Buildings which once covered immense stocks of merchandise are empty, and doors and windows are big yawning holes without glass or boards. The rude signs of "Store," "Assay Office," etc. swing in a crazy manner from the tops of doorways and in front of toppling buildings, and old foundations, overgrown with weeds and partly buried in sand..."

There was a resurgence of activity in the Highland area and the town was occupied again. A decade later, Highland had about forty cabins and around 150 or so tents. Several new stores opened, but once again, the prospects failed to show pay dirt. Highland's residents started leaving, and the town was abandoned, becoming the first ghost town in Pitkin County.

After a few years, rich ore was finally found at the Little Annie claim, not far from Highland. In 1890, a mill was constructed along with several homes. The largest project was the Hope Tunnel, bored three miles eastward in hopes of striking rich ore. Little of value was found, and in the early 1920s, the tunnel was abandoned.

When Muriel Sibell Wolle visited Highland in the late 1940s, one cabin marked the spot opposite the Bavarian Lodge. Today, the area is occupied by modern mountain homes, some of considerable size.

"A Deserted Village," *Aspen Times*, December, 1881.

Don and Jean Griswold, *Colorado's Century of "Cities"*, Self Published, 1958, pp. 216-217.

Len Shoemaker, *Roaring Fork Valley*, Sage Books, Denver, 1958, pp. 26, 36.

Muriel Sibell Wolle, *Stampede to Timberline*, Sage Books, Chicago, 1949, 1974, pp. 228-229.

HOLY CROSS CITY

- *Eagle County, French Creek drainage*
- *Accessible by rough, steep four-wheel drive road*
- *Town had a post office; two standing structures remaining*

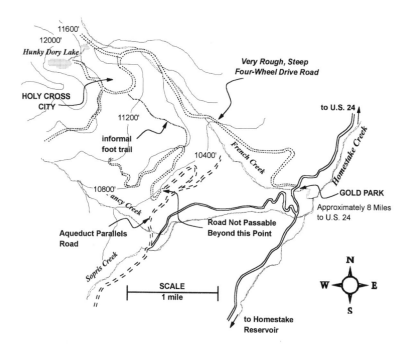

Holy Cross City is located above Gold Park near the end of a rough four-wheel drive road. Using the graded dirt road along the aqueduct, Holy Cross City can be reached on foot over an informal trail marked by cairns.

The Mecca of Colorado ghost towns is Holy Cross City. There are other ghost towns in a better state of preservation, and there are ghost towns with far more interesting buildings. There are also other ghost towns in more remote locations and ones of greater size, but Holy Cross City is attractive because of a combination of factors, including its beautiful location, a rough four-wheel drive road and an obscure history.

A rich deposit of free milling gold was discovered south of Mount of the Holy Cross in August, 1880. The strike was reported in the Leadville *Daily Chronicle* and in the *Summit County Times*. There were stories of how gold ore could simply be picked up off the ground, and as a result of the publicity, the area was soon swarming with prospectors.

Soon the Holy Cross Mining District was formed, optimistically embracing one hundred square miles. As more prospectors arrived, two camps formed. One was Holy Cross City at an elevation of 11,335 feet, which could be occupied only seasonally. The other was Gold Park on Homestake Creek at the bottom of the long two thousand vertical foot, four mile climb.

By 1883, Holy Cross City was listed in a business directory as having a population of 200. It had a post office, justice of the peace, assay office, druggist, the Timberline Hotel, a boarding house, general store, shoemaker, blacksmith shop and two saloons. Most remarkable for this high altitude town was the formation of the Holy Cross School District in 1883, in a place which was only habitable during the summer months.

The buildings at Holy Cross City were in two irregular rows facing each other across a small rocky meadow. The main street ran through the meadow. The Timberline Hotel, assay office and mining headquarters overlooked the town from a hillside. Roads led in several direction to area mines. Other cabins were scattered about and not arranged in any particular order. The small meadow was the only level ground in the general area.

An early photograph from the collection of Fred and Jo Muzzulla, Denver historians, show that Holy Cross City proper once included about a dozen structures. Robert L. Brown took a number of photographs during the 1960s matching the exact location as a historic photograph. He published both photographs in his book, *Holy Cross City: The Mountain and the City.* They revealed that virtually nothing remains of the town except for the two structures still standing today.

A number of mines were responsible for the area's economic growth including the Pelican Mine, about a mile from the town. Ore was recovered using two tunnels, and the approaches to the tunnels were fully covered with snow sheds to allow operation of the mine over an extended season. The Molly Mines were larger than the Pelican and utilized four tunnels. The Comstock Mine was another producer in the area. Other mines included the Belle of the West, Treasure Vault, Tip Top, Backus and Hunkidore.

It might be well to note that the owners of the Treasure Vault Mine wanted to construct their own mill, but use of the road up to Holy Cross City was prohibited by the Gold Park Mining and

This is the larger of the two remaining structures at Holy Cross City, situated in a high meadow at an elevation of 11,408 feet. The meadow, incidentally, was vibrant with wild flowers when this photograph was taken. *(Kenneth Jessen 100A10)*

Milling Company. This forced the Treasure Vault to bring its equipment in over Fancy Pass. So steep are the approaches to this pass that steel pins had to be driven into the rock for securing the cables and rope necessary for moving the heavy milling equipment. After all of this effort, the Treasure Vault Mill operated only for a brief period of time.

From Holy Cross City, gold ore was dumped into a two-and-a-half mile long iron flume which led down to Gold Park where the ore could be processed. Apparently at some later date, the decision was made to construct a mill just below Holy Cross City. Quite a bit of equipment, including several boilers, still sits at this mill site.

The veins were found in crevices, some eighteen inches thick. Assay values ran as high as thirty ounces of gold per ton. The various deposit were not large, however, and most historians say that Holy Cross City was abandoned around 1883-1884 and that only the mine manager and his family remained.

What has been written about Holy Cross City does not agree with postal records. The town was originally in Summit County, then in 1883, Eagle County was carved out of Summit County. The post office remained active from 1882 to 1889, far beyond what others believe was the life of the town. Even more intriguing is that in 1904, the post office was opened once again and lasted until the following year. It is unlikely that there was another town with the same name in Eagle County. A more likely solution is that Holy Cross City probably hung on longer than first believed and after its abandonment, was re-occupied by those who had renewed interest in its gold ore.

Ghost town historian Muriel Sibell Wolle learned of Holy Cross City during World War II. She also found out that it and Gold Park were within the limits of Camp Hale. Worse yet was the discovery that the area was proposed as part of a bombing range. Nothing can disturb a ghost town historian more than the image of a fragile, timberline town, exposed to the elements, receiving a direct hit and being blown to bits.

Such an image made Wolle attempt several times to reach the Commanding Officer at Camp Hale and obtain permission to enter the area. Women at an all-male military base were not especially welcome, but she finally got a signed pass to enter the area.

The old wagon road up French Creek was no longer passable by a vehicle, so she hiked the four miles while friends waited in her car at Gold Park. She covers this lonely and physically demanding trip in her book *Stampede to Timberline.*

The mill below the town was still standing, along with the boarding house. Some of the cabins were made of milled lumber and others of logs, many hidden in the trees at the edge of the meadow where the town was located. She also saw the shaft houses high above the town at the mines.

A number of people, even those with good four-wheel drive vehicles, have concluded that the road to Holy Cross City is so demanding that it takes the fun out of the trip. Others view the road as a challenge. Robert L. Brown probably provides the best description of the road in his book, *Jeep Trails to Colorado Ghost Towns.* The road has been improved somewhat since Brown's visit during the 1960s, especially where it goes through a bog. Brown says, "The distance up from Gold Park to Holy Cross City is only four bone-shaking miles, but you should plan on spending about one and a half nerve-wrecking hours...to get there over one of the steepest, roughest and toughest of mountain roads." He continues to say, "You will drive across paths of old logs that the pioneers called a corduroy road, over broken-down bridges that leave no room for guesswork, through bogs and streams and over huge boulders and sharp, high rocks, strategically emerging from the trail and so placed as to twist the frame of the Jeep in two opposite directions at once. At such times one may hear the comforting sound of fan blades scraping on the housing."

What Robert L. Brown found at Holy Cross City were the remains of a half dozen or so cabins, two still with their roofs and others with partial walls. He reported seventeen foundations in all. Today, the two best-preserved cabins still stand and have been stabilized. They are, however, quite utilitarian and more like miner's shacks than anything else. Only the remains of a few foundations could be discovered among the lush meadows filled with a wide variety of wildflowers. Even without any structures, this is a beautiful place to visit. Ironically, Mount of the Holy Cross cannot be seen from the site.

In recent years, a logging road was graded following the Missouri Tunnel Aqueduct. This provides an alternate, less demanding way to reach Holy Cross City. At the end of the graded portion of the road, a four-wheel drive section continues for another eight-tenths of a mile. A foot trail, which at first follows the logging road, continues on to Holy Cross City. At the end of a switchback that heads northeast, a very faint foot trail marked only by cairns crosses the high meadows to the rough four-wheel drive road originating in Gold Park. It intersects this road just below the mill. This trail is a wilderness experience since only the cairns reflect mankind's presence. The route requires judgement and faith that it leads to Holy Cross City.

This double boiler sits at what was once a mill just below Holy Cross City. Given the nature of the road, it is quite remarkable that such a piece of equipment could be brought to this site. *(Kenneth Jessen 100A6)*

Don and Jean Griswold, *Colorado's Century of "Cities"*, Self Published, 1958, pp. 166-167.

Muriel Sibell Wolle, *Stampede to Timberline*, Sage Books, Chicago, 1949, 1974, pp. 246-251.

Robert L. Brown, *Jeep Trails to Colorado Ghost Towns*, Caxton Printers, Caldwell, Idaho, 1973, pp. 112-116.

Robert L. Brown, *Holy Cross: The Mountain and the City*, Caxton Printers, Ltd, 1970, pp. 123-148.

Thomas Noel, Paul Mahoney and Richard Stevens, *Historical Atlas of Colorado*, University of Oklahoma Press, Norman, 1994, Section 17.

William H. Bauer, James L. Ozment, John H. Willard, *Colorado Post Offices*, Colorado Railroad Museum, Golden, Colorado, 1990, p. 74.

HOPKINS, MEREDITH
And Other Towns Along the Frying Pan River

- *Eagle and Pitkin counties, Frying Pan River drainage*
- *Sites accessible by car; some towns had a post office*
- *Some sites have original structures*

There were a number of small towns founded along the Frying Pan river, stimulated by the arrival of the Colorado Midland Railway in 1887. Most of these communities remain occupied today, however, they are a fraction of their original size.

Hopkins was established by the Colorado Midland Railway and was the home of watchman Frank Blair. Frank worked in a nearby quarry during the day, and at night, he was a "track walker" looking for broken rails, rotten ties and washouts. His wife, Anna, was known by the railroad employees as "Mother" Blair because she fed any railroad worker who stopped to say hello. She was noted for being a good listener and sympathetic to the problems of the railroad employees. She provided a great deal of comfort to lonely men away from their families.

Helpers, in the form of powerful locomotives, were used to push trains upgrade and thus help the lead engine. Once its job was done, the helper would coast back toward Basalt, and the engineers would find some excuse to stop at Hopkins for a piece of Anna's wild raspberry pie. Some of the excuses were thin. Engineers claimed that they had to stop and build up steam where the reality was that no steam was necessary.

Engineers in approaching locomotives would give the Blairs ample warning. The canyon was very narrow at Hopkins, and the Blair's long, frame house was only about fifteen feet from the track. The sound of a whistle meant that they had just enough

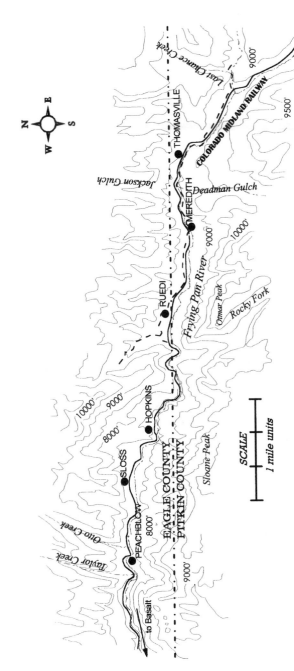

This is how the Frying Pan River drainage looked around the turn of the century. There were a number of small communities associated with the Colorado Midland Railway along the river. It wasn't until the railroad was abandoned in 1918 and the rails removed that a through road was constructed up this canyon.

Ruedi is now below the Ruedi Reservoir and Meredith has been moved a short distance to the east. There is a modern housing development near Peachblow and the old section house still stands at Sloss.

time to get the chickens off the track.

The Blairs had difficulty getting coal to heat their house and for cooking. On locomotives working the heavy grade uphill, the firemen would "accidentally" kick large chunks of coal off the foot plate as they passed Hopkins.

A nice home now occupies the site.

Meredith is now dominated by the Meredith General Store, but it used to be a quarry town. Meredith was started in 1889 by the Meredith Manufacturing Company which opened a limestone quarry. The town was named for Professor Meredith, one of the company owners. The professor was killed in an explosion in the

The Meredith Store is a gathering place for those that live in the area. The store is the only original structure from the Meredith town site a few hundred yards to the west. *(Kenneth Jessen 106A4)*

quarry, and his body is buried about a half mile east of the original town site.

The limestone was heated in a kiln to form lime. The kiln was located conveniently along the Colorado Midland tracks. Lime shipments amounted to only about one carload a week. Stock pens were built, and the railroad added a 12 x 22 foot freight house.

Around 1891, the Miller Creek Lime & Lumber Company purchased the original company and erected a combination office, commissary and boarding house. A sawmill was also constructed, and the lumber business soon exceeded that of the limestone business. A small store was added to Meredith which carried gloves, overalls, tobacco and whiskey for the workers. Eventually the store was expanded to carry groceries, hay and grain. The Meredith post office, opened in 1893, has always been located in the store and remains open to this day.

When the Ruedi Reservoir was constructed, the Meredith store was moved a few hundred yards to the east. The owners of the store say that the other structures at today's Meredith came from various locations. The guest cabins, for example, were moved from another site.

Meredith is easy to reach and is located along 104RD just a quarter-of-a-mile east of the Ruedi Reservoir.

The original town of Peach Blow (sometimes spelled Peachblow) once sat approximately eight and a half miles east of Basalt and was among a number of settlements stimulated in 1888 by the arrival of the Colorado Midland Railway. The site of the original town is abandoned, and a small cluster of houses to the west, just prior to entering the narrow portion of the canyon, now claims title to the name Peach Blow.

Peach Blow was founded by a man named Wilson and its economy was based solely on the fine peach-colored sandstone located on both sides of the river. A rickety-looking bridge, with mining track laid on its deck, was part of a haulage system to bring stone blocks from the quarry on the south side of the river to the railroad on the north side. A mule was used to pull a small mining car across the bridge onto a loading dock.

At first, Peach Blow was called Wilson's Quarries, then when the railroad constructed its siding, the name was changed to reflect the trade name for the peach-colored sandstone.

As the business grew, a few houses were constructed by the workmen at the quarry. One historic photograph shows five structures. Peach Blow was never anything more than a small camp. A post office was opened in 1890, and in 1909, was moved east to Sloss.

Ruedi is a ghost town; the site is under the Ruedi Reservoir. The town was named for Swiss-born John Ruedi who settled along the Frying Pan River in 1880.

The Colorado Midland Railway constructed its line seven years later and built a siding at the ranch. It named the siding Ruedi. The railroad built a depot, section house, bunk house, water tank and pump house at Ruedi.

In 1905, the Roaring Fork Plaster Company constructed a mill at Ruedi. Gypsum was mined from a nearby quarry. The railroad put in a spur track to the mill for the shipment of Plaster of Paris.

As more people moved into the area based on employment at the plaster mill, a town of sorts began to develop at Ruedi. There were about a dozen families living in homes scattered about the area. Historic photographs show that Ruedi did not have a business district or organized street system. John Ruedi opened a post office in 1889 that remained active until 1941. John picked up the mail that was dropped off the train at the water tank. He distributed the mail to his immediate neighbors.

Using the swampy area on his ranch, Ruedi turned the place into fish ponds where he raised trout. He sold the fresh fish to the dining cars on the Colorado Midland. It is said that his customers also included disappointed fishermen who were reluctant to return home with empty creels.

The plaster mill operated until 1918 and was dismantled for scrap. The Colorado Midland was abandoned at this time, and its rails removed.

This is a Colorado Midland section house at Sloss along the Frying Pan River. Few railroad structures like this remain. *(Kenneth Jessen 106A2)*

In 1964, construction of the Ruedi Reservoir dam began and was completed a few years later. The reservoir now inundates the Ruedi site.

Sloss, located between Peach Blow and Hopkins, is another location that served the Colorado Midland Railway. The section house still stands along the road and has been remodeled to serve as a home. The owner is apparently proud of its heritage, since the Sloss station sign hangs on one side along with a historical plaque.

Originally the place was called Sloane, then in 1903, well after the Colorado Midland had constructed its line, Sterling P. Sloss purchased the ranch near the section house. He convinced the U. S. Postal Service to move the post office from Peach Blow to the new location, and it was named Sloss. The railroad changed the name of this location from Sloane to Sloss as a result. The Colorado Midland was abandoned in 1918, but the Sloss post office continued to operate until 1931.

The railroad not only constructed the 24 x 30 foot section house, but also built a bunk house, two outhouses and a telephone booth at Sloss. Sloss became a flag stop where passing trains could be stopped according to demand.

Thomasville is not quite a ghost town, and a few people still live on the site. The town began with the construction of a smelter in 1890, built by the St. Louis and Colorado Smelting Company. The man placed in charge of running the smelter was named Thomas, and the small community which formed near the smelter was logically named Thomasville. The Colorado Midland Railway constructed a spur track between Lime Creek and Thomasville to the smelter located on the hillside north of the

This is one of the cabins in Thomasville, which might date back to the town's beginnings. *(Kenneth Jessen 106A5)*

town. There were also a few lime kilns near the town.

The small town included a store, three saloons, a boarding house, several homes and the Alhambra Hall. A beautiful depot was constructed and was later expanded from its original size. The railroad also built a section house, bunk house, stock pens and had a turntable at Thomasville.

The smelter processed ore from a mine near the Lime-Brush Creek divide and the Bessie Mine near the town. Some ore may have been shipped over the railroad from other mines. The smelter was not profitable, but it kept running until 1892.

The closest post office was at Calcium. It opened in 1888 and was moved to Thomasville in 1890. The post office remained in service until the Colorado Midland was abandoned in 1918.

Today, there is a business on the north side of the road and a few original cabins on the south side of the road that have been restored for seasonal use. The old section house has been moved and modified for use as a garage, and unfortunately, the depot was razed.

Thomasville is located east of Meredith, close to the confluence of Lime Creek and the Frying Pan River on FR105, a paved road.

Clarence Danielson and Ralph Danielson, *Basalt: Colorado Midland Town*, Pruett Publishing Company, Boulder, Colorado, 1965, pp. 61-62, s289-290.

Edward M. McFarland, *A Colorado Midland Guide and Data Book*, Colorado Railroad Museum, Golden, Colorado, 1980, pp. 208-209, pp. 274-276, 301.

Len Shoemaker, *Roaring Fork Valley*, Sage Books, Denver, 1958, pp. 149, 151, 182-183, 191, 200-201, 211.

William H. Bauer, James L. Ozment, John H. Willard, *Colorado Post Offices*, Colorado Railroad Museum, Golden, Colorado, 1990, pp. 27, 97, 111, 125, 133, 141.

INDEPENDENCE
A Town With Many Names

- *Pitkin County, Roaring Fork River*
- *Accessible via paved road plus a short walk*
- *Town had a post office under other names; many standing structures remain*

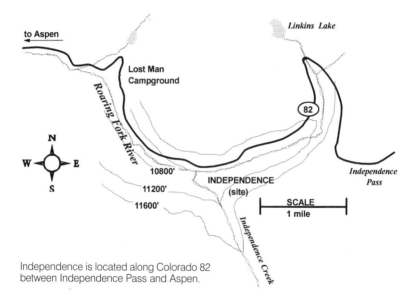

Independence is located along Colorado 82 between Independence Pass and Aspen.

Following the Leadville boom during 1877 and 1878, prospectors began crossing the Continental Divide at Hunter's Pass (now called Independence Pass) looking for other pockets of rich ore. Some gold was discovered at the head of the Roaring Fork River right around timberline. A camp began to form under various names including Farwell and Sparkill. Dick Irwin discovered a lode on the Fourth of July during the early 1880s. When news of

the discovery reached other mining towns, many prospectors
came into the area.

During the summer of 1880, a couple of town promoters
surveyed the town site which was incorporated the following year.
The town was originally named Chipeta in honor of the famous
wife of Chief Ouray. One of these men, William Kinkead, applied
for a post office, and it was granted under the name of Sidney.
The post office lasted a little over two months. Since the date of
discovery was on July 4, the camp was renamed Independence.
The Farwell Consolidated Mining Company applied for a post
office of its own under the name Farwell, and it was opened in
1881. The following year, the name of the post office was changed

This Forest Service photograph, taken in 1939, shows that Independence had weathered the years reasonably well. Most other ghost towns had long vanished by this time. *(U. S. Forest Service)*

to Sparkill and remained open until 1887. During all of its years, never did the post office at Independence reflect the name of the town.

> **Post Office Summary**
>
> | | |
> |---|---|
> | Sidney | January 4, 1881 to March 10, 1882 |
> | Farwell | July 4, 1881 to July 3, 1882 |
> | Sparkill | February 1, 1882 to October 18, 1887 |
> | Chipeta | April 20, 1899 to October 17, 1899 |

Typical of any mining camp, only tents occupied the site at first, then Bill Langstall and Jack Williams constructed a log house. Ted Ackerman started a store in a tent with a stock of goods and soon built a permanent store. It also served as a restaurant and boarding house. Bill Langstall operated a hotel-restaurant in Independence. The town evolved into a stop-over for trips between Aspen, twenty miles to the west, and Leadville, twenty-five miles to the northeast.

In July, 1880, a Leadville newspaper reported that for 75 cents, a meal could be purchased and that oats for the horses were ten cents per pound. Also, the trail over Independence Pass to Twin Lakes went "...across more rocks and swamps than any other hundred miles in the world." There were many toll bridges where the traveler was charged 25 cents, but they were wide enough only for a man and his horse.

The *Aspen Times* sent a correspondent over the route to Leadville in April, 1881. Many accommodations were listed in Independence at this time, among them, the Connor House, the New England House, and the Independence House. The latter was run by Ted Ackerman. Accommodations cost all of $2 per day. The Langstall Brothers were listed as having the largest stock of groceries, wines and liquors in the camp. Cummings & Meany had a general merchandise store while R. H. Jones ran a bar, "...fitted up in style." The town's only drug store was run by C. H. Harding. The *Independence Miner* started publication that year with its first issue on October 8.

The businesses in Independence in 1882 included a number

of new grocery stores and restaurants as well as Briner, Lavender & Company dry goods and clothing. The Bank of Pitkin County had opened and the town even had its own attorney. The Carson Brothers operated daily stages to Aspen, while Rockwell & Bicknell operated daily

There are many interesting structures in Independence, making it one of the best preserved ghost towns in Colorado. *(Kenneth Jessen 092B11)*

stages to Leadville. Con Hansen operated a sawmill, and by this time, the town had gained a barber shop, laundry and meat market. A high percentage of the business enterprises, however, were saloons of various types, some with billiard halls.

By 1888, the population of Independence declined, and most of the business firms closed. The stage service terminated and the town was dying. Ted Ackerman still ran his store, restaurant and post office. He finally gave up and moved to Aspen.

A new group of individuals came along, and maybe to spark interest in the town, the name was changed to Mammoth City. It later became Mount Hope. Neither name was used extensively, and eventually the name Independence returned. Walter Ritchie got a post office established once again, but under the name Chipeta. It lasted from April to October of 1899. The mines continued to operate off and on. In 1920, the mill was torn down and all mining on any large scale ceased.

Independence is located just below Colorado Highway 82 east of Aspen and only about two miles from 12,095-foot Independence Pass. The town site sits at an elevation of

10,800 feet in an open valley near timberline where Independence Creek enters the Roaring Fork River from the south. There is a small parking lot at the east end of the site. The site has the ruins of many cabins spread out over quite an area with some stabilized and partially restored. A caretaker occupies the site during the summer months. It is well worth a visit since all structures are primarily of log construction.

This historic photograph was taken by the Forest Service in 1939, long after the town of Independence had been abandoned. The site is below timberline, but all of the trees were cut to supply lumber for buildings, mine timbers and fuel for the boilers at the mines and mills. *(Denver Public Library, Western History Department MAX 339)*

Frank L. Wentworth, *Aspen on the Roaring Fork*, Francis B. Rizzari (publisher), 1950, pp. 121, 133, 148, 177, 184, 186, 190.

Len Shoemaker, *Roaring Fork Valley*, Sage Books, Denver, 1958, pp. 23, 28-30, 76-77, 145-146.

Muriel Sibell Wolle, *Stampede to Timberline*, Sage Books, Chicago, 1949, 1974, p. 245.

William H. Bauer, James L. Ozment, John H. Willard, *Colorado Post Offices*, Colorado Railroad Museum, Golden, Colorado, 1990, pp. 33, 53, 73, 134.

IVANHOE

A Colorado Midland Section

- *Pitkin County; Frying Pan River drainage*
- *Accessible by automobile over graded dirt road*
- *No original structures remain; public access partially restricted*

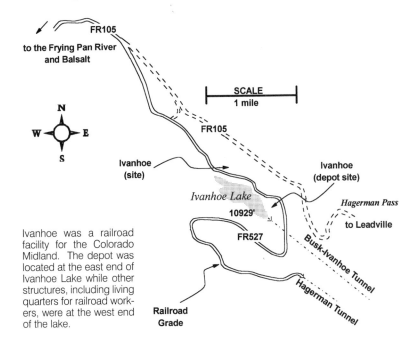

Ivanhoe was a railroad facility for the Colorado Midland. The depot was located at the east end of Ivanhoe Lake while other structures, including living quarters for railroad workers, were at the west end of the lake.

Located in a long, high valley at Lake Ivanhoe was the railroad settlement of Ivanhoe. When the Colorado Midland was first constructed in 1888, the Hagerman Tunnel brought the rails from Leadville under the Continental Divide to Basalt. Because of difficulty keeping the tunnel open in the winter at an elevation of nearly 11,600 feet, a second tunnel, the Ivanhoe-Busk Tunnel, was built about 600 vertical feet lower and was completed in 1893.

Ivanhoe had a railroad station combined with a telegraph office and post office. Not especially attractive, the structure had a mud-room entrance to keep blasts of cold air from entering the interior. It was originally located at the west end of Ivanhoe Lake. When the new tunnel was opened, the depot was moved to the east end of the lake near the portal of the Ivanhoe-Busk Tunnel. The other structures remained at the west end of the lake, and they included a pump house, section house, bunk house, a shed for a hand car, a coal bin, a water tank and sheep pens.

The post office at Ivanhoe has its own checkered history. It first opened in 1888, then closed in 1894 to open again in 1899 and to close in 1912. It opened for the last time in 1912 and was closed in 1918 when the railroad was abandoned. The problems keeping the post office open probably related to finding a reliable postmaster at this remote location.

The winters were extreme at Ivanhoe, and the agent was cut off from the outside world for weeks at a time during heavy storms. Sometimes, supplies were brought to Ivanhoe through the tunnel on a hand car. The first agent committed suicide after the first big storm.

Ivanhoe is a favorite spot for fishermen and is easy to reach over a graded dirt road that is rough in places, but passable by car. The road follows the old railroad grade through Sellar and becomes narrow and exposed at Hell's Gate. Beyond Hell's Gate, the road enters the wide valley where Ivanhoe was once located. No original structures stand, and access to the lower portal is blocked by a gate. At the extreme west end of this valley, a four-wheel drive road leaves the railroad grade and climbs over Hagerman Pass to Turquoise Lake above Leadville.

Edward M. McFarland, *A Colorado Midland Guide and Data Book*, Colorado Railroad Museum, Golden, Colorado, 1980, pp. 33-34, 41-45, 196, 202. 272.

JANEWAY

- *Pitkin County, Crystal River Drainage*
- *Site can be viewed from paved road*
- *Town had a post office; one standing structure remains*

A small cabin, visible from Colorado 133, sits on the gravel flats along the Crystal River just north of where Avalanche Creek enters the canyon. It is said that this is the one remaining structure in the town of Janeway.

Prospecting in the area began in the 1880s, and the Silver Queen Mine was opened on Avalanche Creek. John Mobley set up a place referred to as Mobley's Camp, which acted as a supply point for miners heading up Avalanche Creek. It was also a stage stop on the route to Redstone and Marble. The name was changed to Janeway for Mary Jane Francis, however, it is not clear what connection she had with Mobley or the town. Mobley secured a post office in 1887 and became the postmaster. By the following year, the population of Janeway was fifty people.

By 1898, the Crystal River Railroad was placed in operation from Carbondale to Redstone, and a station was established at Janeway. A siding was built which could hold 29 cars in anticipation of ore shipments from the mines up Avalanche Creek. Buildings at Janeway included a hotel, store, saloon and the post office.

Mrs. Olyn Parker, 89 at the time of this publication, moved to Janeway in 1948. She relates that the old hotel was gone by that time. Her recollection of the location of Janeway places it a short distance up Avalanche Creek. In any event, the Janeway town site was on the east side of the Crystal River, and it is likely that the old cabin north of the bridge across the Crystal River was in or near the town site. Modern homes restrict access to the area.

Dell McCoy and Russ Collman, *The Crystal River Pictorial*, Sundance Publications, Ltd., Denver, Colorado, 1972, p. 29.

Len Shoemaker, *Roaring Fork Valley*, Sage Books, Denver, 1958, pp. 146-147.

Muriel Sibell Wolle, *Timberline Tailings*, Sage Books, Chicago, 1977, p. 193.

Oscar McCullum Jr. Marble, *A Town Built on Dreams*, Sundance Publications, Ltd., Denver, Colorado, 1992, p. 56.

William H. Bauer, James L. Ozment, John H. Willard, *Colorado Post Offices*, Colorado Railroad Museum, Golden, Colorado, 1990, p. 79.

LENADO

On Woody Creek

- *Pitkin County, Woody Creek drainage*
- *Accessible by graded dirt road; private property*
- *Town had a post office; several original standing structures remain*

Up Woody Creek and about four miles northeast of Aspen as the crow flies is the small mining community of Lenado. During the prospecting era of the 1880s, A. J. Varney struck a rich vein containing lead and zinc. The Varney Tunnel Company was

Many of the old structures at Lenado have been restored for seasonal use. There are, however, some abandoned buildings. *(Kenneth Jessen 109C5)*

formed to develop the claim with 150 men at work. The mine was a success and produced a great deal of ore. The settlement of Lenado, populated by about 300 miners, grew up in the vicinity of the tunnel. The first homes in Lenado were built of logs, but after the tunnel company started a sawmill, several frame homes, a boarding house, two saloons and a store were constructed. Isolated at first, a road was constructed up Woody Creek to Lenado, and a mill was built near the tunnel entrance.

In 1888, the Denver & Rio Grande Railroad completed an eight mile grade up Woody Creek to Lenado, however, it never laid any track.

The Lenado post office, established in 1891, operated until 1893 when there was a slump in mining resulting from the repeal of the Sherman Silver Purchase Act. Operations at the mine were resumed after 1900, and mail was carried from Aspen over the Hunter-Woody Creek divide by a horseback rider. The post office was reopened once again in 1905 and remained open until 1907. At that time, about eighty men lived and worked at the town.

The boom to bust to boom mining business struck again with the closure of the mine and mill. The demand for lead and zinc dramatically increased at the start of World War I, and the mine reopened again. A new boarding house was constructed, and some of the homes were restored. Ore was trucked down the railroad grade to Woody Creek for shipment, but after the end of the war, the mine and mill closed for good.

Based on a letter she received, ghost town historian Muriel Sibell Wolle reported that there were fifteen cabins and frame homes as well as the abandoned mill still standing in 1951. A sawmill was the only active business.

There are some newer homes at the site today, as well as some of the original structures restored by their owners.

Len Shoemaker, *Roaring Fork Valley*, Sage Books, Denver, 1958, pp. 96, 180.

Muriel Sibell Wolle, *Timberline Tailings*, Sage Books, Chicago, 1977, pp. 187-188.

William H. Bauer, James L. Ozment, John H. Willard, *Colorado Post Offices*, Colorado Railroad Museum, Golden, Colorado, 1990, p. 88.

MARION

A Coal Town

- *Garfield County, Edgerton Creek drainage*
- *Access limited by private property; foot trail to site*
- *Town had a post office; no standing structures remain;*

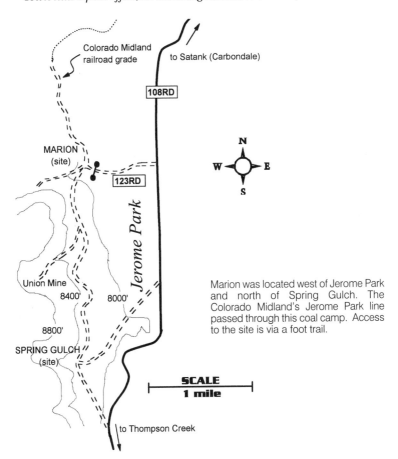

Marion was located west of Jerome Park and north of Spring Gulch. The Colorado Midland's Jerome Park line passed through this coal camp. Access to the site is via a foot trail.

Marion and Spring Gulch were closely related coal mining communities located in Jerome Park and only a mile and a half apart.

Mining began at Marion in 1885 under the ownership of Jerome B. Wheeler. Wheeler sold out to the Grand River Coal and Coke Company which had thirty-five men working at Marion in 1887. By 1889, seventy-five men were working at the mine, and the small community of Marion probably began to develop at this time. The vein sat at a forty-five degree angle and was five-and-a-half feet thick. It was an extension of the same vein at Spring Gulch, but for some reason, the coal could not be converted to coke as easily. A second drift, called the New Marion, was opened. It produced a better quality coal for coke.

Initially, coke ovens were constructed at Marion, but were eventually dismantled, and the brick was used for coke ovens at Cardiff, a Colorado Fuel & Iron town.

The peak year for the population of Marion and for output from the mine was 1890. Although population estimates are hard to find, Marion probably did not grow beyond 150.

The post office opened in 1889 only to close in 1891. It reopened in 1909 only to close that same year. Finally, it opened again and stayed open until the town was abandoned in 1912.

The post office reflects the difficulty of mining at Marion with the first mine closure in 1892. In 1895, it looked like the Marion mine would be abandoned. It was put back into operation in 1898, and under C. F. & I. ownership, a new drift was drilled in 1907 well above the old mine openings. This necessitated construction of a tramway to bring the coal down.

To reach the Marion site, the paved Jerome Park Road runs south from Satank (on the outskirts of Carbondale) to the area where Marion and Spring Gulch are located. The road to Marion is the first right (west) onto a gravel road. There is a parking lot and a sign which indicates that the first quarter of a mile of trail goes through private property. There are gates at either end of this section. After exiting private property, the trail joins the old mine haulage road up Marion Gulch past the tailings piles from various mine openings. Hardly a trace of the town is left and the exact site is difficult to locate.

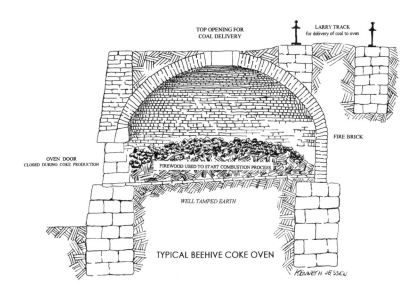

TOP OPENING FOR COAL DELIVERY

LARRY TRACK for delivery of coal to oven

FIRE BRICK

OVEN DOOR CLOSED DURING COKE PRODUCTION

FIREWOOD USED TO START COMBUSTION PROCESS

WELL TAMPED EARTH

TYPICAL BEEHIVE COKE OVEN

KENNETH JESSEN

William H. Bauer, James L. Ozment, John H. Willard, *Colorado Post Offices*, Colorado Railroad Museum, Golden, Colorado, 1990, p. 95.

Anna Johnson and Kathleen Yajko, *The Elusive Dream*, Gran Furnum Printing & Publishing Company, Glenwood Springs, Colorado, 1983, pp. 5, 23, 32, 49-50, 62.

H. Lee Scamehorn, *Pioneer Steelmaker in the West*, Pruett, Boulder, Colorado, 1976, p. 89.

Robert Ormes, *Tracking Ghost Railroads in Colorado*, Century One Press, Colorado Springs, Colorado, 1975, p. 111.

Telephone interviews with Anna Johnson and Kathleen Yajko, June, 1997.

MITCHELL

- *Eagle County, Eagle River drainage*
- *Accessible by paved road*
- *Town had a post office; no structures remain*

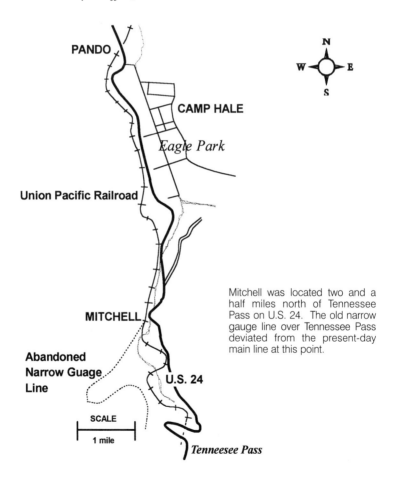

PANDO

CAMP HALE

Eagle Park

Union Pacific Railroad

MITCHELL

Abandoned
Narrow Guage
Line

U.S. 24

SCALE

1 mile

Tenneesee Pass

Mitchell was located two and a half miles north of Tennessee Pass on U.S. 24. The old narrow gauge line over Tennessee Pass deviated from the present-day main line at this point.

The mining town of Mitchell began as Roudebush, named for the prospector that constructed the first cabin in 1878. Other prospectors entered the area and also built cabins. The attraction was gold placer deposits in the Eagle River Valley. The name of the camp was changed to Eagle City in 1879, however, in 1880, the camp got a post office under its original name Roudebush.

A correspondent for the Leadville *Daily Chronicle* described Eagle City as having, "...eight or nine cabins and more going up, and about a dozen tents." The Central City *Daily Register-Call* said that, "The new city consists of six houses and cabins and three or four unfinished cabins."

The gold was soon exhausted and the prospectors moved on. Kilns were built to turn cord wood into charcoal. George Mitchell, one of the early prospectors in the area, rearranged the town around his cabin. A hotel was constructed, and George Mitchell took over the job of postmaster. He managed to change the name of the post office and the camp to Mitchell in 1883.

Mitchell is still indicated on some maps, but the site no longer has any original log buildings. The site is located along Colorado 24 north of Tennessee Pass. The tracks of the Denver & Rio Grande came through this valley in 1881. At that time, the railroad was narrow gauge, and as operations expanded, the track was changed to standard gauge. A passing track was added. In 1935, the Denver & Rio Grande listed Mitchell as having a population of fifty, and its primary industry was lumber. All remains of the original camp were probably cleared as the railroad expanded its operations.

Pando, a mining camp located north of Mitchell, was listed as having a population of forty in 1935. Its original depot closed five years later, but when World War II broke out, a new depot was constructed. Pando was the site of Camp Hale, the training center for the Tenth Mountain Division and home for 15,000 troops. Only the cement foundations are left at Camp Hale and nothing remains at the Pando site.

Central City *Daily Register-Call*, July 15, 1880.

Don and Jean Griswold, *Colorado's Century of "Cities"*, Self Published, 1958, pp. 164-166.

Leadville *Daily Chronicle*, May 28, 1879.

Perry Eberhart, *Guide to the Colorado Ghost Towns and Mining Camps*, Sage Books, Chicago, 1959, p. 175.

Robert A. LeMassena, "Tennessee Pass," *Colorado Rail Annual No. 17*, Colorado Railroad Museum, Golden, Colorado, 1987, pp. 197, 210.

Robert A. LaMassena, *Rio Grande to the Pacific*, Sundance, Denver, 1974, p. 182.

William H. Bauer, James L. Ozment, John H. Willard, *Colorado Post Offices*, Colorado Railroad Museum, Golden, Colorado, 1990, pp. 99, 124.

PLACITA

- *Pitkin County, Crystal River drainage*
- *Accessible via paved road*
- *Town had a post office; several standing structures remain; occupied site*

A small coal mining settlement was created south of Redstone in 1899 by the Colorado Fuel & Iron Company. A coal mine was opened up, and a standard gauge railroad was extended from Redstone to the mine. Coal was shipped directly from the mine to the coke ovens at Redstone.

Apparently the mine did not live up to C. F. & I. standards and was sold in 1901. It continued, however, to supply a limited amount of coal to Redstone.

The town gained its post office in 1899, and it lasted until 1903. The area must have seen some sort of rebirth in 1928 because the post office was established once again. It closed for the final time in 1934.

Placita was also the shipping point for ore coming from the Crystal River mining area and from the marble quarries above the town of Marble. The Crystal River & San Juan Railroad extended the tracks from Placita to Marble in 1906.

Historic photographs taken in the 1920s reveal that only two or three homes were constructed at Placita, along with a railroad depot, a store, stock pens and the coal tipple. After the railroad was dismantled, coal was trucked from Placita. Today, several of the original buildings still stand, converted for summer use.

William H. Bauer, James L. Ozment, John H. Willard, *Colorado Post Offices*, Colorado Railroad Museum, Golden, Colorado, 1990, p. 114.

Oscar McCollum Jr., *Marble, A Town Built on Dreams*, Vol. I, Sundance, Denver, 1992, pp. 111-117.

Tivis Wilkins, *Colorado Railroads*, Pruett Publishing Company, Boulder, Colorado, 1974, p. 123.

Perry Eberhart, *Guide to the Colorado Ghost Towns and Mining Camps*, Sage Books, Chicago, 1959, pp. 310-311.

RED CLIFF
Residents Get The Shaft

- *Eagle County, Eagle River drainage*
- *Accessible by paved road*
- *Town had a post office; occupied town; many original structures remain*

This is how Red Cliff looked in 1910 to photographer George L. Beam who did work for the Denver & Rio Grande. *(Colorado Historical Society F28879)*

Below the spectacular high bridge that carries U.S. 24 over the Eagle River gorge is the old mining town of Red Cliff. It has never been completely abandoned, but does not support the population it once had during its boom years. The town dates back to 1879 when miners from Leadville began prospecting in the area and began the settlement near the confluence of the Eagle River and Turkey Creek. Discoveries were made on Battle Mountain and Horn Silver Mountain. The first cabin was constructed in Red Cliff during that summer by G. J. Da Lee and William Greiner, early prospectors. Around the first of July, a general store was constructed by two merchants, and soon another store opened up using a jack load of goods brought in from Leadville. A mill site was selected, and a town company was formed. The name Red Cliff was agreed upon by the prospectors and miners after the numerous red bluffs that dominate the site.

When news of the Meeker Massacre reached Red Cliff in September, 1879, the miners constructed a log fort for their own safety. The miners sent out a scouting party, but no hostile Indians could be found.

A smelter was constructed by the Battle Mountain Mining and Smelting Company, which owned several of the area mines. It is known that this smelter produced lead bullion, but no mention of any silver output was made. After arrival of the Denver & Rio Grande, the smelter was closed, and ore was shipped to Leadville for processing.

One of the town's big events occurred in 1880 when a sawmill produced the first piece of milled lumber. It was tied to the back of a burro and decorated with evergreens. The burrow, with its single piece of lumber, became part of a St. Patrick's Day parade. Muriel Sibell Wolle, ghost town historian, reported that by the end of the day, all of the parade's

An old barn in Red Cliff sits down by Turkey Creek. *(Kenneth Jessen 102C1)*

participants were drunk, including the burro.

The post office in Red Cliff was opened in 1880 and five years later, changed its name to "Redcliff." After a decade, the post office name was returned to "Red Cliff." Reasons for this are not clear, but the original post office name may have conflicted with some other post office name. The Red Cliff post office closed in 1979.

A death in 1880 precipitated the need for the town's first casket. There wasn't any lumber for its construction, and the casket had to be made from a wagon box plus several packing crates. A man killed by a falling tree was laid to rest in this impromptu coffin. A lawyer agreed to play the role of a minister, and the miners came to the funeral in their very best clothes. This event also marked the opening of the town's cemetery.

The Denver & Rio Grande extended its narrow gauge tracks from Leadville to Red Cliff in 1881. At this time, the town had three businesses, five hotels and a brass band to play at dances. The town also had its own opera house for plays. Red Cliff remained the terminus of the Denver & Rio Grande until 1887. Many stages left Red Cliff for other mining areas to the west during this period of time.

George Crofutt described Red Cliff in his 1885 guide book as, "...a thrifty mining town situated on a triangular piece of land, a miniature valley...The town had a population of about 600 hardy and determined people, who have left the ordinary comforts of life behind them." By this time, Red Cliff had a school, several church organizations and a weekly newspaper, *The Shaft.* Many Red Cliff residents could claim that they got the shaft.

A severe snowstorm in 1884 blocked rail traffic from Leadville, and the newspaper ran out of newsprint. Not wanting to miss an issue, it printed its next issue on wallpaper. The April copy had a dotted background covered with sprays of ivy. The paper played up the fact that April Fools Day had just passed.

Today, Red Cliff is very much alive, with a high percentage of its structures occupied. There are some abandoned buildings, however, to give the town character. The town also has two fine frame churches. Many photographic opportunities exist in this old mining town. The Shrine Pass road also leaves from Red Cliff and provides a scenic way of getting to Vail Pass on I-70.

The Presbyterian Church in Red Cliff, constructed in 1881, is one of several frame churches in the town. *(Kenneth Jessen 102C3)*

Frank Hall, *History of Colorado*, Vol. III. The Blakely Printing Company, Chicago, 1895, p. 124.

George Crofutt, *Crofutt's Grip Sack Guide of Colorado 1885*, Johnson Books, Boulder, Colorado, 1966, 1981, pp. 133-134.

Muriel Sibell Wolle, *Stampede to Timberline*, Sage Books, Chicago, 1949, 1974, pp. 251-254.

Robert Athearn, *Rebel of the Rockies*, Yale University Press, New Haven, Connecticut, 1962, pp. 156, 161.

Robert L. Brown, *Colorado Ghost Towns - Past and Present*, Caxton Printers, Caldwell, Idaho, 1977, pp. 215-218.

William H. Bauer, James L. Ozment, John H. Willard, *Colorado Post Offices*, Colorado Railroad Museum, Golden, Colorado, 1990, p. 120.

REDSTONE
And It's Club

- *Pitkin County, Crystal River drainage*
- *Accessible by paved road*
- *Town had post office; many original structures remain; occupied site*

This school at Redstone was constructed by C. F. & I. for the children of the miners and coke workers. *(Camp and Plant CP096)*

Parry and Griffith noted that an avalanche had exposed the side of the mountain and revealed a coal seam. This discovery was made in 1881 along Coal Creek near Coalbasin, about a dozen miles west of Redstone. Soon, other coal seams were discovered, and a number of claims were filed.

John C. Osgood was a coal prospector working for the Chicago, Burlington & Quincy Railroad (now the Burlington Northern - Santa Fe). He purchased these coal claims in the Coalbasin-Redstone area.

In 1887, Osgood started the Colorado Coal Company which absorbed the Colorado Coal & Iron Company to become the Colorado Fuel & Iron Company in 1892. This grew to become Colorado's largest industry, with forty coal, calcite, lime and iron camps, a steel mill, 15,000 employees and its headquarters in Pueblo. All types of steel products were produced from rails, to nails, to bars, to wire. Most of the coal mined by C. F. & I. was converted into coke for use at the Pueblo steel mill.

According to Norma Kenny in her book, *The Hidden Place: Redstone*, James Leggatt gave Redstone its name around 1890. Initially, log cabins were constructed at Redstone, and when C. F. & I. took over, these primitive structures were razed in favor of company-built homes.

The Redstone post office was opened in 1898, but real growth did not come until it became a C. F. & I. town in 1901. The steel company built coke ovens, houses, two inns, a clubhouse and a school for the children of the working families. Osgood and his wife made Redstone their home and constructed a mansion that they called Cleveholm. The overall architecture selected by Osgood was Swiss-German, giving Redstone a unique look, not typical of a Colorado mining town.

As for the homes of the working men, the C. F. & I. dwellings were built from plans drawn for standard three, four, five and six room houses. To avoid the monotony of the stereotype company town, the different sizes were mixed, and each home was painted a different color. In all, C. F. & I. constructed eighty-four

Almost every C. F. & I. town had its own company physician. This was Redstone's medical doctor. *(Camp and Plant CP054)*

homes in Redstone.

A standard gauge railroad was constructed up the Crystal River from Carbondale to service the coke ovens at Redstone and to bring coal from mines at Placita. A narrow gauge railroad was built from Redstone to Coalbasin also to haul coal. The general idea was to provide coal to the 200 coke ovens in Redstone.

A band was formed in Redstone in 1902. Its members had no previous musical instruction or experience, which was a real challenge for band director Professor Jacoe. Practice sessions took place on the second floor of the new firehouse.

Each band member was issued a uniform and a quality instrument (triple silver plated!), gifts of the Osgoods. The band traveled to other communities to give performances which were reported as quite good. Professor Jacoe had his own agenda, however, since many of the pieces were those he wrote.

The experimentation in clubhouses began in Coalbasin in 1902. The second company clubhouse was constructed in Redstone, but it was far more elaborate than the one in Coalbasin. The building had a basement and stood two-stories high with multiple stone chimneys and decorative false dormers. Columns were used at the main entrance. It was called the Redstone Club, and was governed by a board of elected officers. An initiation fee of a dollar was required to get in, and dues of fifty cents a month were imposed.

Big leather-cushioned arm chairs were placed in the large lounge room. The room also included tables and chairs with fireplaces at either end. A Regina music box, capable of playing a variety of songs from circular steel disks, provided music.

The Redstone Club had a room with billiard and pool tables. There was also a reading room with newspapers in English, Italian and Slavonic, and the club also had a reference library. If this wasn't enough, there was a card room with six card tables, each with its own serving table. Dominoes and checkers were available as well as decks of cards. No gambling was allowed. In the basement were showers, tubs and dressing rooms.

This and other clubs at C. F. & I. camps were meant to discourage the wholesale consumption of alcohol, a common problem in any mining camp. Since the company owned all the land and buildings, it prohibited saloons in most camps. It recognized, however, that to prohibit liquor entirely led to the illegal importation of spirits, usually in large quantities.

The club house was the place the working man could to go for relaxation; women were barred from membership. Women and children, however, could enter during certain hours and on Wednesday evenings.

The best brands of liquor were kept on hand at the bar in the Redstone Club. The bottles were not openly displayed, and the bar was not especially large relative to the other rooms. A rule strictly enforced was no treating of others to a drink. On the subject of alcohol consumption, and as put by C. F. & I. policy, "If he is seen to be getting too much, he is told quietly that he has had enough, and can buy no more at that time." As an alternative to

The C. F. & I. presented this as a Redstone home, but it certainly wasn't a typical home for the working man. It was most likely constructed for a supervisor. *(Camp and Plant CP053)*

drinking, soft drinks, hot chocolate, cake, and sandwiches were available.

The most unusual feature of the Redstone Club was its fully equipped theater on the top floor. It had drop curtains and sets which could be painted. There were dressing rooms, and the stage floor had stage lights.

John C. Osgood provided the funding to construct a stone and wood schoolhouse at Redstone. It was an elaborate building even by Victorian standards and was completed in 1902. It had three large class rooms plus smaller rooms for "domestic science" and manual training. Also there were two exercise rooms with lockers. The school began with grades four through seven, then expanded to include other grades. A night school was started for adults.

For Redstone, the coal and coke era ended in 1910. The town lost sufficient population to result in the closure of the post office in 1918. It was re-established in 1925, only to close again in 1943. As Colorado entered into the post-World War II era of tourism, the town started gaining population, and this prompted the post office to open again in 1954. In 1962, it became a rural station of Carbondale.

Redstone is anything but a ghost town and is filled with restaurants, stores and a number of homes. Cleveholm, Osgood's mansion, is operated as an inn. The Redstone Inn is also open to the public. The entire town is on the National Register of Historic Places.

For a map locating Redstone, see "Coalbasin."

"Club Houses and Recreation Halls," *Camp and Plant*, November 21, 1903, pp. 437-439.
"Excellent Public Schools," *Camp and Plant*, December 26, 1903, p. 565.
Muriel Sibell Wolle, *Stampede to Timberline*, Sage Books, Chicago, 1949, 1974, pp. 226, 228.
Norma Kenny, *The Hidden Place, Redstone*, Redstone Press, Redstone, Colorado, 1992, pp. 13-26.
Sylvia Ruland, *The Lion of Redstone*, Johnson Books, Boulder, Colorado, 1981.
"The Redstone Band," *Camp and Plant*, September 26, 1903, p. 258.
William H. Bauer, James L. Ozment, John H. Willard, *Colorado Post Offices*, Colorado Railroad Museum, Golden, Colorado, 1990, p. 120.

RUBY

On Lincoln Creek

- *Pitkin County, Lincoln Creek drainage*
- *Accessible over four-wheel drive road*
- *Town did not have a post office; several restored structures remain*

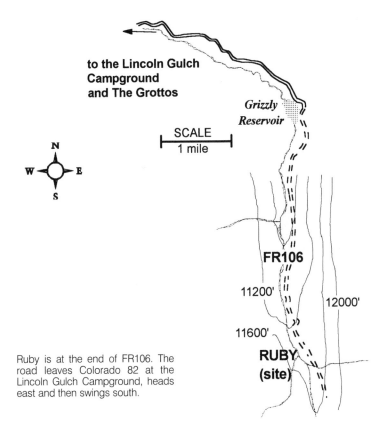

Ruby is at the end of FR106. The road leaves Colorado 82 at the Lincoln Gulch Campground, heads east and then swings south.

Silver ore was discovered in the canyon south of Independence in 1880, and several small mining camps developed. The largest was called Hurt's Camp after one of the prospectors. The area, however, was generally known as South Independence on the South Fork of the Roaring Fork River. The name of the creek was simply too long for one of the prospectors, and he suggested that the name be changed. Since the district was named the Lincoln Mining District, the creek's name was simplified to Lincoln Creek.

At the turn of the century, the Ruby Mining & Development Company took over the silver claims and constructed several large buildings, including a two-story log boarding house capable of housing fifty men. These added to the structures already in place.

A long tunnel was drilled under Red Mountain to reach the ore. Transportation was a severe problem, and in 1906, a wagon road was constructed to the Independence Pass road to allow ore to be hauled to Aspen for smelting. A concentrator was built near the mine to reduce the bulk of ore hauled. The name of the camp was changed to Ruby, and mining lasted until 1912. Others tried their hand, and sporadic mining took place for many years. Eventually, Ruby's only residents were a couple of old prospectors who lived in the boarding house.

In 1947, ghost town historian Muriel Sibell Wolle made her way up Lincoln Creek, past the

The remains of several cabins at the upper end of the valley where the mining town of Ruby was located. *(Kenneth Jessen 109C8)*

Grizzly Reservoir to Ruby at 11,300 feet. She reported that the road beyond the reservoir was very rough. At least a half-dozen sturdy log buildings still stood in the high meadow along Ruby's main street. The mill was still standing as well as the boarding house. One cabin was an assay office that still contained its furnace and

John Nichols lived in this cabin on his mining claim, beginning in 1903, and for the next thirty years. His cabin is located north of the majority of structures defining the ghost town of Ruby. *(Kenneth Jessen 109C7)*

cupels used to heat ore samples. When Robert L. Brown visited the site in the 1960s, only the log boarding house remained standing.

To reach Ruby, drive on Colorado 82 east from Aspen toward Independence Pass. At the Lincoln Creek Campground, turn off and go through the campground. The road is rough, but passable by automobile. The road heads east at first then swings south past the Grizzly Reservoir. It becomes more of a four-wheel drive trail about a half mile beyond the reservoir. At Ruby, there are the remains of many cabins spread out over a wide area. Other cabins have been restored for seasonal use. An interpretative sign along the road tells visitors about the history of the Lincoln Mining District. Ruby's location is among a wall of peaks in excess of 13,000 feet, making the trip worthwhile.

Len Shoemaker, *Roaring Fork Valley*, Sage Books, Denver, 1958, pp. 29, 195.

Muriel Sibell Wolle, *Stampede to Timberline*, Sage Books, Chicago, 1949, 1974, pp. 224-225.

Robert L. Brown, *Ghost Towns of the Colorado Rockies*, Caxton Printers, Caldwell, Idaho, 1977, pp. 295-300.

SATANK
And Its Confusing Past

- *Garfield County, Roaring Fork river drainage*
- *Accessible by paved road*
- *Town had a post office; original structures are unknown*

The original post office at Satank, immediately northwest of the present-day town of Carbondale, dates back to when Satank was founded in 1882. About a mile to the northwest, Captain Cooper and his wife Sarah, filed a plat for a town site in 1884. The Captain named the place Cooperton, but soon changed the name to Rockford. Captain Cooper was a stock holder in the Denver & Rio Grande Railroad. He arranged to have a station established at Rockford.

F. C. Childs was also involved in picking the Rockford site, and he constructed a large general merchandise store. Cooper, in the meantime, conspired to have the post office at Satank relocated to Rockford. Childs became the postmaster, and the town of Rockford turned into Satank leaving the original town of Satank and its neighbor, Carbondale, with no postal facility. Resentment surfaced when the residents of Carbondale named the new Satank site "Yellow Dog."

But Satank, in its new location, grew with the construction of a large brick hotel built by Captain Cooper. He called the place the Hotel Moffat in honor of the banker and president of the Denver & Rio Grande, David H. Moffat. In 1887, Cooper went one step farther to get on the good side of the railroad by renaming the town Moffat. The post office, however, retained the name Satank.

The town of Moffat (formerly Satank, formerly Rockford, formerly Coopertown) continued its growth with three stores and seven saloons. A school was built and a real estate office opened.

The Denver & Rio Grande, influenced by the powerful Colorado Fuel & Iron Company, elected to put its station in Carbondale. This was where a short-lived branch line up Thompson Creek to a coal mine originated.

Captain Cooper died in 1887 and with it, the dream of a great town. By 1892, buildings at Moffat still standing included a single saloon, two stores and the partially complete Moffat Hotel. Only the store was still in business and was run by Ben Davis. Ben's job as postmaster was to carry what little mail there was down to the tracks of the Denver & Rio Grande and toss the mail sac up into a passing Railway Post Office car. The postal worker would kick the incoming mail sac out onto the ground. In 1904, the Satank post office at Moffat closed and the town died.

The original site today is shown on maps as "Sutank" and is, for all practical purposes, part of Carbondale.

Len Shoemaker, *Roaring Fork Valley*, Sage Books, Denver, 1958, pp. 86, 123-125, 171-172.
William H. Bauer, James L. Ozment, John H. Willard, *Colorado Post Offices*, Colorado Railroad Museum, Golden, Colorado, 1990, p. 128.

SELLAR

- *Pitkin County, Sellar Creek drainage*
- *Accessible by graded dirt road*
- *Town had a post office; no standing structures remain*

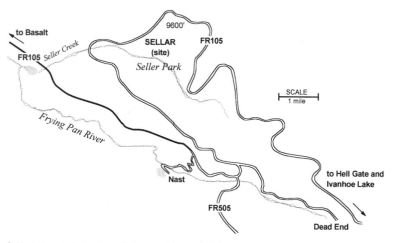

Sellar is located about a mile beyond the end of the paved portion of the road along the Frying Pan River. The graded dirt road is built on the Colorado Midland railroad grade and continues to Ivanhoe Lake.

Sellar was a railroad station and post office on the Colorado Midland with an inn for railroad employees and travelers. It was home to those that maintained the railroad, and also home to those that operated the charcoal ovens.

In addition to the depot, the railroad maintained complete facilities at Sellar including a coal bin, water tank, sand house, section house and a wye for turning locomotives. Sellar was where the rotary snowplows, which ran up to the Hagerman Tunnel to keep the track clear, were turned. At the tail of the wye, the track continued along the line of brick charcoal ovens. Much of the timber in this area was harvested and converted to charcoal for use in smelters at Leadville.

Not much is known about life in Sellar, except that its post office history is quite interesting:

April 12, 1888 to December 17, 1896
December 30, 1896 to July 5, 1898
January 25, 1901 to April 15, 1901
May 22, 1902 to August 14, 1909
Man 11, 1910 to August 10, 1918
(closed permanently when the Colorado Midland was abandoned in 1918)

One of the ovens at Sellar, where timber cut in the immediate vicinity was converted to charcoal. The Colorado Midland had a spur running in front of the ovens. *(Kenneth Jessen 106A7)*

During its thirty-year history, the post office had no less than seventeen postmasters. The availability of a postmaster may have had something to do with its intermittent history.

Sellar is reached from the end of the paved road up the Frying Pan River from Basalt. Where the payment ends, the motorist has two choices; turn right and continue along the Frying Pan River or left to follow the old railroad grade to Sellar. The railroad grade swings around almost 180 degrees and climbs the hillside parallel to the paved road. It turns again into Seller Park. Where the grade becomes covered with cinders, watch for the wye headed off to the right to the charcoal ovens. This is a large beautiful mountain meadow filled with deep grass, and its elevation is 9914 feet. The road is graded and continues past Hell's Gate to Ivanhoe Lake.

Note that Seller Park and Seller Creek are spelled with an "e," while the town, Sellar, is spelled with an "a."

The remains of a large log structure near the charcoal ovens could have been one of the railroad structures or maybe a logger's cabin. *(Kenneth Jessen 106A6)*

Edward M. McFarland, *A Colorado Midland Guide and Data Book*, Colorado Railroad Museum, Golden, Colorado, 1980, pp. 41-43, 205, 274, 301.

Len Shoemaker, *Roaring Fork Valley*, Sage Books, Denver, 1958, pp. 147-148.

William H. Bauer, James L. Ozment, John H. Willard, *Colorado Post Offices*, Colorado Railroad Museum, Golden, Colorado, 1990, p. 130.

SPRING GULCH

- *Pitkin County, Edgerton Creek drainage*
- *Access limited by private property*
- *Town had a post office; no standing structures remain*

C. F. & I. referred to these as "Old Austrian Houses." The company replaced this type of housing with its own standard house design. *(Camp and Plant CP120)*

Coal was discovered in the Jerome Park area in 1882 by William Gray. During 1883 and 1884, a wagon road was constructed from Emma to Marion and Spring Gulch. A mine was opened up at Spring Gulch in 1887 by twenty men working for the Grand River Coal and Coke Company. (C. F. & I. referred to this camp as "Gulch".) The angle of the drift was forty-five degrees, making coal removal difficult. The deposit required three or four cross cuts to intersect the vein.

119

By 1889, seventy-five men were employed at the mine, and the following year, the company constructed four frame houses and a boarding house for miners who wished to live near their work. More houses were added after the purchase of the mine by C. F. & I. in 1892. They continued to operate the mine at Spring Gulch until 1916, when the demand for coke dropped. Coal from Spring Gulch proved ideal for conversion to coke, and so it was hauled to Cardiff, converted into coke, then shipped to smelters throughout the West.

Spring Gulch got its own post office in 1891, and in 1895, the post office changed its name to "Gulch." (The Colorado Midland Railway also used "Gulch" on its time table.) The post office continued to operate until the mine closed in 1916.

By 1905, there were 250 miners living in Spring Gulch, and during the winter of 1906-1907, the town grew to 400 miners with a total population, including families, of more than 1,200. C. F. & I. used one of its standard designs for additional housing at Spring Gulch. Historic photographs show these homes to have two stories with a porch on the rear. Rows of these identical company houses were built along the town's main street.

These neat two-story homes were constructed at Spring Gulch for mine workers by C. F. & I. and represent a standard design. None of these structures are left today. *(Camp and Plant CP018)*

C. F. & I. set up its own company store, the Colorado Supply Company. This store accepted script used to pay miners, but typical of most company stores, it had higher prices than comparable stores in Cardiff or Glenwood Springs. The company took advantage of its monopoly. The miners defeated the monopoly when housewives secretly ordered supplies through Colorado Midland train crews. After an order was placed, the supplies would be carefully tossed off the locomotive before it came into view of Spring Gulch. Someone would be waiting along the track to pick them up.

Historic photographs show Spring Gulch and the mine itself, with its power house, on a knoll above the town. The railroad tracks came into the lower part of town. The residential area was located between the mine and the tracks. In 1901, six men were killed in a mine explosion caused by either methane gas or coal dust released during mining operations.

The best year for Spring Gulch was 1902 when nearly a quarter of a million tons of coal were removed. During this same year, however, the town experienced a severe water shortage. A small spring was its only water source. During this crisis, water probably had to be hauled in by rail.

For a map showing the location of Spring Gulch, see "Marion, a Coal Town." The Jerome Park Road south from Sutank (on the outskirts of Carbondale) goes past the Marion and Spring Gulch sites. Spring Gulch is the second right-hand turn onto a gravel road and heads to the southwest to the base of the mountains. Access to the Spring Gulch site is limited by private property, and the road has been closed in recent years.

Anna Johnson and Kathleen Yajko, *The Elusive Dream*, Gran Furnum Printing & Publishing Company, Glenwood Springs, Colorado, 1983, pp. 6-9, 23, 30-33, 37, 38, 50, 53-56.

H. Lee Scamehorn, *Pioneer Steelmaker in the West*, Pruett, Boulder, Colorado, 1976, pp. 20, 73-74.

Robert Ormes, *Tracking Ghost Railroads in Colorado*, Century One Press, Colorado Springs, Colorado, 1975, p. 111.

William H. Bauer, James L. Ozment, John H. Willard, *Colorado Post Offices*, Colorado Railroad Museum, Golden, Colorado, 1990, p. 67, 135.

SUNLIGHT

- *Garfield County, Fourmile Creek drainage*
- *Access limited by private property*
- *Town had a post office; several standing structures remain*

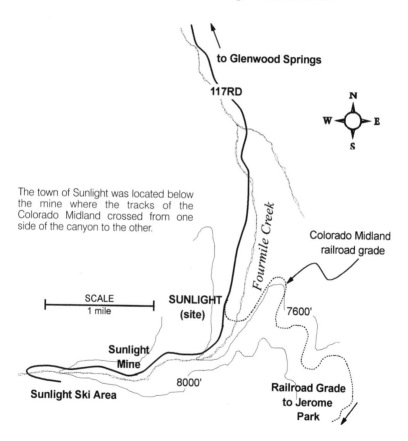

The town of Sunlight was located below the mine where the tracks of the Colorado Midland crossed from one side of the canyon to the other.

to Glenwood Springs

117RD

N
W · E
S

Fourmile Creek

Colorado Midland railroad grade

SCALE
1 mile

SUNLIGHT
(site)

7600'

Sunlight
Mine

8000'

Railroad Grade
to Jerome
Park

Sunlight Ski Area

The first coal mining began in Fourmile Creek in 1887, and by the following year, 35 men were at work on what was called the Sunset Mine. The coal was bituminous, in a nine-foot-thick vein, and good for use in steam locomotives. The next year brought the total number of miners to 150. Because of conflicts with other towns of the same name within Colorado, the name was changed to Sunlight in 1897. The town got its post office which remained open until the following year. In 1899, a post office was re-established and remained active until the town was abandoned in 1912.

A 1905 photograph of Sunlight shows that the mine and the town were pretty well integrated, with the Colorado Midland Railway splitting the settlement. Down on the flats along the creek was the original settlement with a dozen or so irregular log cabins. High above the canyon floor was a neat row of ten identical C. F. & I. homes. Several railroad trestles crossed the canyon. The schoolhouse still stands and has been modified for use as a home. It is located on the north side of the canyon overlooking the town site. The town also had a company store and a boarding house. A map published in *The Elusive Dream* shows that Sunlight also had a saloon, blacksmith shop and mule barn. There was a mine office, a tipple, a powder house and an engine/boiler house.

Due to the nature of the mine and faults that broke through the coal seam, Sunlight required a lot of timbering and was an expensive mine to maintain and operate. It was also a dangerous mine. In September, 1897, an explosion killed a dozen men. C. F. & I. halted production in 1904, but the Midland Mine was worked for a few more years by the Rocky Mountain Fuel Company.

Sunlight is tricky to find because the modern-day road runs on the opposite side of the canyon from the original road, making it difficult to find where historic photographs were taken. When driving south out of Glenwood Springs along Colorado 82, a bridge crosses to the west side of the Roaring Fork River, then parallels 82 for a mile or so. The turnoff to the ski area goes up Fourmile Creek. Scars on the ridge indicate the general area of the mining town site. One lone structure remains in the flat area below the scars. Today, the name Sunlight is associated with the ski area, but the ski area is approximately two miles farther.

This was the C. F. & I. owned company store at Sunlight. Log structures such as this were not typical of C. F. & I. buildings. *(Camp and Plant CP115)*

William H. Bauer, James L. Ozment, John H. Willard, *Colorado Post Offices*, Colorado Railroad Museum, Golden, Colorado, 1990, p. 137.

Anna Johnson and Kathleen Yajko, *The Elusive Dream*, Gran Furnum Printing & Publishing Company, Glenwood Springs, Colorado, 1983, pp. 11, 32-33, 46, 50, 62.

H. Lee Scamehorn, *Pioneer Steelmaker in the West*, Pruett, Boulder, Colorado, 1976, p. 89.

TOURTELOTTE PARK

- *Pitkin County, Spar Gulch drainage*
- *Site not accessible; part of Aspen Mountain ski area*
- *Town had a post office; no standing structures remain*

Henry Tourtelotte first came to Denver in 1878, then traveled to Leadville the following year. He prospected in the Weston Pass area, as well as Big Evans Gulch. Having had no luck, he and his trustworthy jack went over Independence Pass and down the Roaring Fork River. He found a beautiful mountain park above Aspen at the head of Spar Gulch. Along with its beauty, the park had outcroppings of silver ore. It was here that Henry Tourtelotte constructed a cabin. As other prospectors arrived, they too found the place charming, and soon a small community of log cabins formed. The town was informal, and no town survey was made.

The first hotel was constructed in 1885 by Judge Taylor, who named it the Mountain House. He opened the hotel on his birthday and gave a grand ball for the residents. This same year a school was constructed at Tourtelotte Park.

A very rich vein of silver was discovered in 1888 at the Silver Bell Mine, which stimulated the town's growth. The following year the town qualified for its own post office, which remained opened until 1894. An electric tramway was built to haul the ore down to the smelters in Aspen.

Tourtelotte Park no longer appears on contemporary maps. The site is part of the system of ski runs on Aspen Mountain south of the town of Aspen. The site for Tourtelotte Park is approximately one-and-a-half miles south of the Aspen city limits, and ski lifts pass over the area. The structures were probably removed when Aspen Mountain was opened as a ski area.

(Kenneth Jessen 109C6)

Frank L. Wentworth, *Aspen on the Roaring Fork*, Francis B. Rizzari (publisher), 1950, p. 216.
John K. Aldrich, *Ghosts of Pitkin County*, Centennial Graphics, Lakewood, 1987, p. 44.
Len Shoemaker, *Roaring Fork Valley*, Sage Books, Denver, 1958, pp. 38, 95, 42.
Muriel Sibell Wolle, *Stampede to Timberline*, Sage Books, Chicago, 1949, 1974, p. 233.
William H. Bauer, James L. Ozment, John H. Willard, *Colorado Post Offices*, Colorado Railroad
    Museum, Golden, Colorado, 1990, p. 142.

AREA EIGHT $\boxed{8}$

Park County

continued

AREA 8: Park County
Selected Towns

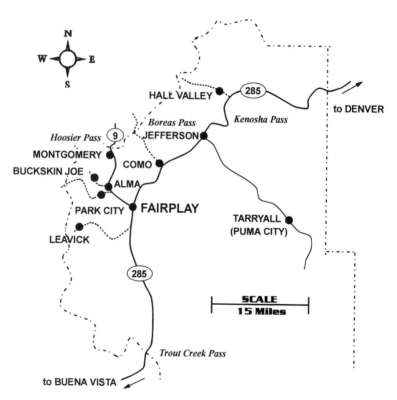

Introduction to Park County

Park County consists of a vast open valley or park surrounded by high mountains on its north and west sides. It was the site of rich gold deposits in the alluvial fill. As these gold deposits were mined, lode deposits were discovered in the surrounding mountains. The first discoveries were made in 1859, and the development of towns began soon after.

Burro Buried on Fairplay's Main Street

Halfway up Fairplay's main street stands a curious monument made of dull, gray cement adorned with ore samples from many of the mines in the Fairplay-Alma area. Etched in the cement is the following expression of respect to one particular burro called Prunes. It reads, "Prunes—

On Fairplay's main street stands this unique monument to a Colorado burro named Prunes. The monument, made of dull, gray cement, is adorned with ore samples from mines in the Fairplay-Alma area. Behind the monument are the ashes of Prunes' last owner, Rupe Sherwood, buried there at his request. *(Kenneth Jessen 083A10)*

a burro—1867 - 1930. Fairplay, Alma—All Mines In This District." Expressed in this simple inscription is the heartfelt praise to this shaggy little servant of Colorado. Ripley, in his "Ripley's Believe-It-Or-Not" syndicated cartoon, made Prunes and his monument famous. Prunes was also featured in 1943 on the radio version of Death Valley Days.

The story of Prunes is also the story of his owner, Rupe Sherwood. When Rupe was twelve, he ran away from home, and after a trip in a covered wagon, ended up hunting with Buffalo Bill. After wandering around the West, Rupe settled in the Alma-Fairplay mining district. For almost five decades, Rupe owned Prunes and boasted that Prunes worked every mine of any consequence in the district at one time or another.

After Rupe "pensioned" his faithful jack, the animal spent its final years making the rounds of Alma's back doors to beg for food. Flapjacks fried in sowbelly grease made old Prunes hee-haw with delight. Residents eagerly gave the old jack food. As the animal approached his 60's, his health began to fail. An examination of his mouth revealed that Prunes was losing his teeth along with his ability to eat.

A blizzard struck Alma in 1930, and the snow drifted deep. The temperature plunged below zero, and Prunes took refuge in an old shed. During the blizzard, the door blew shut, and a snowdrift prevented the old burro from pushing the door open. Residents noticed that the burro was not making his usual rounds. After searching, they found Prunes half-starved in the shed, weak in the legs, and unable to walk. He was showered with food and affection, but did not recover from his exposure to the blizzard.

The miners met in May of 1930 in Alma to decide what to do about the suffering animal. It was a difficult decision, and the miners elected to put an end to the suffering of their little long-eared friend. Prunes was shot as some of the old-timers, including Rupe, wept. His little gray carcass was discarded in a local garbage dump.

A Fairplay cafe owner, with the help of other willing admirers, dug a grave on Fairplay's main street, and here they deposited the remains of Prunes. Over the grave, the miners in the area erected the unique cement monument studded with ore samples from the mines Prunes had worked. Never before had an animal been so honored by a Colorado mining town.

Columnist Arthur Brisbane wrote this about Prunes:

*An old donkey that worked in Colorado mines so long that
few could remember when he started is dead at last. He worked
until he could not work any more, or even eat. They shot him. Now
he is to be honored with a memorial, built of ore samples from all
the mines in which he worked. A touching picture, it will be appre-
ciated by many a two-legged worker, including white-collar
men...they are less fortunate than the old mine burro. Nobody
builds a monument to them and nobody shoots them when they
can no longer earn a living. They are turned adrift.*

Rupe Sherwood composed a long poem titled "Me and
Prunes" which begins:
> *So poor old Prunes had cashed in.*
> *too bad, still in a way,*
> *I'm glad the old boy's eased off*
> *and calling it a day.*
> *I'm going to miss him scandilous!*
> *The world won't seem the same -*
> *Not having him a-standin' here*
> *hee-hawing in the game.*

A year later on August 23, 1931, at the age of 82, Rupe
Sherwood died in the Fairplay hospital. On his deathbed, he realized he was on his last trail. He asked to be cremated and have his
ashes buried behind the monument under which the bones of his
faithful burro were buried. The funeral was attended by about 500
people. A bronze plaque was added to the top of the monument.

Levette J. Davidson, "Rocky Mountain Burro Tales," *1950 Brand Book*, Vol. VI., The Westerner, Denver, 1950, pp. 193-203.

Frank Brookshier, *The Burro*, University of Oklahoma Press, Norman, Oklahoma, 1974, pp. 257-259.

Everett Bair, *This will be an Empire*, Pageant Press, New York, 1959, pp. 174-179.

South Park Salt Works

Precious metal mining was not the only type of mineral recovery carried on in South Park. A couple of brine springs were discovered north of Antero Junction about three-quarters of a mile east of U.S. 285. Before white men came into the area, the Ute Indians knew about these springs. The buffalo and antelope were attracted to the springs, and early settlers also noted the salt marsh in this area.

In 1861, J. C. Fuller purchased some boilers and began producing what he called "Pikes Peak Salt." It is not known what became of this enterprise, but Charles Hall homesteaded at the springs in 1862.

Hall went about manufacturing salt in 1862, and in 1864, he incorporated the Colorado Salt Works. One of the investors was John Quincy Adams Rollins, founder of Rollinsville in Boulder County and a mine owner.

The salt works in South Park as seen from U.S. 285 near Antero Junction. Access is restricted by private property. *(Sonje Jessen SJ120)*

Converted in today's dollar value, investors poured over a half million dollars to erect a sixty-foot high chimney and evaporation kettles. The salt extraction process consisted of boiling the brine from the spring to form a saturated salt solution. Salt crystals were formed in evaporation pans from the solution.

Most of the salt produced was used in the chloridizing process to treat ore. Purity required for consumption was not necessary. The salt sold in bulk for about a dollar a pound.

What became known as the Salt Works Ranch was the only stopping place for travelers between the Fairplay area and Trout Creek or Weston passes.

Legal action over the ownership of the land halted salt production in 1869. The springs did not contain enough saline for the continued economical recovery of salt. A great deal of fuel was required to form the saturated salt solution. Even without income from salt production, the Hall family continued to live on the ranch.

In 1881, a group of investors tried to make money through salt recovery with a thousand-foot deep well. The idea was to try to bring a higher brine concentration to the surface. The Denver, South Park & Pacific arrived in the area providing a more economical means of shipping salt in bulk quantities. This operation continued until 1883.

Bayou Salado was the name commonly used for South Park and is a derivative of the Creole name "Bayou Salade" given to the area by French trappers. This translated to salt marshes.

The salt works can be seen from U.S. 285 to the east side of the road. The brick chimney still stands over a brick building. The site is on private property and is not open to the public.

Virginia McConnell Simmons, *Bayou Salado*, Century One Press, Colorado Springs, Colorado, 1966, pp. 207-213.

Colorado's Worst Serial Killers

Colorado Territory experienced its worst serial murders more than a century ago with the brutal slaying of thirty-three of its citizens. The culprits were two men and a boy, who scrawled their names in blood across the sparsely settled land. It wasn't until twenty-two people had been slain in 1863 that the killers were even identified. They were the Espinosas, and their reign of terror would be the most hideous that Colorado would ever know. The lack of organized law enforcement agencies made it difficult to bring their rampage to an end.

The Espinosas moved to Colorado from New Mexico and settled on the Conejos River in the south end of the San Luis Valley. The 1860 census has Felipe Nerio Espinosa, age 39, and Jose Bibian (Vivian) Espinosa, age 22, living in the area.

After the Espinosas stole the goods they wanted from a wagon headed to Sante Fe, they tied the teamster to the wagon tongue and started the team off at a gallop. Fortunately, a priest was able to stop the runaway horses.

The teamster told the priest what had happened, and the officers at Santa Fe and Fort Garland were informed. In early February 1863, the robbers were identified as the Espinosa brothers, and a military party consisting of Lieutenant Hutt and 15 soldiers were sent out along the Conejos River to capture the outlaws. This action infuriated the Espinosas, and they fled from their home and headed for the Mogote Peaks, north of the Conejos River. They hid in the rocky outcroppings as the soldiers pursued them. An unfortunate soldier came near their hiding place and was shot to death by one of the Espinosas.

The Espinosas left the area and headed northeast across the Sangre De Cristo Mountains and through the Wet Mountain Valley to the Front Range near Pueblo.

A sawmill owner, alone at his sawmill on Hardscrabble Creek near Pueblo, was murdered on March 18 by the Espinosas. The following day the murders continued when another lone sawmill owner was found dead on Fountain Creek, in what is now Dead Man's Canyon, a few miles south of Colorado Springs. The Espinosas then moved to a stage stop and ranch up Ute Pass Road west of Colorado Springs and murdered the owner.

The Espinosas moved across South Park, and within a few days more bodies were discovered between Red Hill and Fairplay. One of the men was a prominent South Park resident, Arnold N. Shoup, the brother of Lieutenant George Shoup. Another was a prospector named Bill Carter who was robbed of his gun, money and clothing. In addition, the murder of two California Gulch residents, Fred Lehman and Sol Seyga, brought the total deaths in South Park to four.

In a *Rocky Mountain News*, April 23, 1863, article, the writer reasoned that Confederate guerrillas were at large. Governor Evans requested the help of Federal troops, but was rejected by Washington D.C. because of the demands of the Civil War.

The residents of South Park were desperate to find the perpetrators and a reason for the killing. They were frustrated in their efforts and had no knowledge of what had happened earlier far to the south in the San Luis Valley. No one dared to venture out on the roads by day or night, and no stranger was above suspicion.

One poor fellow from California Gulch ran from Red Hill to Fairplay to escape an angry posse. Father Dyer, an itinerate Methodist Minister, was able to identify him as John Foster. Foster was new to the California Gulch community, and Dyer saved his life.

A less fortunate fellow named Baxter was staying with a family near Fairplay. A posse surrounded the home and demanded Baxter's surrender. The family refused to release him. After several shots were fired, the posse took Baxter into Fairplay and hung him without a trial. It was evident that little organized law enforcement existed in the territory, and settlers depended on a posse for their protection.

The turning point in the long reign of terror by the Espinosas came near Fairplay. Edward Metcalf was hauling a load of lumber from Alma and became the Espinosa's next intended victim. Just after he passed through a narrow rock outcropping, a shot rang out and a bullet struck him over the heart. It might have killed him except for a memoranda book he carried in his breast pocket. It was this book that stopped the bullet, but the impact knocked him over the load of lumber. Fortunately he had the presence of mind to grab the pole holding the lumber in place. Frightened by the explosive shot nearby, his oxen bolted and ran down the road. Metcalf had the opportunity to see two Mexicans standing by the underbrush as his wagon disappeared over the hill. The rapid flight of the oxen prevented the Espinosas from getting off a second shot, and Metcalf made his way to Fairplay and reported what he had seen.

A mass meeting was called that night, and it was decided that the Mexicans were responsible for all the killing in South Park. Captain John McCannon was designated as the leader of a posse to start after the killers. A call for volunteers resulted in a number of men being selected for the posse. Several men were rejected because Captain McCannon insisted that every posse member be an excellent shot with both a rifle and a sixshooter and be in good physical condition for the rigors of a long chase.

It took some time to gather the necessary supplies and equipment that were needed, and it was not until the morning of the second day that the posse was ready to start on the trail. The *Rocky Mountain News,* May 28, 1863 reported the posse's formation and solicited "...contributions that any of our citizens may feel disposed of to make toward defraying the cost of that expedition." Paid law enforcement officers were few and far between, and posse members joined on a volunteer basis.

When the Espinosas failed to kill Mr. Metcalf, they realized they had been seen and decided to get back into rough country as quickly as possible. They lost no time in making tracks across South Park, avoiding all roads and trails. Their route took them into the rugged foothills north of Canon City. However their horses were in poor condition, so their progress was slow.

Captain McCannon split the posse into two groups. He sent

one group to the northeast under the command of C. T. Wilson, while he took the rest toward the southeast. McCannon's posse immediately began scouting, and on the morning of the second day they found the tracks of two horses leading into the mountains. At the time, no one knew who the riders were, but it was assumed they must be the killers.

The posse built small fires at noon to warm their food and followed the trail long into the evening. No fires were allowed at night to avoid giving away their position, and supper was eaten cold. At dawn, the posse started out once again on the trail.

All the men were under severe mental stress due to the uncertainty of what danger lay ahead. They were very much on the alert because each man realized it was a life and death struggle as they tracked the killers. Tensions grew and finally John E. Endleman could stand it no longer. He began to sing and yell hysterically. John had to be taken by two of the strongest men in the posse to the Addleman ranch in South Park.

The remaining posse members started tracking the two riders at dawn on the third day. Although they pushed all day they saw no sign of the men they were tracking. On the fourth day the trail grew warm, and late in the

A scout for the U. S. Army, Thomas Tobin, was asked by Colonel Tappan at Fort Garland to bring in the heads of the Espinosas. The Espinosas had been on a killing spree, and Tobin carried out his orders. *(Western History Department, Denver Public Library F17565)*

afternoon, the posse came across the burning embers of a recent fire. McCannon surveyed the rolling country of Four Mile Creek (also called Oil Creek) north of Cañon City and ordered the men to make camp. As the full moon rose on the cloudless night, McCannon called for volunteers. Seven men stepped forward, including Joseph Lamb. They traveled light and struggled through the rough country for three miles before crawling into the damp underbrush to wait for the dawn of the fifth day.

Suddenly, near a dense thicket of willows, one of the men whispered "Look!" In a little clearing off the thicket were two horses, one hobbled and the other free. McCannon figured quickly that the two riders must have camped for the night in the thicket and were still there. Again Captain McCannon split up his posse and sent four men around the low hill to get into the gulch below the camp and thus cut off that escape route. McCannon, Joseph Lamb, and two others hid behind some rocks, but within sight of the horses.

Abruptly, the largest of the Espinosas, later identified as Vivian, came out of the thicket and approached the hobbled horse. As he started to remove the hobble, Joseph Lamb, who was closest, slowly pulled a bead on the man and shot him. The rifle ball smashed into Vivian's ribs on his right side and exited through his left side.

A second posse member fired his shotgun at Vivian Espinosa, but the hobbled horse received the brunt of the blast. Vivian raised up on his elbow and returned fire. Another posse member fired next with the ball hitting Vivian squarely between the eyes.

Felipe, the other Espinosa, was startled by the shooting. As he emerged from the thicket, Joseph Lamb, having reloaded his buffalo gun, was in the process of pulling a bead on him when a posse member shouted, "Don't shoot, that's one of our men!" As Lamb lowered his rifle, Felipe Espinosa fired a shot piercing Joe Lamb's hat and then disappeared over the rim of a nearby canyon. Felipe managed to escape.

The posse soon located the Espinosa camp under a high ledge in the gulch. Here they found $125 in gold dust and many items belonging to the victims. While they were examining the camp, the firing lock of a rifle was discovered. The Espinosas were evidently repairing the rifle, but the rifle could not be found. Felipe Espinosa had apparently taken the rifle with him as he escaped and hid it among some rocks on the side of the hill. This rifle was discovered in 1900 by Woody Higgins and Harry Brenton as they were rounding up cattle from the range in that region. The posse left the body where it lay, but gathered up the meager possessions and the startling memo book.

Most of the posse returned to Canon City that night and ate for the first time in thirty hours. Captain McCannon had to hire a wagon to carry three of the posse members because they were too exhausted to ride. The people of South Park rejoiced thinking that the horrible killing had ended at last, but they forgot one thing, Felipe Espinosa was still at large. After his brother was killed, he fled south through the mountains, killing two more men in the Canon City area and then slipped back to his home village on the Conejos River. He was not about to quit his vendetta, and if anything, his thirst for Anglo blood was intensified, but he knew he would need help. He selected a nephew Julio (Julian) who was still in his teens, but as eager as his uncle to kill the hated Anglos.

With revenge in their hearts, the two set out to renew their terrible vendetta. A lone Anglo fisherman on the Conejos River became the next victim.

By early September it was estimated the Espinosas had killed eleven more times, adding to the list of twenty-two victims that Vivian and Felipe claimed they had already killed. (An accurate body count is impossible to recreate, since no organized law enforcement agency existed to investigate and collect evidence.)

The commanding officer at Fort Garland, Colonel Sam Tappan, was told that the Espinosas were in his area. He sent for a man he knew could be trusted to get the job done, a scout named Tom Tobin.

Tobin was a picturesque figure. He rode a black horse and wore a black hat, shirt, trousers and boots. He kept two loaded revolvers in his gun belt, one on each side.

Colonel Tappen gave Tobin specific instructions to "...bring their heads to him." Tobin wanted to hunt the murderers alone, but Tappan insisted that he take some soldiers with him. On September 7, 1863, Tom Tobin, along with Lieutenant Horace W. Baldwin, fifteen soldiers, one civilian and a Mexican boy, left the fort. They located the Espinosas and after a brief battle, both men were shot to death, then decapitated. Tobin put the heads in a gunnysack and rode into Fort Garland with Lieutenant Baldwin and six soldiers. Tobin rode over to Colonel Tappan's headquarters. As Tappan came out, Tobin rolled the heads of the Espinosas out at his feet.

Thomas T. Tobin, "The Capture of the Espinosas," *Colorado Magazine*, Vol. IX. No. 2, March 1932, p 59.

Ralph C. Taylor, *Colorado South of the Border*, Sage Books, Denver, 1963, p. 211.

"Trouble at Fairplay," *Rocky Mountain News*, April 1, 1863.

Captain B. F. Rockafellow, "History of Fremont County," *History of the Arkansas Valley*, Colorado, O. L. Baskin, Chicago, 1881, pp. 575-576.

Henry Priest, "The Story of Dead Man's Canyon and of the Espinosas," *Colorado Magazine*, Vol. VIII. January, 1931 p. 34.

Everett Bair, "Bloody Trail of the Espinosas" *True West*, March-April 1960, Vol. 7 No. 4, p. 51.

Frank Hall, *History of Colorado*, The Blakely Printing Co., Chicago, 1889, Vol. I. p 379. (Capt. Rockafellow's Narrative)

J. Andrew Smith, "A True Account of the Escapades of the Bloody Espinosas," *The Sun* (Canon City) Vol. 9. No. 47, January 28, 1960, p. 9.

Frank R. Lamb, "The Pioneer Story of Joseph Milton Lamb," Master Printers, Canon City, Colorado, 1969, p. II.

Major John H. Nakinvell, "Fort Garland, Colorado," *Colorado Magazine*, January, 1939, pp. 13-28.

Kit Carson III, "The Lives of Two Great Scouts." *Brand Book: Twelve Original Papers Pertaining to the History of the West*, The Westerners, Denver, Colorado, 1947, pp. 197-205.

"The Espinosas, Mysterious Murders Which Caused a Reign of Terror in Colorado", *The Denver Tribune*, March 10, 1884, p. 5.

Virginia McConnell Simmons, *San Luis Valley - Land of the Six Armed Cross*, Pruett Publishing Company, Boulder, Colorado, 1979, p. 80.

Edgar L. Hewett, "Tom Tobin," *Colorado Magazine*, Vol. XXIII, No. 5 (September, 1946), pp. 210-211.

Virginia McConnell Simmons, *Bayou Salado*, Century One Press, Colorado Springs, Colorado, 1966, pp. 114-117.

The San Luis Valley Historian, Vol. XIII, No. 2, 1980, San Luis Valley Historical Society, Alamosa, Colorado, pp. 2-3.

John C. Palmer, "Story of Espinosa Outlaws," *The Canon City Record*, January 31, 1924, Vol. XXXV, No. 5.

Frank R. Lamb, "Additional Facts on Trailing and Capture of the Notorious Espinosa Gang," *The Daily Record* (Canon City), February 7, 1924, Vol. XVIII, No. 32.

ALMA

And Its Suburb, Dudley

- *Park County, Middle Fork of the South Platte River*
- *Accessible via paved road*
- *Towns both had a post office; no standing structures at Dudley; some original structures in Alma*

An early view of Alma's business district. The town was never fully abandoned, even after the end of the mining era. *(Colorado Historical Society F22269)*

Rich silver ore was discovered at the 13,860-foot level of Mt. Bross near Hoosier Pass in 1871 by Captain Plummer. He called it The Moose. Other discoveries came quickly including The Russia and The Dolly Varden, all in the same general area. Within 300 feet of the top of 14,284-foot Mt. Lincoln, the Australia lode was discovered as well.

141

The Moose proved to be the best of the mines and head-quarters for the mining company were established in the town of Dudley, about a mile north of Alma on the Middle Fork of the South Platte River. The town was named for Judson H. Dudley, principal owner of The Moose. By 1872, Dudley had several stores, some saloons, a boarding house, livery stable, hotel, company offices and an assay lab. The largest structure was the mill, which handled ore from all of the area mines. The mill closed after only three years of operation due to the high cost.

Dudley's population fell from 150 to 100 by 1877. It had grown, however, to include the headquarters for the Horseshoe and Lincoln mines. Even though a new smelter was opened, the town was nearly abandoned by 1880. The post office at Dudley opened in 1872 and closed in 1880. By 1890, after yielding an incredible three million dollars in precious metal, The Moose was shut down. With its closure, the town of Dudley was all but aban-

The old Alma Fire House now serves as a museum. It sits along Colorado 9 where the Buckskin Joe Road heads west. *(Kenneth Jessen 099A1)*

doned. Dudley also had competition from Alma as a more desirable place to live.

The daughter of a local storekeeper was Alma Janes. She must have been quite something because the town of Alma was named for her. The town was established in 1873 at the junction of the Middle Fork of the South Platte River and Buckskin Creek, a location essential to its success. Alma was lower in elevation than other towns such as Quartzville, Montgomery or Dudley, yet close enough to the mines to attract the construction of smelters. A branch of the important Boston and Colorado Smelting Company in Black Hawk selected Alma for the site of its smelter in 1873. The Holland smelter was located just three miles to the south. The Denver, South Park & Pacific built a branch to Alma in 1882.

Alma's post office opened in 1873, and by 1874, the town had grown to 700 residents.

Unique to Alma were its many newspapers. *The Mount Lincoln News*, a weekly, was started in 1875. Its editor, W. F. Hogan, moved the paper to Leadville three years later. Between 1880 and 1914, the *Park County Bulletin* was published in Alma. For just a year or so in 1887, the *Park County Miner* also came out of Alma, as well as the *Alma Mining Record*. The latter lasted from 1935 to 1936.

There was a mass exodus from Alma during 1879 to Leadville's silver boom, which left a fourth of the buildings vacant. Many new silver ore discoveries were made up Buckskin Creek, resulting in the return of many of the town's residents. Alma's population peaked in 1884 at around 900. The town now had its own bank. The number of drinking establishments along its main street had also grown, which was offset, somewhat, by three churches.

When the Sherman Silver Purchase Act was repealed in 1893, the U.S. Government was no longer obligated to buy silver at a fixed price. As the value of silver dropped, most of Colorado's silver mines closed. Alma's population also dropped to a third of what it had been.

Large scale hydraulic mining began in 1902 with the Snowstorm Hydraulic Company's acquisition of many of the old placer claims along the Middle Fork of the South Platte River. A system of ditches was used to feed two seven-inch nozzles and one six-inch nozzle called giants. The high pressure water washed down gravel from the ancient stream bed for gold recovery. Tailings from this operation between Fairplay and Alma are quite evident.

A fire in March of 1937 destroyed most of Alma's business district. Only a limited amount of well water was available to fight the fire, and at the time, Buckskin Creek was frozen solid.

Although a relatively small percentage of Alma's original buildings are still standing, it is a town worth visiting. The fire station, located at the corner of Alma's main street and Buckskin Creek Road, is now a museum. As for Dudley, a mountain housing development extending several miles up the Middle Fork of the South Platte River has taken over and none of its original structures remain standing.

John K. Aldrich, *Ghosts of Park County*, Centennial Graphics, Lakewood, Colorado, 1989, p. 8.

Tivis Wilkins, *Colorado Railroads*, Pruett Publishing Company, Boulder, Colorado, 1974, p. 40, p. 45.

William H. Bauer, James L. Ozment, John H. Willard, *Colorado Post Offices*, Colorado Railroad Museum, Golden, Colorado, 1990, pp. 11, 47.

Virginia McConnell Simmons, *Bayou Salado*, Century One Press, Colorado Springs, Colorado, 1966, pp. 120-127.

BALFOUR
An Isolated Mining Camp

- *Park County, Buffalo Creek drainage*
- *Accessible via paved road*
- *Town had a post office; no standing structures remain*

This early photograph of Balfour was said to have been taken when the town was only ten days old. Nothing remains at the site today. *(Denver Public Library, Western History Department X-7168)*

Balfour was one of many isolated mining camps spread out in the vast area of South Park. Unlike other camps, however, Balfour was not in the mountains, but in South Park itself. It was located ten miles south of Hartsel on the north bank of Buffalo Slough. Gold was discovered in 1866 at Balfour, but no effort was made to develop a mine until 1893. This was when the town of Balfour was founded.

The nationality of the miners allowed into the town was the

topic of a debate held in 1894. The result was that Balfour forbid Chinese and Italians, the dominant nationalities in Como, from even entering town.

A weekly newspaper, *The Balfour News,* began publication in 1894 and lasted until 1897. A post office was opened in 1894 and remained active until 1907.

Population figures vary, but Balfour was said to have reached 800 in 1894. The town had three hotels, several stores, a saloon and over 100 log and frame homes. During its peak year, 200 homes occupied the site.

The miners hoped that the same kind of rich gold ore found in the Cripple Creek area would be found here. The volcanic formations may have been very similar, but the ore was not very rich.

During the 1960s, ghost town historian Robert Brown positioned himself in exactly the same location as a historic view of Balfour taken around 1894. The low hills were lined up perfectly. About two dozen structures of various sizes show in the historic photograph. Today, not a trace of this town can be seen, only an open meadow. Ranchers remember when large amounts of lumber could still be found on the site, but South Park storms have eliminated all traces of this town. Colorado 9 runs past the empty site.

Perry Eberhart, *Guide to the Colorado Ghost Towns and Mining Camps,* Sage Books, Chicago, 1959, p. 476.

Robert L. Brown, *Colorado Ghost Towns - Past and Present,* Caxton Printers, Caldwell, Idaho, 1977, pp. 37-40.

Virginia McConnell Simmons, *Bayou Salado,* Century One Press, Colorado Springs, Colorado, 1966, pp. 166-167.

William H. Bauer, James L. Ozment, John H. Willard, *Colorado Post Offices,* Colorado Railroad Museum, Golden, Colorado, 1990, p. 16.

BUCKSKIN JOE

Where Silver Heels Danced

- *Park County, Buckskin Creek drainage*
- *Accessible via graded dirt road*
- *Town had a post office; no standing structures remain*

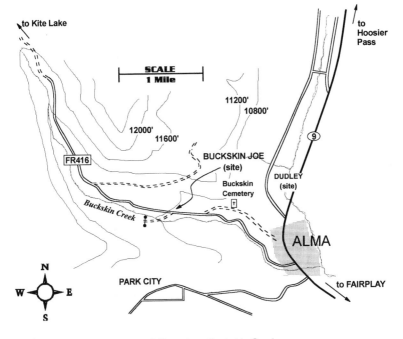

The Buckskin Joe site is west of Alma along Buckskin Creek.

The story of Buckskin Joe, a mining town west of Alma, is close-ly associated with a dance hall girl named Silver Heels. She arrived in Buckskin Joe in 1861 and lived in a cabin across Buckskin Creek from the town itself. When she removed her veil, miners noticed her beautiful face. She got her nickname from the silver heels on the slippers she was wearing the day she arrived. She quickly got a job in Billy Buck's saloon, and became very popular.

Exactly who she was and where she came from has been a point of speculation for many years. One story says she was a young girl named Girda Bechtel who originally came west to help a widow and her children. She quit her job to follow a theatrical career. To test her talents, she came to Buckskin Joe.

A smallpox epidemic swept through the Colorado mining camps during the 1860s, and as the miners became ill, Silver Heels went from cabin to cabin caring for them. Eventually she con-tracted smallpox, which disfigured her lovely face. After the epi-demic passed, the miners took up a collection for Silver Heels as a display of their gratitude. When they came to give her the money, they found a deserted cabin, and no one knew what had become of her. Legend has it that from time to time, a veiled figure visited

This was Buckskin Joe in 1864. It was one of Park County's earliest mining camps. *(Colorado Historical Society F2210)*

the cemetery and that this was Silver Heels paying her respect to those who died in the epidemic. To pay a lasting tribute to this dance hall girl, a 13,822 foot peak, which tow-

This collapsed structure near Buckskin Joe is believed to be the dance hall where Silver Heels danced. *(Kenneth Jessen 098D10)*

ered over the town, was named for her.

Father Dyer, the snowshoe itinerant preacher, held meetings in Buckskin Joe beginning in 1861. One of the meetings lasted two weeks. He commented that he faced every kind of opposition to his religious services, including a dancing institute, theatrical performances, and two murders.

In the fall of 1861, Horace and Augusta Tabor arrived in Buckskin Joe after their stay in Oro City (forerunner of Leadville). They earned a living operating a store. Eventually, Horace opened a second store in Montgomery and was Park County Superintendent of Schools.

The original name for Buckskin Joe was Laurette, and this was the name first used by the post office when it opened in November, 1861. This name came from the town's only two female residents, Laura Dodge and her sister, Jeannette. The name was changed four years later to Buckskin Joe after Joseph Higgenbottom, a prospector who wore leather clothes. Horace Tabor became the first postmaster, and the Buckskin post office continued to operate until 1873.

The first election for county commissioners and the location of the county seat was held December, 1861. The people of

Buckskin Joe cast 382 votes, more than any other Park County town. The county seat was therefore established at Laurett (Buckskin Joe) in January and remained there until 1866, when Fairplay out-voted the other towns. Joseph Higgenbottom's cabin was used as the first courthouse. When the county seat moved to Fairplay, the structure moved with it and sat opposite the red sandstone courthouse. In 1978, the old Buckskin Joe courthouse was moved to South Park City for preservation.

A newspaper was moved from Tarryall to Buckskin Joe in 1862. Sympathetic to the Confederacy, *The Western Mountaineer* lasted from March to December. The town was pro-Union and the paper was boycotted. Confederate money to keep the paper alive failed to materialize. Even though in the minority, a Confederate volunteer company, called the Buckskin Grays, was organized in February, 1863.

Near Buckskin Joe, Stancell Phillips discovered the Phillips lode, a surface vein of gold-bearing quartz, up to forty feet wide. The gold was free milling, meaning that it only had to be crushed and amalgamated to recover its metallic content. Open pit mining recovered over half a million dollars during 1861 and 1862.

Buckskin Joe had nine stamp mills operating at one time, crushing ore around the clock. When the Phillips Mine reached a depth of about thirty feet, the free milling gold ore ran out. The gold was still there, but in the form of sulfides that required smelting.

During its boom years, Buckskin Joe had theaters, saloons, billiard halls, a dancing school, a post office, the Grand Hotel and plenty of stores. There was even a bank run by Stancell Phillips and two others. Stancell had been a door keeper at a theater in Oro City before moving to Buckskin Joe to become the richest man in town, all in less than a year.

William Brewer, a geologist, visited Buckskin Joe in 1869 and reported that only about thirty people remained at the site. Until 1936, the stone chimney of the old courthouse stood at the empty town site. When Muriel Sibell Wolle visited Buckskin Joe in the

1940s, there were only two standing structures. Today, there are no standing structures and only faint traces of foundations.

To reach Buckskin Joe, turn west off of Colorado 9 in the center of Alma onto a graded dirt road which leads up Buckskin Creek. After about two miles, there is a meadow with a side road leading to the right off through the trees. A sign marks this as the way to the cemetery. Buckskin Joe was located in this meadow on the right hand side of the graded road about fifty yards beyond the cemetery turnoff. A second side road leads to the left and

passes the collapsed remains of what is said to be the old dance hall. This road ends at a posted gate. Farther up Buckskin Creek on the left side and just before an old mill is an arrastra down in the creek bed. High on the steep mountainside is the upper station for a tram clinging to the side of a cliff.

Above Buckskin Joe in the creek bed is this circular grove made by an arrastra. This is one of very few arrastras that remain at their original site. *(Kenneth Jessen 098D11)*

Virginia McConnell Simmons, *Bayou Salado*, Century One Press, Colorado Springs, Colorado, 1966, pp. 101-102.

William H. Bauer, James L. Ozment, John H. Willard, *Colorado Post Offices*, Colorado Railroad Museum, Golden, Colorado, 1990, pp. 25, 86.

Thomas J. Noel, Paul F. Mahoney and Richard E. Stevens, *Historical Atlas of Colorado*, University of Oklahoma Press, Norman, Oklahoma, 1993, section 17.

Muriel Sibell Wolle, *Stampede to Timberline*, Sage Books, Chicago, 1949, 1974, pp. 93-96.

Frank Fossett, *Colorado, its Gold and Silver Mines*, C. G. Crawford, New York, 1879, p. 506.

E. J. Amitrani, *A Town is Born*, self-published, 1982, pp. 38-39.

COMO
A Railroad Town

- *Park County; South Platte River drainage*
- *Accessible via paved road*
- *Town has a post office; many original structures remain*

The 1881 Denver, South Park & Pacific narrow gauge stone roundhouse in Como is the very last structure of its type in Colorado and is presently being restored. Como was a railroad town and today retains much of its original character. *(Kenneth Jessen 065D5)*

Como's history is closely tied to the Denver, South Park & Pacific and the King Coal Mine south of town. Como is easy to reach and is located just a mile north of U.S. 285 in South Park. Although only a small percentage of the original structures remain, the town retains much of its original character. There are a number of abandoned buildings mixed with summer homes. There is also a good restaurant in the old hotel. There are efforts to save the historic, stone roundhouse, and restoration work is in process. Funds from the Colorado Historical Society are being used to put a new roof on the structure. Hopefully, tours will some day be given for the general public and Como will become a "must" for travelers in the area.

The Denver, South Park & Pacific began construction in 1872, and was founded by a prestigious group of Colorado business men including John Evans, David Moffat and Walter Cheesman. The general idea was to build a mountain narrow gauge railroad up the South Platte River, across South Park and on to Leadville with a branch over Boreas Pass to Breckenridge. Rails were laid across South Park and reached the site of the future town of Como in 1879. Como was near the point where the route over Boreas Pass split off from the route west over Trout Creek Pass. This, combined with the nearby coal deposits, made Como a logical choice for a division point. At the time, the place was called the Stubbs Ranch and the site was purchased by the railroad. As Italian miners arrived to work the King Coal Mine, they named the town Como after Italy's Lake Como.

By June of 1879, there were a dozen wooden buildings and sixty to seventy tents. It was the temporary end of the track, and many of the residents were transients who would move on as the rails advanced. The most interesting tent structure was the dance hall complete with a wooden floor and a twenty-five foot long bar.

The railroad constructed many buildings in Como which still stand today, including the stone roundhouse built in 1881. A brick hotel was constructed, only to be destroyed by fire in 1896, then rebuilt. A depot with a waiting room, ticket office, baggage room and platform, was built. A machine shop and blacksmith's shop were also constructed along with various storage buildings.

Como was an instant town populated by coal miners and railroad workers. By 1881, the town had 500 residents. Train crews coming in from Denver, Leadville or Breckenridge used Como as a stopover place. Day and night, the whistles of steam locomotives could be heard, and the smell of coal smoke permeated the air as passenger and freight trains came and went to various destinations. Men were constantly coming and going from the roundhouse or the machine shop to town.

In 1880, work began high in Chalk Creek Canyon on the Alpine Tunnel at an elevation well above 11,000 feet. This was the first tunnel drilled under the Continental Divide, and when it was completed, the railroad continued on into Gunnison. At the same time, the line over Boreas Pass into Breckenridge was completed.

Incorporated in 1883, Como's business district included a general merchandise store, a post office and a bakery. There was also a barbershop. A combination saloon and restaurant was located in the downtown area. The I.O.O.F. hall was a two-story structure with the lodge room and office on the first floor and a dance hall up stairs. Wo Lee operated a laundry and nearby was a confectionery store. Facing the Pacific Hotel was a lunch room, a

The Como schoolhouse now serves as the town's civic center. *(Kenneth Jessen 098D6)*

drug store and a pool hall. Other saloons in the business district included Allen's Corner Saloon, the Elkhorn Saloon and Delaney's Turf Saloon. Como's churches included Episcopal, Methodist and Presbyterian, as well as Catholic. Como also had its own town hall, which collapsed during the winter of 1971. Como's post

Como's Catholic church was constructed in 1882 and is among the town's many historic structures. *(Kenneth Jessen 098D7)*

office has operated continuously since 1879.

As mining declined, so did the need for a railroad. As rail traffic was reduced, the number of people living and working in Como also declined. The Alpine Tunnel was closed permanently in 1910. The Boreas Pass line also closed this same year, but by court order, reopened in 1913. In 1935, the wood frame addition to the stone roundhouse burned to the ground, doing extensive damage to a rotary snow plow and two locomotives. A year later, application to abandon the entire railroad was submitted to the Colorado Public Utility Commission. It was granted, and in 1937, the last scheduled passenger train left Como for Denver thus ending the narrow gauge South Park line. The coal mines had been closed for a long time, and the gold in the placer deposits in Tarryall Creek were exhausted. By 1940, Como began its decline into semi-ghost town status.

Como's future is bright, as people continue to come to their summer homes and work progresses on the restoration of the historic Denver, South Park & Pacific roundhouse.

Mary Dyer, *Echoes of Como*, 1879 to 1988, published by George Meyer, 1974, pp. 62, 73.

FAIRPLAY

And Its Fair Deal

- *Park County, Middle Fork of the South Platte River drainage*
- *Accessible by paved road*
- *Town has post office; many original structures remain*

The first two prospectors to enter South Park came over the mountains from Gregory Diggings (Central City) in June, 1859. They were attacked by Indians, but escaped. The men returned along with several others a month later, when all lost their lives in an Indian attack. A third group of prospectors entered South Park and named Kenosha Hill. They discovered some old log cabins left behind by trappers. The group traveled past the present site of Como and up Tarryall Creek where they had good luck panning gold. At the point where Deadwood Gulch and Tarryall Creek join, they staked out 100 foot claims, and established a town. During the summer, several hundred gold-hungry prospectors joined them.

By August, all of the gravel beds at "Tarryall Diggings" were staked out, and latecomers were turned away. The original prospectors, it seems, were unwilling to divide their generous claims, although only a few feet could be worked at a time. The latecomers called the place "Grab-all" and moved on. These prospectors found a good placer deposit where Beaver Creek joins the Middle Fork of the South Platte River. Because of what they believed to be poor treatment in Tarryall Diggings, the prospectors named their place "Fair Play." The name was changed back and forth eight times until the town stuck with its current name of Fairplay.

Fairplay emerged not only as an active mining town, but a crossroads for travel in the region. The trail from Summit County came south over Hoosier Pass through Fairplay as well as the trail over Kenosha Pass. There was also a toll road, opened in 1862, over Weston Pass to Leadville.

The original owner of the town site was William Coleman. He sold the site lot-by-lot. By 1861, the population stood at only 100. A hotel was constructed as more miners continued to arrive in the area. A traveling clergyman from New Jersey, Bayard Taylor, visited Fairplay in 1866 and reported that its population was about 200. He stayed in a log hotel run by James Castello. Taylor found Fairplay quite a lively place.

The first school opened in 1866 and served not only Fairplay, but the surrounding area. Parents from some of the more remote areas would have their children stay with Fairplay families during the school year. The following year, Fairplay became the Park County seat and records were moved from Buckskin Joe. At first, the records were kept in a log structure. After a stone courthouse was completed, the records moved once again.

Father Dyer, a Methodist circuit rider, preached at many of the early mining camps in Park County, Summit County and Lake County and was known as "the snow shoe itinerant." He supplemented his income by carrying the mail over Mosquito Pass, in excess of 13,000 feet. For Sunday services in Fairplay, Father Dyer was forced to use a building with a sign over the door that read "Good

Originally, Father Dyer's church sat along Fairplay's Front Street. It was moved a short distance to become part of South Park City's outdoor exhibit of historical Park County structures. *(Kenneth Jessen 099A11)*

Whisky." He decided that this was not proper for a church, so he found an abandoned two-story log hotel in Montgomery. He personally numbered each log prior to the move to assure it could be reassembled, then paid $100 to have the structure moved to Fairplay. The old log Methodist Church had thirty members and was still used as late at 1877. In 1981, the structure was moved from its original location on First Street to South Park City as part of their outdoor museum of historic Park County structures.

Miners drank a lot of beer, and at the time, beer had to be hauled in from Denver. A German immigrant, Leonard Summer, decided to go into the beer brewing business in Fairplay. In March, 1873, Summer constructed a brewery. It hadn't been in operation six months when a fire spread through Fairplay, wiping out the structure. Summer was unable to replace his loss and left the area. He returned with enough money to construct a brand new brewery made of native stone quarried at Red Hill. A third story was added in 1893. Brewing took place in the cellar. Offices and a tasting room were located on the second floor. Piping carried fresh water throughout the building, and steam power eventually replaced human power for pumping and mixing the

The Summer's Brewery, built by German-born Leonard Summer, is now part of South Park City, but was among Fairplay's original historic structures. *(Kenneth Jessen 086B3)*

ingredients. Summer also had a rehearsal room for the Fairplay Brass Band. It can logically be assumed that band members took fair advantage of the ample beer supply within easy reach.

Summer's product was called South Park Lager and was sold throughout the area. The capacity of his brewery was forty to fifty kegs per day. Summer also owned the Victor Hotel as well as a saloon. His saloon opened in 1879 and was also made of native stone with an unusual stone false front. The brewery and the saloon stand among the exhibits at South Park City, and the brewery is on the National Register of Historic Places.

In the spring of 1879, a drainage ditch on the Fairplay Hotel lot overflowed onto John Hoover's yard. Owner of the Capital Bar and Billiard Parlor, John Hoover was known for his temper, especially when he was drinking. Hoover complained, and Tom Bennett, a young stage coach driver, was hired by the hotel to fix the ditch. Bennett decided to take a break at a local saloon rather than finish the repairs to the ditch. When Hoover returned home, his yard was again filled with water. Hoover got a gun, found Bennett, and put two bullets in the young stage driver.

Bennett died and Hoover remained in the Fairplay jail for a year before standing trial in 1880. Instead of being found guilty of first degree murder, Hoover was found guilty of manslaughter. He received an eight year sentence at the hands of a judge with a record of being soft on criminals. A vigilante group of over one hundred men was formed, broke into the jail, and removed Hoover. Hoover was hanged from the second floor of the courthouse. When the judge arrived in the morning, he found a coiled rope on his desk. This was a sure sign that he would be next, and he needed no encouragement to leave town. The District Attorney left town with the judge!

Fairplay remains a lively place, at least during the summer. It has a number of residents and offers a lot historically in terms of its many original buildings.

E. J. Amitrani, *A Town is Born*, self published, 1982, p. 26.

Robert L. Brown, *Ghost Towns of the Colorado Rockies*, Caxton Printers, Caldwell, Idaho, 1977, pp. 152-156.

Virginia McConnell Simmons, *Bayou Salado*, Century One Press, Colorado Springs, Colorado, 1966, pp. 63-64, 99-101, 110-111, 156-157.

William H. Bauer, James L. Ozment, John H. Willard, *Colorado Post Offices*, Colorado Railroad Museum, Golden, Colorado, 1990, p. 53.

GUFFEY

And Its Mayors

- *Park County; Freshwater Creek drainage*
- *Accessible by paved road; occupied town*
- *Several original structures remain*

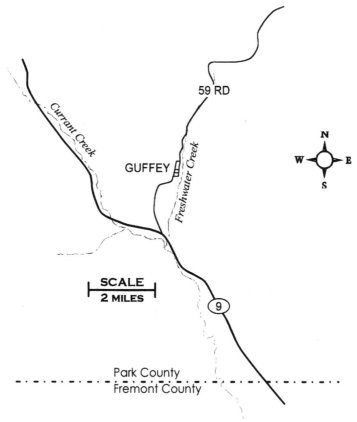

Guffey is located in a remote part of Park County a short distance from Colorado 9.

James Guffey was born in Pennsylvania. During the 1870s, he got in on the ground floor of the oil business. Using money he earned from selling machinery, he began to lease land and sink his own wells. His oil wells eventually extended from Pennsylvania to Texas, and his name was associated with some of the country's major oil fields. In the 1890s, he purchased mining property in the Freshwater Mining District on the south end of South Park. He generously gave the town of Freshwater money for street improvements. For this, the town honored him by changing its name to Guffey.

There is a more colorful story, however, of how Guffey got its name. Senator Joseph Guffey allegedly paid the town of Freshwater $500 to change its name to Guffey. The problem with this story is that Senator Guffey didn't hold office until 1934, well after the town of Guffey was named.

During the 1890s, gold was discovered by Cripple Creek

This is the Guffey Garage, now used as an antique shop under the same name. It is here that Monster, the mayor of Guffey, has his office on a sofa in front of the stove. *(Kenneth Jessen 118D11)*

prospectors. They were drawn to the area by its similar geology. As word got out, over one thousand prospectors came into the area. The town of Freshwater was founded in 1895, and it soon grew to over 500 residents.

Freshwater's main street was lined on both sides with false-front stores. Businesses included three grocery stores, four saloons, three hotels, four restaurants, a couple of bakeries, three hardware stores and two clothing stores. It also had a couple of assay offices and two barber shops. A fruit store, two meat markets and a furniture store rounded out its businesses. Guffey had one lawyer and two physicians. There were four stagecoaches servicing the town during its boom years. Sawmills supplied milled lumber and soon two stamp mills were constructed to process the gold ore.

The residents of Freshwater applied for a post office in 1895. Because there was a Freshwater post office in California, applica-

Colleen Soux sits in front the old Guffey City Hall, constructed in 1896. Her husband, Bill Soux, restored this structure for use by the community. Hundreds of artifacts line its interior walls. *(Kenneth Jessen 118D12)*

tion under this name was denied. Residents then decided on the name Idaville for Ida McClavery Wagner, owner of several mining claims. The following year, the name was changed to Guffey. This post office remains active today.

Metallic ore in the area not only included gold, but some silver. Copper, iron and lead ore were also discovered. Of note is one of the rarest metallic ores, yptotaritralite. Its was used as an alloy.

The first Guffey newspaper came out in 1897. It was called the *Guffy <sic> Prospector*, and it was published until 1903. Other newspapers included the *Guffy <sic> Independent* and the *Freshwater Pilot.*

As with so many other Colorado mining towns, there simply wasn't enough ore to sustain a mining industry. Several tunnels were drilled and shafts were sunk mainly in the area northeast of the town. No large lodes were discovered, and within several years, Guffey was almost disserted. Its economic base became ranching.

Today, 29 people live in Guffey with hundreds more in homes located in the surrounding hills. Guffey is best known for its mayors. In 1988, Park County officials in Fairplay lost the town plat. A new map was drawn and zoning changed what was once residential property to commercial at a substantially higher tax rate. As part of a protest, Guffey residents created a new zone called "ET" for "existing transitional." It applied the ET zoning liberally to town lots.

They also elected a feline mayor, a cat named Paisley. She died of natural causes and was replaced by Smudge le Plume, also a feline. Smudge died mysteriously in 1991 and was believed to have been eaten by an owl. Whifley le Gone, a calico cat, took over the mayoral duties. In 1993, Whifley moved out of town to a ranch.

Shanda, a dog, inherited the position when her master, Bruce Buffington, purchased the general store were the mayor's office was located. The two appeared on the Oprah Winfrey show. During the interview, Shanda preferred to let Buffington do all the talking. By the way, Guffey's two political parties are the "Democats" and the "Repupkins."

Some residents felt that the mayor should be an elected position, and on Halloween, 1998, there was a general election. Monster, a solid black cat, was elected the town's new mayor beating out Lars and Luke, both dogs, and a cockatiel. Monster's office is on an old sofa in front of a stove in the Guffey Garage (an antique shop). Monster has appeared on CNN and America's Greatest Pets. Buffington, by the way, claims this election was invalid, and Shanda doesn't seem to care.

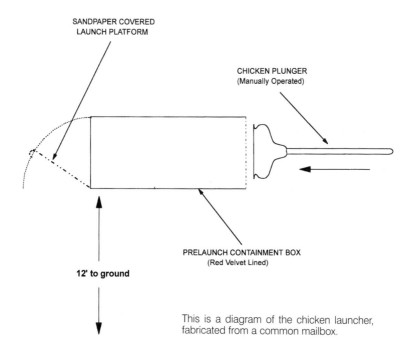

SANDPAPER COVERED
LAUNCH PLATFORM

CHICKEN PLUNGER
(Manually Operated)

PRELAUNCH CONTAINMENT BOX
(Red Velvet Lined)

12' to ground

This is a diagram of the chicken launcher, fabricated from a common mailbox.

Once a year usually on the third weekend in July, Guffey holds a chicken flying contest. For $5, people can rent a chicken. The money goes to city improvements. Those that pay are able to spend quality time bonding with their fowl prior to the event.

From a special containment box twelve-feet above the ground, the chickens are "encouraged" to see how far they can fly.

The record is 138 feet established in 1998.

The process is simple. Each chicken is placed one at a time into the back end of the containment box made from a common mailbox. The back end of the mail box has been removed to allow insertion of the fowl. Event organizers lined the box with red velvet showing their sensitivity to the chicken during the tense moments before a launch. When the front hinged door is opened, most chickens walk then jump. Sandpaper on the inside of the door provides the chicken with a good grip before stepping out into space. For chickens that need encouragement, a chicken plunger is pushed through the back end of the box. In over one thousand flights, no chicken has been injured. After the event, the chickens are returned to their egg-laying duties.

Guffey is worth visiting and can be reached from Colorado 9, which runs south east through South Park or from Cripple Creek on 112 RD then 59 RD.

"Close to Cripple Creek," *Denver Times*, August 7, 1896.
Helen Cahill, editor, *Guffey, One Hundred Years of Memories*, Guffy, Colorado, 1995, pp. 1-5, A-3.
Interview with Bill and Colleen Soux, January 28, 1998.

HALL VALLEY
And Handcart Gulch

- *Park County, North Fork of the South Platte River drainage*
- *Accessible over graded dirt road part of the way*
- *Neither camp had a post office; no standing structures remain*

This privately owned cabin sits up near the Missouri Mine in Hall Valley. The structure has been restored. *(Kenneth Jessen 103D12)*

In 1866, three prospectors left Georgetown and climbed over the mountains into the valley occupied by the North Fork of the South Platte River. They discovered some promising float, staked out a claim and sold it to Colonel J. W. Hall. The valley became known as Hall Valley. The Whale Mine, above 12,500 feet, began operations in 1869. The ore was silver-bearing barite, complex and expensive to smelt. The mining camp was miles from the

Whale and was called Hall Valley. A smelter was constructed there. Hall Valley reached a population of 300 by 1873. An English company took over the mine and, due to poor management, went bankrupt. Although the mine reopened briefly in 1883, the mining camp of Hall Valley was abandoned.

In the 1940s, according to Muriel Sibell Wolle, there was a cabin still standing at the Hall Valley site along with the ruins of a smelter. She also mentioned a stone cellar and a rusting boiler sitting among the ruins of the mill. Today, a Forest Service campground occupies the Hall Valley site, and nothing remains of the old camp.

Handcart Gulch parallels the North Fork of the South Platte River. It was named for the first prospectors in the area who apparently used hand carts to take their possessions over Webster Pass. The valley is filled with prospect holes, but no major mines were developed. The population of Handcart Gulch probably lived in cabins distributed up and down the length of the gulch. Nothing remains today.

Muriel Sibell Wolle, *Stampede to Timberline*, Sage Books, Chicago, 1949, 1974, pp. 101-104.

HAMILTON

And Its Neighbor, Tarryall City

- *Park County, Tarryall Creek drainage*
- *Accessible via graded dirt road*
- *Hamilton had a post office; no standing structures remain*

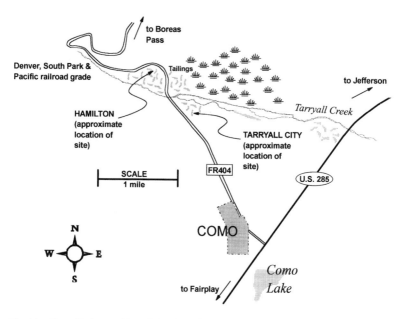

The Hamilton site is near Tarryall Creek on its north bank, while Tarryall City was on the south side of the creek and about a half mile down stream.

Hamilton was established on Tarryall Creek in 1860 and drew thousands of prospectors based on reports that the gravel in the creek bed was rich in gold. The town was named for Earl Hamilton, one of the men involved in the development of the area mines.

Hamilton was built near Tarryall Creek, on its north bank and at the edge of the forest. It had one main street, which paralleled the stream. The town grew quickly to include numerous tents and forty cabins. A stagecoach company built its stables at Hamilton, and a wholesale provision store opened for business. The town also had ten other retail stores, three boarding houses, several saloons, a hotel, a couple of blacksmith shops, a recorder and a justice of the peace. Hamilton's post office opened in 1860 and remained open until 1881. Indicative of the area's population, the Hamilton post office logged upwards to 20,000 names on mail to be delivered to the various prospectors.

Prices in town were outrageous for the time: a sack of flour cost $20 and coffee cost $5 a pound. A day's wages amounted to only $1.50 to $2.00. Most of the prospectors brought their own provisions, enough to last the summer.

Milled lumber was created during the early years by muscle power using a two-man whip saw. Lumber for houses took second place to the demand for sluice boxes used to separate gold from the gravel.

The judicial system was straightforward. McFarland, a man banished from Empire in Clear Creek County, arrived in Hamilton. He received thirty lashes while in Empire and had half of his head shaved for stealing supplies. At Tarryall Diggings, he started robbing sluice boxes of their gold-rich sand. Miners simply got together and hanged McFarland on the spot.

Justice was a potential problem until Colorado became a territory in 1861. South Park was in Kansas Territory, but over Hoosier Pass in Summit County, Breckenridge was in Utah. Central City and Black Hawk were in Nebraska Territory and the San Luis Valley was part of New Mexico. To bring some semblance of order to the area, the United Mining District was created in September, 1860 at the St. Vrain Hotel. Claim size was defined as well as how disputes over claims were to be settled.

In June, 1860, William Holman laid out a competing town called Tarryall City. It was located on the south side of the creek and about a half mile downstream from Hamilton. It amounted to not much more than a cluster of tents and cabins. The cabins were made primarily of hand hewn logs with roofs covered with mud and branches. When the Territorial Legislature met for the first time, it selected Tarryall City as the home of the temporary county seat.

In 1861, Tarryall City became the location of South Park's first newspaper. It was started by *Rocky Mountain News* editor and founder William N. Beyers and three others. Called the *Miner's Record*, it began as a weekly. The first issue was on July 4, and the last issue was that September. The town's population migrated to a warmer climate, but returned the following summer.

Recorded history about these towns is difficult to decipher because the general area was called Tarryall Diggings by the newspapers. Often no distinction was made between Hamilton and Tarryall City.

What caused the end of development to both of these pioneer towns was lack of sufficient water to wash the gold-bearing gravel. A system of ditches only delayed the inevitable abandonment of the two towns. In 1868, Samuel Bowles visited the area, and in his *Our New West*, he remarked that thousands had dug at Tarryall for three or four years, but that only two or three cabins were still occupied. He saw a solitary "dirt-washer," with a dinner pail and pickax, walking along. During this same year, the Schuyler Colfax party visited Hamilton and found fifty empty cabins, two log hotels and only about twenty residents. He described the place as grimy, dirty-looking with manure heaps in front of the houses.

Crofutt reported that only 150 lived in Hamilton in 1880. Frank Hall recorded in 1890 that not one vestige of the town remained. The only evidence of Hamilton or Tarryall City he could find were the piles of rock that were once chimneys.

An early photograph of Hamilton shows that the Peabody Ranch occupied the site and that the ranch house was painted white. There are about six other structures in the photograph, and the Boreas Pass route of the Denver, South Park & Pacific can be seen in the background passing around the mountain.

When the Denver, South Park & Pacific arrived in the area, it built a company town called Como, downstream a short distance from Hamilton and Tarryall. Dredging during the 1930s eradicated any sign of either town, and today, only a willow-covered gravel flat marks the site.

This old cabin is not located at either the Hamilton or the Tarryall City sites, but is the only historic structure in the general area. It sits above the Boreas Pass road between Como and Breckenridge where the road begins its long climb. *(Kenneth Jessen 003B10)*

Don and Jean Griswold, *Colorado's Century of "Cities"*, self published, 1958, pp. 62-63.

Virginia McConnell Simmons, *Bayou Salado*, Century One Press, Colorado Springs, Colorado, 1966, pp. 69-72.

Mary Dyer, *Echoes of Como*, 1879 to 1988, published by George Meyer, 1974, pp. 94-96.

William H. Bauer, James L. Ozment, John H. Willard, *Colorado Post Offices*, Colorado Railroad Museum, Golden, Colorado, 1990, p. 68.

HORSESHOE & MUDSILL
And Other Town Sites

- *Park County, Fourmile Creek drainage*
- *Accessible via graded dirt road*
- *Horseshoe had a post office; no standing structures remain*

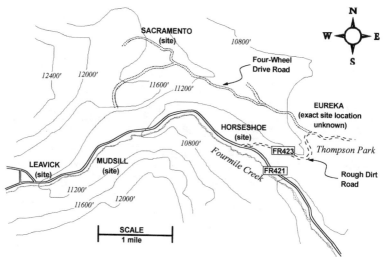

This map indicates the location of Horseshoe and Mudsill and the possible location of Eureka.

Mudsill, at an elevation of 10,921 feet, was a small mining camp which lasted only a few years. It had a small railroad station and a short, four car siding. The railroad built a wye to allow locomotives to be turned. Not much else is known about Mudsill.

The Mudsill mine was located on the north rim of the spectacular Horseshoe Cirque. The mine was opened in 1880, but the silver ore was not especially valuable. "Chicken Bill" of Leadville, however, "enhanced" the ore to make the property more saleable. It was sold for $190,000 to the Lord Mayor of London, who must have felt foolish once the actual value of the mine was determined by assay values. In 1938, the entire Mudsill group of mines, covering 260 acres, commanded a price of only $20,000.

Horseshoe was more of a town than Mudsill and was founded around 1879. Its population soon reached 300 and eventually peaked at 800. Located three miles below Mudsill at 10,500 feet, the town had two hotels, two smelters, two sawmills and several stores. It also had a saloon. A number of cabins were scattered about the area.

The town started out as "Horse Shoe," and the post office was established in 1880 under that name. The name was changed later to "Horseshoe." The Horseshoe post office closed in 1894, but in 1901, the post office opened again at the site under the name of Doran. It closed again in 1907 when the town was abandoned for good.

The U. S. abandonment of the silver standard in 1893 ended the boom years for Horseshoe. In 1896, the Denver, South Park & Hilltop constructed a narrow gauge line up Fourmile Creek, through Horseshoe, to Leavick, thus renewing mining activity stimulated by lower transportation costs.

When ghost town historian Muriel Sibell Wolle visited the Horseshoe site in the 1940s, only two cabins remained standing. There are no standing structures at the site today.

There is quite a bit of confusion over another site in the area called East Leadville. Some historians believe is was an alternate name for Horseshoe. Virginia McConnell Simmons placed it one mile southeast of Sacramento based on an 1898 Forest Reserve map. She referred to a postal directory which lists East Leadville as distinctly different from either Horseshoe or Sacramento. In the definitive work on post offices, *Colorado Post Offices*, East Leadville is not listed.

The mystery continues. *The Fairplay Flume*, May 29, 1879, said that a plat for East Leadville was filed by J. H. B. McFerran and that the town was to be built in Horseshoe Gulch. McFerran was the supervisor or owner of the Last Chance mine on Mt. Sheridan above Horseshoe Gulch. He also owned a smelter in the gulch. A hotel was to have been constructed during the summer of 1879. Simmons states that in 1965, a building was found in the forest southeast of Sacramento, and she speculated that this might have been the site for the town.

McFerran's smelter, the South Park Smelting and Reduction Works, was listed in an 1879 business directory as at Eureka. Eureka was located five miles below Mt. Sheridan, which would place it about a mile east of Horseshoe and above the creek. It may have been on the old road between Horseshoe and Fairplay, which goes up over a small rise east of Horseshoe. The smelter employed forty men and it is not known if they lived at Eureka. Nothing remains at the site.

Virginia McConnell Simmons, *Bayou Salado*, Century One Press, Colorado Springs, Colorado, 1966, pp. 147-148.

George A. Crofutt, *Crofutt's Grip Sack Guide of Colorado 1885*, Johnson Books, Boulder, Colorado, 1966, 1981, p. 104.

Perry Eberhart, *Guide to the Colorado Ghost Towns and Mining Camps*, Sage Books, Chicago, 1959, pp. 133-134.

William H. Bauer, James L. Ozment, John H. Willard, *Colorado Post Offices*, Colorado Railroad Museum, Golden, Colorado, 1990, pp. 46, 74.

Muriel Sibell Wolle, *Stampede to Timberline*, Sage Books, Chicago, 1949, 1974, pp. 96-98.

Mac Poor, *Denver, South Park & Pacific*, Rocky Mountain Railroad Club, Denver, 1976, pp. 273, 290, 424.

JEFFERSON CITY, JEFFERSON and JEFFERSON

- *Park County, Jefferson Creek drainage*
- *Accessible via paved road*
- *Town has post office; many original standing structures*

There were a number of towns that used the name Jefferson. Jefferson City was founded in 1860 at the foot of Georgia Pass. Its location was about six miles to the northeast of Tarryall City. An estimated 2,000 prospectors worked the gravel in the area. This town was the only one shown in South Park on early maps. Jefferson City got its own post office in January of 1860 and was listed as being located in Kansas Territory, a year prior to the establishment of Colorado Territory. The post office closed in December of the same year. Mining continued until about 1864 when the placer gold was exhausted.

A real estate development in 1861 established the new town sites of Jefferson and Palestine, down stream from the Jefferson City site. Buyers from the South Park towns of Hamilton and Tarryall City purchased lots. Some homes were constructed, and the second town of Jefferson got a post office this same year. The post office closed in 1864. The sales of lots apparently did not go well and the town site was abandoned. Bayard Taylor confirmed this in 1866 when he passed through the area.

In 1879, the final town using the name of Jefferson was established near the site of the second Jefferson. Willard Heal laid out the town and was its first resident. He knew the Denver, South Park & Pacific would cross over his cattle ranch and that rail service was required for a successful town. The railroad's survey

Jefferson's second school now serves as a church. It is one of South Park's most charming structures. *(Kenneth Jessen 098D2)*

determined the town's location. He also was a tie contractor for the railroad. Heal opened a store in Jefferson, converted his house into a hotel and stage stop, and was a county commissioner.

Jefferson's population was fifty-five by 1880. In four years, the businesses had increased to include a lumber mill, blacksmith shop, two butchers and a saloon. The railroad constructed a beautiful, classic wood frame depot, which still stands along U.S. 285 in Jefferson. The most unusual business was a cheese factory. It lasted only a year or two, and the building was eventually converted into a community center. Jefferson's second schoolhouse still stands and is used as a church.

Jefferson has changed little over the years and many of its original structures still stand, making it a historic stop along U.S. Highway 285.

William H. Bauer, James L. Ozment, John H. Willard, *Colorado Post Offices*, Colorado Railroad Museum, Golden, Colorado, 1990, p. 80.

Mary Dyer, *Echoes of Como, 1879 to 1988*, published by George Meyer, 1974, p. 107.

Virginia McConnell Simmons, *Bayou Salado*, Century One Press, Colorado Springs, Colorado, 1966, pp. 74-75, 252-253.

KING
Of Coal

- *Park County, Park Gulch drainage*
- *Accessible by graded dirt road*
- *The town had a post office; no standing structures remain*

Built two and a half miles south of Como in the vast rolling high altitude prairie of South Park was the coal mining town of King. A railroad spur was constructed by the Denver, South Park & Pacific to serve the coal mines. As announced in 1880 in the *Rocky Mountain News,* the Union Pacific took over the ownership and operation of the mine. Rows of identical company houses were constructed for the miners, and the number soon grew to sixty frame houses.

King had its own school and provided a home for the teacher. The school doubled as a church on Sundays. It also had a couple of saloons and a company store. The population of King was not sufficient for a post office until 1884. A blacksmith shop, carpenter shop, powder house, and scale house rounded out the structures. There is also a small cemetery at the King site. The nearest hotel was the Thomas, located two miles to the east.

It wasn't coal production that caused the abandonment of King, it was the ignition of coal gas in the confined underground workings. In 1885, thirty-five Chinese were killed at No. 1 mine and their bodies were simply left to rot underground. There were mine fires in 1886 and 1889. An explosion in No. 5 mine in 1896 put an end to coal mining and to the town. The No. 5 mine was the best producing mine at King, and the explosion killed twenty-five Italian miners. Unlike the Chinese, their bodies were recovered and many are buried in the Como cemetery.

177

The post office closed the year of the explosion, and the population dwindled from a high of 400 to a couple of families. One row of company houses was moved to Como to eliminate a housing shortage, and the remainder of the buildings simple deteriorated with time. Today, only the concrete foundations of mining structures remain.

William H. Bauer, James L. Ozment, John H. Willard, *Colorado Post Offices*, Colorado Railroad Museum, Golden, Colorado, 1990, p. 82.

Mary Dyer, *Echoes of Como, 1879 to 1988*, published by George Meyer, 1974, pp. 99-101.

Virginia McConnell Simmons, *Bayou Salado*, Century One Press, Colorado Springs, Colorado, 1966, pp. 164-166.

LEAVICK

- *Park County, Fourmile Creek drainage*
- *Accessible by graded dirt road*
- *Town had a post office; one structure remains*

Leavick in 1900. *(Colorado Historical Society F6528)*

The Hilltop mine has an appropriate name; it is located well above 13,000 feet in South Park high on a mountain in the treeless tundra. It was purchased by Felix Leavick of Leadville in 1892. An incredible two and a half mile long aerial tram brought the ore down to a mill, and the town established at the base of the tram was named Leavick. The town was located at the modest elevation of 11,300 feet.

The story of Leavick really begins with the Last Chance Lode, which was discovered in 1873, in a 12,600 foot saddle between Mt. Sherman and Mt. Sheridan. Nearby, the Hilltop Lode was discov-

179

ered nine years later. The problem with the location was that it was so cold that the interior of the Hilltop Mine was perpetually covered with ice. Miners had to chop ice away from the entrance. A bunkhouse once stood at the mine entrance, indicating that some miners remained at this elevation for at least part of the year.

The mines in this area produced silver with some zinc and lead. Hilltop closed in 1893 with the abandonment of the silver standard by the U. S. government. Unlike other Colorado mines, the Hilltop soon resumed shipping, with zinc as the primary source of revenue. At first, ore was hauled by wagon down to the mill until the aerial tram was constructed. The mine was electrified and new machinery installed in 1901. The Hilltop remained in production until about 1930.

In 1896, the narrow gauge Denver, South Park & Hilltop was incorporated as a subsidiary of the Denver, Leadville & Gunnison. The mine owners financed 49% of the construction. The railroad, completed to the mill at Leavick, hauled coal, supplies and passengers to the town and concentrate from the mill. Serving the Hilltop and the Dauntless mines, the mill continued to operate until World War II. The junction with the South Park line was about three-quarters of a mile from Fairplay. From this junction,

the railroad gained 1,400 feet in elevation to reach Leavick with grades up to 5.85%, making it one of the steepest adhesion railroads in Colorado. Locomotives were able to pull only two or three empty cars up to the mill at a time, and a train consisting of heavy concentrate-filled cars

The old mill at Leavick. Nothing remains of the town itself; the last remaining structures were moved years ago to South Park City outside of Fairplay and placed on display. *(Kenneth Jessen 086B8)*

was very difficult to keep under control coming downgrade. Below Leavick, in Mudsill, a wye was built to turn the locomotives.

The town of Leavick became fully developed during the boom years and had a school, a seasonal barbershop, a dentist and a baseball team. Buildings included two saloons, a boarding house for the miners, a blacksmith shop, a general store, livery barns, a post office, two mills, the lower tram station and an unknown number of homes. A popular brothel was located on the edge of town. The buildings were scattered in a random pattern right at timberline. Population estimates vary, but more than likely, Leavick supported no more than 200 to 300 people.

After the mines closed and the tracks were removed, Leavick was abandoned. It became one of Colorado's most picturesque ghost towns, and for many years its isolation kept vandals away. The old mining road to Leavick was often impassable. In 1948, things changed when the Last Chance Mine reopened. The old right-of-way for the Denver, South Park & Hilltop was purchased and turned over to Park County to maintain as a good, graded, gravel road all the way from U.S. 285 to Leavick. With this change, the town of Leavick became accessible and a popular place to visit and vandalize.

To save what was left of Leavick, the directors of South Park City elected to remove the few remaining structures and place them on display. South Park City is an open air museum adjacent to Fairplay. Without this type of intervention, little would remain of Leavick today.

Today only the mill still stands at the Leavick site. It is in an advanced state of decay and will eventually yield to the heavy winter snows. The upper terminal of the Hilltop Mine can be seen in the far distance from the mill. Scattered remains of the tram towers can also be spotted at intervals on the mountainside. The Leavick site is easy to reach by a good graded road. *See "Horseshoe & Mudsill" for a map showing the location of Leavick.*

Muriel Sibell Wolle, *Stampede to Timberline*, Sage Books, Chicago, 1949, 1974, pp. 96-98.

LONDON JUNCTION
and HOLLAND

- *Park County, South Fork of the South Platte River*
- *Accessible via graded dirt road*
- *Holland had a post office; several original structures at each site*

At London Junction, a branch of the Denver, South Park & Pacific left the main line and began its climb up Mosquito Gulch to the London Mine. This branch was built under the name London, South Park & Leadville. Originally, the main line of the Denver, South Park & Pacific stopped at London Junction, and supplies bound for Alma had to be transferred to a horse-drawn wagon for the remaining mile to Alma. Merchants were quite unhappy with this arrangement.

The railroad constructed a small depot at London Junction, which included living quarters for the agent. The railroad also had a water tank, coal bin, and scale house.

For some reason, London Junction was renamed Alma Junction, and as many as 200 lived there. In 1908, a spur track was built across Mosquito Creek to a smelter. This gave Alma rail service.

A historic photograph taken around 1886 shows five homes at London Junction. Other structures such as the depot also are included. Today, there are several modern homes plus a couple of the original buildings sitting along the road to Park City.

Dwight and Park Holland organized the Holland smelter to treat iron, copper, gold and silver ores in the Alma-Fairplay district. Located three miles south of Alma, Holland was founded as a smelter town in 1874. In February, the town got its own post office, which unfortunately closed in December. Although the town was still occupied a decade later, the smelter was never successful. The smelter was sold at a sheriff's sale in 1875. There are several newer homes at the Holland site. It is not known if any of the original structures remain at the site.

London Junction consisted of a small cluster of cabins. This is one of the original structures, and it sits along the graded dirt road to Park City. *(Kenneth Jessen 099A7)*

Mac Poor, *Denver, South Park & Pacific*, Rocky Mountain Railroad Club, Denver, 1976, p. 424.

Virginia McConnell Simmons, *Bayou Salado*, Century One Press, Colorado Springs, Colorado, 1966, po. 123, 197.

William H. Bauer, James L. Ozment, John H. Willard, *Colorado Post Offices*, Colorado Railroad Museum, Golden, Colorado, 1990, p. 73.

MILL GULCH
Logging Camp

- *Park County, Mill Gulch drainage*
- *Access by foot trail*
- *No standing structures on site*

Dusty Arnold, Ben Jessen, and Brooke pose by a cabin below a small lumber camp located in Mill Gulch south of Guanella Pass. The name of this camp remains a mystery. *(Kenneth Jessen 109B9)*

High in Mill Gulch at an elevation of 11,000 feet, south of Guanella Pass, stands a ghost camp which supported a small lumber mill. The name of this place is a mystery. The remains of two substantial log cabins sit in an open meadow, while below in the trees a short distance away once sat a larger structure, possibly a boarding house. Facing into a small gully is the foundation of a small lumber mill as evidenced by the piles of slash and mounds of sawdust. Down the steep access road in a meadow about a half-mile away is a cabin in relatively good condition.

This lumber camp is but a short distance west of the abandoned Geneva Basin Ski Area, however, access up Mill Gulch is restricted to foot travel. The original access road is between Duck Creek and the Guanella Pass road. It is blocked off at one end by a berm placed there by the Forest Service and at the other end by private property. A ford across Duck Creek leads into Mill Gulch, and from the ford, it is a pleasant two mile hike to the logging camp. The entrance to Mill Gulch is, by the way, close to the Geneva Park Campground.

This site does not appear in the traditional ghost town books and is an example of the many abandoned camps yet to be discovered in the Colorado high country.

MONTGOMERY
Sent To A Watery Grave

- *Park County, Middle South Platte River drainage*
- *Accessible by graded dirt road*
- *Town had a post office; site under water*

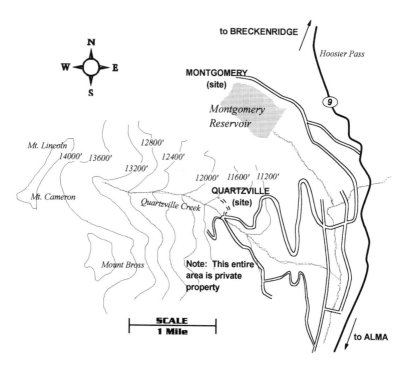

The Montgomery site is south of Hoosier Pass, and most of the site is below the waters of the Montgomery Reservoir.

Gold flakes were discovered in the vast gravel deposits in South Park in 1859, and Montgomery became one of the Park's earliest settlements in 1861. The town was located at 10,800 feet immediately south of Hoosier Pass and was part of the Snow Blind Mining District. This district was reorganized as the Montgomery Mining District in August, 1861. The town got its post office in 1862, and it remained active until it was moved to Dudley in 1872. Montgomery regained its post office in 1882 with a resurgence in mining activity. It lost its post office for the final time in 1888 when the town's population began to fall.

Father Dyer visited Montgomery in 1861 to preach a sermon. He was not successful in getting the miners away from their claims. One man, however, took time to visit with Dyer and ask him to join him for a meal. The meal was served on the ground since the man had not yet had time to build a cabin.

By the fall of 1861, Montgomery had two hotels and seventy cabins. There was also a store and a couple of sawmills running day and night to keep up with the demand for milled lumber.

The following year, Montgomery's population exploded to a thousand or so with over 150 cabins. The town also had six mills processing gold ore. Montgomery had gained a drug store and a doctor. There was also a bakery, mercantile store, dry goods store, more hotels and five sawmills. In Montgomery's two-story, 50 by 100 foot hotel, public dances were held on the second floor, with people coming from the surrounding area to participate. Touring variety shows stopped at Montgomery.

Even though both the Methodists and Presbyterians held weekly church services, Montgomery gained a reputation as a wild mining town. To celebrate Colorado becoming a territory, Montgomery sent President Lincoln a bar of gold, and the town's people named one of the highest peaks in the area for Lincoln.

Bayard Taylor visited Montgomery in 1866 and reported a population between 300 and 400. Taylor assumed that the town had decreased in size. To Taylor, the lack of abandoned buildings simply meant that the surviving residents used the lumber in their fire places to keep warm. After the placer gold was exhausted, silver ore was discovered in 1881, and the town was revived. Another boom occurred in 1898 and continued past the turn of the century.

Most of the town was located in a relatively flat meadow at the headwaters of the Middle South Platte River. Some of the town, however, was up on the hillside as evidenced by an early photograph. A mine called Robber's Roost required climbing a frightening ladder with 200 rungs.

When ghost town historian Muriel Sibell Wolle visited the Montgomery site in 1947, the ruins of cabins and a faint trace of

When Montgomery was still a boom town in 1867, this photograph was taken showing the town's size. Today, most of the site is under the Montgomery Reservoir. *(Colorado Historical Society F6433)*

the foundations were all that remained. There was evidence of three principal streets.

A century after Montgomery was founded, Colorado Springs purchased the site and cleared out what remained. A dam was built and now a reservoir covers the old Montgomery site.

The site can be reached by a graded dirt road, which leaves Colorado 9 about a mile south of Hoosier Pass and angles down toward the Montgomery Reservoir. There is access to the reservoir near the dam as well as access to the upper portion of the reservoir via a graded dirt road.

William H. Bauer, James L. Ozment, John H. Willard, *Colorado Post Offices*, Colorado Railroad Museum, Golden, Colorado, 1990, p. 100.

Virginia McConnell Simmons, *Bayou Salado*, Century One Press, Colorado Springs, Colorado, 1966, pp. 108-109.

Robert L. Brown, *Ghost Towns of the Colorado Rockies*, Caxton Printers, Caldwell, Idaho, 1977, pp. 224-228.

Muriel Sibell Wolle, *Stampede to Timberline*, Sage Books, Chicago, 1949, 1974, p. 99.

MOSQUITO

And The London Mine

- *Park County, Mosquito Creek drainage*
- *Accessible by graded dirt road*
- *Town did not have a post office; no standing structures remain*

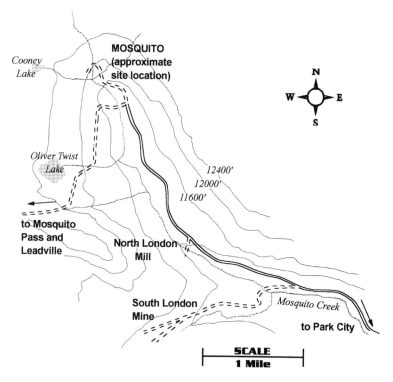

This map indicates the location of the London Mill and approximately where the mining camp of Mosquito once stood.

The name of this small camp is possibly its most interesting historical fact. Miners at the upper end of Mosquito Creek were having trouble deciding on the name for their mining district and for their new camp. Several names were suggested, but they could not reach an agreement. The place for the name was left blank in a ledger. When the miners met again, the secretary opened the book and saw the smashed remains of a large mosquito right in the blank spot for the camp's name. It was agreed that the camp be called Mosquito.

Mosquito was located at the very end of the Mosquito Creek drainage where the graded dirt road makes its turn and begins the climb toward Mosquito Pass. The camp's elevation was just below 11,600 feet. When the wagon road over the pass was completed in 1879, the camp became a stage stop. Prior to the construction of

The London Mill and its associated office building is all that remains in the general area where the town of Mosquito once stood. The actual Mosquito site is farther up the Mosquito Creek drainage beyond the Mosquito Pass road. *(Kenneth Jessen 065D)*

railroads into South Park and the Arkansas Valley, the pass itself was the busiest stretch of road in the Rocky Mountains. Because of its incredible altitude of 13,186 feet, it was called "The Highway of Frozen Death." The pass was closed in 1910 and remained closed until post-World War II improvements.

Mosquito did not last long and remains of the camp are very difficult to find. The area is poorly drained and snow fields linger through the summer. This swampy area is thick with mosquitos as the name suggests, and vegetation has covered whatever was left of the camp.

The London Mine was divided into the North London and the South London. The mine was opened in 1874 and continued to produce gold, silver and lead for many years. At first a stamp mill in Mosquito Gulch was used to reduce the ore, then in 1882, the London, South Park & Pacific narrow gauge railroad was built to the North London mine. An aerial tramway transported ore directly to the railhead where it could be hauled to smelters in Alma or to the company-owned mill at London Junction.

On the other side of the ridge, however, the South London was the biggest producer of the two mines. A mill was constructed in 1883 to handle its ore. During the 1890s, a tunnel was drilled through the ridge to connect both mines and to allow transportation of ore to the railhead from the South London. It continued to operate until 1943.

The lower tram station for the North London mine, an office building and outhouse still stand in the wet, marshy area along Mosquito Creek. Scattered lumber and a collapsed building suggest that there were a number of structures on this site. The faint remains of the railroad grade can also be located.

John K. Aldrich, *Ghosts of Park County*, Centennial Graphics, Lakewood, Colorado, 1989, p. 30.

John L. Dyer, *The Snow Shoe Itinerant*, Father Dyer United Methodist Church, Breckenridge, Colorado, 1976, (originally published by Cranston & Stowe, Cincinnati, Ohio, 1890), p. 151.

Muriel Sibell Wolle, *Timberline Tailings*, Sage Books, Chicago, 1977, p. 92.

Virginia McConnell Simmons, *Bayou Salado*, Century One Press, Colorado Springs, Colorado, 1966, pp. 127-128.

PARK CITY

- *Park County, Mosquito Creek drainage*
- *Accessible via graded dirt road*
- *Town had a post office; several original structures remain*

In 1878, a group of Denver and Fairplay investors, including H. A. W. Tabor, incorporated the Mosquito Pass Wagon Road Company which ran up Mosquito Creek, over Mosquito Pass above 13,000 feet, and on to Leadville. The road over the pass was opened in 1879 and became a major route from Denver to Leadville. There were many stage stops along the way, including Fairplay. Up to four stage companies used this route.

This two-story log home is one of several original structures in Park City. *(Kenneth Jessen 099A6)*

In 1882, a branch of the Denver, South Park & Pacific was constructed up Mosquito Creek to serve the London mine at an elevation of 11,462 feet. From London Junction, about a mile south of Alma, the railroad gained 1,200 vertical feet in 7.4 miles.

At the mouth of Mosquito Creek, a town called Park City developed in 1879. About twenty people moved to Park City along the busy Mosquito Pass route. The town gained a dozen or so businesses and four hotels. Its post office opened in 1879 under the name of Park.

The need for stagecoach service declined in 1882 with the arrival of the railroad, which constructed its line over Trout Creek Pass to Buena Vista then up Chalk Creek Canyon. Park City began to lose population, and the post office closed in 1891.

Today, Park City is worth a visit. It typifies a small mountain community, and several of its original log structures have been restored for use as seasonal housing.

For a map which shows Park City, see "Buckskin Joe."

Virginia McConnell Simmons, *Bayou Salado*, Century One Press, Colorado Springs, Colorado, 1966, p. 145.

William H. Bauer, James L. Ozment, John H. Willard, *Colorado Post Offices*, Colorado Railroad Museum, Golden, Colorado, 1990, p. 111.

PUMA CITY

- *Park County, Tarryall Creek drainage*
- *Accessible via paved road*
- *Town had post office; no original structures remain*

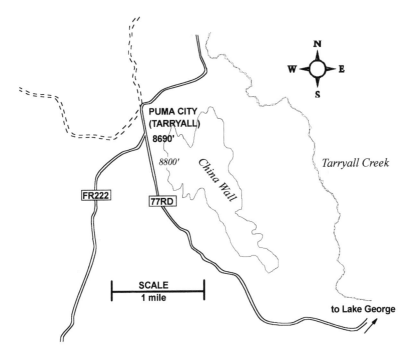

Puma City/Tarryall is located along 77RD north of Lake George. The actual town site is nothing more than a meadow, and a recent mountain property development sits adjacent to the site.

There is always confusion when one town is abandoned and another town uses the same name. Such is the case for Tarryall. An outcropping of gold, silver and lead ore was discovered by Rocky Mountain Jim (not to be confused with Rocky Mountain Jim Nugent killed in Estes Park). The float was found at the southeast corner of South Park northwest of Lake George, in 1896. Rocky Mountain Jim did not file a claim at first, but brought back two partners. The claim was in an open meadow at 8,500 feet and west of Tarryall Creek. This was far removed from the active mining areas of Fairplay, Alma, Tarryall City and Hamilton.

Near the claim, Puma City was founded, named for the nearby Puma Hills. C. W. Gilman from Denver laid out the town which covered fifty acres. Puma City grew quickly to include fifty houses, tents and log cabins. The town soon had three hotels and a boarding house. There were two general stores, a blacksmith shop and a livery stable. Sawmills turned out milled lumber and five saloons provided residents with entertainment. By 1897, the population of Puma City peaked at 1,000 people.

The mail arrived daily from Lake George, thirteen miles to the south. The town newspaper was the *Puma Ledger*. In 1896, the post office opened, but under the name Tarryall. The original Tarryall City, near Hamilton, had been abandoned long ago and the name was simply reused. The post office remained open until 1909. In 1914, during its second boom, the Puma City post office reopened and remained open until 1933.

One of the principal mines was the Boomer, with assayed values between $85 to $100 per ton in gold, silver and lead. Other mines included the June and the Hard to Beat. The No Name mine had its assay run from $25 to $58 per ton in gold. All of the mines looked good initially. Ore was hauled by wagon south to the Colorado Midland Railway for shipment to smelters in Denver. In all, there were about twenty mines in the area.

The best years lasted until 1905, then the population dwindled to twenty-five. The general store stayed open as well as a meat market and the office of a notary public. As people left

Tarryall, they sold their property to Mr. Derby who, in time, ended up owning most of the town.

Ranching became the stable economic basis for the town. In 1922 during its second boom, a school was built in Puma City.

Colorado 24 runs through Lake George. A short distance north of Lake George, 77RD turns off and heads north to Puma City/Tarryall. As shown by ghost town historian Robert L. Brown in his before and after photographs of the site, a dozen or so ramshackle buildings once made up downtown Tarryall. At this same location today, there is only a meadow. Mountain property adjacent to the site, however, has brought the population back to twenty-five.

Midge Harbour, *The Tarryall Mountains and the Puma Hills*, Century One Press, Colorado Springs, Colorado, 1982, pp. 42-46.

Robert L. Brown, *Ghost Towns of the Colorado Rockies*, Caxton Printers, Caldwell, Idaho, 1977, pp. 286-290.

William H. Bauer, James L. Ozment, John H. Willard, *Colorado Post Offices*, Colorado Railroad Museum, Golden, Colorado, 1990, p. 140.

QUARTZVILLE

- *Park County, Middle South Platte River drainage*
- *Accessible by graded dirt road*
- *No standing structures; access to site itself restricted by private property*

High above Alma is the ghost town of Quartzville. Little remains today of this once sizable town as modern mountain homes encroach on the site. *(Kenneth Jessen 107A3)*

The Independent Mining District was formed in 1861, in an area northeast of the summit of Mt. Bross, elevation 14,172 feet. Silver ore was discovered in this region, and a small mining camp called Quartzville grew below the mines. The camp itself was located at 11,400 feet.

By the end of 1861, Quartzville had about fifty cabins spread out in a sunken meadow. The resident population was between sixty and one hundred men. One of the first visitors to the town was Father Dyer, the snowshoe itinerant preacher. In August, he

gave a sermon to about thirty miners in this lofty place. During
the 1870s, Quartzville continued to grow, and by 1872, the estimated population was 200.

The primary mines were the Moose, at 13,800 feet, located
just below the summit of Mt. Bross and the Russia Mine, just
below 14,000 feet. The combined output of the Moose and the
Russia was worth over three million dollars.

The ore was exhausted toward the end of the 1870s, and
Quartzville went into a period of decline. Revitalization occurred
in 1884 when the Quartzville Tunnel was drilled to access several
lodes. The final blow came in 1893 with the repeal of the Sherman
Silver Purchase Act. Quartzville became a ghost town.

Reaching Quartzville during the 1940s was an arduous task
for Muriel Sibell Wolle, author of *Stampede to Timberline.* It
required a hike from the valley floor, four and a half miles through
swamps and across streams, as well as bushwhacking through
dense stands of trees. At Quartzville, she found many cabins still
in reasonable condition, some hidden in the trees and others in a
small meadow. She found two large log houses and deep ruts
where the main street had been located.

Another ghost town historian, Robert Brown, found ten to
fifteen standing cabins in the 1960s, a testimony to the size of
Quartzville. Today, there are the remains of only three cabins, all
in a row, and almost flat to the ground. A mountain property
development has made it easy to visit the site, but new construction has all but obliterated Quartzville. Private property now limits access to the site. In a decade or less, nothing will remain.

Although there is not much to see at Quartzville, it is easy to
reach. From Alma, head north on Colorado 9 toward Hoosier
Pass. Take the second graded dirt road to the left which is marked
County 6. This road parallels Colorado 9, but runs along the
South Platte River through a mountain property development,
while Colorado 9 climbs toward Hoosier Pass. Look for a left turn
marked Quartzville Road. Follow the Quartzville Road up to
11,400 feet, ignoring numerous side roads. The road ends at the

Quartzville site located in a meadow where a four-wheel drive road (Forest Service Road 437) takes off up Mount Lincoln past several mines. The site is surrounded by private property, and one home overlooks this meadow.

It is beautiful place with Mount Bross and Mount Lincoln, both over 14,000 feet in elevation, immediately to the west. Tucked away between these two high peaks is yet another peak over 14,000 feet in height, Mount Cameron. To the east sits 13,822 foot Mount Silverheels.

For a map showing the Quartzville site, refer to "Montgomery."

Muriel Sibell Wolle, *Stampede to Timberline*, Sage Books, Chicago, 1949, 1974, p. 85.

Robert L. Brown, *Ghost Towns of the Colorado Rockies*, Caxton Printers, Caldwell, Idaho, 1977, pp. 291-292.

Virginia McConnell Simmons, *Bayou Salado*, Century One Press, Colorado Springs, Colorado, 1966, p. 108.

SACRAMENTO, COLORADO

- Park County, South Platte drainage
- Accessible over a four-wheel drive road, some walking may be required
- Town did not have a post office; a number of standing structures remain

A number of cabins are still standing at the remote mining camp of Sacramento. *(Kenneth Jessen 097C3)*

At an altitude of well over 11,000 feet and at the head of Sacramento Gulch, rich silver ore was discovered in 1878. An early shipment of nine and a half tons yielded $1,346. For a one month period, $39,000 was recovered.

A group of miners founded the Sacramento Mining Company in 1878 to develop the mine. The October Tunnel was driven into the side of the mountain, and a smelter was built at the mouth of the gulch to serve the mine. Although the ore was very rich, the ore body was exhausted by 1895.

What was called Sacramento City or Sacramento Flats was located just below timberline on the ridge between Sacramento Creek and Fourmile Creek. The town consisted of twenty cabins, seven of which remain standing today.

To reach Sacramento can be tricky. Take the graded dirt road up Fourmile Creek from U.S. 285, about a mile and a quarter south of Fairplay. Drive to the Horseshoe town site, then take the steep dirt road to the right that angles up the side of the valley. This is Forest Service 423. When the road starts back downhill after crossing over a shallow pass, turn left on the Thompson Park Road (which may or may not be marked). Ignore the side road, which will be on the right after about a mile. In slightly over two miles, take the right fork in the road at a small meadow. Note the remains of a cabin. Then drive up this road through heavy timber to the ghost town of Sacramento. In 1996, the road was blocked by windfall about a half mile from the site. Cabins are scattered on both sides of the road, and one cabin appears to have a double roof, possibly for added insulation.

For a map showing the site, see "Horseshoe & Mudsill."

Frank Fossett, *Colorado, its Gold and Silver Mines*, C. G. Crawford, New York, 1879, p. 507.

Robert L. Brown, *Ghost Towns of the Colorado Rockies*, Caxton Printers, Caldwell, Idaho, 1977, pp. 307-311.

Virginia McConnell Simmons, *Bayou Salado*, Century One Press, Colorado Springs, Colorado, 1966, p. 147.

SOUTH PARK CITY
Preserves History

- *Park County, South Platte River drainage*
- *Accessible by paved road*
- *Site an outdoor museum adjacent to the town of Fairplay*

A lthough South Park City, adjacent to the town of Fairplay, looks like an old mining town, it really never existed. It was created as a means of preserving historic structures found in Colorado mining towns before the turn of the century. A variety of abandoned buildings in Park County were moved to South Park City and combined with existing buildings at the north end of Fairplay's main street. This forms an outdoor museum with universal appeal to both young and old.

The original Park County courthouse, on the left, was built in 1862. On the right is a cabin from Garo, constructed during the mid-1890s. *(Kenneth Jessen 099A12)*

203

At the end of a long, dusty, rough dirt road, historians are sometimes rewarded with a cluster of ramshackled buildings of an abandoned mining town. The visitors to such places can stand on the main street and imagine what life must have been like in a high mountain meadow surrounded by majestic peaks. To find an old ghost town like this is quite exciting, but the hard reality is that precious few towns exist. As time passes, so do the ghost towns.

Is it better to rescue old structures and relocate them for the sake of preservation or is it better to simply let the ghost towns rot away and return to dust? Lacking preservation efforts, it is painfully obvious that nothing will remain for future generations.

The South Park Historical Foundation thought it best to move representative samples of old structures from area mining towns into an outdoor museum. Experts were brought in to stabilize and restore these structures. The end result is an artificial mining town composed of historic structures representing life during the late 1800s. Hopefully, South Park City will be around for generations to come.

Such an ambitious endeavor usually has a single individual behind the effort. In this case, the individual was Leon Snyder of Colorado Springs. His favorite fishing holes were in South Park, and he passed by the remains of many once bustling towns such as Leavick, Tarryall, Horseshoe, Mosquito, and North London. Snyder could visualize what these towns must have looked like during their boom years. He could see in his mind's eye an old drug store fully stocked with various remedies, some containing a great deal of medicinal alcohol. He could also see a bar with its bottles lined up next to stuffed novelty owls typical of the day. Snyder's idea was to bring what was left of some of these towns into one place for preservation.

The South Park Historical Foundation was formed in 1957 and soon included many leading historians. With luck, Snyder was able to purchase the partially abandoned north end of Fairplay's Front Street. Plans were formulated for the restoration of the existing structures on both sides of the street including the

Denny House, the old stone Summer Brewery, Colonel Mayer's home, and a stone saloon. To this core other buildings were added to fill out the town. Foundations were built, wooden flooring replaced, period furniture brought in ... all to recreate a mining town. Donations included an old printing press for the newspaper office. The entire contents of an old drug store were purchased and put on display.

By the end of the summer of 1957, the three remaining structures at Leavick had been moved to South Park City as well as other structures from Alma and Fairplay itself. More buildings were added the following year. Board walks were built, and mining equipment was brought in to complete the picture. Soon twenty-two buildings lined the main street of the newly created town of South Park City.

The most ambitious move was an inn from its original site near the top of Mosquito Pass at 13,180 feet. Snyder had seen this magnificent, two-story structure many times. It was a massive building and made up of hand-hewn timbers as thick as 18 inches. There was only a primitive, rock-strewn trail leading to the inn. The movers raised the building off the ground, and a bulldozer cleared a path ahead of the structure. During the trip, it slipped off a flat bed truck twice, but the old inn arrived in fine condition with most of the chinking between its massive logs intact.

South Park City needed a newspaper office, so it was decided to move an old

Moved in 1958 from the North London mine, this structure served as the assay office. It is now part of the exhibit at South Park City. The mine was developed in the 1880s, and it is believed that the assay office was constructed after 1890. *(Kenneth Jessen 099A10)*

schoolhouse from Lake George. The building, with its false front, was moved 45 miles over Wilkerson Pass. The old general store at Dudley was carefully taken down, log-by-log, from its original location and reassembled in South Park City. From the North London mine, the old assay office was moved.

At an elevation of 11,300 feet, Leavick was fast rotting away. All of the remaining buildings, except the mill, were moved to South Park City. This included a small trappers cabin, a miner's cabin and a blacksmith shop.

In 1959, a century after the first gold rush to Colorado, the South Park Historical Foundation's museum opened to the public. It is well worth the visit and takes about one to two hours to tour.

The Rost Barn, originally located at 2nd and Main in Fairplay, was used by the Rost family for a small dairy herd. It escaped the fire of 1873, was moved to South Park City in 1985 to become part of an agricultural exhibit. *(Kenneth Jessen 086C9)*

E. J. Amitrani, *A Town is Born*, self published, 1982.

WESTON
Wild and Wicked

- *Park County, South Platte River drainage*
- *Access restricted by private property*
- *Town had a post office; no standing structures remain*

Not really a true mining town, but rather a mining supply point for tons of material bound for Leadville, Weston was located at the east end of the road over Weston Pass. More specifically, it was three and a half miles southwest of Garos where the Weston Pass road crosses the old railroad grade of the Denver, South Park & Pacific.

The town was typically piled high with freight waiting to be hauled over the pass. There were three transfer companies operating in Weston in 1880. The number of passengers that passed through town was around one hundred per day. To take care of all the visitors, Weston had an extraordinary number of restaurants, eleven in all, plus a number of saloons and gambling halls.

Colonel Robert J. Spotswood controlled the flow of traffic and was responsible for keeping up a steady stream of wagons. Spotswood's experience was in supervising a division on the Overland in Northern Colorado.

The Oyster Bar and Johnny Nugent's Tontine were among the most popular places in Weston. Nugent also owned a stage stop in Mosquito Gulch. When Weston faded, he moved his business to Newett on Trout Creek Pass. When Newett's population fell, he moved on to Cripple Creek and Manitou Springs.

The wildest place in Weston was Frank Morgan's. He had twenty females working there who were said to have "assorted talents." His place offered one-stop shopping for entertainment and combined a saloon with a gambling house and a dance hall.

A post office opened in Weston in November, 1879 only to close in February of the following year. This may be an indication of how short-lived Weston really was.

The Denver, South Park & Pacific reached Weston in 1879, and the town became a forwarding point for supplies arriving from Denver. It wasn't long, however, until the railroad continued construction over Trout Creek Pass to Buena Vista. Once Leadville was connected by rail, the need for Weston Pass was eliminated along with the town of Weston.

William H. Bauer, James L. Ozment, John H. Willard, *Colorado Post Offices*, Colorado Railroad Museum, Golden, Colorado, 1990, p. 151.

Perry Eberhart, *Guide to the Colorado Ghost Towns and Mining Camps*, Sage Books, Chicago, 1959, p. 135.

Virginia McConnell Simmons, *Bayou Salado*, Century One Press, Colorado Springs, Colorado, 1966, pp. 175-176.

AREA NINE

9

Lake County

continued

AREA 9: Lake County
Selected Towns

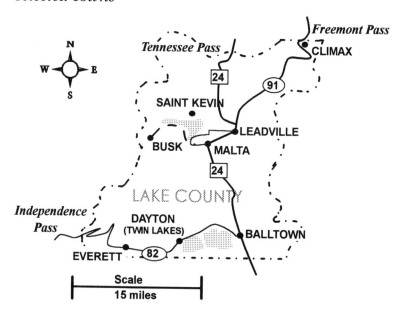

Introduction to Lake County

The distribution of population in most Colorado counties during the mining era was not usually concentrated in one area. Lake County is an exception, and its development centered around Leadville. There are a few abandoned town sites outside the Leadville area, but they do not amount to much.

The first discoveries made in the Leadville area were placer deposits in California Gulch, which runs east and west. Oro City was formed as a result of this discovery. After the placer gold was exhausted, lode or hard rock mining began at the head of California Gulch. With the discovery of lead-silver carbonates, exploration defined a large area of mineralization bounded on the south by Iowa Gulch and Evans Gulch on the north. The area was about two miles long and a mile and a half wide. Leadville evolved on the western edge of this deposit, and a high ridge, consisting of peaks over 13,000 feet, defined the eastern side of the deposit.

There are a number of ghost towns in this area which were Leadville satellite towns including Evansville, Ibex, Adelaide, Stumptown and Finntown. To the south of Leadville, where the smelters were located, the towns of Jacktown, Stringtown, Bucktown and Malta evolved. There were also several ghost towns associated with either the railroads or with small mining claims north of Leadville along the East Fork of the Arkansas River. These include the sites of Tabor City, Alicante, Birds Eye, Worton and Howland. Some mining was done to the west, near Turquoise Lake, and to the south at Red Mountain, west of Twin Lakes. Placer deposits were also worked south of Leadville in Chaffee County along the Arkansas River and its tributaries. Few other towns were established. Because the sites are concentrated, visiting ghost towns in Lake County is relatively easy.

Although many interesting people came to Leadville and left their mark, the stories of the following two men are especially interesting.

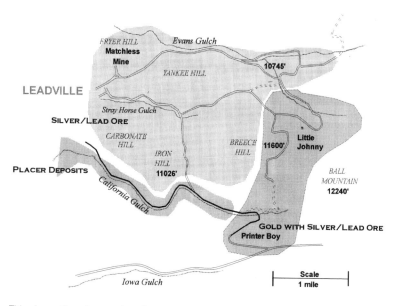

This shows the primary mineralized areas near Leadville and explains why the towns in Lake County were concentrated in one area.

H. A. W. Tabor

More has been written about Horace Austin Warner Tabor and his first and second wives than practically any other historical figure in Colorado. As put by Rene L. Conquoz in his booklet, *The Saga of H. A. W. Tabor*, "From poverty to wealth, from wealth back to poverty - the story will be told over and over again."

Horace Tabor married his boss's daughter, Augusta. Instead of remaining in Maine, where Horace would have taken over his father-in-law's business, they moved to the Kansas prairie. When it seemed like Kansas might become a battlefield during the rising conflict between the North and the South, Tabor, his wife and small son moved to Denver in 1859 to be counted among the first gold seekers. With a wagon drawn by an ox, the quest for gold drove the Tabors to Payne's Bar near the future town of Idaho Springs. Augusta was the first woman at this place and spent her time selling pastries and bread. The Tabors returned to Denver after Horace was cheated out of his placer claim.

Their next adventure was south to Colorado Springs and over Ute Pass. The Tabors were, in fact, the first pioneers to take a wagon over the pass. They traveled across South Park, got lost several times, and somehow managed to find Trout Creek Pass. They traveled down from the pass to the Arkansas River then upstream to Kelley's Bar, one of the very first settlements in the area. Horace panned gold at Cache Creek to the north, but the black sand mixed with the gold made recovery of the precious metal difficult.

They stayed at Cache Creek for about a month when they heard about a new gold field farther to the north in California Gulch. They arrived at the site of Oro City in May, 1860. At the time, the miners had run out of food and faced starvation. The Tabors slaughtered their ox and divided the meat among the camp.

When the placer gold was just about exhausted, the Tabors moved over the mountains into South Park and settled in

Buckskin Joe (west of Alma) in 1862. Here they opened a grocery store, which was to be the first of a number of stores opened by the Tabors. Horace spent much of his time prospecting while Augusta ran the store and raised their son. Horace was elected to the school board and also served as post-master. When the placer gold was exhausted, Horace decided to move back to Oro City since lode mining in California Gulch had taken over as the

H. A. W. Tabor became one of the wealthiest men in the West based on a grubstake he gave to two German prospectors. He lost his wealth and died in poverty. *(Kenneth Jessen collection)*

major economic activity. In 1868, Horace was appointed postmaster in Oro City, and Augusta opened up a store using the stock from their Buckskin Joe store. Oro City, however, was not in the same location. During the Tabors' absence, the settlement moved up the gulch to the Printer Boy Mine to form "new" Oro City.

A new settlement, which Horace referred to as Slabtown, formed about one half mile from the old site of Oro City. At about the same time, the Tabors opened a store in Malta to the west of California Gulch. In 1877, Horace must have seen some potential in Slabtown; he moved some of his goods from his other stores and opened a new store at the site. The name of this town changed to Leadville, and it outgrew all other mining towns in Colorado.

A fourth-class post office was set up in Tabor's Leadville store, and residents had to come to the store to get their mail. A long line formed outside his store on the mornings when mail was delivered. This brought business to his store, and he had to hire extra clerks.

How the Tabors went from poverty to wealth probably had more to do with luck than skill. Back when Horace and Augusta operated their store in Buckskin Joe, a man named William Van Brookly came into the store and wanted a grubstake. Horace was out at the time so Augusta took care of the man. He offered Augusta a mining claim in exchange for board. She said no, the man sold the claim to a couple of prospectors for $100, and later the new owners recovered $80,000. This taught Horace to always grubstake prospectors.

Just as Horace was opening his Leadville store on a Monday morning in 1878, a couple of German immigrants walked in and asked about a grubstake. This was not an uncommon event since Tabor had given grubstakes to many prospectors. Both of the men had been shoemakers, and their names were August Rische and George Hook. They outlined a plan for Tabor and demonstrated good knowledge in prospecting.

Tabor provided the men with picks and shovels, food for a week plus a jug of whiskey. The two men set out for Fryer Hill and worked on a prospect near the New Discovery.

Rische and Hook toiled for a week in the rocky soil, digging a shaft. They ran out of food and returned to Tabor for a second grubstake. They also updated Tabor on their progress, and nothing indicated that it was anything more than a "dry" hole void of ore.

The men reached the depth of ten feet, enough to file a claim. At the depth of twenty-seven feet, the Germans struck carbonate ore containing 200 ounces of silver to the ton. This was on May 15, 1878, and the

Augusta Tabor was Horace Tabor's first wife. Without her business abilities, it is safe to say that Horace would never have become a millionaire. *(Colorado Historical Society)*

mine was given the name the Little Pittsburg. When the news spread of the discovery, Tabor left Augusta and their son to investigate the find. The grubstake agreement, which cost Tabor all of sixty or so dollars, gave Tabor a third of the claim. By the end of the summer, each man was $10,000 richer. Hook sold out and moved away from Leadville. Later that year, David Moffat and H. A. W. Tabor purchased Rische's third for a little over a quarter of a million dollars. Incidentally, the carbonate ore was the origin of the black sand that caused Horace Tabor so many problems at Cache Creek.

The ore body in the Little Pittsburg was exhausted in just two years. The property produced $1.8 million dollars in that short time, and Tabor wisely sold his share in the mine for a million dollars. After the sale, the ore ran out. The Chrysoite, Tabor's second mine, did just about as well for him financially. Tabor purchased the Matchless Mine for $117,000 and had to spend another $30,000 in legal fees to establish its title. The mine had been

Baby Doe Tabor was Horace Tabor's second wife. She was quite a bit younger and married Horace before the divorce from his first wife was final. *(Colorado Historical Society)*

passed from promoter to promoter and was thought to be worthless. In 1880, Tabor's miners were driven out by flooding. Afterwards, he hired a new superintendent and soon a rich ore body was struck. Returns were staggering at two thousand dollars a day. One shipment alone contained 10,000 ounces of silver to the ton, valued at little over a dollar per ounce. For Tabor, mining silver ore was the next best thing to having a license to print money!

Tabor invested heavily in Leadville's future. Along with Rische, he opened the Bank of Leadville in 1879. Tabor was a shareholder in the Leadville Illuminating Gas Company to provide lighting for the town. He spent $78,000 on the Tabor Opera House and was one of the financiers of the Tabor Grand Hotel. He owned the Leadville *Daily Herald.* He also constructed several buildings in Denver, including a large structure which occupied a city block where the Tabor Center is located today.

A twenty-five year old divorcee named Elizabeth Bonduel McCourt Doe, better known as Baby Doe, came to Leadville to live in 1880. Horace and Baby Doe met, and there was immediate chemistry between the two. For a while, Horace and Baby Doe met discretely, then Horace moved out of his home. He tried to get a divorce from Augusta, but she refused. He became desperate and had his business associate secure a divorce in Durango. It was not legal, however. Instead of waiting, Horace and Baby Doe were secretly married in St. Louis in 1882. Horace continued to have his business associate work on getting a legal divorce, while Augusta got wind of the attempted divorce in Durango. She also found out that Horace had gotten married, and she went after as much of his estate as she could get. The estate at the time was estimated at nine million dollars, but Horace claimed it was far less. In a hearing, the judge agreed with Horace. H. A. W. Tabor's social status suffered in the scandal while Augusta came away with a tidy alimony. Horace, however, got Baby Doe.

Tabor was elected to Lieutenant Governor of Colorado, but had higher political ambitions; he wanted to become a United States Senator. When Senator Henry Teller vacated his position, Tabor used his money and influence to wrangle an appointment to fill out Teller's term. Tabor served as a United States Senator from February 3 to March 4, 1883. Baby Doe was now legally his wife, but as news of the details of the scandal, infidelity and bigamy became public knowledge, not even the politicians in Washington could tolerate the situation. It was much to their relief that Tabor's tenure was short lived.

This is one of the last photographs taken of Baby Doe Tabor. She lived out her final years at the Matchless Mine east of Leadville and was found frozen to death in her cabin. *(Colorado Historical Society F30239A)*

The magic touch that brought Horace Tabor fame and fortune did not continue. His rich mines on Fryer Hill played out, but he kept on investing in other mines which proved worthless. After the silver crash of 1893, his fortunes declined rapidly. Tabor was a man who lived for the moment and did not save for the future and fell for many schemes and scams such as a mahogany forest in South America. He finally purchased a mine near Ward and was so broke that he put on miner's clothing and worked it himself. His last piece of property was sold at auction in 1897 to pay off a mortgage. At the age of 69, Tabor passed away in Denver's Windsor Hotel from appendicitis. At the time, he was Denver's postmaster. Close to the time of his death, he told Baby Doe to hang on to the Matchless Mine, since it had been the source of millions of dollars for Horace.

Baby Doe lived in poverty, and the only thing she could afford was to move back to Leadville from Denver and live in the shack located next to the Matchless. During the winter of 1935 while living alone, she broke a trail through the deep snow and walked the mile or so to a grocery store in Leadville. Her feet were wrapped in gunny sacks and she wore a terribly torn old black dress. A delivery truck took her back toward the Matchless, stopping as close as possible. Baby Doe got out, waved good-bye to the driver, and trudged back to her shack carrying her groceries.

Her closest neighbor watched out for the old woman. After several

The Matchless Mine, where Baby Doe was found frozen to death in 1935, is now a tourist attraction. *(Kenneth Jessen 082C1)*

days, she didn't see smoke coming from the chimney of Baby Doe's shack. The neighbor tried to reach it, but the snow was too deep. She got some help, and when they reached the cabin, they found Baby Doe frozen to death, stretched out stiff on the floor. When Baby Doe's estate was settled it consisted of no money and only trunks of personal items stored in a Denver warehouse.

Mart Duggan, Leadville Lawman

The first marshal in Leadville was T. H. Harrison. He held the job only a few days, however, because threats from the lawless element convinced him he would live longer in some other location. On April 2, 1878, George O'Connor was elected by the Leadville City Council to replace the prudent T. H. Harrison.

On April 25, Marshal O'Connor stopped at Billy Nye's saloon in the course of making his rounds. He was enjoying a mug of beer, courtesy of the management, when one of his junior officers, James M. Bloodsworth, pushed his way into the saloon. He approached O'Connor at the bar.

"I hear that you called me a coward and a guy," Bloodsworth said. (A guy was a term generally used for a man who acted effeminate.)

O'Connor promptly set the record straight by denying having said such a thing about one of his own men. Nevertheless, in an instant the junior officer drew his revolver and fired point blank at O'Connor. The first shot hit the marshal in the stomach, and the second hit him just below the heart. The impact threw O'Connor back against the bar. As O'Connor slumped to the barroom floor, Bloodsworth pumped three more rounds into his victim, then fled. Bloodsworth mounted his horse, and rode out of town, never to be seen in Leadville again.

Mayor H. A. W. Tabor offered six hundred dollars for the arrest,"...and return of the body of James Bloodsworth." Marshal O'Connor lived a few hours, but even before he was dead, Mayor Tabor called a special meeting of the Leadville City Council to replace the marshal. Martin "Mart" Duggan, an Irishman, was appointed the new city marshal the next morning. Born in County Limerick, Martin was brought to the United States by his parents as part of their baggage. Mart lived for a while in New York State, then the family moved to Illinois, South Dakota, and Nebraska. In 1861, the Duggans finally settled in Colorado. Mart Duggan became a bronco buster living in Utah and Montana. During a wagon trip in Montana, he was surrounded by Indians and ended up in a brisk fight.

While living in Virginia City, Montana, he stole food to stay alive. He became a dancer at one of the parlor houses performing the Irish Jig. On a trip to Salt Lake City with a herd of wild broncos, he broke 38 of them.

Duggan arrived in Denver in 1867, with no hat, few clothes, and no money. He took odd jobs in Central City, Nevada City, and Georgetown before moving to Custer City, South Dakota. After Custer City, he became a faro dealer at a saloon in Cheyenne and ended up cutting timber in Del Norte. After living in Dolores and becoming a saloonkeeper in Ouray, Duggan moved to Leadville. His size and physical strength got him a job as a bouncer at a dance hall.

One night, a guest began shooting out the candles. Duggan put a stop to it by grabbing him by the scruff of the neck. Just as Duggan was about to pitch the man out, the guest shouted, "You can lick me with your fists, but you can't do it in a fair fight with guns. Gimme my shooter and I'll give you all the fun you want, you bully."

"I'm no bully," replied Duggan, "and if you must have a fight, I'll accommodate you. Come outside, and we'll settle it."

On the snow covered road, the two men faced each other at twenty paces. A referee, standing in the doorway of the dance hall, raised his own revolver and fired a shot into the air. The two adversaries advanced toward each other, firing as they walked. Duggan's third shot put a hole in the man's breast, and the man fell face first into the snow. This, and several other incidents,

Martin Duggan, Leadville City Marshal, used strong-arm tactics to bring law and order to town. After stepping down as marshal, he shot Lewis Lamb to death over a minor dispute. In front of the Texas House, Duggan was gunned down eight years later. *(Denver Public Library, Western History Department F4527)*

gave Duggan the reputation of a fearless man.

Martin Duggan was of medium height, but had a compact, massive build. He was very strong. He had a square face, a broad forehead, and fine features. His light hair and fair complexion complemented his blue eyes. As a lawman, Duggan was not overly concerned with "due process." He fought for law and order using the same methods as the lawless. Duggan wasted no time in establishing his version of the law, and for his efforts, he received $125 a month.

As marshal, Duggan had his work cut out for him in Leadville. It was a dangerous job; he was the town's third marshal in just two months. Soon after becoming town marshal, Duggan received written notice to leave town within twenty-four hours or follow George O'Connor. He didn't let the threat interfere with his work, but he took every precaution.

Law and order was a new concept in Leadville, and many a crusty miner did not want to have a stranger tell him how to act. Leadville also had a lawless element.

Duggan felt that the law applied to everyone in Leadville regardless of social standing. Not many days after H. A. W. Tabor appointed Duggan city marshal, August Rische became drunk and disorderly. Rische was Mayor Tabor's partner in the fabulous Little

Pittsburgh mine. Mart Duggan hauled Rische into jail, charging him with drunkenness and resisting arrest.

The Mayor was astonished when he learned about his partner's jail sentence. The following morning Tabor stopped by to ask Duggan, "I hear you got my business associate in your lock up?"

"That's right, Mr. Mayor," replied Duggan.

"What's the fine on him?" Tabor asked.

"No fine," was Duggan's terse reply.

Tabor still did not take Duggan seriously and told the marshal, "That's what I like, an understanding marshal. Give him a scare, a night in jail."

"He's in for ten days," was Duggan's next dry remark.

"Now look here, Duggan, I'm the mayor of this town," said the now irritated Tabor.

"And I'm the law here, Mr. Tabor. Rische owes the City of Leadville ten days." Duggan was unflinching. "You can pick him up when he's paid."

At that, Tabor threatened to relieve Duggan of his duties. Duggan resented having Tabor telling him how to run his office and threatened to lock him up if he didn't shut up and move on. Tabor knew he had hired a man with high principles.

The *Leadville Chronicle* said of Martin Duggan, "Sober, there was no more courteous, obliging person. But under the influence of liquor, he was the incarnation of the devil, and had as little regard for human life as a wild beast."

Marshal Mart Duggan's appointment ran out in April, 1879, and he decided not to accept a second term. He and his wife traveled to Flint, Michigan, to visit her relatives. In the meantime, the rough element in Leadville began again to make itself known, as the new marshal was unable to keep things under control. After a particularly bad sequence of violent events, including a double lynching by citizens who realized that the Leadville marshal was ineffective, a wire was sent to Duggan. He was asked to reconsider his decision to resign. In December, Mart Duggan was once again Leadville's city marshal. In April, 1880, his second term expired, and again he refused to serve another term. He went into the livery business and indulged in horse racing.

On Monday, November 22, Duggan was asked to deliver a sleigh to Winnie Purdy. She was one of Leadville's ladies of pleasure and lived in the red light district. Duggan set out across the fresh snow in a sharp looking cutter pulled by a pair of spirited black horses. As he rounded the corner of Pine and Fifth he almost knocked down Lewis Lamb. Lamb demanded an immediate apology, and the two men exchanged a few heated words. Duggan drove off, which should have ended the matter, but his Irish temper got the best of him, and he turned the sleigh. Lamb drew his revolver. Duggan not only drew, but fired his revolver. The bullet entered Lamb's mouth, breaking his jaw and stopping in his spinal column which caused instant death. Witnesses testified that Lamb's gun was loaded, cocked and ready to fire.

Duggan voluntarily surrendered to the police captain and later was found innocent by virtue of self defense. Ironically, Duggan had never killed a man during his term as city marshal.

Louis Lamb had been a local miner and a family man. His wife vowed eternal hatred for the ex-marshal, and she promised to wear her "widow's weeds" until Duggan was dead. She then vowed to deliver these weeds to Mrs. Duggan upon Mart's death.

In April, 1888, Duggan was at the Texas House, a popular Leadville gambling establishment, when he got into an argument with owner Bailey Youngson. Duggan was drunk and upset with one of the dealers for some unknown reason and threatened to run the fellow out of town. When Youngson attempted to defend his dealer, Duggan asked him to get his gun and meet him out in the street.

Duggan's friends convinced him to leave and go home. Early that morning, a shot rang out, and several men began shouting for the police. They found Martin Duggan lying in a pool of his own blood on the boardwalk in front of the Texas House. A bullet had entered his head behind the right ear, and it was amazing that he was still alive. The powder burns indicated that he had

Lewis Lamb's widow danced in front of the Texas House, the building with the awning the center of this photograph, upon learning that her husband's murderer, Martin Duggan, had died. *(Colorado Historical Society)*

been shot at close range.

When daylight came, Duggan regained consciousness at his home. His injury was too great, however, and he soon died. It was almost five years to the day since he had first walked the streets of Leadville wearing the badge of city marshal.

Mrs. Lamb did leave her widow's weeds at the front door of the Duggan home. She also danced in front of the Texas House where Mart was shot.

Caroline Bancroft, *Silver Queen, The Fabulous Story of Baby Doe Tabor*, Johnson Publishing Company, Boulder, Colorado, 1955, pp. 78-80.

Rene Coquoz, *The Saga of H. A. W. Tabor*, Johnson Publishing Company, Boulder, Colorado, 1973, pp. 7-37.

Edward Blair, *Leadville: Colorado's Magic City*, Pruett Publishing Company, Boulder, Colorado, 1980, pp. 86-87, 161, 168-173, 201-202

Bartlett, G. W., "Mart Duggan, Fighter." *The Rocky Mountain Magazine* Number 10, December 1903.

Don and Jean Griswold, *History of Leadville and Lake County*, Colorado Historical Society, Denver, 1996, pp. 149, 160-161, 735. (also the Leadville Chronicle, April 10, 1880)

Edward Blair, *Leadville: Colorado's Magic City*, Pruett Publishing Company, Boulder, Colorado, 1980, pp. 105-106, 111, 116-117, 120-122.

Robert K. DeArment, "Mart Duggan: Leadville Lawman." *Frontier Times*, February, 1985, pp. 11-15.

ADELAIDE (ADLAIDE)

- *Lake County, Stray Horse Creek drainage*
- *Accessible via graded dirt road*
- *Town had a post office; no standing structures remain*

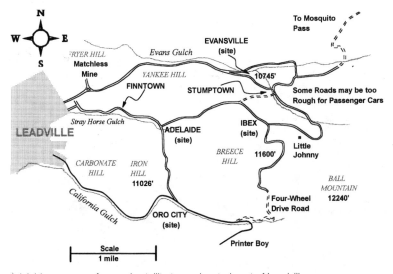

Adelaide was one of several satellite towns located east of Leadville.

L ike many other Colorado mining towns, Adelaide has a confusing history over the exact spelling of its name. Frank Walls
and A. B. Powell discovered rich silver ore in the vicinity of this
mining town in 1876. They staked out the Adlaide claim and the
town that developed near the mine became Adelaide City. The
"City" was dropped later, and the name "Adelaide" came from the
Adelaide Silver Smelting Company. It is not known why the
smelter company selected a slightly different spelling.

225

Park City was established in Stray Horse Gulch before Adelaide. It is a predecessor of Adelaide and was located at or near the same spot.

A post office was established in 1878. Seventy men worked at the Adlaide Mine and a dozen or so worked at the smelter. Frank Fossett visited the town in 1879 and reported that its population was several hundred and increasing rapidly. By this time, the town had seven streets, thirty-six log cabins, twenty-eight frame buildings, four saloons, a drug store, a grocery store, two laundries, a variety store, the Adelaide smelter and mining offices.

The post office remained active until 1901, and as the mines

When photographed, this mining town was called Park City. Then Park City became Adelaide. The Evergreen Saloon is on the left side of its dusty main street. In just a few years, every tree in the area was cut for use in the mines, for the construction of buildings or for fuel. Today, the location is a meadow called Adelaide Park, and not a single structure remains standing. *(Colorado Historical Society F8762)*

were exhausted of their ore, the town was abandoned. Strong winds and blowing snow coming up Stray Horse Gulch eventually destroyed all of Adelaide's structures. The site today is a meadow void of all structures, and is marked by a sign, "Adelaide Park." From the site, the high mountains west of Leadville are in view.

In 1879, there were two fatal shootings in Adelaide. Henry Wilson and John Smith spent most of the night at several drinking establishments located along the road in Stray Horse Gulch. They ended up at an Adelaide saloon, where they started playing cards. An argument erupted, they drew their guns, and Wilson fired first. The round, delivered at point blank range, mortally wounded Smith, who died four days later.

Wilson tried to deflect any blame for the death of Smith by saying that they were just having fun and his gun went off by accident. This did not agree, however, with eyewitnesses who saw the men were quarreling. It is not known what happened to Wilson.

Just weeks later, W. C. Keeler and a lady friend were walking along one of Adelaide's streets. They met a couple of drunkards, not uncommon in a mining town. The drunks made foul remarks, and Keeler called them down. The two drunks drew their revolvers and fired at Keeler, giving him a grazing scalp wound. Charles Johnson came to his door to see what the shooting was all about and was wounded in the hip for his curiosity.

Men from a boarding house ran into the street, and they too were fired upon. One man died of his injuries. Later, two suspects were arrested, but could not be positively identified.

Don and Jean Griswold, *History of Leadville and Lake County*, Colorado Historical Society, Denver, 1996, pp. 131, 170, 200, 245, 333, p. 141, 693-694, 1875-1876, 1984.
Don and Jean Griswold, *Colorado's Century of "Cities"*, Self Published, 1958, pp. 156-157, 256, 266.
William H. Bauer, James L. Ozment, John H. Willard, *Colorado Post Offices*, Colorado Railroad Museum, Golden, Colorado, 1990, p. 9.

ALICANTE

- *Lake County, upper Arkansas River drainage*
- *Site not accessible; private property*
- *Town had a post office; no standing structures remain*

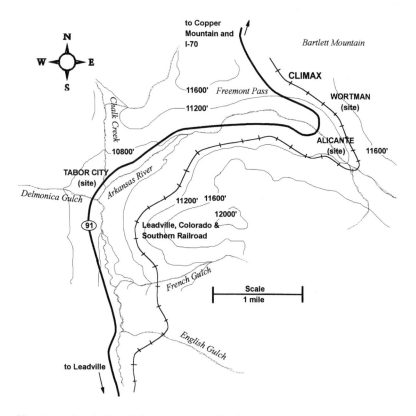

Alicante was located in a high meadow just below Fremont Pass.

This small camp was situated below Fremont Pass (Climax) on the Leadville side next to the tracks of the Denver & Rio Grande (not to be confused with the Denver, South Park & Pacific which ran through the same valley). Alicante was founded in 1880 to serve the Walter Scott Mine high above the camp. A two thousand foot long tram was used to bring ore down to Alicante to a twenty stamp mill. The camp lasted until 1888, with a peak population of about one hundred. Alicante was named for a city in Spain and did have a post office from 1881 to 1887. After its closure, the post office was moved up to Climax on Fremont Pass.

Early photographs of Alicante show a two-story boarding house with a false front, a store, a small station and a barn. The settlement was at an elevation of about 11,000 feet, and a curved snow shed protected the track. The snow became so deep during 1886 that the snow shed was completely buried. Railroad employees living at Alicante were pressed into service to clear the tracks.

The Alicante site is located close to Colorado 91 on the Leadville side of Fremont pass where it reverses direction just below Climax.

Another camp, Wortman, was not very far away.

David Digerness, *The Mineral Belt*, Vol. II, Sundance Publications, Silverton, Colorado, 1978, pp. 234, 248.

Dolores Osterwald, *High Line to Leadville*, Western Guideways, Lakewood, Colorado, 1991, p. 39.

Don and Jean Griswold, *History of Leadville and Lake County*, Colorado Historical Society, Denver, 1996, p. 1741.

Mac Poor, *Denver, South Park & Pacific*, Rocky Mountain Railroad Club, Denver, 1976, pp. 384, 449.

William H. Bauer, James L. Ozment, John H. Willard, *Colorado Post Offices*, Colorado Railroad Museum, Golden, Colorado, 1990, p. 11.

BALL TOWN

- *Lake County, Lake Creek drainage*
- *Accessible via paved road; private property*
- *Town did not have a post office; several standing structures remain*

Ball Town was originally called Lake Creek Station by the Denver & Rio Grande. Trains stopped to let passengers off for the trip to Twin Lakes. A wooden sign suspended between two poles read "Twin Lakes" and originally marked the location.

Most structures at Ball Town are in excellent condition. This collapsed cabin may date back to the formation of the place as a stopover for travelers headed to and from Twin Lakes. *(Kenneth Jessen 103B9)*

William H. Ball and his wife worked a placer claim and lived near there. When travelers became stranded at the station, the Balls took them in as guests. Eventually, they constructed guest cabins, and Mrs. Ball served fresh trout dinners.

A hack provided service between the resort hotels at Twin Lakes and Ball Town. A round trip cost $3, relatively high for a time when a day's wages could be far less.

There are guest cabins at the site today, and the tradition established a century ago continues.

Don and Jean Griswold, *History of Leadville and Lake County*, Colorado Historical Society, Denver, 1996, p. 680.

BIRDS EYE

Named for Feldspar

- *Lake County, upper Arkansas River drainage*
- *Accessible via paved road*
- *Town did not have a post office; no standing structures remain*

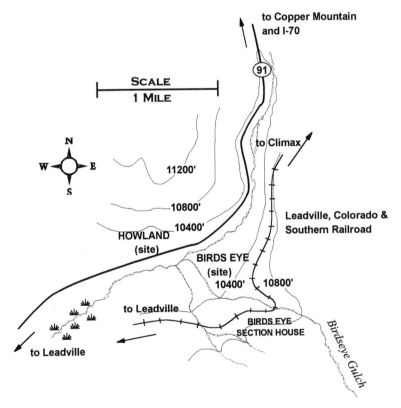

Birds Eye and Howland were located a short distance apart with Howland on the north side of the Arkansas River.

Birds Eye was a small camp located down in the swampy flat area along the East Fork of the Arkansas River at the mouth of Birds Eye Gulch. Nothing remains of the camp today, but a log home can be seen near the mouth of the gulch. Private property restricts access to this area, and the site is filled with willows. The Denver, South Park & Pacific built a section house and tool house high above the camp along their highline from Leadville to Climax. With time, the railroad structures have become known as Birds Eye.

The town of Birds Eye was named for large feldspar crystals embedded in the igneous porphyry. The crystals resembled a bird's eye. The remains of a stamp mill were once evident at the site.

Dolores Osterwald, *High Line to Leadville*, Western Guideways, Lakewood, Colorado, 1991, p. 31.
Perry Eberhart, *Guide to the Colorado Ghost Towns and Mining Camps*, Sage Books, Chicago, 1959, p. 204.

BRUMLEY

Near Independence Pass

- *Lake County, Lake Creek drainage*
- *Site close to paved road*
- *Town did not have a post office; collapsed remains of three structures*

As ghost camps go, Brumley sits in one of the most scenic spots in Colorado. Its three collapsed cabins are in a beautiful meadow near Colorado 82, two miles from the first switchback on the east side of Independence Pass. The site is located at 10,400 feet and is still shown on topographic maps.

Brumley was both a stage station and a mining town. The toll gate for the toll road over Independence Pass was located in Brumley. Supported by nearby mines, the town got its name from the owner of a hotel, a man named Bromley. The spelling of the town's name was changed for some unknown reason.

The biggest mine in the area, Champion Mine, was north of Brumley at 12,800 feet on Mt. Champion. The ore was carried by tram north to the Champion Mill in the Halfmoon Creek drainage.

To reach the site, which is in plain view of Colorado 82, Lake Creek must be crossed. This can prove challenging during spring runoff.

(Kenneth Jessen 105C10)

Perry Eberhart, *Guide to the Colorado Ghost Towns and Mining Camps*, Sage Books, Chicago, 1959, pp. 226-227.

BUSK

- *Lake County, Busk Creek drainage*
- *Accessible by graded dirt road*
- *Town had a post office; no standing structures remain*

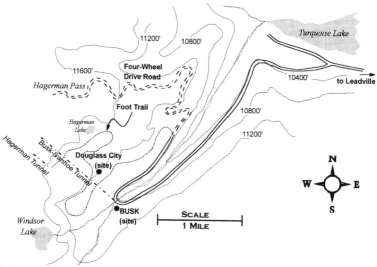

Busk was located at the east portal of the Busk-Ivanhoe Tunnel, used by the Colorado Midland Railway.

Busk was less of a town and more of a construction camp. It then became a railroad station. It was located at the east portal of the Colorado Midland's Busk-Ivanhoe Tunnel. There were at least four structures on the south side of the portal at one time. One structure was the Busk Station, which was important to the regulation of train traffic through the tunnel. A control rod was carried by the train crews as they passed through the two mile tunnel and had to be placed in a receptacle at the other end to insure that opposing trains never met inside the tunnel.

The Colorado Midland was the first standard gauge railroad through the Colorado mountains and stretched for over 200 miles, ending at New Castle with a branch to Aspen.

Busk was also the site for a construction camp from 1890 to 1893. It was named for J. R. Busk, one of the large stockholders in the Colorado Midland. The Hagerman Tunnel was the first passage used by the Colorado Midland under the Continental Divide. Considerably higher in elevation, snow removal was a severe problem. The approaches to the Hagerman Tunnel simply could not be kept open during severe storms. The Busk-Ivanhoe Tunnel was constructed by a separate company at a lower elevation, then leased to the Colorado Midland. It opened for train traffic in December, 1893. Eventually the Colorado Midland purchased the tunnel.

After the tunnel was abandoned and the tracks removed in 1918, the tunnel became an automobile toll road for many years. It is still used to transport water from Lake Ivanhoe on the Western Slope to Busk Creek, which empties into Turquoise Lake.

During the time the tunnel was under construction, several hundred men lived in Busk. A post office was established in 1890 and remained open until 1894. Several homes were constructed at Busk to house the railroad employees, but today, no structures remain.

Edward M. McFarland, *A Colorado Midland Guide and Data Book*, Colorado Railroad Museum, Golden, Colorado, 1980, pp. 23-24, 33-34, 38-43, 269, 270.

William H. Bauer, James L. Ozment, John H. Willard, *Colorado Post Offices*, Colorado Railroad Museum, Golden, Colorado, 1990, p. 26.

Perry Eberhart, *Guide to the Colorado Ghost Towns and Mining Camps*, Sage Books, Chicago, 1959, p. 230.

CLIMAX
Founded on Molybdenum

- *Lake County, Arkansas River drainage*
- *Site on private property; no access*
- *Town had a post office; original structures unknown*

These are company houses in Climax, located at the base of Bartlett Mountain. *(Colorado Historical Society F13634)*

Charles Senter, a solitary prospector, searched for gold ore on Bartlett Mountain in 1879 in an area that had already been carefully combed by others years before. What Senter found was not gold ore, but rather a curious yellow-colored mineral. He broke some of the mineral apart, exposing a light gray mineral. Within the sample were veins of a darker material, which had a greasy feel. Senter reasoned that this was graphite. He filed three claims on Bartlett Mountain hoping to find deposits of precious metal ores. Senter lived about three miles away in a cabin situated at the head of Tenmile Canyon.

The Denver & Rio Grande extended its narrow gauge line

from Leadville over Fremont Pass in 1880, and since it was the highest point on their line, they named the place Climax. The Denver, South Park & Pacific built its narrow gauge railroad over the pass four years later. Because Fremont Pass was at the end of a long grade, water tanks, turntables, and coal tipples were added. The South Park also had a telegraph office and siding at Climax.

In 1890, Denver prospectors staked claims near those of Charles Senter. The assay incorrectly showed the presence of lead sulfide. Senter sent his samples to the Colorado School of Mines, and their assay identified the mineral as antimony and graphite. Senter recorded his claims in 1893, and in 1895, the mineral was correctly identified as molybdenum disulfide or "molybdenite."

In 1887, there were enough people living at Climax to merit a post office. At an elevation of 11,320 feet, it became the highest post office in the United States. Remaining active until 1917, the office was then moved to Alicante on the Arkansas River side of Fremont Pass. Eventually, the post office became a branch of the one in Leadville.

At the time, the mineral molybdenite was regarded as virtually worthless, but this soon changed as World War I approached. This rare metal, when combined with steel, resulted in an alloy considerably tougher than normal steel. By 1917, mining was conducted on a large scale, and the community of Climax had an estimated population of 200. The demand for molybdenum continued to rise, and in 1936, Climax Molybdenum constructed 100 modern homes with three to six rooms, 43 apartments, a large hotel and a dining hall capable of seating over 300 miners. As time progressed, more homes and apartments were added. During the 1990s, there was a surplus of molybdenum and the mine closed.

Mac Poor, *Denver, South Park & Pacific*, Rocky Mountain Railroad Club, Denver, 1976, p. 447.

Muriel Sibell Wolle, *Stampede to Timberline*, Sage Books, Chicago, 1949, 1974, p. 68.

Stephen Voynick, *Climax*, Mountain Press Publishing Company, Missoula, Montana, 1996, pp. 1-6, 140, 211.

William H. Bauer, James L. Ozment, John H. Willard, *Colorado Post Offices*, Colorado Railroad Museum, Golden, Colorado, 1990, p. 34.

DAYTON

Becomes Twin Lakes

- *Lake County, Lake Creek drainage*
- *Accessible by paved road; access limited by private property*
- *Town was the county seat and had a post office; many structures remain*

When Lake County was created in 1861, the big mining boom was in California Gulch with Oro City as the population center. The Colorado Territorial Legislature designated Oro City as the Lake County Seat because it was the largest town in the county and was growing rapidly.

Some fine old homes can be found in Twin Lakes. The name of the town was originally Dayton. When the mining boom ended, Dayton was abandoned. When the area was rediscovered, it became the resort town of Twin Lakes. *(Kenneth Jessen 105C8)*

Near Twin Lakes, Ira King tried to capitalize on the many miners passing through his property. It was located a little north and west of the inlet to the upper lake. The traffic was created by the nearby discovery of complex galena ore rich in silver in the Red Mountain Mining District to the west of Twin Lakes. King purchased some milk cows and began selling dairy products. Level ground, cool summer evenings and Twin Lakes, which was a short distance away, contributed to the area's appeal. Others liked the site King selected and set up their tents. This was soon followed by the construction of cabins. Some of these people, including King, were from Ohio and named the place Dayton.

There were a sufficient number of people living in this part of Lake County to warrant a voting precinct. These individuals mustered enough votes to move the county seat at Oro City to Dayton. Another story credits George Leonhardy, county assessor at Oro City, with moving the offices to Dayton. He decided that Dayton had more promise and moved to Dayton in 1866, taking the county seat with him. The following year, the Lake County courthouse was established on the second floor of Dayton's Masonic Hall.

A post office was requested in 1866 and granted as Dayton became an official town. Milled lumber was supplied by a sawmill located along a creek below the lowest lake. Within a very short period of time, four or five hundred people moved to the town.

Bayard Taylor, a world traveler, lecturer and author, visited Dayton in the summer of 1866 and noted that it was located on a triangular piece of meadow where the inlet to the upper lake was located. He also noted that, "The people, with singular perversity, have selected the only spot where a view of the beautiful lakes is shut out for them."

The boom was not to last. The ore was a non-renewable resource, and the amount of mineralization was unpredictable. As the summer of 1868 passed, practically all of Dayton's residents abandoned their cabins and moved to Granite. Postal authorities then recognized Granite as the replacement for Dayton, and in

November, the post office at Dayton closed. The county offices moved to Granite. Also, the entire log Masonic Hall was laboriously skidded down to Granite.

During the summer of 1873, General William Palmer, founder and first president of the Denver & Rio Grande, visited the Twin Lakes area. He camped by the upper lake and reported that Dayton was abandoned, calling it Deserted Village. The author of an article describing the trip noted, "It is full of sad suggestions of human hope and despair ... Through these vacant darkened houses once shone the evening light of welcome warmth to guide and cheer the chilled and weary miner." They noted that the town had a milliner shop, stores, and about two dozen cabins, but no church. Few historic photographs of Dayton survive, but one shows approximately forty structures of varying size.

Northwest of Dayton is Colorado's highest peak, Mount Elbert, at 14,433 feet. Other peaks above 14,000 feet are north and south of Dayton. The town was also on the busy toll road from the east to Aspen over Independence Pass. The visitors coming through the area wrote articles in newspapers, including the *New York Times*, extolling the virtues of the area and the great fishing.

This log structure probably dates back to the time Twin Lakes became a resort town. It is boarded up for the winter. *(Kenneth Jessen 105C7)*

It was only a matter of time until Dayton was rediscovered, not by miners, but by tourists.

In 1879, when a new post office was established, Dayton was reborn in the same spot as the new town of Twin Lakes. Court Derry started a resort by opening the Twin Lakes Hotel. Twin Lakes came into its own when two railroads constructed their lines along the Arkansas River just six miles below the town. The Denver & Rio Grande came through in 1880 with its narrow gauge line from Denver and was followed by the Colorado Midland, a standard gauge line from Colorado Springs. There was a station at Ball Town, where tourists could hire a hack to take them to Twin Lakes. Tourists were drawn from Leadville as well as from Denver and Colorado Springs.

Mining continued as part of the economy of Twin Lakes. There were several mines above the town toward Mount Elbert, and gold dredging was profitable in the gravel deposits west of the lakes.

The toll road over Independence Pass, originally called Hunter's Pass, was completed in 1881. As the shortest route from Denver to Aspen, it was very busy. This also helped the economy of Twin Lakes as the jumping off place for the arduous and harrowing journey over the pass.

Twin Lakes is a worthwhile town to visit and is far from a ghost town, but is fully occupied by seasonal residents. There are many original log structures, some over a century old.

Don and Jean Griswold, *History of Leadville and Lake County*, Colorado Historical Society, Denver, 1996, pp. 66-67, 104-107.

Leadville Carbonate Chronicle, November 11, 1901.

Muriel Sibell Wolle, *Stampede to Timberline*, Sage Books, Chicago, 1949, 1974, p. 158.

Perry Eberhart, *Guide to the Colorado Ghost Towns and Mining Camps*, Sage Books, Chicago, 1959, p. 215.

Virginia McConnell Simmons, *The Upper Arkansas*, Pruett Publishing Company, Boulder, Colorado, 1990, pp. 58, 291-292.

William H. Bauer, James L. Ozment, John H. Willard, *Colorado Post Offices*, Colorado Railroad Museum, Golden, Colorado, 1990, pp. 42, 144.

DERRY RANCH PLACER

- *Lake County, Box Creek drainage*
- *No access; private property*
- *Many standing structures remain*

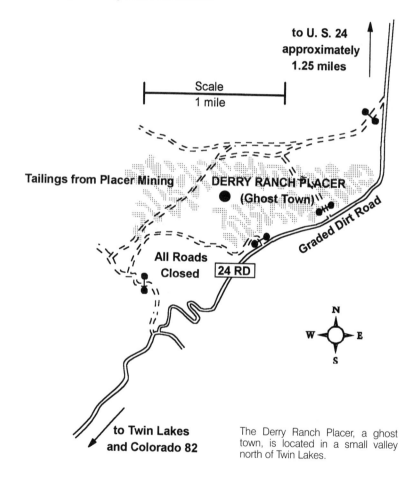

The Derry Ranch Placer, a ghost town, is located in a small valley north of Twin Lakes.

From a public road, this is the Derry Ranch Placer sitting in a shallow valley formed by Box Creek and Corske Creek. *(Sonje Jessen SJ100)*

One of the most interesting ghost town sites exists in a small valley north of Twin Lakes. It can be viewed from a gravel road, which runs from Colorado 82 north from the lower of the Twin Lakes, climbing past a campground, then north and east to intersect Colorado 24 north of Kobe. There is a cluster of abandoned buildings sitting between the piles of rock discarded from a dredge operation, which lasted until 1950. Little is known about this small mining town, who lived there, or when it was founded.

Gold was discovered in the Derry Ranch Placer in the 1860s. The Derry Gold Dredge Company operated a dredge in the deposit until about 1913, then there was a lull in mining activity until 1916. From that point on until 1924, a second dredge worked Box Creek and Corske Creek, recovering placer gold valued at a low of five cents per cubic yard up to $3 per cubic yard. Once the initial claim was depleted of its gold, the dredge company tried to extend its operations to the east. The land owner would not sell, and, in 1924, the dredge was dismantled. Land dredging, using a dry plant for separation, continued up until 1950. At today's price of gold, about $26 million was removed from the area (68,837 ounces).

To reach a point where the Derry Ranch Placer town can be seen, exit Colorado 24 south of Leadville on a secondary paved road about a half mile north of Kobe. For a short distance, this road parallels Colorado 24, then turns west and climbs the ridge. The road becomes graveled. From the ridge, the Derry Ranch Placer town is to the north and sits between fingers of waste rock from the dredging operation.

Ben H. Parker, Jr., *Gold Panning and Placering in Colorado*, Colorado Geological Survey, Denver, 1992, p. 54.

Don and Jean Griswold, *History of Leadville and Lake County*, Colorado Historical Society, Denver, 1996, pp. 2252-2253.

Twin Lakes Miner, November 25, 1911.

Virginia McConnell Simmons, *The Upper Arkansas*, Pruett Publishing Company, Boulder, Colorado, 1990, p. 139.

DOUGLASS CITY

A Construction Camp

- *Lake County, Busk Creek drainage*
- *Accessible by foot trail*
- *Town did not have a post office; several collapsed cabins remain*

Douglass City was a construction camp for the Colorado Midland Railway during the time the grading was done from Leadville to the Hagerman Tunnel. It was named for a subcontractor, W. A. Douglass. He had the responsibility of drilling the tunnel from its east portal to meet the opposing construction crew drilling from the west portal. It was also the center of the grading required to reach the tunnel site.

Douglass City began to take shape during May, 1886, when machinery and supplies were unloaded at the Denver & Rio Grande depot in Leadville. The freight was put on wagons and, along with over one hundred men, a great caravan was formed to take the wagons to the site of Douglass City. The town sprang up on a Saturday upon the arrival of the caravan, and by Monday morning, Douglass City was fully occupied and cabins were under construction.

A machine shop, commissary and many cabins were built first. Then work started on the tunnel about half a mile away. Initially, the Douglass City area was home to 400 men, but as the grading began, a total of 1,570 men and 350 burros worked in the area. It is not likely that all lived in Douglass City. Nationalities included Italians, Irishmen, Norwegians and U.S. born citizens.

An enormous amount of supplies flowed from Leadville up to the various construction sites. One newspaper article estimated that at its height, 350,000 pounds of supplies per month were transported on the backs of draft animals.

The town had but one street, Douglass Avenue. A company office was constructed, and the town also had a dry goods store, shoe shop, bunk houses, and a residence for the supervisor. At its height, the town had eight saloons and a dance hall where a full orchestra played.

Leadville's famous ex-marshal, Mart Duggan, moved to Douglass City to run a saloon. Violence was common, and any laborer caught traveling alone to Leadville was usually held up and robbed. Duggan had killed several men and was ideal for the job.

A peddler named Fiede began selling jewelry in town during the summer of 1887. He went from saloon to saloon showing the items to the "professional" girls hired to hustle drinks and entertain men in assorted activities. Mart Duggan entered one of the saloons and was shown a recent purchase. Duggan just laughed at the outrageous price the girl had paid for an imitation gem passed off by the peddler as the real thing. He suggested to the girls that they locate the peddler and get their money back. On second thought, he volunteered to do the job himself. Soon the peddler was confronted by Duggan and "arrested." A mock trial was held and the money was returned. After the shakedown, Mart Duggan style, the peddler went straight to authorities in Leadville and filed assault charges against Duggan. The judge dismissed the charges after hearing all of the story.

The biggest paying job in Douglass City was that of a check broker, a man who cashed payroll checks for a commission. The average laborer earned about $70 a month for six day work weeks, and the unconscionable broker took 20% of that amount.

In September, 1887, Douglass City passed into history as the rails of the Colorado Midland advanced through the Hagerman Tunnel and down the Frying Pan River. Douglass City can be reached by a trail established by the Forest Service to allow visitors to walk the old Colorado Midland grade up to the tunnel. The parking area is about a mile beyond Busk and is marked by a sign. It is about a mile hike to the Douglass City site. The remains of many log cabins are present, but it is difficult to imagine the original size of this town, which was the temporary home to at least 400 men.

For a map showing the location of Douglass City, see "Busk."

One of the cabins left at the construction camp of Douglass City, home to at least 400 men during the construction of the Colorado Midland Railway. *(Kenneth Jessen 011D1)*

Don and Jean Griswold, *History of Leadville and Lake County*, Colorado Historical Society, Denver, 1996, pp. 1743-1745, 1751, 1860, 1864-1868, 1879, 1931-1932.

EVANSVILLE

- *Lake County, (Big) Evans Gulch drainage*
- *Site accessible by graded dirt road*
- *Town did not have a post office; no standing structures remain*

An early view of Evansville, located in Evans Gulch east of Leadville. The town shows up on most early maps and was important to the area. Nothing remains today at the site. *(Denver Public Library, Western History Department X-374)*

Little is known about Evansville (also called Evans or Gig Evans Gulch). It was founded in 1879 during the Leadville silver boom and shows up on most historic area maps. Despite the lack of information, Evansville's location on the north side of the primary area of mineralization was important. It did not have a post office, but the resident population has been estimated at 400. In the 1879 election, 140 votes were cast by its residents. The town constructed a school with initial enrollment of about two dozen students.

The Denver & Rio Grande passed through Evansville and called its station Evans. The line made a loop from the north side of Big Evans Gulch to the south side, where the town was located. Beyond this point, the railroad climbed up to Ibex.

The site can be reached by driving east out of Leadville on the road leading to Mosquito Pass, also called the Evans Gulch Road. Immediately out of Leadville, this road passes the Matchless Mine of H. A. W. Tabor fame where his second wife, Baby Doe, froze to death in 1935. The Evansville site is where Lincoln Gulch enters Evans Gulch, but before the road crosses from the north side of the creek to the south side. Beyond this point, the road heads to a junction where, in an easterly direction, it goes over Mosquito Pass and to the west climbs to the site of Stumptown and Ibex.

For a map showing the Evansville site, see "Adelaide."

Don and Jean Griswold, *History of Leadville and Lake County*, Colorado Historical Society, Denver, 1996, pp. 378, 2150.

Perry Eberhart, *Guide to the Colorado Ghost Towns and Mining Camps*, Sage Books, Chicago, 1959, p. 203.

EVERETT

Stage Station on Road to Aspen

- *Lake County, Lake Creek drainage*
- *Site near a paved road; no access to site itself; private property*
- *Town had a post office; no structures remain*

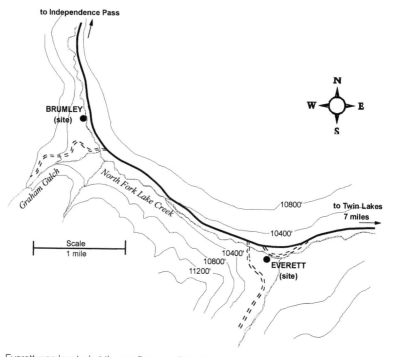

Everett was located at the confluence of the North Fork and South Fork of Lake Creek.

Near the confluence of the South Fork and North Fork of Lake Creek is the Everett site, situated in a small meadow below modern day Colorado 82. Today, the site is fenced and posted. Nearby is a parking area for those wishing to climb 14,336 foot La Plata Peak.

The original road through Dayton (Twin Lakes) up Lake Creek went to the Everett site, but turned up the South Fork to the Red Mountain mining district. In response to the increasing demand for a shorter route to Aspen, the Twin Lakes Toll Road was formed in 1880, and a crude wagon road over Independence Pass was completed the following year up the North Fork.

C. M. Everett laid out the town at the junction of the two creeks in anticipation of a thriving business. A stage station and a hotel, called the Everett House, were constructed. A post office opened in 1881, but was closed six years later when the population of Everett declined and traffic over the pass diminished as a result of competition from railroads.

The population of Everett never grew beyond fifty or so. The town was all but abandoned by 1890, but the empty hotel stood until 1954, then collapsed. From the road, it does not look as if any structures stand today.

Marshall Sprague, *The Great Gates*, Little, Brown and Company, Boston, 1964, pp. 256-257.

Virginia McConnell Simmons, *The Upper Arkansas*, Pruett Publishing Company, Boulder, Colorado, 1990, p. 140.

William H. Bauer, James L. Ozment, John H. Willard, *Colorado Post Offices*, Colorado Railroad Museum, Golden, Colorado, 1990, p. 53.

FINNTOWN

- *Lake County, California Gulch drainage*
- *Accessible via graded dirt road*
- *Several standing structures remain*

Little is known about Finntown. It was located immediately east of Leadville on the road to Adelaide, where miners of Finnish descent were concentrated. John Aldrich, in his *Ghosts of Lake County* booklet, writes that Finntown was originally called Cleator Moor Gulch when it was occupied by immigrants from the mining area of Cleator Moor, England. The English residents moved on to other areas, leaving the town occupied predominately by Finnish and Swedish immigrants. The name was then changed to Finntown.

One of two surviving structures at Finntown, east of Leadville. *(Kenneth Jessen 105C5)*

In 1911, a cave-in imprisoned three miners at Shaft No. 5 of the Morning Star Mine near Finntown. The men were working on the third level when the timbers in the shaft above them gave way. The timbers were forced out into the shaft by the rock fall, partially blocking the shaft such that the man cage could not be raised to the surface. The foreman instructed his men to cut the cage loose, letting it fall down the shaft. In the meantime, the foreman scratched a message in Finnish on a piece of wood and put it in a gunny sack. The sack was then tied to the end of the severed cable. By jerking on the cable, they signaled the hoist operator to raise the cable.

The hoist operator saw that only the gunny sack was attached to the cable's end where he was expecting the man cage. He untied the gunny sack and was confused by the message on the piece of wood. He sent his son to Finntown to get help. The word about the cave-in was spread, and experienced miners from nearby properties came to help with the rescue. A plan was formulated, and after sixty hours of work, the trapped men were brought to the surface.

Don and Jean Griswold, *History of Leadville and Lake County*, Colorado Historical Society, Denver, 1996, p. 2240.
John K. Aldrich, *Ghosts of Lake County*, Centennial Graphics, Lakewood, Colorado, 1990, p. 17.

HOWLAND

- *Lake County, Arkansas River drainage*
- *Accessible via paved road; exact location of site uncertain*
- *Town had a post office; no standing structures*

Howland's exact location is difficult to determine despite the fact that it is on an 1879-1880 map, compiled from government surveys. It was located somewhere opposite Birdseye Gulch on the north side of the Arkansas River. This would place it close to Birds Eye. No trace of the town exists today.

Howland was named for Colonel Henry Howland who managed the Birdseye Lumber Company. Howland constructed a road up Birds Eye Gulch to intersect the Mosquito Pass Road. Mail was received daily and Colonel Holwand was the postmaster. The saw mill employed fifty men, and population estimates for the town were on the order of 100.

Howland got its own post office in 1879. The Gold Metal Mine in Birdseye Gulch also supported Howland. When the mines began to close, the population dropped. In 1882, when it reached twenty, the post office was closed.

William H. Bauer, James L. Ozment, John H. Willard, *Colorado Post Offices*, Colorado Railroad Museum, Golden, Colorado, 1990, p. 75.

Don and Jean Griswold, *History of Leadville and Lake County*, Colorado Historical Society, Denver, 1996, pp. 361, 370.

Perry Eberhart, *Guide to the Colorado Ghost Towns and Mining Camps*, Sage Books, Chicago, 1959, p. 204.

Leadville Evening Chronicle, October 8, 1879.

IBEX

Mining Complex

- *Lake County, Evans gulch drainage*
- *Accessible via graded dirt road*
- *Town had a post office; only mining structures remain*

Ibex is often listed in ghost town books, but it was a mining complex with many railroad spurs and mine structures. There were some miner's cabins scattered in no particular order throughout this area, but historic photographs show no well-defined town.

It was at Ibex where James Brown, the husband of Margaret "Molly" Brown, got his start as the superintendent of the Ibex Mining Company's mine. Molly Brown, survivor of the sinking of the Titanic and rescuer of some of its passengers, became known

Ibex was once a large mining complex with structures and cabins spread out over the treeless expanse of this heavily mined area. The ore bin is about all that is left. *(Kenneth Jessen 104A6)*

as the "Unsinkable Molly Brown." James owned the Little Johnny Mine, which was close by, and this was the source of his great wealth. In 1893, the Little Johnny was shipping a million and a third dollars in ore per year. In today's economy and adjusting for inflation, this would be nearly fourteen million dollars.

Ibex was among only a few major gold producing mines in the Leadville area and was not effected by the silver crash of 1893, when the United States went off of the silver standard. The mines at Ibex got so deep, however, that pumping costs began to exceed profit. Mining in this area was saved by the Yak Tunnel, drilled at the lower end of California Gulch. When the Yak tunnel reached the Ibex group of mines in 1903, it was 1,500 feet below the surface. At this depth, the tunnel allowed the owners of the Ibex complex of mines to drain the workings.

Ibex was served by the Denver & Rio Grande, and at an elevation of 11,500 feet, it was the highest point on the railroad. A number of snow sheds protected the tracks from severe winter storms. Ibex also had a post office, which opened in 1896 and closed in 1905.

To reach Ibex, drive up Evans Gulch. Turn right after passing the Evansville site. Cross the creek and head up the steep graded dirt road. Continue climbing until a flat area at the base of Ball Mountain is reached. An automobile can usually make the trip. A modern mine, fenced on all sides, occupies part of what was called Idaho Park. This was where the Ibex complex of mines was located. A large ore bin still stands, but little is left of other structures.

For a map showing where Ibex was located, see "Adelaide."

Don and Jean Griswold, *History of Leadville and Lake County*, Colorado Historical Society, Denver, 1996, pp. 729, 1820, 2008, 2022, 2153, 2159, 2206.

William H. Bauer, James L. Ozment, John H. Willard, *Colorado Post Offices*, Colorado Railroad Museum, Golden, Colorado, 1990, p. 76.

LEADVILLE
The Cloud City

- *Lake County, Arkansas River drainage*
- *Accessible via paved roads; occupied town*
- *Active post office; many historic structures remain*

By a considerable margin, more information, books and booklets have been published about Leadville than any other Colorado mining town. This reflects its importance to the State of Colorado.

Leadville is not a ghost town nor has it ever been abandoned, but like any mining town, it has had its ups and downs. A brief history of Leadville is presented here. In addition, Leadville's history is tied to that of Oro City. Refer to "Oro City, Pioneer Town" for details.

The house with the eye was built by Eugene Robitaille, a Canadian, in 1879. The brow dormer represents the all-seeing "Eye of God." *(Kenneth Jessen 103B11)*

257

Oro City, located in California Gulch, became the Lake County seat when the county stretched all the way to the Utah border and was larger than many states. By 1865, the placer gold in California Gulch began to dwindle. Oro City lost its population and also its status as county seat. Dayton (the predecessor to Twin Lakes) took over as county seat.

Soon, the source of the gold in California Gulch was discovered in its upper regions. This first successful lode mine was the Printer Boy, and a stamp mill was constructed to pulverize its gold-bearing quartz. Once this first discovery was made, other lode mines opened in the immediate area. The original town site was abandoned in favor of the new Oro City near the Printer Boy.

By 1872, the towns in the upper Arkansas River were all but deserted except for the new Oro City. Even the new tourist town of Twin Lakes, which succeeded Dayton, had but four visitors for the entire year. Cache Creek, an early placer towns, was now a ghost, and only a few people remained at the old Oro City site.

William Stevens and Alvinus Wood teamed up to reprocess the placer gravel deposits in California Gulch using more efficient

One of Leadville's most famous residents, H. A. W. Tabor, lived in this modest frame home. *(Kenneth Jessen 103B10)*

means of gold recovery. Their tests showed that a great deal of gold had been discarded due to primitive mining methods. An eleven mile long ditch was constructed to bring water to this operation.

It was probably Alvinus Wood, a mining engineer and metallurgist, who first recognized the potential significance of heavy black sand that clogged the riffles in the sluice boxes, making gold recovery more difficult. Samples of the black sand revealed a high concentration of lead combined with silver. In 1865, the two men secretly explored the area above California Gulch and staked out claims where they discovered outcroppings of the dark colored mineral. It wasn't until the winter of 1875-1876 that they began mining by opening the Rock. Miners couldn't understand why these men were paying them to dig out what seemed worthless black material that didn't contain gold.

Stevens revealed that what was being mined was carbonate of lead containing silver. Carbonates had been detected before and even mined on a limited basis, but Stevens and Wood made it profitable. Through the purchase of other claims combined with new claims, the two men controlled the entire area.

A new camp to the north of the original Oro City was established. It was dubbed "Slabtown" by H. A. W. Tabor, a pioneer merchant, who through a lucky grubstake, later became one of the wealthiest men in the Rocky Mountains.

Edward Blair in his book, *Leadville: Colorado's Magic City,* covers the first settlers in Slabtown, later to be named Leadville. He credits George Albert Harris with being the first to camp at the site, but Charles Mater established the first retail business. Mater was from Granite, having worked his way West in 1860. This Prussian immigrant settled in Granite in 1867, where he built a general store. In 1877, he moved some of this stock to Slabtown and constructed a twenty-by-thirty foot log merchantable store. George Albert Harris, in the meantime, built the camp's first hotel. At one and a half stories high, it could sleep eight to ten men. Named the City Hotel, Edward Blair suggests that the actual capacity of the hotel, "...probably varied with the occupant's size, how well they knew each other, and how recently they had had a bath."

In 1868, H. A. W. Tabor constructed a store in "new" Oro City and another in Malta. Tabor must have seen potential in Slabtown and responded in 1877 by constructing a store just up the street from Mater's store. The mail arrived at Tabor's store, giving him the edge in business.

A few weeks after Tabor opened his store, William Nye saw an enormous hole in the range of businesses. He constructed the one business common to practically every mining town, a saloon. After remodeling, it became the Bon Ton Billiard Hall.

In August, 1877, a reporter wrote that the future Leadville had six buildings including the two stores, the hotel, a drug store, a wagon shop and a sampling works for analysis of ores.

George L. Henderson, a business man involved in a number of enterprises, met with the residents of Slabtown and suggested that a new name would be more dignified. Under consideration were "Carbonate," "Cerrusite," "Meyer," and "Leadville." Leadville was accepted, and in June, 1877, the United States Postal Service accepted an application under that name. H. A. W. Tabor was elected the town's first mayor.

As the mines developed, so did Leadville. It grew to become the largest mining town in Colorado, and as the sphere of prospecting expanded, rich new deposits of lead-silver ore were discovered. The mines on Fryer Hill, in particular, made millions for the various owners. The richest mine was the Robert E. Lee. One miner approached its owners and offered $200,000 just to work the mine for thirty-six hours. The mine was so rich that the owners refused. During one seventeen hour period, this mine yielded over one hundred thousand dollars in mineral wealth. One writer said that to improve on such a record, miners would have to strike a pocket of coined silver dollars!

In 1877, there stood a quiet forest with a small cluster of log structures. In just two years, the place was a large bustling town sitting on a treeless expanse of rock. The streets of Leadville were clogged with people, horses and ore wagons. There was an unending noise from the rumble of the wagons, the crack of a bull whip and the shouts of the drivers. At night, the parlor houses, dance halls and saloons operated until dawn.

Thousands arrived to seek their own fortunes, and the

clamor of new construction filled the air. Little thought was given to urban planning, and Leadville was a rough, frontier town. Historic photographs show how each merchant built his own board walk with no regard for the height or position of the adjacent board walk. The simple act of walking required concentration since the path between stores was filled with unexpected hazards. The streets were a quagmire of mud in the spring and dust in the summer. Garbage was tossed onto the street to be trampled into the dust. Tree stumps, along with discarded merchandise, barrels and lumber, formed the shoulders.

By the summer of 1879, an estimated five thousand lived in Leadville proper with another five thousand in the surrounding camps. By the end of the year, Leadville's population climbed to an estimated ten thousand within the city limits. The New Year's Eve edition of the *Leadville Chronicle*, 1880, placed Leadville's population at 30,000, probably an exaggeration.

As for the "suburbs" of Leadville, there were many. Lack of space and chronic housing shortages forced many to seek other areas. Historic photographs show that many miners lived in houses interspersed among the mines themselves. It was helter-skelter with no regard for order.

Practically all ethnic groups were represented in Leadville. The Irish led the immigrants in number and lived up on Chicken Hill, above the town. The Cornish congregated to the south end of town near the smelters. A number of Negroes had fled the South after the end of the Civil War and formed a colony in Leadville. Swedes, Finns and Norwegians also entered Leadville.

One group intentionally excluded were Orientals. The miners were suspicious that the Chinese would accept work at substantially lower wages and cause unemployment.

With inadequate housing, survival during the winters was difficult. Leadville is above 10,000 feet and sub-zero weather is common. Cooking was also a challenge since the boiling point of water is substantially less.

Smelters were constructed to process the carbonate complex

ore, but the entire economic development of the region would have stalled without rail transportation. For one thing, the smelters could not have continued to operate on cord wood since the supply in the immediate area was exhausted. Coal hauled in by rail was essential. The narrow gauge Denver & Rio Grande arrived in 1880, followed four years later by another narrow gauge line, the Denver, South Park & Pacific. The Colorado Midland, a standard gauge railroad, reached Leadville in 1887. Abundant ore, good transportation, and a population of skilled miners assured the town's continued growth.

In 1893, the Sherman Silver Purchase Act was repealed by Congress. This released the United States Government from being forced by law to purchase a fixed amount of silver every year. This

The Tabor Grand Hotel, located in Leadville's central business district, was partially financed by H. A. W. Tabor. It was completed in 1885. *(Kenneth Jessen 095A3)*

event was combined with a reduction in silver purchases by
Britain. The price of silver, which had been artificially established,
dropped, and by the middle of the summer, ninety percent of
Leadville's work force was idle. The short-term effect was devastating, but soon many of the mines reopened. Some were rich in
gold, and silver production was a minor portion of their output.
In other cases zinc mining developed, especially after the turn of
the century. Lead was in constant demand. As World War I
approached, the production of molybdenum took off. "Molly"
was essential to the production of tough steel needed for the war
effort. The mine was located on Fremont Pass north of Leadville
at Climax.

Leadville was home to many famous people including not
only H. A. W. Tabor, but people like Charles Boettcher, a hardware
store owner, who gained his wealth in the mines. He continued
by building a financial empire in Denver. Meyer Guggenheim was
also made wealthy by his mines, the Y. A. and Minnie. One of the
founders of the May D&F Department Store chain, David May,
opened his first store in Leadville. Margaret Tobin Brown became
a heroin when she helped save fellow passengers on the Titanic.
She became known as the "Unsinkable" Molly Brown. Notables
like "Doc" Holliday and "Soapy" Smith also visited Leadville.

Leadville today is a historic treasure well worth a visit.
Many of its original structures have been preserved, and abandoned buildings can be found scattered about the town. There
are also several museums including the Healy House, the National
Mining Hall of Fame and the *Herald Democrat.*

D. Ray Wilson, *Colorado Historical Tour Guide*, Crossroads Communications, Carpentersville,
   Illinois, 1990, pp. 221-226.

Don and Jean Griswold, *History of Leadville and Lake County*, Colorado Historical Society, Denver,
   1996, p. 426.

Edward Blair, *Leadville: Colorado's Magic City*, Pruett Publishing Company, Boulder, Colorado,
   1980, pp. 1-21, 40, 51, 55, 58, 174.

Lawrence Von Bamford, *Leadville Architecture, Architecture Research Press*, Estes Park, Colorado,
   1996, pp. 55-56.

MALTA

- *Lake County, Arkansas River drainage*
- *Accessible by paved road*
- *Town had a post office; one standing structure remains*

Malta is approximately two and a half miles west of Leadville on Colorado 24. The old schoolhouse sits at the site, but otherwise, little remains of this pioneer smelter town. Malta's first smelter was built in 1875. Smelters were essential to the recovery of precious metals, lead and zinc from the complex ore found in area lode mines. Originally, Malta was called Galena. One of the major investors was named Swill, and Swilltown was suggested. This name, however, carried a negative connotation that this was the place where there were sloppy, beer guzzling drunkards. The

The Malta schoolhouse is one of the few remaining structures at this early smelter town site. *(Kenneth Jessen 098B7)*

smelter was constructed by the Malta Smelting and Mining Company Works, so it was only logical to pick Malta as the name of the town.

In 1876, Malta had a population of 150 with two grocery stores, one blacksmith shop and a butcher shop. The post office, which opened the previous year, was located in the butcher shop. One of the stores was operated by H. A. W. Tabor who would eventually end up as one of the wealthiest men in Colorado, only to die in poverty. William Nye operated the town's only saloon at this time.

The smelter was located just 400 yards north of the town. Constructed by a Cincinnati-based company, owners of the smelter realized that part of its roasting and smelting efficiency was lost by constant replacement of poor quality fire brick used in the furnaces. New fire brick was ordered from England.

Initially, Malta had the only smelter in the area, but in 1877, a new smelter was constructed at the head of California Gulch to handle ore from the Printer Boy Mine. As other, larger, more modern smelters were constructed on the south side of Leadville, business at Malta began to decline.

The post office closed in 1887, but with a resurgence in population, reopened in 1890 and remained upon until 1950.

In 1878, the Malta smelter complex had grown to include a 140-foot ore shed, engine house, crusher room, sampling room, and a blast furnace. A bath house was added to allow smelter workers to wash and guard against lead poisoning. It employed twenty-five men.

By this time, Malta consisted of two hotels and fifty cabins. In 1881, there were four hotels, a brewery, several saloons and a population of more then 300. A race track nearby provided additional business.

Malta was a stage stop on the Barlow & Sanderson route from South Park. It became a railroad junction for the Denver & Rio Grande where their main line over Tennessee Pass deviated from their line through Leadville and over Fremont Pass.

Don and Jean Griswold, *History of Leadville and Lake County*, Colorado Historical Society, Denver, 1996, pp. 44, 127, 128, 135, 140, 159, 164, 171.

George Crofutt, *Crofutt's Grip-Sack Guide of Colorado 1885*, Johnson Books, Boulder, 1966, 1981, p. 117.

Perry Eberhart, *Guide to the Colorado Ghost Towns and Mining Camps*, Sage Books, Chicago, 1959, p. 202.

William H. Bauer, James L. Ozment, John H. Willard, *Colorado Post Offices*, Colorado Railroad Museum, Golden, Colorado, 1990, p. 93.

ORO CITY
Pioneer Town

- *Lake County, Arkansas River drainage*
- *Access by paved road*
- *Town did have a post office; no standing structures remain*

This photograph was taken in 1881, well after placer gold brought thousands into California Gulch to live in Oro City. *(Colorado Historical Society F7794)*

A. G. Kelley is generally credited with finding the first gold along the upper Arkansas River in 1859. The following year, three prospecting parties entered the upper Arkansas, and one of them broke off from the others. This party headed north (upstream), past Kelley's initial discovery. The members of this third party agreed among themselves to systematically explore the gulches in the upper part of the valley. They also swore that if any member made a discovery, the rest of the party would be alerted. It was Abe Lee who dug down into the gravel and panned out a good quantity of gold flakes on April 26, 1860. He told those who were nearby. A large bonfire was lit, and guns were fired into the air to alert the others.

After the other members of the party were present, a mining district was organized to define the size of a claim and to bring order to the process of filing claims. Abe Lee was elected recorder and collected a fee from each claim holder.

How the place was christened California Gulch depends on the source. Some say Abe Lee likened his first pan of gold flakes to that first discovery in California during the gold rush of 1849. But others dispute this, saying the prospectors from California made up the majority of the men.

During the spring and summer of 1860, an estimated five thousand prospectors came into the area. This figure doubled by the end of the summer. The entire gulch, from its mouth all the way east for six miles, was filled with the one hundred foot claims allowed by the mining district. Members of the first party had already staked out the richest gold-bearing gravel, and Abe Lee got claim number one.

In the rush to pan as much gold as possible, little thought was given to the construction of cabins. California Gulch is well over 10,000 feet and summers are short. Most prospectors lived in their wagons or in tents.

Horace Tabor and his family were exceptions. They had just arrived from Cache Creek, located farther down the Arkansas River. Horace apparently saw the potential of California Gulch and built an 18-foot by 32-foot log cabin about one-half mile above the present Leadville city limits. As autumn approached and the weather turned cold, a few log cabins began to appear, with each miner selecting a spot on his claim. Men with carpentry experience helped with the construction of cabins and shanties. From Tabor's store to the east and to the west, cabins were scattered randomly up and down California Gulch.

The placed was named Oro City, "oro" meaning gold in Spanish. Oro City was not pretty, as evidenced by early photographs. In a maze of heaps of gravel are a variety of cabins and shanties scattered over a wide area amid hundreds of tree stumps.

Estimates on just how much gold was removed during 1860 vary from $80,000 to ten million. Abe Lee reported removal of $60,000 during the summer of 1860. The miners working claims number 5 and 6 recovered $65,000 in gold. Up to claim number 56, the average prospector could expect to make $19 per day in panning. This may not sound like much, but this was at a time when the average wage was $1 to $1.50 per day. The price of gold, incidentally, was fixed at $18 per ounce.

The price of supplies in Oro City was quite high, and those who couldn't make money panning or at another trade were forced to leave. Flour sold for a dollar a pound and bacon sold for fifty cents a pound. Fresh meat was not a problem. Deer were shot to supply meat, and there was an ample supply of trout in the streams.

Augusta Tabor became postmistress; a letter from Denver cost 75 cents to transport to Oro City. The Oro City post office opened in February, 1861, and remained active until 1895.

The placer gold was soon exhausted and, during the summer of 1865, those who returned found little value in their pans. The population dropped to less than 400, and two years later the place was a ghost town. Lake County encompassed all of Chaffee County, and by 1870, a census showed only 522 residents.

In the very upper part of California Gulch, a lode of gold-bearing quartz was discovered. The simple tools of the prospector had to yield to more expensive mining methods. Such tools as sluice boxes and gold pans were no longer of value. The mine was named the Printer Boy, and outside capital was secured to develop the claim. Oro City was moved two and a half miles up California Gulch. This included Tabor's store. The original Oro City site later became part of Leadville.

The story of mining, however, was just beginning. A couple of clever prospectors, Alvinus Wood and William Stevens, identified the black sand, which clogged the sluice boxes and got in the way of gold mining, as carbonate of lead containing a high percentage of silver. Some of the miners who stayed on in Oro City were hired to work a claim called the Rock.

By 1878, the area was filled once again with prospectors as word of the discovery spread. The site of the second Oro City is indicated by a small metal sign along the paved road in California Gulch. No structures remain standing at the site.

For a map showing the location of "new" Oro City, see "Adelaide."

Don and Jean Griswold, *History of Leadville and Lake County*, Colorado Historical Society, Denver, 1996, pp. 2-3.

O. J. Hollister, *Mines of Colorado*, Promontory Press, New York, 1974, (originally published in 1867 by Samuel Bowles & Company), pp. 316-317.

William H. Bauer, James L. Ozment, John H. Willard, *Colorado Post Offices*, Colorado Railroad Museum, Golden, Colorado, 1990, p. 108.

SAINT KEVIN

- *Lake County, St. Kevin Gulch*
- *Condition of access road unknown*
- *Town had a post office; no standing structures remain*

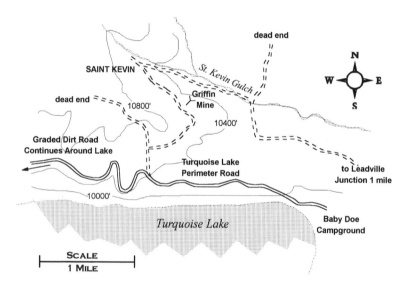

Saint Kevin (or St. Kevin) sounds more like a monastery than it does a mining camp. Originally the drainage was called Sowbelly Gulch, a much more colorful name, but it was changed to Saint Kevin. The Griffin, St. Kevin and Belle silver mines were developed in the area and along with them, a small mining camp formed. Under the name Saint Kevin, the camp got its own post office in 1886.

Transportation costs were high and ore had to be hauled by wagon down from the mines, across Tennessee Park, then up to

270

the smelters in Leadville. A concentration mill was constructed in Saint Kevin to reduce the tonnage hauled. About forty to fifty men worked at the mines and a few more at the mill. By 1890, the population had dwindled to the point where the post office was closed.

Don and Jean Griswold, *History of Leadville and Lake County*, Colorado Historical Society, Denver, 1996, p. 1267, 1445, 1572, 1639, 1855, 1996.

John K. Aldrich, *Ghosts of Lake County*, Centennial Graphics, Lakewood, Colorado, 1990, p. 38.

William H. Bauer, James L. Ozment, John H. Willard, *Colorado Post Offices*, Colorado Railroad Museum, Golden, Colorado, 1990, p. 126.

SNOWDEN

- *Lake County, Arkansas River drainage*
- *Site accessible via paved road*
- *No standing structures; remains of railroad grade only*

Snowden, associated with the Colorado Midland, was a station along the main line. In 1888, to avoid the steady grade up through Leadville, then back downhill, the Colorado Midland constructed a bypass around the town from Snowden directly along the Arkansas River. At a place it named Arkansas Junction, the main line headed west through either the Hagerman tunnel or the Busk-Ivanhoe Tunnel to the Fryingpan River drainage. Service to the numerous Leadville mines was now a branch line.

Snowden was located south of Malta and got its own post office in 1890. The post office closed in 1893, however. The Colorado Midland constructed a depot, section house, bunk house and water tank at Snowden. After the railroad was abandoned in 1918, the railroad structures at Snowden were probably removed. The station was originally called Crystal Lakes.

Don and Jean Griswold, *History of Leadville and Lake County*, Colorado Historical Society, Denver, 1996, p. 2035.

Edward M. McFarland, *A Colorado Midland Guide and Data Book*, Colorado Railroad Museum, Golden, Colorado, 1980, pp. 23, 300.

William H. Bauer, James L. Ozment, John H. Willard, *Colorado Post Offices*, Colorado Railroad Museum, Golden, Colorado, 1990, p. 133.

SODA SPRINGS and EVERGREEN LAKES

- *Lake County, Lake Fork of the Arkansas River drainage*
- *Accessible by paved road*
- *Place had a post office; original structures unknown*

Soda Springs has been listed among Colorado's ghost towns, but it was not based on mining. Soda Springs was a resort area dominated by the Mount Massive Hotel. A second hotel, The Soda Springs House, was smaller and more primitive. The site is located south of Turquoise Lake and was quite popular among Leadville residents during the 1880s.

The Mount Massive Hotel had stables, croquet courts, a baseball diamond and picnic tables. Nearby was a horse track for trotters. The hotel boasted of its interior plastered walls and a great fire place next to the dining room. The hotel was a log structure, two stories high. In the winter, the hotel offered sleigh rides. A horse drawn hack provided service between Leadville, Evergreen Lakes and Soda Springs.

A post office opened in 1879, about the time the two hotels opened, and it closed in 1902.

During this same period of time, a second resort area was developed farther to the south at Evergreen Lakes. A connecting road was constructed between the two areas, and in 1883, a small hotel was built between the second and third lakes. The area was incorporated as the Evergreen Lakes and Mineral Springs Improvement Company with H. A. W. Tabor as one of the owners. A town site was planned in conjunction with the acquisition of one thousand acres. A restaurant, hotel and two houses were constructed, but it never became a town. The restaurant was quite elaborate with a veranda overlooking the lakes, private rooms for parties, a billiard room and a parlor. A dozen rowboats were brought in for use by guests.

Private property borders the paved road, and the site is not accessible. There is a pull-off beside the road at the springs.

The Leadville Ice Palace, 1896 *(Colorado Historical Society F6637)*

Don and Jean Griswold, *History of Leadville and Lake County,* Colorado Historical Society, Denver, 1996, pp. 286-287, 316, 342, 379, 404, 426, 877, 993-994, 2150.

STRINGTOWN

And Other Leadville Suburbs

- *Lake County, Arkansas River drainage*
- *Accessible via paved road*
- *Town did not have a post office; several original structures remain*

Stringtown was but one of several suburbs to the south of Leadville, and a number of its homes are occupied today. These suburbs were located in a shallow valley at the mouth of California Gulch to the southwest of Leadville. It was the smelter area, including the Arkansas Valley Smelter, and closer to Leadville, the Western Zinc Mining & Reduction facility. Stringtown was also where the American Association of Workingmen, a labor group, was organized in 1888. The group was concerned about the influx of foreigners, which drove out American laborers by accepting lower pay.

Stringtown had a grocery store, several saloons, the Great Northern Hotel and a number of cabins and shanties. A school opened in the fall of 1893.

Jacktown was located between Stringtown and Leadville. It consisted of forty-five cabins. Bucktown was to the south of Stringtown. Across the Arkansas River near the smelters was yet another suburb called Little Chicago. Brooklyn Heights was also located somewhere in this general vicinity. Official maps made during the 1800s fail to reveal their exact locations.

To reach Stringtown, drive south out of Leadville on Colorado 24, and between Leadville and the Malta school is Stringtown. There are a number of old frame buildings along the road, which probably date back to the turn of the century or before.

Don and Jean Griswold, *History of Leadville and Lake County*, Colorado Historical Society, Denver, 1996, pp. 1323, 2014, 2150, 2187.

STUMPTOWN

- *Lake County, South Evans Gulch drainage*
- *Accessible via graded dirt road*
- *Town did not have a post office; several standing structures remain*

There are a large number of abandoned structures, such as this old store, in the general vicinity of Stumptown. *(Kenneth Jessen 104A3)*

Stumptown was a place of strong women. The two most noted were Mrs. Anton Anderson and Molly Brown. Anton Anderson lost control of an enraged bull at his Stumptown ranch. The animal charged, horns down, and ripped his leg open, cutting the femoral artery. He bled to death well before a physician could arrive. After the neighbors carried his body into his home, they decided to put the bull to death as a form of retaliation. Just before they carried out their plan, Mrs. Anderson arrived. She drove her buggy into the yard as a dozen neighbors gathered to tell her of the death of her husband. She reacted in a calm manner, and when the neighbors told of their plan to dispatch the bull, she said, "Don't kill the poor brute..."

In the meantime, the bull continued to bellow and snort in the barn. The neighbors could hear the animal racking his horns over the wood. They could see the walls shake as the animal butted the side of his stall. But the minute Mrs. Anderson walked into the barn, all the commotion stopped. Mrs. Anderson led the bull from the barn, and he walked meekly behind her into a pen.

Mrs. Anderson went into her house where her dead husband had been placed, and she showed the same courage in dealing with his death as in dealing with the bull.

The most famous residents who lived in Stumptown were Mr. and Mrs. James J. Brown. At the time, he was superintendent of the Ibex Mining Company. Later in her life, Mrs. Margaret Brown survived the sinking of the Titanic and helped rescue fellow passengers. For this, she became known as the "Unsinkable" Molly Brown.

Stumptown sits below Ibex and above Evansville at the head of South Evans Gulch. A barn, several cabins and mine structures mark the site. Over a small rise are the remains of a false front store. It was apparently not a town with an orderly street system. The closest post office was at the top of the hill at Ibex.

See "Adelaide" for a map locating Stumptown.

An old Stumptown barn. *(Kenneth Jessen 104A2)*

Don and Jean Griswold, *History of Leadville and Lake County*, Colorado Historical Society, Denver, 1996, pp. 2210, 2225, 2232.
Leadville Herald-Democrat, September 7, 1911.

TABOR CITY
Battle Over Its Name

- *Lake County, upper Arkansas River drainage*
- *Site near paved road*
- *Town had a post office; no standing structures remain*

Like other towns along the upper Arkansas River, Tabor City was a very small camp located southwest of Fremont Pass near Colorado 91. It was situated a dozen miles northeast of Leadville near the mouth of Chalk Creek. The camp gained enough population to merit a post office in 1879, only to have it close two years later. The camp also had the advantage of being along the tracks of the Denver & Rio Grande Railroad.

A plat for Tabor City was made on what was originally called Chalk Ranch. Colonel Taylor was responsible for creating the town and owned half interest. He wanted to change the town's name to his own, but the other residents didn't agree. The first sign was put up by Taylor and it read "Taylor City." Residents countered with a sign one-third larger which read "Tabor City." Taylor then announced plans to construct a three-story building and install a sign on its side of even larger proportions.

Before the building could be started, the fortunes of Colonel Taylor declined, while those of Horace Tabor grew to enormous proportions. Tabor became one of the richest men in the West. The residents ignored the attempted name change and stuck to Tabor City. After all, who would want their town named for a has been? The Leadville *Evening Chronicle*, realizing that Taylor had lost, commented, "...Taylor will have to find some other introduction to prosperity."

In just two years, the placer deposit was exhausted and

Tabor City was abandoned. The place returned to its original name of Chalk Ranch. Nothing remains at the site, in fact, the exact location is difficult to determine.

For a map showing the approximate location of Tabor City, see "Alicante."

Don and Jean Griswold, *History of Leadville and Lake County*, Colorado Historical Society, Denver, 1996, pp. 307-308.

Don and Jean Griswold, *Colorado's Century of "Cities"*, Self Published, 1958, p. 158.

William H. Bauer, James L. Ozment, John H. Willard, *Colorado Post Offices*, Colorado Railroad Museum, Golden, Colorado, 1990, p. 138.

WORTMAN

- *Lake County, upper Arkansas River drainage*
- *Site not accessible; private property*
- *One structure remains*

Wortman was located near and above another obscure mining camp called Alicante. Both were located in a high valley immediately below Fremont Pass (Climax). Wortman had its own post office from 1900 to 1908, and then again from 1916 to 1919. The camp consisted of a collection of cabins near the Wortman Mine below Clinton Peak.

Mining at Climax has obliterated the town site, leaving one lone cabin sitting in a meadow above Wortman. *See "Alicante" for a map showing Wortman's location.*

A lone cabin is all that is left to mark the site of Wortman. *(Sonje Jessen Sj101)*

David Digerness, *The Mineral Belt,* Vol. II, Sundance Publications, Silverton, Colorado, 1978, p. 212.
William H. Bauer, James L. Ozment, John H. Willard, *Colorado Post Offices,* Colorado Railroad Museum, Golden, Colorado, 1990, p. 154.

AREA TEN 10

Teller County

continued

AREA 10: Teller County
Selected Towns

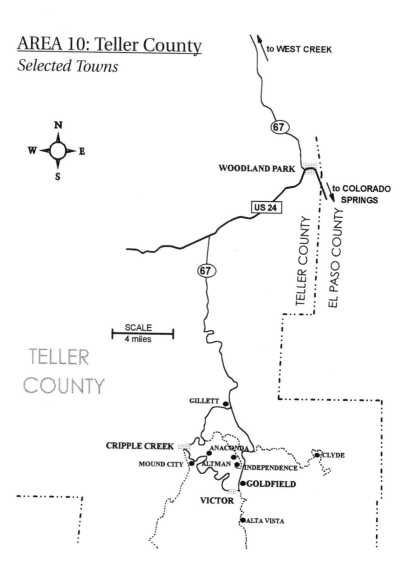

Introduction to Teller County

The Cripple Creek District was the last great gold rush in Colorado. It began with the substantial gold ore discoveries in 1891, although local rancher and prospector Bob Womack discovered gold at a much earlier date. Within this district, the towns were concentrated in a relatively small area making it easy for the ghost town explorer to see every site within a day. The towns of Cripple Creek, Victor and Goldfield were never completely abandoned and were the principal towns in the region. Other small satellite towns, however, are gone. Included among these towns are Mound City and Anaconda in Squaw Gulch, both destroyed by fire. Arequa, Beacon Hill and Eclipse in Arequa Gulch were eventually buried under mine tailings. Some of these ghost towns still have standing structures such as Independence, Altman and Midway. Others are void of structures, such as Stratton and Cameron east of Cripple Creek. Gillett, to the north of the District, still has one occupied home. Most of this site was plowed under and the town site returned to pasture land. Well outside of the Cripple Creek Mining District, but included in this area, is West Creek north of Woodland Park. To round out this area are some of the abandoned town sites associated with the railroads. This includes Alta Vista and Adelaide on the Florence & Cripple Creek Railway and Clyde on the Cripple Creek &

After years of prospecting, Bob Womack discovered gold ore in the Cripple Creek region. In 1890, he officially filed a claim. This was the beginning of the region's gold rush that made many men rich. Bob sold his claim for precious little and died in poverty.

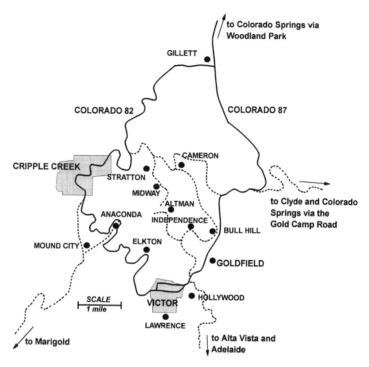

This is an overview of the towns in the Cripple Creek area showing only contemporary roads, both paved and dirt.

Colorado Springs District Railway.

    The story of how the Cripple Creek area was settled is tied to the life of Bob Womack. He and his brother William moved to Cripple Creek in 1876. They took over the ownership of a ranch owned by the Welty family for $500 and two pigs. Bob believed that the 1873 United States Government sponsored survey, which mentioned the possibility of gold in the region, was correct. Between his duties operating the ranch, he explored the region looking for gold ore. Bob Womack was skilled at tracking and hunting, making him well qualified for prospecting.

    The reason others had not recognized the area's potential for precious metal mining has to do with the nature of the mineralization. The gold is found as a complex telluride ore in the form of sylvanite or calaverite. Neither mineral has the look or feel of typical gold ore associated with decomposed quartz. It is also complex ore requiring high heat to free the gold.

In 1879, Bob found a piece of float in the streambed near his ranch. His efforts to discover the origin of the float intensified, and eventually, he correctly identified a vein of sylvanite. He named his claim The El Paso. His propensity to drink then brag about his discoveries, however, hurt his credibility. Sylvanite ore requires capital to develop. Due to his reputation for drinking, he was unable to convince Colorado Springs businessmen to loan him the required money to sink a tunnel and begin mining. In 1886, Womack staked out a placer claim, and in 1890, Womack officially filed a claim for the El Paso Lode near Poverty Gulch. It wasn't until the following year, however, that others came along and verified that a vast deposit of gold ore occupied the ancient volcanic crater in the Cripple Creek region. Other than recognition, Womack received precious little for his discovery and died in poverty.

How Cripple Creek was Named

There are differences of opinion on how Cripple Creek was first named. Probably the most authoritative account is in Marshall Sprague's book, *Money Mountain*. As his account explains, Levi Welty traveled from his Ohio home to make a living in Colorado. He brought with him his four children and settled near Colorado Springs, making a living as a rancher. As more people moved into the area, the grass became overgrazed. At this time, cattle rustling was also common.

These problems bothered Welty. He rode up over Ute Pass to Florissant, then he headed south to the forested foothills near an old volcanic cone called Mount Pisgah. In a shallow valley near the cone, Welty spotted a winding stream and plenty of grazing land. Welty and his boys constructed a cabin at the spring, which was the source of the small creek. Welty moved his family and cattle up into this area which was void of population.

To keep the animals away from the pure clear water coming out of the spring, Welty went about constructing a spring house. One of his boys accidentally rolled a log on his brother. In the excitement, Levi Welty accidentally discharged his shotgun. A piece of buckshot nipped the flesh in his hand, temporarily crippling him. At the same time, a pet calf was frightened by the blast and tried to jump the stream. The calf's leg was broken in the process, and to this Welty remarked, "Well boys, this sure is some cripple creek."

Cripple Creek's Red Light District

By the turn of the century, Cripple Creek had become prosperous beyond all expectations. More than 50,000 people lived in the Cripple Creek Mining District with approximately half calling the town of Cripple Creek home. Annual gold production was eighteen million dollars and the number of miners working in the area was around eight thousand. The town had electric lights, telephone service, a water supply system and a city government. There were two electric trolley car systems, the High Line and the Low Line, which provided light rail service to almost all the region's mines and towns.

As Cripple Creek grew in size, Bennett Avenue became the respectable business district with stock exchanges and banks. Fine stores lined both sides of the street. In contrast, Myers Avenue had evolved into the honky-tonk part of town. Its businesses consisted of brothels, saloons, gambling halls, dance halls, parlor houses and the like.

The first madam to set up shop in Cripple Creek on Myers Avenue was Blanche Burton. Typical of most "business" girls, her background remained a mystery. For many years, she operated her Cripple Creek brothel, then retired to Colorado City after the turn of the century. She was quite generous with her money and purchased coal for poor families. In 1909, an oil lamp exploded, and Blanche Burton died of her burns at the age of 50. For seven

decades, her grave went unmarked, then the former mayor of
Colorado Springs, Bill Henderson, had a marker made.

The majority of the establishments on Myers Avenue were
between 3rd and 5th streets. This included such notable places
as the Old Homestead, Opera Club, The Library, Last Chance,
Miners Exchange, Old Yellowstone, and The Dawson Club.
Employment levels for prostitutes were in the hundreds and possibly as high as 300.

East of 3rd Street, the road was called Poverty Gulch. This
was Cripple Creek's slum. The more adventurous male could find
girls of color working in cribs along Poverty Gulch. National origins included Japanese, Mexican, Native American, Spanish,
Chinese, French and a few black girls. These girls were individual
operators and not part of a brothel. Prices were quite a bit lower
than the "sporting" houses on Myers Avenue.

A typical crib had two rooms including the bedroom in the
front and a small kitchen in the rear. A city ordinance required
that the window shades be drawn at all times. This must have
made for a drab existence. In addition, a tax of $6 a month was
imposed for each working girl. Madams had to pay $16 a month.
Physical examinations were also required.

Robert Brown, Colorado historian and author, reports in his
book, *Cripple Creek, Then and Now,* that there was an exchange of
services between the girls on Myers Avenue and restaurant owners
on Bennett Avenue. The girls could discreetly leave their brothels
and walk over to Bennett Avenue for a free meal when business
was slow. The restaurant owner could later "collect" for the meal
by visiting that particular girl.

The most famous establishment on Myers Avenue was at
353. Known as the Old Homestead, its first madam was Hazel
Vernon. One of many wood-frame structures along this street, it
was destroyed in one of the 1896 fires. Rebuilt as a two-story brick
building, the Old Homestead remains standing today and is operated as a museum. Probably the most expensive and sophisticat-
ed brothel in all of the region, each of the Old Homestead's second

story rooms used for entertaining gentlemen was heated by a charcoal stove. A staff of seven, including maids, butlers, a porter and musicians, saw to the needs of the patrons. The Old Homestead had other amenities including electric lights, running water, a telephone and even an intercom.

Between five and six carefully selected girls worked at The Old Homestead. For potential customers to look over the

The Old Homestead is one of the few surviving parlor houses in Colorado and is now operated as a museum. One of Cripple Creek's new casinos towers over the old structure.
(Kenneth Jessen 111C8)

"merchandise," a unique viewing room was located at the top of the stairs. The exterior of each of the bedroom doors had a brass cardholder. The girl who occupied that particular room could post her cards in the holder in case her gentleman client cared to remember her name. As would be expected of a first class brothel, the Old Homestead served the finest food and drink. The place attracted groups from other towns and visits had to be planned. Lavish parties were also held in the establishment.

The best known madam was Pearl DeVere. She added to the elegance of the Old Homestead with her costly clothes and red hair.

Mabel Barbee Lee, just eleven years old at the time, had a fascination with Pearl. She later provided vivid descriptions of Pearl in her book *Cripple Creek Days.* Pearl drove around town in a phaeton pulled by a pair of high-stepping black horses. She held the reins in a firm, rigid position and looked neither right nor left to avoid eye contact with any of her customers.

Pearl often wore a taffeta dress with a wide, velvet hat. Her auburn hair would be adorned with willow plumes. Dressed either in brown or black, she used plenty of makeup to emphasize her long dark lashes and pale skin.

In 1897, Pearl was found dead in her room from an overdose of morphine. Mabel Barbee Lee provided her readers with a description of the corpse as she took one last look at Pearl DeVere. In death, Pearl looked so natural that it seemed as though she could have opened her eyes at any moment. The mortician tried his best to put Pearl's hair back to its familiar color, but the dye he used caused it to become dirty pink.

Some facts about Pearl DeVere that appeared in the *Victor Daily Record* probably surprised many townspeople. When she first arrived in Cripple Creek, she went under the name of Isabelle Martin. She was the wife of C. B. Flynn of Monterey, Mexico. At one time, she had been very wealthy and was a world traveler. For a while, she lived with a gambler named Dietz. Dietz gained notoriety by breaking the bank at Monte Carlo.

When Pearl died, her sister from Evanston, Indiana was notified. She came to Cripple Creek to claim the body. She had no idea of Pearl's occupation, and when she was told that Pearl was a madam, she disowned her sister. She referred to Pearl as a stain on her family and that the stain was as red as the dye on her hair. The sister said she would take no responsibility for Pearl's burial.

Many residents stepped forward to help with the funeral expenses, but a mysterious admirer sent an unsigned letter containing a thousand dollars in crisp new bills. Pearl's funeral was elaborate to say the least. The Elk's brass band played a funeral march as they stepped down Cripple Creek's main street just ahead of the hearse. The casket, lavender in color, was almost hidden by a blanket of red and white roses. Pearl's own carriage followed with a man walking beside the empty rig, driving the black horses. The seat held a large cross of shell-pink carnations.

Another madam named Lillian Powers began her "practice" in Denver, but she soon moved to Cripple Creek. She opened a house with a few girls. Unlike most houses, however, Lil kept her place spotless, including clean linens, curtains and other details. She had a place where gentlemen could relax and drink a beer or two. She made more in tips and in the sale of alcoholic beverages than her competitors made selling sex. Her success was her downfall, and competition and pressure from other madams forced her to leave town.

One dark side of prostitution was the frequent suicide of the girls. Although to their male clients, they seemed happy and pleasure-giving, the girls lived drab, lonely lives isolated from proper society. A 1900 Cripple Creek newspaper reported the passing of Blanche Garland, an employee of the Bon Ton Dance Hall. She injected chloroform into her veins. An "inmate" of the Mikado, Lucille Morris, died what was probably a painful death from carbolic acid. The *Cripple Creek Times* reported that Nellie Rolfe was discovered dead in a crouched position on the floor of her bedroom. Her address was given as 377 Myers Avenue. Hypodermic syringes and empty bottles of morphine were found near her body.

A decline in mining activity produced a decline in Cripple Creek's population. The brothels began to close, and they had fewer wealthy clients. Mine ownership was being consolidated under corporate ownership, and wealthy mine owners were becoming a thing of the past. The prostitutes either retired or moved to other towns.

Labor Strikes Lead to Death and Destruction

A struggle began in the Cripple Creek Mining district between mine owners and the miners, leading to multiple deaths and the destruction of a great deal of property. At issue was the

During the labor violence of 1904, Union terrorist Harry Orchard and Billy Aikman set off a dynamite explosion that killed fourteen non-union miners. This is what remained of the Florence & Cripple Creek depot in Independence. One wall was blown away and the force of the explosion disintegrated the entire platform. Many standing on the platform, waiting for the arrival of a train, were blown to bits. *(Denver Public Library X-9529)*

length of the workday and pay. Most miners worked ten-hour shifts for $3 under poor and dangerous working conditions. Many miners lost their lives in accidents. More miners died an early death from the combination of poor ventilation and rock dust produced during the drilling process.

In 1893, the Sherman Silver Purchase Act was repealed by Congress. In effect, the United States was no longer forced to purchase a certain amount of silver every year, or for that matter, maintain a fixed ratio between silver and the dollar. The price of silver fell to almost half of its previous price, closing most Colorado silver mines. Only the richest silver mines were able to survive.

A recession followed with many miners out of work. The price of gold, however, was unaffected, and Cripple Creek mines kept on producing. Many unemployed miners from Leadville, Aspen, Silverton, Georgetown and other areas flocked to Cripple Creek in hopes of getting hired. This created a labor surplus that benefited only the mine owners.

The first strike was by the Western Federation of Miners in 1894. It was won by the union for a wage of $3 per day for an eight-hour shift. When 1903 came along, however, the mine owners were in a position of strength. Because of this, the secretary of the Western Federation of Miners recruited Harry Orchard to stir up trouble. Harry Orchard was born Albert Horsely and came from Ontario, Canada. He began work at Idaho's Coeur d'Alene mine. During a labor dispute, Orchard blew up a mine and eventually killed the governor of Idaho in a dynamite explosion at the governor's home. By the time Orchard arrived in the Cripple Creek area, it was said that he was responsible for the deaths of twenty men.

The unrest began in Altman with a branch of the Western Federation of Miners called the Free Coinage Union No. 19. They held out for $3 per day and an eight-hour shift. The mine owners simply replaced the striking miners with unemployed silver miners. Only two of the fifty mines in the Altman area gave in to the union demands.

The Orpha May, a typical Cripple Creek mine, is located near Bull Hill along the Range View Road. This mine enjoyed a life span of five decades and eventually reached a depth of 1,264 feet. Present open pit mining will eventually undercut this old mine along with many others in the area. *(Kenneth Jessen 096D1)*

Vandalism and threats against non-union workers prompted the Colorado National Guard to be called in. The Colorado Militia also pitched its tents just below Altman. Military camps were also established at other towns.

In September, 1903, a bullpen was constructed by the National Guard at Goldfield to hold union leaders forcibly removed from their homes. This included the staff of the pro-union *Victor Daily Record.* See "Goldfield" for more details.

Soon after, Harry Orchard and an assistant, Billy Aikman, set off over fifty pounds of dynamite at the six-hundred-foot level in the Vindicator Mine hoping to kill as many non-union miners as possible. The miners were working at the seven-hundred-foot level, however, and Orchard had misjudged their location. Instead, two union men were killed.

The American Eagle Mine above Victor is open to the public. This is the blacksmith shop. *(Kenneth Jessen 111C6)*

The culmination of the district's labor problems came when terrorist Harry Orchard planned to kill as many people as possible at the Florence & Cripple Creek depot at Independence. His specific targets were the scabs hired by mine owners to replace the striking union workers. Orchard got the help of Steve Adams, and the two purchased two boxes of dynamite, some caps and some acid.

Orchard also worked on his alibi. He went on a camping trip the evening of June 5, 1904, at Cheyenne Mountain with some friends and took a saddle horse with him. During the night, Orchard quietly rode back to Independence.

Adams and Orchard worked on a bomb during the night; it used a tilt-up device for detonation. When a wooden frame was pulled into an upright position by a wire, bottles of acid spilled onto the dynamite caps causing them to explode. The caps, in turn, set off the primary dynamite charge.

Under the cloak of darkness, the men placed the device under the depot platform. The corks on the acid bottles were removed, arming the bomb. A wire was stretched across the railroad track to an ore house where Orchard and Adams hid.

Around 2:00 a.m., just prior to the arrival of a passenger train, a number of non-union miners began to congregate on the depot platform just over the bomb. When the men were bunched together and as the train approached, Orchard pulled on the string which tilted up the device. The explosion ripped the depot platform apart, blowing off one of the depot walls in the process. There were twenty-seven men on the platform at the time, and thirteen were killed instantly, their bodies blown to bits. Body parts even fell on the hillside above the depot. Among the injured, six were saved by amputation of arms and legs. One man died later of his injuries.

A special train carrying doctors and nurses was sent to the scene. Sheriff Robertson called upon his men to hunt down the killers. Bloodhounds were brought in to help in the search. Orchard and Adams had soaked their shoes in turpentine and successfully threw the bloodhounds off their trail.

Orchard rode hard back to his camp. When the others in his party woke in the morning, they had no idea Orchard had left the camp during the night. Adams also made a clean getaway. Sheriff Robertson, unable to apprehend the terrorists, was forced to resign or be hanged. Peace was finally restored and the mines continued to operate under the $3 per ten-hour shift plan.

The day after the explosion, a Florence & Cripple Creek train headed south with twenty-five union activists on board. They were dumped in New Mexico in a remote area near Raton and warned never to return to Cripple Creek.

Drainage Tunnels Save Cripple Creek Mines

As the mines around Cripple Creek became deeper, water problems began to appear. This was especially true below the 800-foot level. A layer of impervious granite kept the ground water at this depth, and the cost of pumping became prohibitive. Large steam-powered underground pumps were common to all deep mines. The sustained cost of coal to keep the pumps operating was expensive, and only the richest mines could afford to go deep into the earth. If a pump broke down, the mine could flood so quickly that the chances of loss of life were high.

After the turn of the century it looked like many Cripple Creek mines would have to close. The Carlton brothers, Bert and Leslie, were gaining a foothold through the purchase of many of the area mines. They stood to lose much of their investment if water forced the closure of their mines.

The most common method of solving this problem consisted of boring a drainage tunnel at an elevation lower than most area mines. The El Paso Drainage Tunnel was the first attempt to drain the Jack Pot and El Paso mines, but the tunnel was inadequate. This led to the development of the Roosevelt Deep Drainage Tunnel, which was started in 1902 and financed by Bert Carlton. It bored through the tough layer of granite and took until 1910 to complete. The tunnel, 15,737 feet in length, ran from the Victor-Cripple Creek area to the southwest, and cost just over half

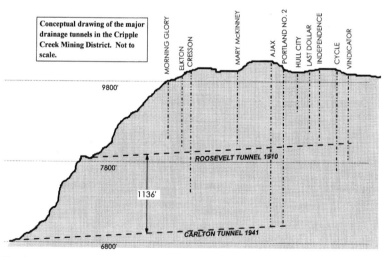

CRIPPLE CREEK MINING DISTRICT

The Roosevelt and Carlton drainage tunnels were expensive projects, but they greatly extended the productive life of many Cripple Creek mines.

a million dollars. It intersected the area's mines at about the 8,000 foot level and extended their lives by two decades.

By 1930, the mines had reached well below the Roosevelt Tunnel. A new tunnel, 1,136 feet lower than the Roosevelt, was started. Bert Carlton spearheaded the idea, but passed away before the tunnel was completed. It seemed only fitting that the tunnel be called the Carlton Tunnel.

At a cost of 1.25 million dollars, the Carlton Tunnel was over six miles in length, with its portal at Marigold. The project was complete in 1941, and allowed mines like the Ajax and Portland No. 2 to reach depths well below three thousand feet. This drainage tunnel allowed the area's mines to continue to operate profitably until recent times. As haulage technology advanced, it became more efficient to use open pit mining methods combined with heap leaching.

REFERENCES FOR CRIPPLE CREEK'S RED LIGHT DISTRICT

Bill Grimstad and Raymond Drake, *The Last Gold Rush*, Pollux Press, Victor, Colorado, 1983, pp. 11-12.

Clark Secrest, *Hell's Belles*, Hindsight Historical Publications, Aurora, Colorado, 1996, p. 94.

"In Morpheus' Deep Embrace," *The Victor Daily Record*, June 6, 1897.

Leland Feitz, *Myers Avenue - A Quick History*, Little London Press, Colorado Springs, Colorado, 1967, p. 17, pp. 24-25.

Mabel Barbee Lee, *Cripple Creek Days*, Double Day & Company, Garden City, N. Y., 1958, pp. 75-84.

Robert L. Brown, *Cripple Creek, Then and Now*, Sundance, Denver, 1991, pp. 48-55.

REFERENCES FOR LABOR STRIKES LEAD TO DEATH AND DESTRUCTION

Bill Grimstad and Raymond Drake, *The Last Gold Rush*, Pollux Press, Victor, Colorado, 1983, pp. 109-110, p. 112.

Brian H. Levine, *Lowell Thomas' Victor*, Century One Press, Colorado Springs, Colorado, 1982, pp. 33-45.

Marshall Sprague, *Money Mountain*, Little, Brown and Company, Boston, 1953, pp. 253-256.

Robert L. Brown, *Cripple Creek, Then and Now*, Sundance, Denver, 1991, pp. 93-98.

REFERENCES FOR DRAINAGE TUNNELS SAVE CRIPPLE CREEK MINES

Bill Grimstad and Raymond Drake, *The Last Gold Rush*, Pollux Press, Victor, Colorado, 1983, pp. 48-49.

Mabel Barbee Lee, *Cripple Creek Days*, Doubleday & Co., Garden City, New York, 1958, pp. 237-238, pp. 254-264.

ALTA VISTA and ADELAIDE
Railroad Towns

- *Alta Vista, Teller County, Millsap Creek drainage*
- *Adelaide, Fremont County, Eight Mile Creek drainage*
- *Accessible via graded dirt road*
- *No standing structures remain at either site*

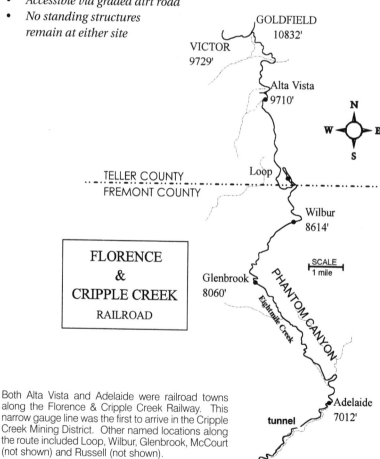

Both Alta Vista and Adelaide were railroad towns along the Florence & Cripple Creek Railway. This narrow gauge line was the first to arrive in the Cripple Creek Mining District. Other named locations along the route included Loop, Wilbur, Glenbrook, McCourt (not shown) and Russell (not shown).

A lta Vista was located three miles south of Victor and began as a stage stop. The narrow gauge Florence & Cripple Creek, the first railroad into the Cripple Creek District, provided service to the area for 23 years. The railroad was constructed in 1894, and Alta Vista was selected as the location for the railroad yards. At the time, there wasn't enough room in the Victor-Goldfield area for the yards. Only a few homes were constructed at the Alta Vista site for employees of the railroad. When the railroad was abandoned in 1912, so was Alta Vista.

All that remains of Adelaide is this stone-lined well and the railroad grade. In addition to railroad structures, Adelaide once had a store and a boarding house. *(Kenneth Jessen 111D6)*

The Alta Vista site is in an open meadow with a beautiful view of the Millsap Creek drainage. It is difficult to identify today with only a trace of the wye where helper locomotives were turned after the long climb up Phantom Canyon. The Alta Vista depot was moved many years ago and now serves as the visitor's center for Victor.

Adelaide was located 23 miles from Cripple Creek, well down Phantom Canyon. Originally named Robinson, the name was changed to Adelaide when the railroad was constructed through the site. It had several railroad structures including a section house, depot, water tank and passing track. There was also a small store and a story-and-a-half boarding house at the site. The small community got its own post office in 1894, which remained open until 1901.

In 1895, a cloudburst destroyed much of Adelaide including the boarding house where three people lost their lives. In addition, three others were killed in this flood. Almost ten miles of track and roadbed were damaged or destroyed by the flood. A freight train was trapped in the canyon for five weeks until the damaged track was replaced.

The year after the flood, the railroad relocated Adelaide on a shelf cut into the side of the hill and well above flood level. The depot was moved, and a new water tank was constructed.

Today, nothing remains at Adelaide except for a stone-lined well below the railroad grade.

Other locations along the railroad include Loop, Wilbur, Glenbrook, and Russell.

Leland Feitz, *Ghost Towns of the Cripple Creek District*, Little London Press, Colorado Springs, 1974, p. 4.

Tiv Wilkins, *Colorado Railroads*, Pruett Publishing Company, Boulder, 1974, p. 103.

Tiv Wilkins, *The Florence & Cripple Creek and Golden Circle Railroads*, Colorado Railroad Museum, Golden, Colorado, 1976, pp. 39, 54, 67, 69.

William H. Bauer, James L. Ozment and John H. Willard, *Colorado Post Offices*, Colorado Railroad Museum, Golden, Colorado 1990, p. 9.

ALTMAN

Highest Town in the Area

- *Teller County, Grassy Creek and Wilson Creek drainages*
- *Access by graded dirt road to the American Eagles Mine*
- *Several structures remain*

This drawing of Altman, from Bull Hill looking toward Pikes Peak, was based on an 1894 photograph when the camp reached its peak. Little is left today at the Altman town site.

Located at an elevation of 10,629 feet, Altman claimed to be the highest incorporated city in the World. There were other cities in South America, however, that easily exceeded Altman's elevation. Named after sawmill owner Sam Altman, the town was platted during the gold rush in 1893. Altman got its own post office the following year. When the mines began to develop, Sam Altman constructed the area's first stamp mill to crush gold ore.

John Calderwood, a union organizer, got virtually every Altman resident to join his small union, which became part of The Western Federation of Miners. This union combined with others in the surrounding towns until two thirds of all the miners in the Cripple Creek District were union members. The miners fought with the Colorado Militia during strikes in 1894 and 1904.

During its boom years, Altman had two hotels, three grocery stores, four boarding houses, a drug store, an assay office, two shoemakers and nine saloons. The saloons included the Thirst Parlor, Monte Carlo and Silver Dollar. Social life pivoted around a half-dozen fraternal lodges and the union. Altman also had several churches and a school.

In 1896, Altman was incorporated, and by 1897, it had a population of nearly 2,000 people. Mining in the area began to decline, and by the turn of the century, the population had fallen to well under 1,000. The Western Federation of Miners loss to the mine owners during the 1904 strike was responsible for the departure of many residents. By 1908, only one hundred residents still occupied the town. Its buildings, situated on a high saddle, deteriorated, but a few residents hung on to maintain the waterworks

Possibly this was a boarding house. It is located at the Altman site along the new road leading to the American Eagles Mine. *(Kenneth Jessen 111B12)*

or to work in some of the mines. In 1911, the post office closed. The 1920 census listed 42 residents.

By the 1940s, according to ghost town historian Muriel Sibell Wolle, all that remained in Altman were three or four frame homes, some mine buildings and a rusting fireplug. Robert L. Brown visited Altman during the 1960s when he was working on *Jeep Trails to Colorado Ghost Towns.* There were several buildings still standing, and he discovered a safe in one structure. Only the foundation of the Union Hall was visible at the lower end of the town's main street.

In 1988, Robert Brown used a historic photograph of Altman to position his camera in exactly the same spot. There were over seventy-five structures in the historic photograph while Brown's photograph showed that Altman had dwindled to only a dozen structures. Today, it's hard to even identify Altman's streets, and only five structures remain.

At the top of the hill overlooking the Altman site was a mine called the Pharmacist. It was started by a couple of druggists new to mining and prospecting. As the story goes, they were prospecting and didn't know where to begin digging. They tossed their hats in the air and dug into the ground where they landed. The mine eventually produced a half-million dollars in gold.

To reach Altman, take the graded dirt road from Victor to the American Eagles Mine. The mine is owned by the Cripple Creek & Victor Gold Mining Company and is open to the public. This road can be driven by automobile. Above Victor, this road joins the road from Independence and climbs past the Altman site. Altman is on the right hand side when headed uphill to the American Eagles Mine.

See "Introduction to Teller County" for Altman's general location relative to other ghost towns in the Cripple Creek area.

An old double hip roof home is one of the few remaining structures at the ghost town of Altman. Someday this structure will yield to open pit mining, which has encroached on the site. *(Kenneth Jessen 111C1)*

Leland Feitz, *Ghost Towns of the Cripple Creek District*, Little London Press, Colorado Springs, 1974, p. 6.

Marshall Sprague, *Money Mountain*, Little, Brown and Company, Boston, 1953, pp. 136-144.

Muriel Sibell Wolle, *Stampede to Timberline*, Sage Books, Chicago, 1949, pp. 476-477.

Muriel Sibell Wolle, *Timberline Tailings*, Sage Books, Chicago, Illinois, 1977, p. 88.

Robert G. Taylor, *Cripple Creek Mining District*, Filter Press, Palmer Lake, Colorado, 1973, pp. 101-102, 136.

Robert L. Brown, *Cripple Creek, Then and Now*, Sundance, Denver, 1991, pp. 112-113.

Robert L. Brown, on *Jeep Trails to Colorado Ghost Towns*, Caxton Printers, Caldwell, Idaho, 1963, pp. 36-38.

William H. Bauer, James L. Ozment and John H. Willard, *Colorado Post Offices*, Colorado Railroad Museum, Golden, Colorado 1990, p. 11.

ANACONDA and MOUND CITY

Squaw Gulch Towns

- *Teller County, Squaw Gulch drainage*
- *Accessible by graded dirt road*
- *No structures remain*

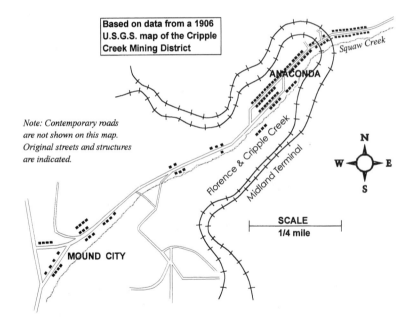

Based on data from a 1906 U.S.G.S. map of the Cripple Creek Mining District

Note: Contemporary roads are not shown on this map. Original streets and structures are indicated.

ANACONDA

Squaw Creek

Florence & Cripple Creek

Midland Terminal

MOUND CITY

SCALE
1/4 mile

N
W — E
S

Anaconda began as a mining camp called Squaw Gulch and then became the town of Barry. As this map shows, it was situated at the head of Squaw Gulch and included a substantial business district and many homes. Mound City was located near the mouth of Squaw Gulch, and its economy was supported by two mills.

Anaconda went through several name changes. When George Carr was prospecting in the hills around his Broken Box Ranch, he accidentally uncovered the remains of an Indian squaw. The gulch below this discovery was named Squaw Gulch.

In 1891, the Blue Bell Mine was developed on the hillside above Squaw Gulch, and during that year, a modest amount of ore was shipped. The mining company built a boarding house in the gulch, and several cabins were constructed by the miners. This cluster of cabins was also named Squaw Gulch.

Vinton and Bill Barry laid out a town in 1892 which encompassed the mining camp of Squaw Gulch. They named the town Barry. The Barry brothers then purchased the Anaconda Mine, a property with good potential. The mine's output increased during 1893, and the following year, the town of Barry was renamed Anaconda. By the turn of the century, the population was over one thousand.

The Anaconda Mine was soon overpowered by the Mary McKinney Mine. To prevent burying the railroad tracks which circled around the head of the gulch, cribbing was used to hold the

The Deerhorn Boarding House sat on the hillside above Anaconda's main street. The two men on the left wearing aprons probably worked in the kitchen. *(Denver Public Library X-6604)*

tailings in place on the hillside. Over the years, this cribbing grew to enormous proportions until it formed a long, high wall which remains standing today.

The Florissant House, a typical false-front Anaconda business, once stood along the now vacant main street. *(Denver Public Library X-6603)*

Anaconda had two business blocks which included such establishments as hotels, saloons, a drug store and several grocery stores. The town had approximately sixty structures of various sizes and a town center consisting of a row of false-front stores. All types of occupations were represented in Anaconda's population, including lawyers, dressmakers, an optician and several physicians. Anaconda also had a fine schoolhouse.

The post office opened under the name Barry in 1892. During the following year, the name was changed to Anaconda. The post office remained open until 1909, then reopened in 1911 and remained active until 1917.

The Cripple Creek Morning Times on January 1, 1899, remarked that in Anaconda, "The class of homes is the very best - nice cottages dotting the hills on either side of the stream."

Anaconda had three rail lines, including an electric trolley line, which allowed workers to commute to other areas in the district.

Horace Barry boasted (maybe tongue in cheek) that the town was the cultural center of the entire Cripple Creek Mining District. The proof was in the Squaw Gulch Amusement Club with a membership of 400. Of these, Barry said that 399 were from aristocratic families. The president of the club got his job

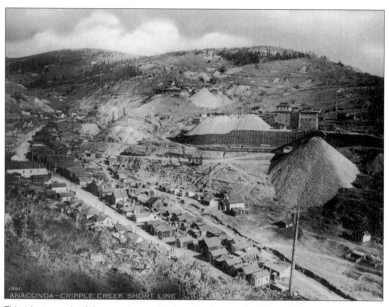

This photograph of Anaconda emphasizes the impressive Mary McKinney Mine on the right. Nearly 100 structures appear in this photograph illustrating the town's size. All of the structures in the main part of town were destroyed by fire in 1904. *(Denver Public Library MCC-1951)*

because of his ability to call square dances. The sergeant-at-arms was Bob Womack, the very same prospector credited with the discovery of rich ore in the Cripple Creek District. He was posted at the door to keep prostitutes from entering and preserve the club's dignity. Womack, however, thought all women were wonderful irrespective of their occupation. He was the wrong man for the job and allowed ladies of the evening free access to the club.

Anaconda was destroyed by fire in November, 1904, and was not rebuilt. Dynamite was used to try to form a firebreak, but all the dynamite did was provide kindling for the fire's advance. Residents decided to move to Victor or Cripple Creek. By 1908, Anaconda still had 250 residents living in structures not consumed by the fire.

The Anaconda town site today has no standing structures, however above the town are a couple of weathered buildings associated with the Anaconda Mine. There are also two abandoned houses behind the Mary McKinney Mine, but these are on private property.

Mound City, at the extreme lower end of the gulch, was settled in 1891 and grew up near two large mills which provided employment. About 500 to 600 people lived in Mound City by 1893.

The town consisted mainly of frame shanties and a few log cabins scattered about the floor of the gulch, with no particular regard to "city planning." The buildings did not even define a main street. The town had several businesses including three grocery stores, two meat markets and a couple of saloons. Mound City also had a barbershop, hotel and clothing store.

A typical miner's shack in Mound City was made up of exterior vertical milled boards with smaller boards nailed over the seams. Inside, newspapers were used for insulation. The interior had horizontal boards to cover the newspaper. The ceiling was often covered with canvas. A coal stove provided warmth, and its pipe went directly up through a hole in the roof. Trash collection was simple. Garbage was tossed out the front door, and what wasn't eaten by wandering burros is probably still there. Running water was extremely rare, and an outhouse behind the structure completed the picture.

The Brodie Mill, using the cyanide leaching process, was the primary employer. This was the first mill of its type and could eco-nomically process large amounts of low-grade gold ore. A second mill, the Rosebud, also added to the economy. The Rosebud was destroyed by fire in 1894 and never rebuilt. The Brodie Mill operated until 1900 when competition from other, newer mills made

Once part of the mining structures at the Anaconda Mine, this building can be seen by tourists riding the Cripple Creek & Victor Narrow Gauge Railroad. *(Kenneth Jessen 092D4)*

continuation uneconomical.

The town's most famous resident was Judge Melville B. Gerry. In 1883, Gerry sentenced cannibal Alfred Packer for eating his fellow companions. At the time, Gerry was a judge in Lake County and held court in the Lake County Court House in Lake City.

Today, the Mound City site is void of any structures, and even the foundations of its many buildings are difficult to locate. The stone foundations for both the Brodie and Rosebud mills remain.

Mound City, located a short distance below Anaconda, consisted of board and batten miner's shacks, a few log structures and a two-story, false-front store. None of these structures remain today. *(Denver Public Library X-11200)*

Don and Jean Griswold, *Colorado's Century of "Cities,"* self-published, 1958, pp. 253-254.

Leland Feitz, *Ghost Towns of the Cripple Creek District*, Little London Press, Colorado Springs, 1974, pp. 10-14, 18, 42-43.

Leslie Doyle Spell and Hazel M. Spell, *Forgotten Men of Cripple Creek*, Big Mountain Press, Denver, 1959, pp. 47, 59, 71.

Marshall Sprague, *Money Mountain*, Little, Brown and Company, Boston, 1953, pp. 102, 301.

Muriel Sibell Wolle, *Stampede to Timberline*, Sage Books, Chicago, 1949, pp. 476-477, 462.

Robert G. Taylor, *Cripple Creek Mining District*, Filter Press, Palmer Lake, Colorado, 1973, pp. 102, 104.

Robert L. Brown, *Cripple Creek, Then and Now*, Sundance, Denver, 1991, pp. 117-118.

Robert L. Brown, *Ghost Towns of the Colorado Rockies*, Caxton Printers, Caldwell, Idaho, 1977, pp. 230-234.

William H. Bauer, James L. Ozment and John H. Willard, *Colorado Post Offices*, Colorado Railroad Museum, Golden, Colorado 1990, pp. 12, 17.

AREQUA, BEACON HILL and ECLIPSE

- *Teller County, Arequa Creek drainage*
- *Sites are buried under mine tailings*
- *Towns did not have post offices; no structures remain*

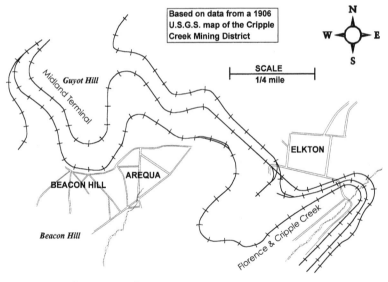

Note: Contemporary roads
are not shown on this map.
Original streets are indicated.

Derived from a 1906 map, Arequa and Beacon Hill are shown but not Eclipse. Eclipse was located to the east near the head of the gulch indicated by the hairpin turns in the railroad tracks. The roads indicated on this map are those that existed at the turn of the century. The modern-day paved road follows the grade of the Florence & Cripple Creek.

The oldest settlement in the Cripple Creek Mining District, Arequa, was settled prior to 1890. Founded by Ben Requa, the town never grew beyond a population of one hundred or so. The town was named after its founder, but for some unknown reason, an "A" got added to the name "Requa."

Employment was provided by the Arequa Mill, which treated low-grade ore. Unlike other Cripple Creek District towns, Arequa was not close to the major producing mines, therefore, its growth was limited. Arequa did not last long; in fact, the town had the distinction of having the shortest-lived post office in the area. Its post office opened on July 9, 1894 and closed less than two months later. The old town site has been buried under the tailings from the Golden Cycle Mill.

Beacon Hill was located to the west of Arequa and is shown on the maps of the day as a distinct settlement. Little else is known.

Another small satellite town was Eclipse. Its economy was supported by the large Economic Gold Extraction Company mill using the chlorination process. Workers at the mill constructed homes in Arequa Gulch near the mill.

On the other side of Squaw Mountain in Victor, tailings from the Gold Coin Mine threatened to overrun the town. The Woods Investment Company drilled a transportation tunnel to carry ore out to the Economic Gold Extraction mill at Eclipse. The mill burned in 1908, but by then, its process was obsolete. Sparks ignited homes in Eclipse and they too were destroyed.

Eclipse was located below Colorado 67 just south of Elkton, but before the road enters Victor. The site is buried under tons of tailings from the present heap leaching operation.

Leland Feitz, *Ghost Towns of the Cripple Creek District*, Little London Press, Colorado Springs, 1974, pp. 15-17.

Mabel Barbee Lee, *Cripple Creek Days*, Doubleday & Co., Garden City, N. Y., 1958, p. 236.

Muriel Sibell Wolle, *Stampede to Timberline*, University of Colorado Press, 1949, p. 462.

Robert L. Brown, *Cripple Creek, Then and Now*, Sundance, Denver, 1991, p. 122.

William H. Bauer, James L. Ozment and John H. Willard, *Colorado Post Offices*, Colorado Railroad Museum, Golden, Colorado 1990, p. 13.

BULL HILL

- *Teller County, Wilson Creek and Grassy Creek divide*
- *Accessible by paved road*
- *Town did not have a post office; several structures remain*

One of several abandoned railroad cars at Bull Hill. This particular car once served on the Colorado Midland and was eventually relegated for use by maintenance workers. *(Kenneth Jessen 023C34)*

Bull Hill, located north of Goldfield and near Independence, was the site of the Midland Terminal Railway yards and supported a modest population of railroad workers. The railroad reached Bull Hill in 1894 and built coal facilities and a water tank. At an elevation of 10,199 feet, it was the highest point on the Midland Terminal. The Bull Hill depot was moved to Anaconda and, during the 1960s, was moved again to Cripple Creek to serve as the depot for the Cripple Creek & Victor Narrow Gauge

Railroad. This two-foot gauge railroad runs as a tourist attraction.

Bull Hill had two large mills, one five stories high. The Colorado Springs & Cripple Creek District Railway also had facilities at Bull Hill.

Today, an attractive two-story brick home marks the site. The remains of two passenger cars and a freight car can be seen in the general area, but are located on private property.

Theresa Mine near Bull Hill. *(Kenneth Jessen 118D4)*

Edward M. McFarland, The Cripple Creek Road, Pruett Publishing Company, Boulder, 1984, pp. 38, 97, 102, 137.

Leland Feitz, Ghost Towns of the Cripple Creek District, Little London Press, Colorado Springs, 1974, p. 19.

CAMERON

Location of Pinnacle Park

- *Teller County, Grassy Creek drainage*
- *Accessible by graded dirt road*
- *No structures remain*

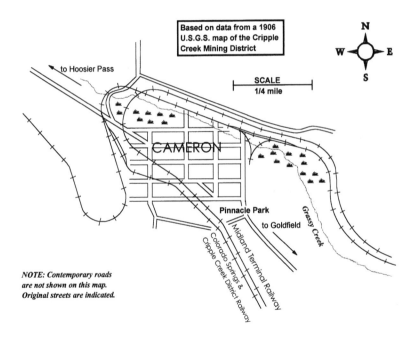

Cameron's building lots were not completely filled, but with nearly forty structures, it was a good-sized town for the Cripple Creek area. Note the swamp along Grassy Creek.

Cameron included an amusement park called Pinnacle Park. As seen in this photograph, the town was scattered across the meadow, despite the fact that there was a well-defined street system. None of these structures remain today. *(Denver Public Library X-609)*

At one time, the people living at Cameron proposed that the town be called Cripple Creek. A rival town, Fremont, took that name and grew into the largest town in the region. Cameron was called Gassy at first. Allen Gullion owned a ranch in the area and had a digestive problem; this led to the name Gassy. Feeling that this might have been a little too descriptive, local residents then changed the name to Grassy.

Growth was stimulated by the arrival of the Midland Terminal in 1894. For a while it was the terminus for the railroad, and a few boarding houses were built. The Woods Investment Company purchased the 183-acre Grassy town site in 1899, under the ownership of the Cameron Mines, Land and Tunnel Company. At that time Grassy became Cameron, and many improvements were made, such as graded streets and boardwalks. The Woods Brothers insisted on the use of fire resistant material in the eight-block business district, taking a lesson from the disastrous fire that destroyed other area towns.

Despite an organized street system, the blocks in Cameron were not filled with structures. This gave the town a spread out appearance with buildings interspersed with vacant lots.

Mining in the immediate area was sparse relative to Cripple Creek or Victor. The Lansing Mine was close to town and produced a quarter of a million dollars in gold. Elsmere No. 1, No. 2

and No. 3 shafts were also in or adjacent to the town site but the ore was not of sufficient value to fully develop these mines.

What set Cameron aside from all other communities in the region, however, was the construction of Pinnacle Park. Built on the south side of Cameron in a wooded area covering about thirty acres, Pinnacle Park officially opened on June 2, 1900. The park included picnic grounds, a small zoo and an athletic field that could seat 1,000 spectators. Over the years, many thousands of visitors enjoyed the park's attractions.

Scattered throughout the park were caged animals including bears. A large log restaurant and a dance pavilion were also located within the park. Children were entertained by a carousel. Normal admission was a dime, but on holidays and special occasions, the admission was a quarter. This might not seem like much today, but on a miner's daily wage of $2.00 to $3.00, it was quite a bit.

A double arch walkway allowed pedestrians to cross safely over the parallel tracks of the Colorado Midland and the Colorado Springs & Cripple Creek District Railroad. The latter railroad offered trolley car service from other towns in the district. On Labor Day, 1900, an estimated 9,000 people came to enjoy the park. Pinnacle Park remained popular until its closure in 1912.

Within its sixty blocks, Cameron grew to a population of 400. The business district consisted of a hotel, jail, two saloons, a printing office, meat market, three grocery stores, four restaurants, a billiard hall, barber shop and a school. Services included a physician, an insurance agent and a justice of the peace. Cameron's post office opened in 1901 and remained active for eight years. *The Golden Crescent* was the town's newspaper, and Cameron had a fully functional government that met in the city hall.

Today, little is left to mark the Cameron town site or Pinnacle Park. Above the town site are two old structures that were once part of the town. The meadow where the main portion of the town was located has returned to its natural state. Prior to the present-day fence and no trespassing signs, ground searches by other historians revealed the remains of the dens where the bears were kept, as well as various foundations. The parallel grades of the two railroads, however, are quite evident.

Mollie Kathleen Mine near Cripple Creek. *(Kenneth Jessen 118D10)*

John K. Aldrich, *Ghosts of Teller County*, Centennial Graphics, Lakewood, 1986, p. 16.

Leland Feitz, *Ghost Towns of the Cripple Creek District*, Little London Press, Colorado Springs, 1974, p. 21.

Marshall Sprague, *Money Mountain*, Little, Brown and Company, Boston, 1953, p. 33.

Robert G. Taylor, *Cripple Creek Mining District*, Filter Press, Palmer Lake, Colorado, 1973, pp. 86-87.

S. E. Poet, "The Story of Cameron, Colorado," *Colorado Magazine*, Vol. IX, No. 5, September, 1932, The State Historical Society, Denver, pp. 194-198.

Tivis Wilkins, *Short Line to Cripple Creek*, Colorado Railroad Museum, Annual No. 16, 1983, p. 150.

William H. Bauer, James L. Ozment and John H. Willard, *Colorado Post Offices*, Colorado Railroad Museum, Golden, Colorado, 1990, p. 27.

CLYDE

Located Along the Railroad

- *Teller County, Middle Beaver Creek drainage*
- *Accessible by graded dirt road*
- *Town did not have a post office; no original structures remain*

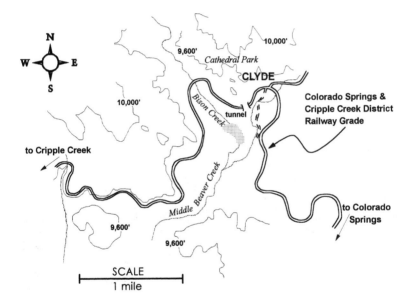

Clyde is located along the grade of the Colorado Springs & Cripple Creek District Railway east of the highest tunnel on the line. This grade is known today as the Gold Camp Road. The original structures are gone, but modern mountain homes now occupy the town site.

Constructed in 1901, Clyde was a stop along the Colorado Springs & Cripple Creek District Railway. Originally the location was called Seward. The railroad built a station and water tank. The station, constructed in 1902, included a waiting room and a telegraph office. A small lake at Clyde was developed by the railroad into a recreation area. The town also had a sawmill and a few homes. The population of Clyde couldn't have been much over twenty.

Under the Seward name, the location got its own post office in 1896. This would tend to indicate that the place had some population prior to the arrival of the railroad. The name was changed to Clyde in 1899, and the post office remained open until 1909. The railroad was abandoned through Clyde in 1923.

A pavilion, with open sides and a corrugated roof, was

Clyde, originally called Seward, got its own post office in 1896. The Colorado Springs & Cripple Creek District Railway built its standard gauge short line through Clyde in 1901. Clyde then became a recreation area with excursion trains, such as this one, making regular trips. *(Denver Public Library X-7493)*

constructed near the lake. This provided a place for evening dances. Small boats could be rented for excursions on the lake. The railroad owned all of the facilities at Clyde, including the boats. On Sundays and holidays, excursions from Cripple Creek to Clyde were quite popular.

Today, modern homes are located at the Clyde site, but the small lake remains alongside the railroad grade.

Independence Mine near Victor *(Kenneth Jessen 119A6)*

Doris Wolfe, *The Gold Camp Road*, self-published, 1991, p. 35.

Tivis Wilkins, *Short Line to Cripple Creek*, Colorado Railroad Museum, Golden, Colorado, 1983, pp. 148-150.

William H. Bauer, James L. Ozment and John H. Willard, *Colorado Post Offices*, Colorado Railroad Museum, Golden, Colorado 1990, pp. 35, 131.

CRIPPLE CREEK

Destroyed by Fire

- *Teller County; Cripple Creek drainage*
- *Accessible by paved road; occupied town*
- *Has an active post office; many original structures*

A very early view of Cripple Creek shows many of the wooden structures that were consumed by the 1896 fires. The majority of buildings were replaced by more substantial structures made of stone and brick. *(Denver Public Library X-806)*

Never a ghost town, Cripple Creek's history is rich and detailed. It represents the last boomtown in Colorado and is the principal city in the region.

The story of Cripple Creek begins with a cowboy named Bob Womack. He spent endless hours prospecting in the region believing that vast deposits of gold lay beneath the soil. He did discover gold ore in a place called Poverty Gulch in 1878, staking his first claim in 1886. It would be several years before the area blossomed into a full-scale gold rush, however.

This 1876 photograph predates Cripple Creek by many years. It shows the Broken Box (or Welty) Ranch where Bob Womack worked as a ranch hand. Note that the spring-house appears to be draped in canvas. In his spare time, Bob prospected in the region and is credited with making the first gold discovery. *(Denver Public Library X-811)*

The Broken Box Ranch superseded Bob Womack's original ranch and was eventually owned by the Houseman Cattle and Land Company. Its principal owners were Horace W. Bennett, Julius A. Myers and Alexander Horseman. Since the gold rush began in 1891, prospectors began trespassing on their land. They decided to plat a town rather than contend with evicting prospectors. The prospectors were offered town lots with the condition that when they left, all improvements would remain behind. The town was named Fremont.

This strategy rewarded the Houseman Company with brisk sales. A 25-foot by 125-foot lot sold for $25; corner lots commanded a price of $50. This was quite high for the times considering that these lots sat at an elevation of about 9,500 feet and included no sewage facilities, water or even streets.

Success attracts competition. On a nearby mining property called the Hayden Placer, its owners established a 140-acre town site to compete with Fremont. Town lots were offered on a payment plan. Gambling and the sale of liquor were forbidden. In contrast, Fremont had no such restrictions. This may explain why Fremont became more of the business center and Hayden Placer became more residential in nature. Near what is today the intersection of Fourth and Myers Avenue in Cripple Creek, the first business was built. It was a barbershop connected to an out-door saloon, an interesting combination. Photographs taken in 1892 show the primitive nature of the town's structures. Many were tents or partially wood and partially canvas. Outhouses appear to be dispersed randomly between the various buildings. Muddy paths made up the street system.

A hotel was built in Freeman called The Headquarters. It was a two-story log structure with a large common sleeping room for its guests who had to set aside any desire for privacy. A second hotel was built in Hayden Placer with eight rooms.

By the end of 1891, the combined population of the two towns was around 800. As the two towns grew, the boundary between them became indistinguishable. In the meantime, lot prices rose to $250 or more. Since the name of the mining district was Cripple Creek, the two towns were generally referred to as Cripple Creek.

The Houseman Company applied for a post office under the name of Fremont, and was granted a post office in July, 1891, only

This photograph of Bennett Avenue during the Cripple Creek fire of April 29, 1896 shows merchants moving their goods into the street while others are using wagons to escape to safety. A high percentage of the town's businesses were destroyed. *(Denver Public Library X-868)*

to have it close in December. The reason given by the United States Postal Service: several other towns in the West were named Fremont. At this same time, the Hayden Placer officials filed for a post office under the name of Morland. Postal records show that Fremont became Morland, but no mention was made of the physical location for the post office. The Morland post office lasted two months, when decision was reversed changing the name back to Fremont. Ed De La Verge is credited with suggesting that the place be called Cripple Creek. The combination of Fremont and Hayden Placer officially became Cripple Creek in February, 1893.

The three active gold mines near Cripple Creek grew to fifty by the end of 1892. By the end of 1893, there were 150 active mines in the area. Saw mills operated around the clock to keep up with demand for lumber and heavy mine timbers. Tent structures yielded to frame structures. A toll road was constructed from Florence through Phantom Canyon, and a shelf road was built along Cripple Creek to Canon City. A third road came south from Divide for easy access to Colorado Springs.

The newly formed town of Cripple Creek got off to a good start with a population of 6,000. Not only was there a long list of traditional businesses including 49 grocery stores, Cripple Creek had forty stockbrokers and a stock exchange. There were also a number of banks, and the town's first newspaper was called *The Crusher*. The town provided a living for 72 lawyers, no doubt spending most of their time on mining claim litigation.

Myers Avenue took on its own garish personality with dance halls, variety theaters, parlor houses and cribs. Sprinkled among these places were most of the town's 73 saloons.

Like so many other Colorado mining towns, Cripple Creek suffered devastating fires. Few of the original frame structures survived, and what the visitor sees today, especially in the business district, are buildings constructed since 1896. Old Cripple Creek was filled with row upon row of wooden structures adjacent to each other, and construction materials included highly flammable tarpaper covering. Lack of a trained fire department and a water main unable to supply sufficient water to a major blaze made the town ripe for destruction.

At the time of the first fire in 1896, Cripple Creek had a population of about 16,000. Because of soaring production from the mines, the population increased at a very rapid rate, making exact estimates difficult. The city had a water system with fire hydrants fed from a small reservoir above the town. Fire alarms were placed along the major street. The fire department was composed of 175 volunteers, three hose carts, a hook and ladder truck, and a pumper tank. All were hand drawn or horse drawn.

The first fire broke out April 25, on the second floor of the Central Dance Hall. Although historical accounts vary, Jennie LaRue, a prostitute, quarreled with her boyfriend, and during a struggle which followed, a gasoline stove was overturned on the dry plank floor, starting the fire.

As the fire spread through the building, six shots were fired into the air. This was a prearranged signal among the residents that a major fire had broken out. A street side fire alarm was sounded as well as a whistle located at the power plant.

Before the first hose was laid, the wind spread the fire to the Union Dance Hall and Casey's Second Hand Store. After the firemen got a second hose in operation, it looked like the fire might be extinguished. Unfortunately the hose burst, and during the time it took to replace it, the fire spread beyond control. The firemen bravely manned their hoses until the walls of the false-front stores began falling into the street. Soon the fire leaped across Myers Avenue. It became abundantly clear to the merchants along Bennett Avenue that little could be done to stop the fire, and it would be best to load up wagons with their merchandise. When the post office went up in flames, 35,000 pieces of mail were destroyed.

A second front was staged along the masonry wall separating the oncoming lanes on Bennett Avenue. Hoses were manned in an effort to keep the fire from jumping the street. By this time, the air was superheated, creating a firestorm. The intense heat

The Gold Mining Stock Exchange and the First National Bank on Bennett Avenue were just a few of the financial institutions in the town during Cripple Creek's boom days. *(Denver Public Library X-877)*

forced the firemen to move. Prisoners held in the jail at City Hall were released just in time to keep from getting cooked alive.

As more hoses were added, the water pressure dropped to the point where none of the firemen could effectively fight the blaze. The water main from the reservoir to the hydrants was simply insufficient.

To create a firebreak, dynamite was used to blow up buildings in the path of the fire. In many instances, the dynamite accelerated the fire due to the amount of kindling created. In all, about twenty buildings were blown to bits in this futile, desperate attempt to bring this fire under control.

An estimated 5,000 people were left homeless. Using tents, some businesses were able to reopen. This included several brothels. Millionaire Winfield Scott Stratton formed a relief committee and sent two trainloads of food and building supplies from Colorado Springs to Cripple Creek. Saint Peter's Catholic Church in Cripple Creek opened its doors as a shelter for mothers and their small children.

As incredible as it seems, the Saturday fire was followed by a second major fire on Wednesday. One of the cooks at the Portland Hotel turned over a grease-filled kettle. The grease ignited on the hot stove sending flames up the stovepipe. The overheated stovepipe set the upper portion of the building on fire. The fire spread to the Palace Hotel where a boiler explosion amplified the damage. However, this was only a preliminary blast. When the fire reached one of the grocery stores, the building was blown into kindling. There had been 700 pounds of dynamite in stock. A bank, harness shop and ten saloons were quickly reduced to ashes. When the fire burned itself out, the majority of structures in the business district had been destroyed. In addition, many homes were gone.

The era of shacks and the predominance of wood frame businesses ended with the fires of 1896, giving the townspeople a chance to construct a more substantial Cripple Creek. Most of the buildings along Bennett Avenue were replaced by brick or stone structures. Many of these buildings survive to this day.

After the turn of the century, gold production began to decline and the rapid growth experienced during the 1890s came to a halt. In 1903, the Western Federation of Miners struck, idling 3,500 men. The consolidation of mining properties began after the strike ended. In addition, better mining methods requiring fewer men were used.

As the mines got deeper, water became a problem, and the cost of pumping became a significant portion of the cost of mining. The Roosevelt Tunnel, three-miles long, was drilled in 1911 to drain the mines and allow them to be taken to greater depths. Thirty years later, a second drainage tunnel was necessary. It was the six-mile long Carlton Tunnel. (see "Drainage Tunnels Save Cripple Creek Mines" in the introduction)

A mining boom, of sorts, occurred in 1934 when the price of gold was increased from $20 an ounce to $35 an ounce. After World War II, mining tapered off. Today, underground mining has been replaced by massive open pit mining. The operation is virtually removing all of the hills between Cripple Creek and Victor. The gulches are being filled with tailings.

Limited stakes gambling was approved by Colorado voters, and casinos began to operate in Black Hawk, Central City and Cripple Creek on October 1, 1991. Buildings once abandoned were again occupied, the town's empty streets once again filled and Cripple Creek was reborn. New casinos also appeared on once vacant lots.

The Crusher was Cripple Creek's first newspaper. The town was called Fremont at the time, and it became part of Cripple Creek when Fremont combined with Morland (Hayden Placer). Note the paperboy in the foreground. *(Denver Public Library X-862)*

Leland Feitz, *Cripple Creek! A Quick History*, Little London Press, Colorado Springs, Colorado, 1967, pp. 52, 57.

Leland Feitz, *Ghost Towns of the Cripple Creek District*, Little London Press, Colorado Springs, Colorado, 1974, pp. 9, 10-14, 16, 18.

Lester L. Williams, *Cripple Creek Conflagrations*, Filter Press, Palmer Lake, Colorado, 1994, p. 2.

Marshall Sprague, *Money Mountain*, Little, Brown and Company, Boston, 1953, pp. 18, 40-45.

Robert L. Brown, *Cripple Creek, Then and Now*, Sundance, Denver, 1991, pp. 83-87.

"The Story of the Day," *The Denver Republican*, April 30, 1896.

William H. Bauer, James L. Ozment and John H. Willard, *Colorado Post Offices*, Colorado Railroad Museum, Golden, Colorado 1990, p. 101.

DUTCHTOWN, HOLLYWOOD and MARIGOLD

- *Teller County, various drainages*
- *Sites accessible by graded dirt roads*
- *Unknown number of structures*

There were a number of small mining communities whose history is lost to time and to consolidation with other towns. Dutchtown was located two miles south of Victor. Hollywood, a suburb of Victor, is shown on historical maps as immediately to the east of the city limits.

Marigold, still shown on contemporary maps and with some seasonal residents, was a stop on the stage road between Victory and Canon City. It became a construction camp for the Carlton Tunnel, started in 1930 and completed in 1941. The tunnel undercut the major mines in the Cripple Creek District and provided drainage. Marigold's post office opened in 1895 and closed in 1902. (see "Drainage Tunnels Save Cripple Creek Mines" in the introduction.)

Leland Feitz, *Ghost Towns of the Cripple Creek District*, Little London Press, Colorado Springs, 1974, p. 47.

William H. Bauer, James L. Ozment and John H. Willard, *Colorado Post Offices*, Colorado Railroad Museum, Golden, Colorado, 1990, p. 95.

ELKTON
At the Head of Arequa Gulch

- *Teller County, Arequa Creek drainage*
- *Access to site restricted by private property*
- *Town had a post office; several structures remain*

L ike the majority of mining towns, Elkton was not a planned community. It grew up near the Elkton Mine at the head of Arequa Gulch. Elkton was served by the narrow gauge Florence & Cripple Creek, the standard gauge Midland Terminal, and the standard gauge Colorado Springs & Cripple Creek District electric line. The railroads passed through on various levels of track cut into the hillside.

The initial discovery of gold ore was made by William Shemwell, a blacksmith from Colorado Springs. He found the ore on the side of Raven Hill near the head of Arequa Gulch, and there the Elkton Mine developed. It became the second largest gold producer in the Cripple Creek district.

When Shemwell registered his claim, he needed to call it something. He remembered a pair of bleached antlers lying on the ground near his prospect hole. Thus the name Elkton was given to the property.

Shemwell had previously given up half interest in any claim he made to a pair of Colorado Springs grocers. Shemwell had received $36.50 in groceries in exchange for his half interest in a mine that would ultimately produce fifty million dollars in gold. The grocers, Sam and George Bernard, lost interest in selling goods to the public, as the output of the Elkton Mine shot up by astounding amounts. They bought Shemwell's share and hired noted local miner, Ed De LaVergne, to take over the Elkton's management.

The Bernards began to sell lots in Elkton, but never bothered to plat the town. The town did take on a rectangular street system. A great deal of the economic impetus for Elkton's survival came in 1899, with the construction of the Economic Mill.

The town got its own post office in 1895, which remained in operation until 1926. There were three grocery stores, a drug store, the Sheldon Hotel and four saloons. The town also had a church, public school, boarding house and a butcher shop.

About a mile away and above the town of Elkton, Richard Roelef, a mining engineer, was hired to look over the Cresson Mine on behalf of its Chicago owners. Roelef deepened the mine and removed vast amounts of low-grade ore from what had been a marginal property. All of this changed, however, on November 24, 1914. Roelef woke up Hildreth Frost, a respected lawyer, and mining expert Ed De LaVergne. The men were taken to the

The Elkton Mine buildings had an orderly appearance. The town of Elkton can be seen in the background and consisted of a variety of board and batten shacks. This photograph was taken on September 3, 1894. *(Denver Public Library X-8178)*

Cresson Mine and down to the twelfth level. Roelef led them into a vug, or natural cave, to witness an incredible find. Usually such caves are filled with beautiful crystals, but contain little in the way of valuable ore. This vug was different; its walls were covered with gold-bearing sylvanite crystals.

Small cavities were filled with fractured sylvanite which could be mined by simply scooping the material off the floor. So rich was this deposit that two steel doors were installed at the entrance to the cave, and armed guards stood duty around the clock. The highest-grade ore, scraped from the side of the cave, was placed directly in sacks and hauled to the surface. Ore of lesser value was screened, then placed in sacks. Third rate ore was still so rich it was shipped as regular ore. Some forty thousand dollars in gold ore was removed during the first week of mining. One single 150-ton shipment of ore brought in nearly half a million dollars. Nearly fifty million dollars in gold was removed from the Cresson Mine over the years.

Elkton's population grew to 200 by the turn of the century, and the town extended over four city blocks. The Economic Mill burned in 1908, and at the time, Elkton had 400 residents. During the next decade, its population dwindled to 150. In 1950, census records show only 6 residents. The town was abandoned by the 1960s, but its buildings still stood along what was once the main street.

Large-scale open pit mining began above Elkton, and by 1990, the Cripple Creek and Victor Gold Mining Company had fenced in the town site. For a while, there were still a few of Elkton's old buildings, but by 1998, none of the structures remained. As for the Cresson Mine, it is part of the large open pit mine and is still giving up its gold.

For a map showing Elkton's location, see "Arequa, Beacon Hill and Eclipse."

Bill Munn, *A Guide to the Mines of the Cripple Creek District*, Century One Press, Colorado Springs, Colorado, 1984, p. 26.

Brian H. Levine, *Cities of Gold,* Stonehenge Books Denver, 1981, pp. 68-70.

"Cave of Gold," *The Colorado Springs Gazette*, December 15, 1914.

John K. Aldrich, *Ghosts of Teller County*, Centennial Graphics, Lakewood, 1986, pp. 21-25.

Leland Feitz, *Ghost Towns of the Cripple Creek District*, Little London Press, Colorado Springs, 1974, pp. 24-25.

Marshall Sprague, *Money Mountain*, Little, Brown and Company, Boston, 1953, p. 301.

Robert G. Taylor, *Cripple Creek Mining District*, Filter Press, Palmer Lake, Colorado, 1973, pp. 63, 88, 133.

Robert L. Brown, *Ghost Towns of the Colorado Rockies*, Caxton Printers, Caldwell, Idaho, 1977, pp. 145-151.

William H. Bauer, James L. Ozment and John H. Willard, *Colorado Post Offices*, Colorado Railroad Museum, Golden, Colorado, 1990, p. 50.

GILLETT

And Its Bull Fight

- *Teller County, West Fork Beaver Creek drainage*
- *Accessible by paved road*
- *Town had a post office; several structures remain*

Gillett was a substantial town as evidenced by this photograph of its business district. None of these structures remain today. *(Denver Public Library X-8654)*

The Gillett town site, north of Cripple Creek in Beaver Park, is located along Colorado 67 and is typically the first site most visitors pass by coming from Woodland Park.

Gillett began with one log cabin belonging to rancher Jim Miller. Anticipating the arrival of the Midland Terminal Railway, the Beaver Park Land Company was formed and purchased the valley. A plat for a town was filed in 1894, and at that time the railroad line from Divide came through the valley on its way to

Cripple Creek. The new town was named Gillett for W. K. Gillett, a passenger agent for the Sante Fe Railroad. Apparently, Gillett raised the necessary money to build the Midland Terminal. Employment was dependent on several mills and the railroad. The largest combination mill and smelter was the El Paso Reduction Company, served by its own rail spur. (NOTE: Some sources indicate that Gillett was once called Cripple Creek City or Gateway City.)

In 1896, Gillett reached its peak of development. A January, 1897 issue of the Colorado Springs *Gazette* described the town as "...a very new, very raw, very Western town. The principal street (Parker) is at the crossing where the train stops. There are two rows of wooden buildings, mostly one story, stretching out eastward on either side of the street." Gillett reached a population of 1,200 to 1,800 and had its own railroad depot, as well as a substantial business district. This included twenty five saloons, five dance halls, a casino and the area's only racetrack. Incidentally, after the casino closed, the building was converted into the town's schoolhouse. The town's newspaper was called *The Gillett Forum.* Gillett also had the only bank outside of Victor and Cripple Creek.

Originally, this was the Monte Carlo Casino. After it went out of business, the building was converted into Gillett's No. 2 school. *(Denver Public Library X-8652)*

The Gillett post office opened in 1894, and except for an eight-month period, remained open until 1913. Looking at Gillett's nearly vacant town site today, it is hard to believe that most of its structures have vanished over the years.

During the summer of 1895, Joe Wolfe, a con man on the run from Oklahoma, arranged for a bullfight to be held in Gillett using the racetrack. He entered a partnership with another "operator" named Arizona Charlie Meadows. They formed a company with the name of Joe Wolfe Grand National Spanish Bullfight Company. The pair arranged to bring Mexican bulls, matadors and picadors in for the event.

What the promoters failed to take into consideration was the reaction of the Colorado Humane Society. The Society got an injunction to stop the bulls from entering the United States. Therefore, the bulls, along with the matadors and picadors, were held at the Texas border. As the dates for the bullfights approached, Wolfe and Meadows became desperate enough to purchase seven farm bulls from ranches in Phantom Canyon. These bulls weren't the least bit aggressive since they had not been bred to fight. The real bulls, however, arrived in time for the event.

The event was widely advertised, and on August 24, 1895, an estimated 50,000 people descended on Gillett either by the Midland Terminal Railway or wagon from the surrounding area.

Also arriving in Gillett was Colorado's most famous con man, Jefferson Randolf "Soapy" Smith. He traveled from Denver to "work the crowd." He did such a good job of fleecing the potential audience that a number of seats were not filled.

Those that could not afford to get into the racetrack sat on the nearby hills. Accounts of the event itself vary. Some witnesses reported that the bulls didn't put up much of a fight, but that several were killed. Another account says that protesters stopped the bullfight after the first animal was slaughtered. In any event, the planned three-day celebration was canceled, and the meat from the slaughtered animals (or animal) was distributed to the poor. Several historical sources claim that this was the only bullfight ever staged in the United States.

By the turn of the century, Gillett began to decline in size and importance. Better milling facilities at Colorado City (outside of Colorado Springs) forced the closure of Gillett's mill. Gambling and other forms of entertainment became available in Cripple Creek and Victor. By 1908, only thirty people remained in Gillett, but sixty structures were still standing. The valley was purchased for ranching in 1911, and all but a few of Gillett's structures were razed. The streets were plowed under, and the area was seeded for pasture.

The St. Dimas Chapel, with its rounded roof, stood abandoned in Gillett for many years. During the 1940s, ghost town historian Muriel Sibell Wolle visited the Gillett site and described the sad condition of the church by saying, "The interior was a depressing sight for everything had been removed. Broken plaster littered the ground and nothing but cattle had found shelter in it for years." Fire gutted the structure in 1952, and today, only the stone pillars, which once supported the roof, remain.

There is an occupied two-story home at the site with two other abandoned homes. The deteriorating remains of one of the commercial buildings sit along the highway. All of the land is private and posted limiting exploration of the town site.

Brian H. Levine, *Cities of Gold*, Stonehenge Books, Denver, 1981, p. 91.

Leland Feitz, *Ghost Towns of the Cripple Creek District*, Little London Press, Colorado Springs, Colorado, 1974, pp. 30-34.

Muriel Sibell Wolle, *Stampede to Timberline*, University of Colorado Press, Denver, Colorado, 1949, pp. 478-480.

Robert G. Taylor, *Cripple Creek Mining District*, Filter Press, Palmer Lake, Colorado, 1973, pp. 88, 102, 138.

Robert L. Brown, *Cripple Creek, Then and Now*, Sundance, Denver, 1991, pp. 55, 107.

The Gillett Forum, December 31, 1898.

William H. Bauer, James L. Ozment and John H. Willard, *Colorado Post Offices*, Colorado Railroad Museum, Golden, Colorado, 1990, p. 60.

Ghost town historian Muriel Sibell Wolle took this photograph of Gillett's St. Dimas Chapel long after it had been abandoned. Only the stone supports for its roof remain today. *(Denver Public Library X-3936)*

Sitting alone in a fenced field, the St. Dimas Chapel at Gillett is just about to crumble into history. *(Kenneth Jessen 111B4)*

GOLDFIELD
And Its Bull Pen

- *Teller County, North Fork Wilson Creek drainage*
- *Accessible by paved road; partially occupied town site*
- *Town had a post office; many original structures remain*

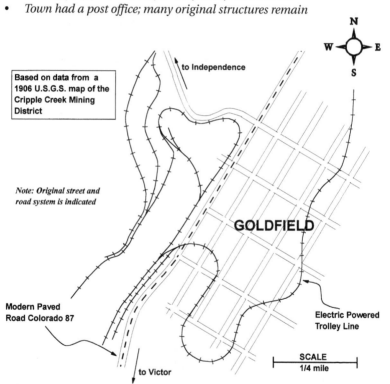

Only a small portion of the extensive railroad yards are shown on this map. In addition, to the southwest and northwest of Goldfield were numerous mines. An electric trolley car line ran right through the town and its grade is still visible today.

Portland mine owners James Doyle and James Burns founded Goldfield in 1895, as a company town for their miners and supervisors. The town was laid out in a large open meadow a short distance from Victor at an elevation of 9,903 feet. The Gold Knob Mining and Townsite Company sold lots in Goldfield. Due to its close proximity to the area's mines, the town quickly filled with homes.

Goldfield became known as the "City of Homes," a family town, as schools and churches were constructed. After a year from the date of its founding, Goldfield's population exceeded 2,000 making it the district's third largest town. Sidewalks were installed as new homes were built. A substantial business district formed along its main street. Goldfield got its own post office in 1895, which remained open until 1932. At that time, the population of the town could no longer justify a post office. Goldfield could also claim to have the longest continuously operating Sunday school in the Cripple Creek Mining District.

The town of Independence formed near the Independence Mine on the hillside above Goldfield. Eventually, the two towns grew together, and by the turn of the century, the combined

Goldfield, once the third largest town in the Cripple Creek Mining District, can be seen in the background behind the Eagle Sampler. *(Denver Public Library X-9754)*

population was around 3,500. This was only exceeded in size by the towns of Cripple Creek and Victor.

All three railroads serving the district ran through Goldfield. Below the town, in an open meadow, rail yards and freight storage facilities were constructed. An electric trolley line curved around the hillside and passed directly through Goldfield. An astounding 75% of all the ore mined in the district was shipped from the Goldfield-Independence area.

Very much like other towns in the district, Goldfield was a stronghold for members of the Western Federation of Miners. During the 1903-1904 conflict, the State Militia camped at Goldfield. At the end of the strike, the mine owners won, and some of Goldfield's union residents were deported.

In September, 1903, Governor Peabody sent the Adjutant General Sherman Bell to Cripple Creek to return law and order. Bell immediately built a "bull pen" in Goldfield to hold prisoners arrested during the war between the miners and the union. Within a few hours, a county commissioner and a judge were tossed into the heavily guarded bullpen. Heliograph stations were set up on the tops of the surrounding hills for direct communication between the various militia camps. Telescopes, manned by troops, scanned the county side for any act of violence. Bell also brought several Gatling guns and small field artillery pieces.

The "mouthpiece" for the Western Federation of Miners was the *Victor Daily Record.* A sizable force of soldiers, led by Major McClelland, arrested five newspaper employees, including the editor, during the late morning hours. All were taken to the Goldfield bullpen.

The wife of one of the Linotype operators and the business manager completed that day's edition. The newspaper was ready to be circulated by 3:00 a.m. the following morning, and its headline read, "SOMEWHAT DISFIGURED, BUT STILL IN THE RING." A copy was delivered to the bullpen much to the delight of the editor.

Robert Brown used his "then and now" technique in Goldfield to match a historic photograph with one of his own taken from the same spot along the main street. The historic photograph shows fifteen structures; today, only a store, home and the City Hall remain.

Goldfield is located just outside Victor and is serviced by a paved road. There are a number of homes dating back to the mining era, and many of the buildings are still occupied. The City Hall has been restored recently.

The Goldfield City Hall and Fire Station sat abandoned and deteriorating for decades. It is now in the process of being restored. *(Kenneth Jessen 111C12)*

Brian H. Levine, *Lowell Thomas' Victor*, Century One Press, Colorado Springs, Colorado, 1982, pp. 36-39.

Marshall Sprague, *Money Mountain*, Little, Brown and Company, Boston, 1953, p. 251.

Robert L. Brown, *Cripple Creek, Then and Now*, Sundance, Denver, 1991, p. 123.

Robert L. Brown, *Ghost Towns of the Colorado Rockies*, Caxton Printers, Caldwell, Idaho, 1977, pp. 184-188.

William H. Bauer, James L. Ozment and John H. Willard, *Colorado Post Offices*, Colorado Railroad Museum, Golden, Colorado, 1990, p. 63.

INDEPENDENCE
And Winfield Scott Stratton's Close Call

- *Teller County, North Fork of Wilson Creek*
- *Accessible via graded dirt road*
- *Town had a post office; several structures remain*

The Palace Hotel in Cripple Creek hosted the meeting between Winfield Scott Stratton and L. M. Pearlman. Stratton watched as Pearlman's option burned in the hotel's fireplace. This was Stratton's salvation and his first step toward becoming Cripple Creek's first millionaire. *(Denver Public Library X-820)*

Independence began as Hull City located adjacent to the Hull City Placer. It was a true mining town in every sense with some homes located near the Florence & Cripple Creek Railway, while other homes were dispersed among the mines. Photographic evidence shows that Hull City's original cabins were all of log construction. There were defined streets, however, and a small business district. Under the name Macon, a post office was

344

established in 1895. The Macon post office was changed to Independence in 1899, and it remained open until 1954.

Since Macon wasn't incorporated, it was absorbed into Goldfield, a mile to the south. When the Independence Town and Mining Company began to develop the Independence Mine, the company bought back twenty lots and the town of Independence was formed. Some of the commercial buildings were supported by stilts to make them level on the hillside. The exact location of Independence was farther up the hill from Hull City.

Along with the narrow gauge Florence & Cripple Creek Railroad, the Colorado Springs & Cripple Creek District electric rail line as well as the Midland Terminal Railway ran through Independence. Stimulated by the arrival of the railroads, Independence grew to a population of over one thousand.

Very little is left of this once great town today. A cluster of homes sits in a shallow gulch on the hillside overlooking the many mines in the area. The graded dirt road, which runs from Bull Hill to the American Eagle Mine, provides access to Independence.

Winfield Scott Stratton was the Cripple Creek area's first millionaire, and it was the Independence Mine that made him rich.

Some of the businesses in Independence were supported on stilts. This is the California Hotel, located along the town's main street. *(Denver Public Library X-9523)*

His story is one of extraordinary luck and good fortune. On July 4th, 1891, Stratton was prospecting on the side of Battle Mountain, which at the time, was free of other mining claims. Based on the geology of the area, he reasoned where rich ore could be found. As he searched for gold, Stratton could hear shots fired into the air as miners began their celebration of the 4th of July. That day, Stratton found what he wanted and staked out the Washington and Independence claims.

Stratton came from a humble background and was a carpenter by trade. He was grubstaked by Leslie Popejoy in Colorado Springs. When an assay came back from samples Stratton carried back to Colorado Springs, it showed gold content amounting to $380 per ton of ore from the Independence. This delighted Popejoy since the grubstake he provided Stratton amounted to less than $50.

When Stratton returned to Battle Mountain, he staked out two more claims which he called Professor Lamb and Black Diamond. Nearly broke, Stratton could not afford the development work required on each claim to hold title.

Stratton was forced to return to Popejoy for supplies and money. He took more samples from the Independence for analysis. This time, the results were poor at only $11.20 per ton, not worth the effort to mine. The total amount Popejoy had given

This is an early photograph of Stratton's modest home in Independence. Stratton made his fortune from the nearby Independence Mine. *(Denver Public Library X-548)*

Stratton was now $275. Stratton proved quite clever by offering Popejoy promissory notes amounting to $275 plus interest for Popejoy's half interest in the Independence. Since Popejoy believed the claim to be worthless, this was an easy sell. Popejoy reasoned that he would at least recover his investment and break-even.

This situation, however, forced Stratton to sell a lot he owned in Denver as well as his Colorado Springs home. This brought in $750, enough to pay off his debt to Popejoy and a little to live on.

KENNETH JESSEN

Winfield Scott Stratton, Cripple Creek's first millionaire. While working as a carpenter, Stratton spent time prospecting in the Cripple Creek area. He eventually struck it rich, and showed remarkable restraint by limiting his daily gold output to $2,000.

Stratton moved to Battle Mountain and erected a tent surrounded by a log fence. He tried to borrow money from his friends, but with no luck, offering half interest in all four claims for $500 in cash. In the meantime, none of the four claims produced any substantial assay value.

In October, 1891, Stratton struck a deal with Sam Altman for half interest in the Independence in exchange for doing the development work. After Altman spent $950 sinking a shaft during the following three months, he failed to strike any worthwhile ore and gave up. In the meantime, the demand for milled lumber in the Cripple Creek area had increased. Sam Altman established the town of Altman, a short distance from the Independence, and started a sawmill. This left Stratton with full ownership of the Independence.

In February, 1892, Stratton struck a rich vein of gold ore in the Washington and sold the claim to a mining company for

This is a recent photograph of the Vindicator Mine located immediately below Independence. Miners could walk from their homes to this and several other mines. *(Kenneth Jessen 097A9)*

$10,000 in cash and a $70,000 bond. The mining company, in turn, tried to raise money through the sale of stock. The vein of ore "pinched" out, and the company forfeited the bond. This put the title to the Washington back in the hands of Stratton.

Stratton continued to work alone to develop his claims and struck yet another rich vein of gold ore in the Washington. This time he sold his claim to a California company for $150,000. Stratton retained the right to continue mining until the claim was paid in full. During this thirty day time period, he shipped out $25,000 in gold ore. The investors backed out of the deal, and Stratton once again retained title.

After nearly two years, Stratton became discouraged with his results in the Independence Mine and secured a "sellers" assay. This inflated the value of the ore through manipulation of the assay. One day in 1893, Stratton found L. M. Pearlman waiting in his shack near the Independence. Pearlman represented a San Francisco mining syndicate, who initially wanted to buy the Washington. Stratton steered him toward an option on the

Independence and asked the ridiculous price of $155,000 for a mining property which had not proved to be worth a cent. Stratton did not like Pearlman and simply wanted to get rid of him. However, Pearlman wrote out a check for $5,000 for a thirty-day option with the $150,000 balance owed if the option was exercised. In today's money, this was equivalent to well over a million and a half-dollars.

Under the agreement, Stratton was required to remove his equipment immediately so that the syndicate could begin exploration work. The shaft was only eighty-five feet deep, and at its bottom, there were four exploratory crosscuts radiating out in different directions. Stratton went about removing his equipment from three of the four. He checked the fourth crosscut which he had abandoned. The debris had to be removed first, and Stratton crawled in to discover a rusty drill bit. He poked around and rock fell away from the outer edge of a thick vein of rich gold ore. Astounded, Stratton then made every effort to determine the vein's value. After he took a few samples, he replaced the debris to keep his discovery a secret. When the assay results came back, Stratton realized that if the option were exercised, he had given up three million dollars in gold ore, all within easy reach.

The lease expired on July 28, 1893, and Stratton had to sweat it out. He was forced to act disinterested around Pearlman as though the Independence was totally worthless.

On the night before the option was to expire, Stratton invited Pearlman out for dinner at The Palace in Cripple Creek. The hotel had a huge fireplace, and to take the chill off of the night air, there were always a few burning logs.

Stratton and Pearlman sat in the easy chairs near the fireplace after a full meal and talked about mining in the Cripple Creek District. To Stratton's relief, Pearlman revealed that his men had hardly found enough ore in the Independence to cover the cost of the option. Pearlman planned to have the abandoned fourth crosscut examined by his crew the following morning. On the other hand, he hated to spend another day's wages on a worthless mine. He related to Stratton that what he really wanted was to leave Cripple Creek in the morning and offered Stratton back his option.

Stratton trembled at the thought and, holding back his emotions, casually asked Pearlman to toss the option into the fire. As the two men watched the option burn, turn black and shrivel into ashes, Stratton privately rejoiced.

Stratton immediately set about developing the Independence and exercised a great deal of self-control by limiting his net to $2,000 a day (over $20,000 in today's money). This immense source of wealth came to a man who had spent most of his life

working as a carpenter for $3 a day. During the life of the Independence, it yielded twenty-six million dollars.

For a map showing the location of Independence, see "Midway."

There are quite a few abandoned structures within Independence. The town still had a few residents into the 1950s. *(Kenneth Jessen 097A11)*

Frank Waters, *Midas of the Rockies*, Covici Freide, New York, N. Y., 1937, pp. 124-129.

Don and Gene Griswold, *Colorado's Century of 'Cities,'* self-published, 1958, p. 293.

Leland Feitz, *Ghost Towns of the Cripple Creek District*, Little London Press, Colorado Springs, 1974, pp. 35-37.

Marshall Sprague, *Money Mountain*, Little, Brown and Company, Boston, 1953, pp. 121-124, 253-259, 301.

Muriel Sibell Wolle, *Stampede to Timberline*, Sage Books, Chicago, 1949, p. 475.

Robert L. Brown, *Cripple Creek, Then and Now*, Sundance, Denver, 1991, p. 125.

William H. Bauer, James L. Ozment and John H. Willard, *Colorado Post Offices*, Colorado Railroad Museum, Golden, Colorado, 1990, pp. 77, 92.

LAWRENCE

Older Than Victor

- *Teller County, Wilson Creek drainage*
- *Accessible via graded dirt road*
- *No standing structures remain*

Lawrence, founded by the Woods Investment Company, was located along Wilson Creek below present-day Victor. The building in the center foreground was the Lawrence House, and it advertised meals available at all hours. *(Denver Public Library X-12001)*

Lawrence was located immediately south of Victor on Wilson Creek at the base of Straub Mountain. The settlement predates Victor, and for a time, it acted as the commercial center for the southern end of the Cripple Creek Mining District.

About 300 people lived in Lawrence. The buildings themselves were primarily made of logs. The name Lawrence was taken from a ranch at the same site.

The Woods Investment Company started the town in 1892. A post office opened that same year and remained open until 1898, when it was combined with Victor's post office.

The large Lawrence Gold Extraction Mill was one of the area's first mills successful in processing the area's complex ore. As Victor began to grow into the region's second largest town, many of Lawrence's residents may have moved the short distance to Victor.

In 1974, there were a few original structures still standing in Lawrence, but today, there are none. To reach the site, head south on 2nd Street in Victor and follow this street down to Wilson Creek. Here, the road turns west and eventually comes to a dead end.

Abandoned home in Goldfield *(Kenneth Jessen 118D2)*

John K. Aldrich, *Ghosts of Teller County*, Centennial Graphics, Lakewood, 1986, p. 31.

Leland Feitz, *Ghost Towns of the Cripple Creek District*, Little London Press, Colorado Springs, 1974, pp. 38-39.

Muriel Sibell Wolle, *Stampede to Timberline*, Sage Books, Chicago, 1949, p. 466

William H. Bauer, James L. Ozment and John H. Willard, *Colorado Post Offices*, Colorado Railroad Museum, Golden, Colorado 1990, p. 88.

MIDWAY

And The Grand View Saloon

- *Teller County, Grassy Creek drainage*
- *Accessible by graded dirt road*
- *Town did not have a post office; several structures remain*

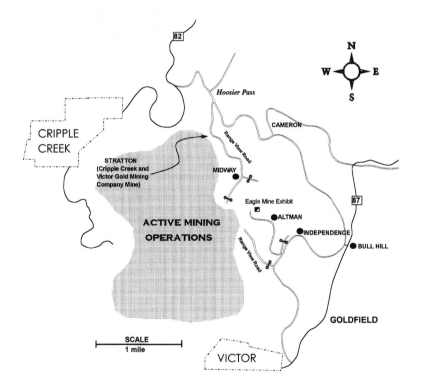

Midway is located south of Hoosier Pass on a graded dirt road. The road continues south of Midway, but has been blocked in recent years as open pit mining operations expand.

In 1942, Muriel Sibell Wolle took this photograph of the Grand View Saloon in Midway. The structure remains standing today, surrounded by a chain link fence. *(Denver Public Library X-3777)*

Midway was serviced by the Cripple Creek & Colorado Springs District Railway, which ran its electric trolley cars through town. Known as the High Line, it allowed its miners to commute to their jobs. The town of Midway was situated about halfway between Victor and Cripple Creek at an elevation of 10,487 feet.

Midway's most prominent structure was the two-story, false-front Grand View Saloon. It stood by itself for years, but weather and vandals began to take their toll. The wood which made up the front of the structure began to disappear. It remained one of the most photographed ghost town buildings in the area. To preserve it, a chain link fence has been erected around the structure. The fence makes it difficult to photograph.

Historic photographs show that Midway was never a large settlement and had less than twenty structures, including sheds associated with the railroad.

To reach Midway, drive south from Hoosier Pass to the Range View Road. Continue up this road past the Stratton site where the Cripple Creek & Victor Gold Mining Company has its

This is the Grand View Saloon today. The structure is deteriorating and soon will fall to the ground unless stabilized. *(Kenneth Jessen 111B8)*

offices and buildings. At Midway, there are about six or seven structures, some sitting below the town site in the trees. Most of the area is posted no trespassing.

Sandra Dallas, *Colorado Ghost Towns and Mining Camps*, University of Oklahoma Press, 1985, p. 135.

Leland Feitz, *Ghost Towns of the Cripple Creek District*, Little London Press, Colorado Springs, 1974, pp. 10-14, 18, 40.

Robert L. Brown, *Cripple Creek, Then and Now*, Sundance, Denver, 1991, pp. 106, 109.

STRATTON
And the Wine Glass Theory

- *Teller County, Grassy Creek drainage*
- *Accessible by graded dirt road*
- *Town did not have a post office; no structures remain*

The first settlement at the Stratton site was called Summit, located between Midway and Hoosier Pass. It was nothing more than an informal mining camp for the Deerhorn Mine. Summit became a company town in 1900, when Winfield Scott Stratton's mining company purchased the site and nearby mines. Previously, W. S. Stratton had sold his vast holdings in the Cripple Creek area for eleven million dollars. He used the proceeds to test what was referred to as the "Wine Glass" or "Bowl of Gold" theory. Presumably, deep within Cripple Creek's volcanic bowl, the veins of gold telluride converge much like the stem of a wineglass. The richest ore, according to the theory, would be found in the stem, and Summit was over that point. W. S. Stratton used his newly founded town, which he named Stratton, as his headquarters for the systematic exploration of the mineralization of the district. He passed away before his theory could be tested.

Neat red brick and white frame structures were built. The buildings included dormitories, a dining hall and mining company offices. Several of these structures were two stories high. With no business district, residents of Stratton used the electric trolley cars, operated by the Cripple Creek & Colorado Springs District Railway, to get to and from Cripple Creek or Victor for supplies.

In 1980, the buildings at Stratton were razed to make way for the Cripple Creek & Victor Gold Mining Company offices.

This company has open pit mining and heap leaching operations throughout the district. NOTE: Some sources refer to this site as Winfield.

For a map showing the location of Stratton, see "Midway."

KEN JESSEN

John K. Aldrich, *Ghosts of Teller County*, Centennial Graphics, Lakewood, 1986, pp. 33-34.

Leland Feitz, *Ghost Towns of the Cripple Creek District*, Little London Press, Colorado Springs, 1974, p. 45.

Leslie Doyle Spell and Hazel M. Spell, *Forgotten Men of Cripple Creek*, Big Mountain Press, Denver, 1959, p. 91.

Robert L. Brown, *Colorado Ghost Towns Past and Present*, Caxton Printers, Caldwell, Idaho, 1977, pp. 305-311. (Note that Robert L. Brown confuses Summit with Summit Park. The latter became Woodland Park.)

Robert L. Brown, *Cripple Creek, Then and Now*, Sundance, Denver, 1991, p. 107.

VICTOR
The City of Mines

- *Teller County, Wilson Creek drainage*
- *Accessible by paved road; occupied town*
- *Town has a post office; many original structures remain*

This overview of Victor predates the devastating fire of 1899. The Gold Coin Mine dominates the town's structures to the left center. Most of the structures in this photograph were destroyed by the fire. *(Denver Public Library X-571)*

Victor never quite became a ghost town although during its lean years, a significant portion of homes was abandoned. In addition, much of the town has been razed or destroyed by fire. With the advent of limited stakes gambling in 1991 in nearby Cripple Creek, Victor is undergoing a revitalization. People who work in the gaming industry have moved to Victor. The town is making strides in developing its tourist trade.

Frank and Harry Woods paid $1,000 in 1893 for a 136-acre

placer claim and laid out the town of Victor. They named the place for Victor Adams, one of the original homesteaders at Lawrence, an early community along Wilson Creek below Victor.

Since the town was built on a placer deposit, the Woods brothers spread the word that every lot was a gold mine. Certainly each lot had potential, and the lots sold well. The brothers decided that the growing town needed a first class hotel. While Frank Woods was grading the foundation, he struck a twenty-inch vein of rich gold ore on a claim called the Gold Coin. Frank purchased the claim and a shaft was sunk. Within a few months, the Gold Coin was bringing in a respectable $50,000 a month.

The Woods brothers had their fingers in just about every economic pie in the region. They not only owned a number of mines, but constructed large mills to process the ore. They founded a number of towns, built an amusement park east of Cripple Creek and were major real estate developers.

Although Victor was founded two years later than Cripple Creek, it soon grew almost as large. The two towns were not at all alike, however, as Cripple Creek became the business and entertainment center of the region. Victor became "The City of Mines" with the richest mining area, Battle Mountain, immediately above town.

The Woods brother's Gold Coin

The DeCaffery building in Victor is a reminder of more prosperous times. Note the brick and stone construction. *(Kenneth Jessen 097A6)*

Mine dominated Victor's business district, and on the edge of town was the head frame of the Strong Mine. The Independence was a short distance away on Battle Mountain, and towering over Victor were the Portland and Ajax mines.

Victor had a rough and tumble appearance, with mine structures, shacks, homes, head frames and false-front stores all intermingled. Railroad tracks cut through town at odd angles, and a trolley car line ran down its main street. The streets were dirt and the business district was serviced by wooden boardwalks. Only two or three bathtubs existed since water was scarce. Water sold for five cents a bucket from a horse drawn tank wagon. However, these primitive conditions failed to keep Victor from growing to nearly 8,000 by 1896.

In August, 1899, Victor suffered a disastrous fire. It started in a shack behind the 999 Dance Hall and destroyed 200 buildings leaving 3,000 people homeless. The firemen were hopelessly understaffed and lacked sufficient fire-fighting equipment. Also, there wasn't enough water to put out the blaze.

By noon the next day, Victor started to rebuild. The post

After its 1899 fire and reconstruction using brick and stone, Victor was ready for the next century. The new brick Gold Coin Mine shaft house, an elaborate structure with unique stained glass windows, dominates the business district. *(Denver Public Library X-577)*

office was back in business. By nightfall, several saloons and restaurants were open using tents. The fire destroyed the surface structures of the Gold Coin Mine in the town center. It also consumed the elegant Gold Coin Club, built by the Woods brothers for the entertainment of Victor's residents.

The hoist house for the Gold Coin was soon rebuilt of brick. Sporting stained glass windows, it was the most elaborate mining structure of its type in the West. A bath and lockers were included for the miners along with a reading room complete with tables, the latest periodicals and the best books. No money was spared rebuilding the Gold Coin Club either, also constructed of more durable brick. The new building contained a gymnasium, bowling alleys, ballroom, indoor pool, and game room. For the intellectual, it also had a 700-volume library. After the mining boom was over, the Gold Coin Club became a hospital, then a private home.

Victor was served by three railroads. The first one to arrive was the narrow gauge Florence & Cripple Creek from the south. It came into town in 1894, followed by the Midland Terminal. At the turn of the century, the Colorado Springs & Cripple Creek District Railway arrived.

The most famous resident of Victor was news correspondent Lowell Thomas. Lowell was born in 1892 in Iowa to Dr. and Mrs. Harry Thomas, and the family moved to Victor in 1900. After graduating from the Victor High School, Lowell went to college and returned to Victor to become editor of the *Victor Daily Record*. In 1912, Lowell became editor of the *Victor News* with an increase in pay. His big break came when he was hired as a reporter for the *Chicago Evening Journal*.

Lowell began his broadcasting career in 1925, and it lasted for more than four decades. In 1940, he also became the first television news broadcaster. Involved with Cinerama, the first widescreen movie system, Lowell also narrated the Fox-Movietone News shown before every movie. In 1976, President Gerald Ford presented Lowell Thomas with the Medal of Freedom, the country's highest honor for a civilian.

Today, there are a number of attractive frame homes in Victor, making a drive around town worthwhile. *(Kenneth Jessen 111C11)*

Leland Feitz, *A Quick History of Victor*, Little London Press, Colorado Springs, Colorado, 1969, pp. 5-18.

Marshall Sprague, *Money Mountain*, Little, Brown and Company, Boston, 1953, p. 165.

Muriel Sibell Wolle, *Stampede to Timberline*, Sage Books, Chicago, 1949, pp. 466-469.

Brian H. Levine, *Lowell Thomas' Victor*, Century One Press, Colorado Springs, Colorado, 1982, pp. 92-99.

WEST CREEK

And Confusion With Pemberton

- *Douglas County, West Creek drainage*
- *Accessible via graded dirt road*
- *Town had a post office; several structures remain*

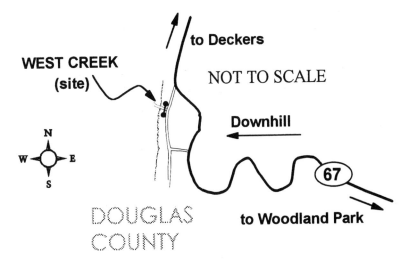

West Creek is located west of Colorado 67 and north of Woodland Park.

West Creek (also spelled Westcreek) is a very ghostly place. At the site are four abandoned shacks, with a fifth shack off in the trees. These buildings sit on private property, behind a fence. This may be why West Creek is so well preserved. A dirt road runs by the buildings and off into the forest. But looks are deceptive; these buildings could be nothing more than abandoned sportsman's cabins built well after the short-lived mining boom in the area.

In August, 1895, Captain George Tyler sent his son to Denver with samples of what appeared to be promising gold ore. The Captain had found the samples on his ranch. A mining company was formed, although the samples were not rich in gold or silver. Everyone in the area knew of the millionaires who struck it rich to the south in Cripple Creek.

In 1896, 500 square miles of public land was opened to prospecting. It was hoped that the gold-rich volcanic formation at Cripple Creek surfaced near West Creek.

As prospectors came into the area, a number of small camps were formed including West Creek, Tyler, Pemberton, North West Creek, North Cripple Creek, Ackerman, Trumbull and Griven. By 1897, prospectors were arriving from Deckers and from Palmer Lake. Estimates vary, but sources say that 5,000 prospectors once occupied the area.

A somewhat socialistic approach was taken in finding ore in this region. Each man had to do so many days of work on a given claim, but he was not given title, even if all of the development work was completed. Others did the same thing. If any one struck it rich, the claim would be divided evenly among those agreeing to this plan.

The first wagon load of ore was shipped to a smelter in 1896. Assay results must have been encouraging since it was decided to tunnel 500 feet into the mountain on the most promising claim. The miners became "subscribers" and received three shares of stock for each shift they worked. Again, the general idea was to share the wealth.

Samples of ore from a mine near Pemberton showed beads of gold on the quartz after the sample was roasted. Unfortunately, the deposits were not rich, and no mining development took place. A small fortune was made by two ladies, however, who baked bread for the hungry prospectors.

Pemberton, the largest town in the West Creek area, was

located at the bottom of the hill along the road from Woodland
Park. It had forty structures and even telephone and telegraph
service. Since Pemberton sat along West Creek, the name of the
town was changed to the name of the creek. There was another
town to the south called West Creek. By the time the name
change occurred, the original West Creek was abandoned.

This situation led to an interesting incident when Muriel
Sibell Wolle, ghost town historian and author of *Stampede to
Timberline*, was doing her fieldwork at Pemberton during the
1940s. After sketching one of its old structures, she was told about
a less traveled road to Florissant. (Today, this road is FR200 and
goes up Trail Creek.) After she drove a mile from West Creek, she
came to a fork in the road with highway signs. One sign pointed
the way to Florissant, but the other pointed to West Creek. The
direction was opposite from where she had just been. Puzzled,
she wondered how she could reach West Creek by driving away
from the town. She continued, however, and reached a deserted,
false-front store in the middle of a field. She found an occupied

This could be the ghost town of West Creek (also spelled Westcreek) dating back to
1895. But looks are deceptive; these abandoned structures could also be nothing more
than sportsman's cabins constructed after the mining boom. *(Kenneth Jessen 111B2)*

cabin and knocked on the door. The lady who answered explained that the building was an old hardware store and that it was all that remained of the original town of West Creek. Mrs. Wolle firmly stated that she had just driven from West Creek. The lady explained that that was Pemberton, but it was now called West Creek. Since the original town of West Creek was deserted, no objections were raised to the name change or the resulting confusion.

West Creek got its own post office under the Pemberton name in 1896, and in 1902, the name became "Westcreek." The post office remained open until 1919. It was established again in 1935 and remained open until 1968.

To reach West Creek (Pemberton), drive north from Woodland Park on Colorado 67 through a beautiful forest broken occasionally by vast meadows. A bike trail follows Colorado 67 for about seven and a half miles to Manitou Park Lake. Another five miles or so beyond the lake, the road makes its descent into the West Creek drainage. The abandoned town is a short distance west of Colorado 67 on a graded dirt road. Modern homes occupy part of the site.

Muriel Sibell Wolle, Timberline Tailings, Sage Books, Chicago, 1977, pp. 96-97.

Muriel Sibell Wolle, Stampede to Timberline, Sage Books, Chicago, 1949, pp. 480-482.

Robert L. Brown, Jeep Trails to Colorado Ghost Towns, Caxton Printers, Caldwell, Idaho, 1973, pp. 223-225.

William H. Bauer, James L. Ozment and John H. Willard, Colorado Post Offices, Colorado Railroad Museum, Golden, Colorado 1990, p. 112, p. 150.

AREA ELEVEN

Chaffee County

continued

AREA 11: Chaffee County
Selected Towns

Introduction to Chaffee County

Exploration by white men in this region began in 1859 with prospectors searching for gold in the gravel deposits along the Arkansas River. From that point on up until 1867, nearly six million dollars in gold was removed from the area north of Salida up to Leadville, with most of it coming from California Gulch. At the time, what is now Chaffee County was included in Lake County. Aside from California Gulch, the richest deposits were near Granite, while smaller gold deposits were found along the banks of the Arkansas River and other watercourses. As is always the case, the placer deposits were quickly depleted, and the miners turned toward lode or underground mining. The richest ore was found near St. Elmo, Monarch Pass, Turret and along Clear Creek west of Granite. The mines supported a number of small towns. When the ore was depleted, most of them were abandoned.

Other mineral deposits also contributed to Chaffee County's early economy. Iron ore was mined at Calumet by Colorado Fuel & Iron for their blast furnaces at Pueblo. Granite was quarried north of Salida, and a large limestone quarry was developed below Monarch Pass.

Agriculture initially supported mining. Farms and ranches began to dot the bottomland along the Arkansas River during the 1860s and 1870s. Cattle ranching was common. Crops, such as potatoes, turnips and even lettuce, were sold to stores in the mining towns. Raising hay and oats for the many draft animals was also a major agriculture activity.

A logging industry flourished on both sides of the Arkansas River to supply the mines with timbers and for the construction of the buildings in the mining towns. Timber was also cut and converted to charcoal.

Today, Chaffee County has a varied economy with tourism dominating much of the activity.

The Lake County War

Violence in rural Colorado was relatively rare during the 1800s. This makes the Lake County War not only significant but an unusual event in Colorado history. It was less of a war and more of a case of lawlessness carried to the extreme by vigilantes. It certainly gave the area a bad reputation. Some historians have gone so far as to speculate that Chaffee County was split from Lake County in 1879 as a direct result of the war.

The Lake County War began as a feud in July, 1874 between George Harrington, an area rancher, and his neighbor, Elijah Gibbs. Harrington tried to put out an arson-caused fire in his small grocery store located behind his home. While throwing water on the fire, he was shot in the back and died instantly.

It was likely that Harrington was gunned down by Elijah Gibbs. The two men had argued previously over water rights in a ditch they held jointly. Gibbs needed more water for his cattle and claimed that during the argument, Harrington had tried to hit him with a shovel. Gibbs fired his gun presumably at Harrington but missed. He later claimed it discharged accidentally.

Following Harrington's assassination, Gibbs was arrested on circumstantial evidence. The local sheriff believed Gibbs would be lynched before the trial, and therefore, the case received a change of venue to Denver. Gibbs was acquitted, probably because of lack of evidence. After the trial, Gibbs returned to his ranch, but was unable to live a peaceful life.

During this period, mill owner Charles Nachtrieb and others formed a vigilante group called the "Committee of Safety." Their sole purpose was to run Gibbs, his family and friends out of the area. No one remotely connected with Gibbs was safe.

In January, 1875, a mob of at least fifteen vigilantes attacked the home of Elijah Gibbs, located near Gas Creek at Lands Hill. (This location is approximately halfway between Salida and Buena Vista near Centerville.) At the time, Elijah's pregnant wife Mary and three small children were home. Also in the cabin were a neighbor woman and her child.

The heavily armed vigilantes called out to Gibbs to leave his cabin. When there was no response, brush was piled around the windowless north wall and set on fire. There wasn't any regard for the innocent women and children inside, but fortunately, the fire had little effect. Next, wood and hay were piled up at the front door. When one of the vigilantes, Samuel Boon, tried to light the material, Gibbs fired and hit Boon in the right breast.

The vigilantes rushed the cabin as Gibbs began firing his revolver, trying to defend himself and his family. The bullets found their mark and two men fell hit in the legs. One of them

This was the town of Granite in about 1875 when Judge Dyer was shot to death while sitting in his office in the Lake County Courthouse. It culminated a long reign of terror by vigilantes known as the Lake County War. *(Denver Public Library, Western History Department X-8753)*

was holding a loaded, cocked shotgun, which discharged as he fell. The blast mortally wounded Dave Boon, brother of Samuel.

Gibbs had the advantage of being able to fire through narrow chinks in the logs. The moon reflected on the snow providing Gibbs with good visibility. He also wounded vigilante Finley Kane.

The vigilantes were outgunned and retreated. Gibbs ran for help down Gas Creek to his father's home. In the meantime, the vigilantes returned and picked up their three wounded men. David Boon died the following day. The day after David died, Samuel passed away. Finley Kane passed away on January 22.

Upon hearing that he had killed two men outright and caused the death of a third man, Gibbs turned himself in to local authorities at Browns Creek. He pleaded self-defense and was promptly released.

He and his immediate family, brother and father-in-law decided to escape and rode out of the area, only to find that the vigilantes had blocked all of the roads. They were stopped by a gang of men including the local sheriff. Somehow, the Gibbs family escaped to Colorado Springs and then to Denver, all the time followed by the sheriff. Denver police placed Gibbs in protective custody, and he was never seen again.

With the Gibbs family out of the way, the Committee of Safety began a reign of terror by rounding up sympathizers. Many were pulled up by the neck using a hangman's noose to near suffocation. Upon being released, these individuals were given thirty days to leave the area. Using these terror tactics, the vigilantes managed to drive off about forty settlers.

That spring, Charles Harding was brave enough to speak out against the vigilantes. His body was discovered on April 2, 1875, lying on a road east of the Arkansas River not far from vigilante member William Bale's home. He had been shot three times.

The most grievous assassination was that of Judge Elias Dyer, son of the beloved itinerant preacher, Father John Dyer. The vigilantes gave Judge Dyer three days to resign and move out of the area. To that, Dyer issued arrest warrants for twenty-eight vigilantes, commanding them to appear in his Granite courtroom.

The vigilantes showed up at court on July 3, 1875, and were heavily armed. Although they were asked to surrender their arms, Judge Dyer adjourned the court for safety reasons until the following morning. While sitting at his desk in the courthouse, Judge Dyer was fatally shot in the head. The round was delivered at such close range that powder burns were left around the bullet hole behind his ear. A second round went through Dyer's wrist. That very morning, Judge Dyer had written his father a wonderful letter relating, among other things, how proud he was to be the son of Father Dyer. Buried at Castle Rock, his tombstone includes the inscription, "I died for law, order, and principle."

A great deal of testimony was taken from various witnesses who were in the general area at the time of the shooting. James Woodward got a good look at one man holding a gun on the platform just outside the office of Judge Dyer. Woodward refused to testify for fear of his life. Later, Woodward was shot to death while riding on his ranch.

Law and order was eventually restored to the area, but no one was convicted of Judge Dyer's murder or any other victim of the Lake County War.

Chaffee County Formed

The rapid growth of Leadville during 1878 precipitated a change in the size of Lake County. Lake County included what is now Chaffee County. The county seat was Granite, which was inconvenient for Leadville residents. The population in the Leadville area alone exceeded that of the rest of the county. On February 8, 1879, the Colorado State Legislature carved Lake County from Carbonate County. Carbonate County was on the north end and included Leadville. The dividing line was just north of Granite. A couple of days later, the Legislature changed its mind and named Carbonate County Lake County. The southern portion was then named Chaffee County.

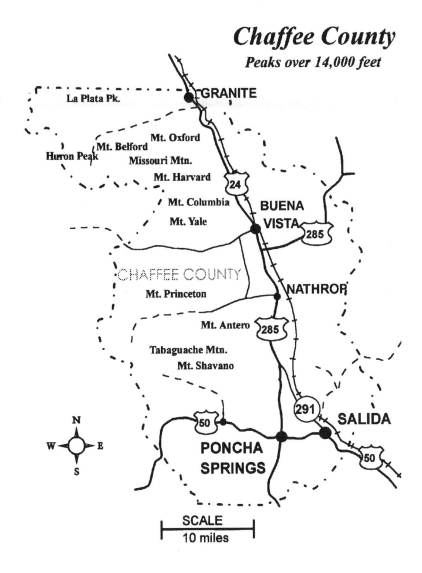

Chaffee County
Peaks over 14,000 feet

County Line Dispute

It is rare indeed when one county would capture a portion of another county. It happened as election hopes ran high for Fremont County Clerk Joseph Milson. He saw a way to capture a large portion of Chaffee County legally and end up a hero. Within the target area were a number of mining camps including Whitehorn. Milson reasoned that he would be elected if he could place these towns on Fremont County's tax rolls.

Since mining in Whitehorn was closely linked to Turret to the west and Salida to the south, residents were notably upset over these developments. Little could they do since a valid survey had been made in 1883, clearly placing Whitehorn in Fremont County. It simply had not been acted upon.

The case landed in the courts in 1899 and was settled in favor of Fremont County. Ironically, Whitehorn and the other camps faded away and became ghost towns soon after.

A History of Chaffee County, edited by June Shaputis and Suzanne Kelly, Buena Vista Heritage, Buena Vista, Colorado, 1982, pp. 14-15.

History of the Arkansas Valley, Colorado, O. L. Baskin & Co., Chicago, Illinois, 1881, p. 477.

June Shaputis, *Where The Bodies Are*, Arkansas Valley Publishing Company, Salida, Colorado, 1995, pp. 11-12.

Rev. John L. Dyer, *The Snow-Shoe Itinerant*, Cranston & Stowe, 1899, pp. 285-321.

ALPINE
Didn't Last Long

- *Chaffee County, Chalk Creek drainage*
- *Accessible by paved road; town had a post office*
- *Occupied site; no original structures remain*

Alpine's main street in 1881. The Badger Hotel, on the right, was named for the Badger State of Wisconsin by its owners. None of the structures shown here remain today. *(Denver Public Library, Western History Department X-6504)*

Alpine was one of the many short-lived camps in the Colorado mountains. The first cabin was constructed at the site in 1877 where Baldwin Creek enters Chalk Creek. It was Col. Chapman that stimulated the town's development with the construction of a smelter. In 1879, Alpine was incorporated, and Chapman became its first mayor. By 1882, the town had about 500 residents, but the town's boom years ended suddenly. At this time and farther up Chalk Creek, the Mary Murphy Mine above Romley was developed. Smelters were constructed at St. Elmo, and a smelter was built at Romley near the lower station of the tram from the mine. The smelter at Alpine was relegated to processing small amounts of ore from local mines. St. Elmo, located below Romley, became the area's residential and commercial center. With their prospects dim, many Alpine residents packed up and moved upstream.

The ore supplied to the smelter at Alpine was insufficient to allow economical operation and it soon closed. The Foster Smelting Company purchased the smelter and rebuilt it in 1880 as

A group of men can be seen standing on a raised wooden platform at the combination depot and freight room at Alpine. Empty sacks used for ore are piled on the platform. Alpine was a small mining community located along Chalk Creek and serviced by the narrow gauge Denver, South Park & Pacific Railway. *(Denver Public Library, Western History Department X-6506)*

a sampling works. It ran for many years and employed forty men. Long after the buildings were gone, its smokestack still stood.

In 1881, the narrow gauge Denver, South Park & Pacific Railroad completed its main line up Chalk Creek Canyon through the Alpine Tunnel to Gunnison. A small, attractive depot was constructed at Alpine. The depot included a freight room and living quarters for the agent. In addition, Alpine had a water tank and siding. For some reason, the railroad changed the name of its depot to Fisher in 1899, and the post office followed suit. It only remained open until the following year.

Aside from several stores and a liquor store, Alpine had two hotels, The Badger Hotel and The Arcade. The Badger Hotel was named for the Badger State of Wisconsin, the home state of its owners Captain Ford and John T. Swain. Alpine also had twenty-three saloons and a two-story dance hall. Eventually, a school was constructed, but Alpine lacked a church.

By 1937, all that was left of Alpine was the brick smokestack and the remains of two log cabins. In 1950, ghost town historian Muriel Sibell Wolle took a photograph of Alpine's main street showing a single cabin. Only the smokestack for the smelter remained in 1977 when she returned.

The town site eventually ended up in the hands of one owner, Bird Fugua, who was purchasing land in the area. As the road up Chalk Creek Canyon was improved, transients took refuge in the one remaining cabin. Preservation was hopeless, and the cabin, plus the remains of other structures, were razed. Modern homes now occupy the site.

Mac Poor, *Denver South Park & Pacific*, Rocky Mountain Railroad Club, Denver, 1976, p. 429.

Robert L. Brown, *Ghost Towns of the Colorado Rockies*, Caxton Printers, Caldwell, Idaho, 1977, pp. 36-38.

History of the Arkansas Valley, Colorado, O. L. Baskin & Co., Chicago, Illinois, 1881, pp. 494-495.

Virginia McConnell Simmons, *The Upper Arkansas*, Pruett Publishing Company, Boulder, Colorado, 1990, pp. 117-119.

William H. Bauer, James L. Ozment and John H. Willard, *Colorado Post Offices*, Colorado Railroad Museum, Golden, Colorado 1990, p. 54.

Muriel Sibell Wolle, *Stampede to Timberline*, Sage Books, Chicago, 1949, pp. 149-150.

ARBOURVILLE

And Frank Gimlett

- Chaffee County, South Arkansas River drainage
- Accessible by paved road; town had a post office
- Several structures at site, vintage unknown

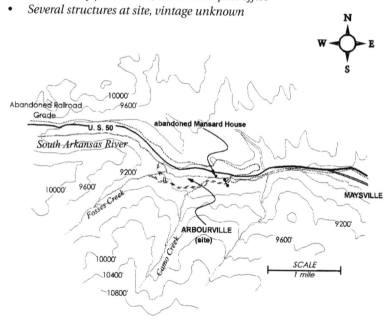

Arbourville's location is approximately four miles above Maysville. Some historians, however, disagree. Robert L. Brown placed Arbourville well above Garfield close to Monarch many miles west of Maysville. Brown based this on a historic photograph and the alignment of the mountains in the background.

Arbourville (also spelled Arboursville, Arborville and Arbour-Villa) would have been just another small mining camp in the Colorado Rockies if it hadn't been for its one notable residents, Frank Gimlett.

Arbourville was a small mining camp located approximately four miles upstream (west) of Maysville along the South Arkansas River. It was started in 1879 by Pap Arbour who planned to establish the town as a stage coach stop along the new Monarch Pass Toll Road. Construction on the toll road proceeded so slowly that Pap opened a parlor house and dance hall. (Parlor house was often used as a polite term for a brothel.) There was also a small smelter at the site to treat ore from area mines. Arbourville's population probably never exceeded 150.

The same year as the town was founded, a post office opened, and two years later its name was changed to Conrow. The post office was closed in 1882 as the town's population fell. It is not clear why the name of its post office was changed to Conrow, but the town itself remained known as Arbourville.

As Arbourville was abandoned, Pap Arbour's dance hall was

A small false-front office building in Arbourville. The photograph was taken by renowned pioneer photographer William Henry Jackson during the 1880s. *(Denver Public Library, Western History Department X-6673)*

moved log by log to Salida and erected on a vacant lot on West First Street. A grand reception was held to mark the opening of this establishment in its new location.

Arbourville did not have a church, and the Congregational minister from Maysville made regular visits. The town did, however, have its own school.

By the 1940s, Arbourville was a ghost town except for its lone hermit, Frank Gimlett. He was a miner with literary aspirations who wrote and published a number of booklets. Although Gimlett rambled from one subject to the next, his caustic criticisms of U. S. Government policy were quite clear. In his *Over Trails of Yesterday*, subtitled "Stories of Colorful Characters that Lived, Labored, Loved, Fought and Died in the Gold and Silver West," Gimlett refers to himself as the Hermit of Arbor Villa. After a trip to Washington DC, Gimlett reported to his readers that it was, "...the Mecca for racketeers, work evaders and time killers."

The exact location of Arbourville has been in question. When Muriel Sibell Wolle was working on her book, *Stampede to Timberline*, she quoted a letter stating that it was located four miles above Maysville. This agrees with the location given in the 1881 book, *History of the Arkansas Valley*. Perry Eberhart followed suit in his *Guide to the Colorado Ghost Towns*. When Robert L. Brown was putting together his

This abandoned Mansard house sits just below U.S. 50 and four miles above Maysville. It overlooks the Arbourville site. Although in dispute, this location is where most historians place Arbourville. *(Kenneth Jessen 100A3)*

Colorado Ghost Towns, Past and Present, he used a format where a contemporary photograph was taken at exactly the same site as a historic photograph. When it came time to photograph Arbourville, he discovered that the physical features of the surrounding mountains would not line up properly until he was well above Garfield and nearly to Monarch. This was many miles from where other accounts placed Arbourville. Was Brown wrong or were the earlier accounts of the town's location incorrect? The map in this section places Arbourville below Garfield where Fosses Creek and Como Creek enter the South Arkansas River. An abandoned Mansard style house, with concrete walls, sits above the site. Further investigation is limited since the site is fenced and posted no trespassing.

This is the Hermit of Arbourville, Frank Gimlett. He had literary aspirations and wrote a number of booklets which he sold to tourists for a quarter each. He used the booklets for his caustic criticisms of the United States Government.

Virginia McConnell Simmons, *The Upper Arkansas*, Pruett Publishing Company, Boulder, Colorado, 1990, p. 131.

History of the Arkansas Valley, Colorado, O. L. Baskin & Co., Chicago, Illinois, 1881, p. 499.

William H. Bauer, James L. Ozment and John H. Willard, *Colorado Post Offices*, Colorado Railroad Museum, Golden, Colorado 1990, pp. 13, 37.

George A. Crofutt, *Crofutt's Grip-Sack Guide of Colorado*, 1885 Edition, Johnson Books, Boulder, Colorado, reprint 1981, p. 68.

BEAVER CITY, VICKSBURG, WINFIELD

And other Clear Creek Towns

- *Chaffee County, Clear Creek drainage*
- *Accessible by graded dirt road; some towns had a post office*
- *Original structures remain at some sites; all on private property*

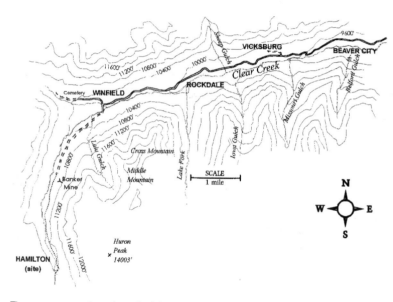

There were a number of small mining camps along Clear Creek west of Granite. Today, Beaver City, Vicksburg, Rockdale and Winfield are seasonally occupied and are serviced by a graded dirt road.

Although a mining district was founded during the 1860s, mining activity in Clear Creek didn't begin until 1880. Up to this time, the only significant activity was ranching. As silver ore was discovered, the new mining camps of Beaver City, Vicksburg, Silverdale, Rockdale and Winfield were established.

Closest to the mouth of the Clear Creek Canyon was Beaver City where prospectors constructed twenty cabins. The first cabin was built by Cooley and Babcock. They were quite friendly and offered a free reading room to their fellow prospectors. Beaver City never quite got enough population to merit a post office, and today, there are two cabins at the site.

Vick Keller founded Vicksburg, about two miles farther up Clear Creek. The small camp got its own post office in 1881 under the spelling, "Vicksburgh." Just four years later, the post office closed.

An ad in an 1881 issue of the *Chaffee County Times* lists two billiard parlors at Vicksburg. One was called Peck's Palace, where

Winfield did not grow to sufficient size to merit a post office until 1881. Lots were simply given away to anyone who wanted to build a cabin or a commercial building. This is the old schoolhouse, now serving as the town's museum. *(Kenneth Jessen 095B1)*

wine and liquor could be purchased, and the other was Ben Pelton's establishment. Every morning, a stagecoach left Granite for Vicksburg. By 1882, Vicksburg had grown to forty buildings, including two billiard halls, a couple of saloons, two hotels, boarding house, assay office, livery stable, blacksmith shop, and a school. By 1885, population estimates for Vicksburg varied from 150 to 600, depending on the source.

The most striking feature of Vicksburg, unique among Colorado mining towns, is its neat line of Balm of Gilead trees along the main street. The trees were paid for by town residents who wanted some shade. Also unique are the two irrigation ditches which parallel either side of Vicksburg's shaded main street. A majority of Vicksburg's log cabins have been restored for seasonal use.

Located two miles west (upstream) of Vicksburg is the old mining town of Rockdale. Another town called Silverdale was founded by a mining company in 1881 on a 136-acre site next to Rockdale. Silverdale was to have been a company town with a post office, boarding house, assay office, store and an office for the mining company. Contracts were let for the construction of a large mill that apparently was never completed, and the plans for the company town fell through. A post office opened in January, 1882, but closed just four months later.

The area around Rockdale is surrounded by high peaks such as Huron at 14,003 feet, Browns at 13,523 feet, Iowa at 13,831 feet, Missouri at 14,067 feet and Belford at 14,196 feet. To the north, hundreds of mining claims were made on Mount Hope, 13,933 feet, in hopes of striking it rich.

There are several log structures at Rockdale used as summer homes. Although these structures could easily pass for vintage mining cabins, they may have been built after the original town was abandoned. When she was writing *Stampede to Timberline*, Muriel Sibell Wolle visited the various sites along Clear Creek during the 1940s. She clearly states that, "No sign was left of Beaver City, nor of Silverdale, nor Rockdale..."

Winfield, founded on silver mining, did not grow to sufficient size to merit a post office until 1881. As with many other mining towns, Winfield had several other names. Apparently it was once called Florence or Lucknow. The town site was laid out this same year on 120 acres and was divided into 50-foot by 100-foot lots. These lots were simply given away to anyone who wanted to build a cabin or commercial building. The town peaked in 1890 and had three saloons, three stores, two hotels, a boarding house, a mill and smelter, a church and a school. The schoolhouse is still standing and serves as a small museum.

When the United States abandoned the silver standard in 1893, most silver mining activity in Colorado came to a halt. Winfield was likely abandoned at this time. The last ore to be hauled out of the upper Clear Creek area was in 1918, six years after the Winfield post office had closed.

There are about a half dozen structures at Winfield and some date back to the mining era. There are also several private homes at the site of more recent vintage.

Shown on topographic maps

Vicksburg was founded by Vick Keller, and this small mining camp got its own post office in 1881. At one time, there were forty structures in the town. Its most unique feature among Colorado mining towns is the neat line of trees along the main street. *(Kenneth Jessen 095A9)*

is yet another town at the head of Clear Creek south of Winfield. This was Hamilton, a mining camp for the Hamilton Mining and Tunnel Company. Although only a meadow marks the location of the camp today, there were once four or five log cabins.

This photograph by Muriel Sibell Wolle was probably taken during the late 1940s and shows one of the log cabins at Vicksburg. This particular cabin still stands and sits off by itself from other cabins located along Vicksburg's tree-lined street. *(Denver Public Library, Western History Department X-4791)*

Chaffee County Times, September 23, 1881 (reproduced in Portal into the Past).

Jim and Louise Rowe, "Clear Creek Canyon," *A History of Chaffee County*, edited by June Shaputis and Suzanne Kelly, Buena Vista Heritage, Buena Vista, Colorado, 1982, pp. 132-133.

Jim and Louise Rowe, *Portal into the Past*, Clear Creek Historical Society of Chaffee County, Granite, Colorado, 1971.

Muriel Sibell Wolle, *Stampede to Timberline*, Sage Books, Chicago, 1949, p. 146.

William H. Bauer, James L. Ozment and John H. Willard, *Colorado Post Offices*, Colorado Railroad Museum, Golden, Colorado 1990, pp. 132, 146, 153.

BROWNS CANYON
and RIVERSIDE

- *Chaffee County, Arkansas River drainage*
- *Access limited by private property; each town had a post office*
- *Original structures unknown*

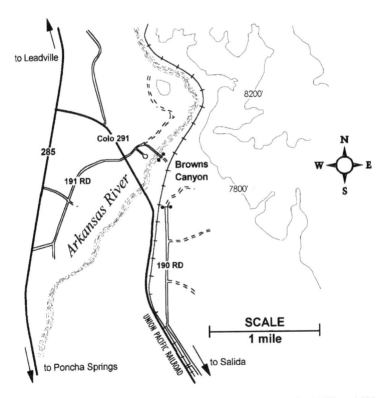

Access to the Browns Canyon site is blocked by posted gates for both 191 RD and 190 RD. At one time, as many as twenty carloads of charcoal were shipped each day from the kilns located at Browns Canyon.

Located along the main line of the Denver & Rio Grande Railway and seven miles northwest of Salida was a small camp originally called Kraft, then renamed Brown's Canyon, and later simplified to Browns Canyon. The specific location of this camp was at the southern end of the canyon formed by the Arkansas River. Today, it is a popular place for white water rafting.

Railroad workers and placer miners lived at Browns Canyon. Its main economic activity, however, was its charcoal kilns.

H. D. McAllister constructed seven kilns at Browns Canyon and owned other kilns throughout Chaffee County. The abundant supply of timber on the hills above the railroad was converted to charcoal. As many as twenty carloads of charcoal were shipped each day. The trees were hauled to the kilns where they were cut into cordwood. The brick kilns stood about twenty feet high with a ramp to access the arched entrance. About twenty-five or more cords of wood were used in each kiln. Once stacked, the wood was ignited and after the fire became hot, the front entrance was blocked with either brick or stone leaving small openings for air to enter. After four days of smoldering in a reduced oxygen environment, the entrance would be opened and the hot charcoal racked out to cool. It was then loaded into railroad cars for shipment to smelters. The Leadville smelters probably purchased most of the output of these kilns. Charcoal is required as a reduction agent for the metallic oxides formed during precious metal smelting.

Browns Canyon got its own post office under the name Kraft in 1882. In 1888, the name was changed to Browns Canyon, and the post office remained open until 1893. In 1904, it reopened only to close permanently four years later. Browns Canyon had a population of about seventy-five residents.

As the local supply of wood was exhausted, Browns Canyon dropped in size. The hillsides were eventually denuded by hundreds of woodcutters, and little was done in terms of reforestation. The railroad workers became the small camp's last remaining residents. Today, the site is on private property.

Riverside was a small community approximately nine miles

north of Buena Vista, located on the banks of the Arkansas River. The site can be seen from U. S. 24, and it is still indicated on maps. Virginia McConnell Simmons provides some detail about this community in her book, *The Upper Arkansas.* The area was first settled by a Frenchman named Frank Mayol. George Leonhardy purchased the property and constructed a tollgate for a road running from the river west through the hills over Trout Creek Pass. This was a shortcut over other routes for mail and freight destined for Leadville coming via South Park. When mail started coming over the road in 1872, a post office was established.

When the Denver & Rio Grande laid its narrow gauge track along the Arkansas in 1880, it made Riverside one of its stations. A depot was constructed and a water tank installed. The railroad added a section house and bunkhouse for track maintenance workers.

In addition to the railroad, Riverside was supported by ranching, some placer mining, and a sawmill. A school was also constructed. The Riverside post office remained in operation until 1905. Riverside probably never grew much beyond a population of one hundred. Access today is limited by private property.

Dick Dixon, "Other Camps in the Ute Trail Area of Chaffee County," *A History of Chaffee County,* edited by June Shaputis and Suzanne Kelly, Buena Vista Heritage, Buena Vista, Colorado, 1982, p. 166.

June Shaputis, "Riverside," *A History of Chaffee County,* edited by June Shaputis and Suzanne Kelly, Buena Vista Heritage, Buena Vista, Colorado, 1982, p. 149.

Virginia McConnell Simmons, *The Upper Arkansas,* Pruett Publishing Company, Boulder, Colorado, 1990, pp. 70, 80, 171, 231, 233.

William H. Bauer, James L. Ozment and John H. Willard, *Colorado Post Offices,* Colorado Railroad Museum, Golden, Colorado 1990, pp. 24, 83, 122.

BUENA VISTA

Captures County Seat

- *Chaffee County, Arkansas River drainage*
- *Accessible via paved road; Occupied town*
- *A number of original structures remain*

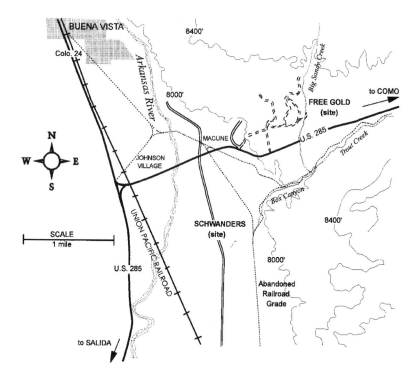

Free Gold was a small mining camp located southeast of Buena Vista near the mouth of the canyon formed by Trout Creek. The abandoned grade of the Denver, South Park & Pacific Railway is also indicated on this map.

NOTE: A brief history of Buena Vista is presented here as a matter of completeness. This community has never been a ghost town. Free Gold is also covered in this section.

As homesteads were established beginning in the mid-1860s, the Upper Arkansas River Valley became dependent on ranching and agriculture rather than mining. Among the early settlers were James and Hugh Mahon. Their homestead was on the west side of the present-day town of Buena Vista at the golf course. The Mahons operated a stage station, and in 1876, a post office was established under the name of Mahonville.

Other settlers formed the nucleus of a town along the Arkansas River adjacent to Mahonville. Charles Dearhiemer, a carpenter, is credited with constructing the first cabin. Alsma Dearhiemer named the place Buena Vista, Spanish meaning "beautiful view." Buena Vista grew and Mahonville stagnated. In 1879, Buena Vista was incorporated, and the post office was moved from Mahonville. At this time, Buena Vista had 150 residents and among them, 45 registered voters.

A photograph of Buena Vista's main street, taken between 1880 and 1885, shows a number of false front business buildings. Careful examination of this photograph reveals the Hardware Miners Supplies store, Martin's Coffee and Chop House, the El Paso Livery Stable and Captain Burke Place. *(Denver Public Library, Western History Department X-7277)*

The Maxwell Park Schoolhouse was built in 1889 and has been restored by volunteers. It is located southwest of Buena Vista on 321 RD. *(Kenneth Jessen 104C12)*

The following year, with the support of votes from Nathrop, Buena Vista won a majority to have the county seat moved from Granite. The people in Granite didn't take kindly to this turn of events. A raiding party from Buena Vista commandeered a Denver & Rio Grande locomotive and flat car. They rode north during the night to Granite and broke into the courthouse unnoticed. The records were removed and transported to Buena Vista. A new courthouse was constructed in 1883, and today, it is listed on the National Register of Historic Places. In 1928, Buena Vista lost its position as county seat to Salida.

Above all, Buena Vista was a transportation and supply center starting with the 1880 arrival of two narrow gauge railroads, the Denver, South Park & Pacific and the Denver & Rio Grande. For a while, the two railroads used the same track under a joint operating agreement. With little land left for a viable right of way, the standard gauge Colorado Midland was forced to build across the hillside above Buena Vista at Wild Horse in 1887. Numerous stagecoaches and freight wagons also passed through Buena Vista.

The town's first newspaper was the *Chaffee County Times* with a publication date of 1880. The following year, the *Buena Vista Herald* began publication, and the *Buena Vista Democrat* came along in 1883.

Until the city fathers passed a series of ordinances, livestock roamed the streets at will. They ripped the paling from fences and destroyed any attempts at backyard gardening. Animals that died on the city streets were left to rot. In addition, Buena Vista citizens were armed and settled their differences with gun fights. Trash was dumped wholesale into the Arkansas River or tossed into the bushes. In summary, Buena Vista was a rough place to live.

A hint of how violent Buena Vista was during its early days comes from the turnover rate among its town marshals. Perley Wasson was the first town marshal, beginning in December, 1879. He lasted three months and was replaced by W. B. Jenness. Jenness resigned after two weeks on the job. William Thompson took his turn but resigned in April of the following year. Mr. Mix was next and left at the end of his first week. And so it went until the lawless element in Buena Vista was driven out of town.

School started in rented facilities in 1880, and in 1893, a schoolhouse was constructed. Several churches were constructed, and from its early days, Buena Vista had a substantial business district. Among its businesses were thirty-two saloons. The first telephone arrived in 1893 and was placed at a central location in a wooden box with a hand crank.

This old store in Buena Vista faces the railroad tracks. *(Kenneth Jessen 095B2)*

Over the years, Buena Vista has made the transition from mining to becoming a business center for the region. It now relies heavily on tourism.

Located not far from Buena Vista was a small mining camp called Free Gold. It got its own post office in 1880, but the office closed a year later. Aside from a stamp mill, the small town had several homes, a store and a saloon. Its peak population is estimated at fifty miners. Historian Virginia

The tunnels at Wild Horse above Buena Vista. The standard gauge Colorado Midland was forced to build across the hillside above Buena Vista in 1887, and due to rugged terrain, the railroad had to tunnel through rock outcroppings. *(Kenneth Jessen 103B5)*

McConnell Simmons wrote that the location was said to have been chosen by a spiritualist with psychic powers. Remodeled in recent years, the red brick schoolhouse is one of Free Gold's original structures. The Free Gold site is located immediately north of U.S. 285 and west of Johnson Village.

Judy Porrata, *Buena Vista*, Little London Press, Colorado Springs, Colorado, 1979, pp. 14-17.

June Shaputis, "Buena Vista," *A History of Chaffee County*, edited by June Shaputis and Suzanne Kelly, Buena Vista Heritage, Buena Vista, Colorado, 1982, pp. 121-122, 140.

William H. Bauer, James L. Ozment and John H. Willard, *Colorado Post Offices*, Colorado Railroad Museum, Golden, Colorado 1990, pp. 59, 93.

Virginia McConnell Simmons, *The Upper Arkansas*, Pruett Publishing Company, Boulder, Colorado, 1990, pp. 144, 70.

CACHE CREEK

One of the Region's Earliest Towns

- *Chaffee County, Cache Creek drainage*
- *Accessible via graded dirt road*
- *Town had a post office; no structures remain*

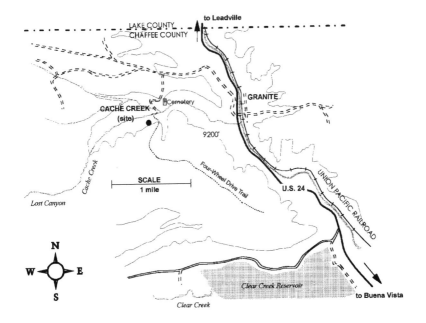

Cache Creek was one of the earliest towns in the Arkansas River drainage, and its site is about a mile and a half west of Granite. Nothing remains at the site today except for the piles of waste rock from decades of placer mining.

Gold was first discovered by A. G. Kelley in 1859 in the upper Arkansas River Valley. The gold was in the form of flakes found in the gravel brought down from the mountains by glaciers during the last Ice Age. Kelley waited until the following spring before returning to the site of the discovery. This early placer deposit became known as Kelley's Bar. Just two miles to the north, more gold flakes were discovered at a place called Georgia Bar at the point where U.S. Highway 24 crosses Clear Creek.

The richest find, however, was at Cache Creek where gold was discovered in 1860. This creek empties into the Arkansas River at a point nearly opposite Granite. About two miles west of Granite, the town of Cache Creek was founded by the placer miners. Cache Creek got its own post office in 1862 under the name "Cash Creek." The post office remained active for nine years, the same length of time Cache Creek remained a viable town. Incorporated in 1866, Cache Creek was home to approximately 200 to 300 miners. The town consisted of cabins of assorted sizes, located randomly about the creek on a dry sagebrush-covered hillside.

Using an extended form of a sluice box called Long Toms, the yields were quite good, ranging from $2 to $20 per day per man. The rules for the mining district allowed 100 feet of creek bed for each miner. All of the placer miners had the right to the water in the creek.

The name Cache Creek is thought to have come from French trappers who operated along the Arkansas during the early 1800s. They were said to have hidden or cached their pelts along the creek.

In 1865, the Gaff Mining Company of Cincinnati, Ohio, purchased the claims in the vicinity of Cache Creek as well as other placer deposits in the general area. A two-mile flume was constructed to supply more water to the area and allow the expansion of mining operations. The Gaff Mining Company was superseded by the Twin Lakes Hydraulic Gold Mining Syndicate. The latter employed sixty men to work the placer during the 1880s. The biggest investment, however, was a water tunnel under the ridge separating Cache Creek from Clear Creek. The tunnel was dug from either end and from a central shaft sunk at midpoint. It was completed in 1884, and gold production along Cache Creek tripled.

Horace Tabor lived to become one of the richest men in Colorado, and later in his life, he had a profound influence on the State. It was at Cache Creek that Horace Tabor got his humble introduction to placer mining. He, his wife and child arrived in Denver during the winter of 1859. When spring came, Horace was determined to try his hand at prospecting and ventured over Ute Pass west of Colorado Springs. He and his family traveled across South Park to the Arkansas River to dig in the gravel for gold at Cache Creek. They didn't get rich and after a few months, they moved farther up the Arkansas to California Gulch. Tabor was the twelfth man to file a claim in this mineral rich area. While Horace was prospecting and mining, Augusta cooked for the miners and watched their baby son. The couple eventually opened a small store at what became Oro City.

At the Cache Creek site, contemporary ghost town historian Robert L. Brown carefully positioned himself to take a photograph from the very same place as a historical photograph. As shown in his book, *Colorado Ghost Towns, Past and Present,* not a single structure survives today.

To reach the Cache Creek site, take the Lost Canyon Road south of Granite, but north of the highway bridge over Cache Creek. This dirt road climbs around the hillside to the west. Where it divides, the left branch continues down to the Cache Creek cemetery and to the town site. Irregular gravel piles from years of hydraulic mining are visible along the creek.

Virginia McConnell Simmons, *The Upper Arkansas*, Pruett Publishing Company, Boulder, Colorado, 1990, pp. 45-46.

Robert L. Brown, *Colorado Ghost Towns, Past and Present,* Caxton Printers, Caldwell, Idaho, 1977, pp. 63-66.

William H. Bauer, James L. Ozment and John H. Willard, *Colorado Post Offices*, Colorado Railroad Museum, Golden, Colorado 1990, p. 31.

Frank Hall, *History of Colorado*, Vol. IV., The Blakely Printing Company, Chicago, Illinois, 1895, p. 78.

History of the Arkansas Valley, Colorado, O. L. Baskin & Co., Chicago, Illinois, 1881, p. 485.

CALCITE

A Colorado Fuel & Iron Town

- *Fremont County, Howard Creek drainage*
- *Accessible via graded dirt road; town had a post office*
- *Private property restricts access; no structures remain*

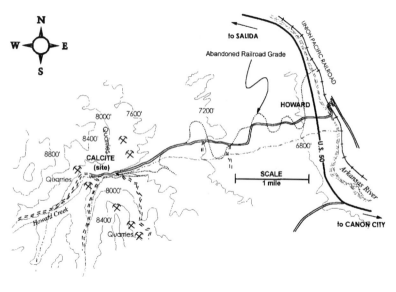

The Calcite site is located west of Howard on 4 RD. Lower, middle and upper Calcite sites are marked by signs. At one time, the town was served by a branch of the Denver & Rio Grande Railroad.

NOTE: Although Calcite is located in Fremont County, it is included here because of its proximity to Salida and other towns in Area 11.

Calcite was a company town owned by Colorado Fuel & Iron Company in Pueblo. Its sole purpose was to quarry limestone for use as a flux in the steel-making process. The Calcite quarries were opened in response to an increase in demand beyond the supply in the Pueblo area. There were three separate but adjacent quarries at Calcite. The first contained saltwater limestone used for making iron. The second limestone quarry contained magnesium required for furnace linings. The last and uppermost quarry was composed of limestone produced by fresh water. It was used for making open-hearth steel.

When the town of Calcite was established, along with its quarries in 1904, it also got its own post office. At the time, the place was called Howard's Quarry. The quarries continued to produce limestone until 1930, and at this time, the post office was closed and the town abandoned. As was the case for other C. F. & I. towns, the homes were either moved or sold in place to local residents.

Typical of other C. F. & I. towns, Calcite had a clubhouse for the quarry workers and a company-owned store. There were numerous company houses, including bungalows and a boarding house. Much of this information was derived from a search of the site itself since little photographic evidence survives.

A branch of the Denver & Rio Grande Railroad was constructed in 1903 from its main line near Howard up to Calcite. The railroad used a series of giant "S" curves to gain altitude, and near the top of the grade, there was a switchback. The rails remained in place until 1936, six years after the quarries closed. Possibly the Denver & Rio Grande believed that the quarries would be purchased and reopened.

The Calcite site can be reached by driving southeast from Salida on U. S. 50 to Howard. From Howard, 4 RD runs west through a cut below the Howard schoolhouse and turns into a graded dirt road. Just past marker 4 is a sign noting the lower portion of Calcite at the first quarry. There are a number of cement foundations located on private property, and are visible from the

This staircase leads nowhere, but at one time, it came from the basement of a large building at the upper Calcite town site. There are many more foundations in the area, and Calcite may have had forty or more structures located in the canyon formed by Howard Creek. *(Kenneth Jessen 109A12)*

road. Farther up this road, a second sign marks the middle camp. Several large foundations, both of stone and cement, mark the site. A modern home sits at this site, and both sides of the road are posted. Another quarter of a mile up the road is the upper Calcite camp with many more foundations. Judging from its size and shape, one foundation supported either an office or boarding house.

H. Lee Scamehorn, *Pioneer Steel Maker in the West*, Pruett Publishing Company, Boulder, Colorado, 1976, p. 105, p. 115.

Robert LeMassena, *Rio Grande to the Pacific*, Sundance Publications, Denver, 1974, pp. 80, 149.

Robert Ormes, *Tracking Ghost Railroads in Colorado*, Century One Press, Colorado Springs, 1975, pp. 53-54.

William H. Bauer, James L. Ozment and John H. Willard, *Colorado Post Offices*, Colorado Railroad Museum, Golden, Colorado 1990, p. 27.

CALUMET, CAMP JEFFERY
and HEMATITE

- *Chaffee County, Railroad Gulch drainage*
- *Calumet accessible by graded dirt road; other sites require walking*
- *No standing structures remain at Calumet or Hematite*

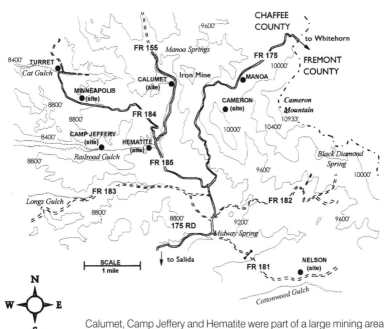

Calumet, Camp Jeffery and Hematite were part of a large mining area northeast of Salida. The region's largest town became Turret.

Calumet was an iron ore mining camp, located northeast of Salida in the low mountain range dividing Chaffee County from Fremont County. The camp and the Calumet Mine were owned and operated by Colorado Fuel & Iron Company for its steel mill in Pueblo. Only the stone foundation of one structure remains today. The camp once had a boarding house, powder house, mine office, some small dwellings, mining structures and two tramways.

Due to its bulk and weight, iron ore required rail transportation. The Denver & Rio Grande Railroad constructed a branch line in 1881 up Railroad Gulch to Calumet. The Calumet Branch connected to the Rio Grande's main line at Hecla Junction along the Arkansas River.

For the first five and a half miles, the grade was a staggering seven percent. Surveyors limited normal narrow gauge railroads to four percent. Beyond the end of the first five and a half miles, the grade eased to six percent. This steep grade made operating this branch dangerous and expensive. It was relatively easy to get

A section gang on the Denver & Rio Grande Calumet Branch. For the first five and a half miles, the grade was a staggering seven percent and beyond that to the end of track, it was six percent. This was well beyond the normal narrow gauge limit of four percent. *(Denver Public Library, Western History Department X-11000070)*

empty cars up to the mine, but a fully loaded train coming down grade was difficult to control. The brakes on each car often were locked such that the wheels slid along the steep track. Adding to the operating problem were floods that damaged the track in the narrowest places along the route.

The Calumet Mine was located on the southwest facing side of a mountain and was operated from two ore haulage tunnels separated vertically. A pair of tramways was built in 1882 to allow ore cars to be lowered by cable down the mountain to a loading tipple next to the railroad tracks. Ore output amounted to ten to fifteen cars a day. Each day, as many as three trains had to negotiate the steep track from the Arkansas River.

Approximately one hundred men were required to operate the mine, and because of its isolation, it can be presumed that they lived in Calumet. The camp got its own post office in 1882, but it lasted only three years.

In October, 1881, a fire destroyed Big Jake's saloon in Calumet. It nearly spread to other cabins and shanties in the camp. Big Jake had a Denver & Rio Grande superintendent, along with ten other men, arrested for starting the fire. The case was dismissed when Big Jake failed to show up to press charges. Apparently Jake's actions were not popular among Calumet's residents. Jake was afraid to show his face again in the camp and sent a driver with an empty wagon up to get his belongings. Calumet residents turned the wagon back, and the driver was told to deliver a threatening message to Big Jake.

Eventually, all of the best ore was removed and what was left contained too much sulfur. In the meantime, Colorado Fuel & Iron opened up another mine at Orient. This mine was located at the northeast end of the San Luis Valley and was far less isolated. In contrast to Calumet, constructing a railroad to Orient was quite easy. As Orient became the primary source of iron ore, operations at the Calumet mine were scaled back. The mine closed in 1897 and the camp was abandoned. The following year, however, the demand for steel was such that the Calumet Mine was reopened and operations continued until 1899. At this time, the mine was closed permanently and the buildings were dismantled. Some of the structures were moved to Orient. A disastrous flood destroyed the railroad in 1901 in a narrow section of Railroad Gulch known as Box Canyon.

Today, mineral collectors venture into the abandoned iron mine. It is quite dangerous because of falling rock in the large cavities left by mining operations. Nevertheless, exquisite specimens of calcite and epidote have been recovered.

Along the right of way for the Calumet Branch and five miles above the Arkansas River was a place called Camp Jeffery. Originally named Hancock for a local mine, the place was founded in 1882. Its main purpose was for the railroad section hands. Buildings included a section house for the workers, plus a couple of small houses. All were constructed of milled wood and neatly painted. A siding allowed narrow gauge trains to pass. The name change to Camp Jeffery took place in 1891, and the name was selected for the Denver & Rio Grande's new president, Edward Turner Jeffery. A two-room cabin can be found near the railroad grade today, but it is privately owned and occupied.

The most knowledgeable historian on this part of Colorado is Dick Dixon. In *Trails Among the Columbine 1995/1996,* he speculated that Camp Jeffery must have been a nice place to live. Although isolated and accessible only by rail, it was located where Railroad Gulch widened above the confines of Box Canyon. The town received the winter sun and had a mild climate. Because it was in a protected canyon, it probably was not exposed to high winds, and there was an ample supply of water. Later, prospectors entering the area added to the buildings at Camp Jeffery.

Where the Turret Road passes Railroad Gulch (185 RD) and at the base of the switchbacks to Turret was another small mining camp. It was originally called Venice and was located a little over a mile from Camp Jeffery. Railroad workers as well as prospectors lived in Venice, and after the Calumet mine was closed and the railroad abandoned, it was reborn as Harrington. It was named for a local prospector who lived at the site. In 1904, a town site was surveyed by the Oklahoma Mining Company. At this time, Turret was growing, and there was speculation that another town would be needed for all the prospectors coming into the area seeking gold ore. The mining company named the site Hematite, electing not to use either of the two previous names. Had the railroad been rebuilt after a flood in 1901, Hematite would have become the transfer point for freight and passengers headed to Turret. A historic photograph shows that it amounted to very little and had only five structures including a store and a saloon.

A fluorite quarry opened up many years later, and during the 1940s, some of the workers lived at Hematite. Waste rock

buries part of the site today, and a small shack still stands below the road among the trees. Reaching the site requires only a short walk from 185 RD down Railroad Gulch.

This stone foundation is about all that remains at the Calumet site. To the east and high on the side of the mountain are the large tailing piles for the iron mine. *(Kenneth Jessen 103B3)*

Dick Dixon, "The D&RG's Calumet Branch," *Trails Among the Columbine 1995/1996*, Sundance, Denver, 1996, pp. 15, 19, 28, 37-40, 43, 45, 58, 69-73, 79.

William H. Bauer, James L. Ozment and John H. Willard, *Colorado Post Offices*, Colorado Railroad Museum, Golden, Colorado 1990, p. 27.

CAMERON, MANOA and NELSON

- *Chaffee County, Ute Creek drainage*
- *Access limited by private property*
- *Towns did have a post office; no standing structures remain*

Manoa is located along FR 175, and there are two structures on the site. In recent years, it appears as though the buildings are being restored. *(Kenneth Jessen 009D11)*

Dick Dixon, a journalism and history teacher at Salida High School, has contributed an incredible amount of information about these obscure mining camps located in the hills northeast of Salida. Cameron, Manoa and Nelson were centered around

Cameron Mountain where gold was discovered during the late 1890s.

The Manoa site is located on FR 175 and east of Turret. It was founded in 1897. With a reliable supply of fresh water, it was a good town site. Its original founders called it Paradise Camp, but the name was changed to Manoa. Manoa was believed to be the Indian word for mountain of gold, reflecting the optimism of the early settlers. There are two original structures on the site, and in recent years, it appears as though they are being restored.

No great quantity of gold ore was discovered, but this didn't stop an English company from investing in the town's mine and in the town site itself. J. Hershberger built a house in Manoa in 1899 while working on his tunnel. Apparently he failed to find enough good ore and proposed the creation of a game preserve on his claim, hoping to boost the sales of stock in his mine. He began by feeding the wild animals to try to keep them around. His feed bill, however, became greater than the returns from his mine.

That November, the first and probably the last baby was born in Manoa. In 1900, the camp did get its own post office, and in 1904, Manoa's population was twenty-five. The town had a grocery store and a general store. There was also a dairy which sold milk and cream. For a while, the place also had a boarding house. Most residents were content to live in canvas structures with log cribbing around the base.

As mining declined in the area, the one remaining store in Manoa closed in 1907. The post office also ceased operation. By the end of 1908, residents had abandoned Manoa and moved on to other areas. The store was skidded to Whitehorn where it too was later abandoned. Nothing remains at the site today, and access is restricted by private property.

Starr Nelson was both a rancher and a railroad engineer for the Denver & Rio Grande. His ranch was in a meadow on the south side of Cameron Mountain where today's FR 182 ends.

While Starr was away working for the railroad during the spring of 1897, prospectors began to invade his range. His father,

G. S. Nelson, divided part of the ranch and started selling lots. Starr returned to find a mining camp situated in the middle of his ranch. Starr took over the sale and management of the camp and liquidated 62 lots at $25 each. In response to his sale of lots, he reported to a Salida newspaper that initially, he knew little about mining but was learning fast.

Soon the town of Nelson had eight to ten cabins. It also had a restaurant and a saloon. Under Starr's management, application was made for a post office. Nelson did get its own post office, but under the name Cochem. It opened in June, 1897, and closed one year, eleven months later.

As prospecting expanded to the north side of Cameron Mountain, the mining camp of Cameron was established. It was named when Orlando Preston dug into the mountain and found gold in February, 1897. His fellow prospectors broke a bottle of champagne over the rock and christened the place Cameron. The name came from area rancher Thomas Cameron.

By spring, sixty-seven lots had sold and there was a grocery store, bunkhouse, combination saloon and restaurant, plus a number of cabins. Many lived in tents.

As the number of claims grew, conflicts between the prospectors also increased. To guarantee some set of rules for things like claim size, a procedure for filing a claim was devised. A mining district was formed by fifty-six prospectors from the surrounding camps. Starr Nelson became secretary. In May, 1897, a number of miners formed the Cameron and Orton Ridge Prospectors and Miners Mutual Protective Association to prevent mine owners and promoters from taking unfair advantage of their labor. Arthur L. Whitehorn was one of those assigned to draw up the bylaws.

An inventive miner, W. H. Shook, built a tramway that automatically dumped its ore out of a mine car when it reached the end of the track. This saved Shook a trip up his incline each time he wanted to haul ore to the surface.

As Turret, located to the west, grew to become the economic

center of the area, many of the prospectors and miners moved out of these smaller camps. By 1902, Cameron was abandoned, and in October, the Sunset Consolidated Company purchased the town site, including all five of its log structures. A contractor was hired to move the buildings to the Sunset Mine. Before the buildings could be moved, an arsonist burned the town to the ground. Nothing remains at Cameron, and access is limited by private property. The town site is south of FR 175 on the west side of the pass over Loco Ridge.

For a map showing the location of these towns, see "Calumet, Camp Jeffery and Hematite."

Dick Dixon, "Cameron," *A History of Chaffee County*, edited by June Shaputis and Suzanne Kelly, Buena Vista Heritage, Buena Vista, Colorado, 1982, pp. 127-128.

Dick Dixon, "Manoa," *A History of Chaffee County*, edited by June Shaputis and Suzanne Kelly, Buena Vista Heritage, Buena Vista, Colorado, 1982, pp. 142-143.

Dick Dixon, "Nelson (Cochems)," *A History of Chaffee County*, edited by June Shaputis and Suzanne Kelly, Buena Vista Heritage, Buena Vista, Colorado, 1982, pp. 147-148.

William H. Bauer, James L. Ozment and John H. Willard, *Colorado Post Offices*, Colorado Railroad Museum, Golden, Colorado 1990, pp. 35, 95.

CLEORA

Named for Saloon Keeper's Daughter

- *Chaffee County, Arkansas River drainage*
- *Accessible via graded dirt side road; private property*
- *Several structures remain*

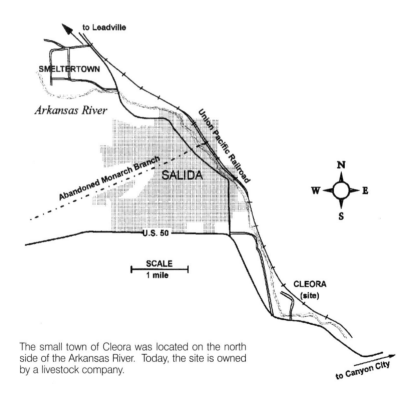

The small town of Cleora was located on the north side of the Arkansas River. Today, the site is owned by a livestock company.

William Bale was an early rancher in the Salida area and when the opportunity presented itself, he moved to a new town site along the Arkansas River. This site was selected by the Atchison, Topeka & Santa Fe Railroad as their division point. Bale named the new town for his daughter, Cleora. Bale constructed a combination stage station and tavern on the site. It was a two-story log building and included guest rooms. Bale, incidentally, was one of the vigilantes involved in the Lake County War. (See *The Lake County War* in the Introduction for more details.)

Cleora was a town based on speculation that the Santa Fe would win the right to construct its line through the Royal Gorge west of Canon City. After a court battle, the Denver & Rio Grande emerged victorious and constructed its main line to Leadville right through Cleora. It established its own facilities to the north at a place originally named South Arkansas. This grew to become the town of Salida.

The Cleora post office was established in 1876, and it remained open for a half-dozen years. By 1885, Cleora was almost deserted, and some of its residents moved to Salida. Even a few of the buildings were moved. Today, the site is a ghost town with two frame cottages still standing. A livestock company owns the site.

One of the few structures left at Cleora is this building constructed by the Denver & Rio Grande Railroad, possibly for one of its maintenance-of-way workers. *(Kenneth Jessen 108D1)*

George A. Crofutt, *Crofutt's Grip-Sack Guide of Colorado*, 1885 Edition, Johnson Books, Boulder, Colorado, reprint 1981, p. 81.

Muriel Sibell Wolle, *Stampede to Timberline*, Sage Books, Chicago, 1949, pp. 295-296.

William H. Bauer, James L. Ozment and John H. Willard, *Colorado Post Offices*, Colorado Railroad Museum, Golden, Colorado 1990, p. 34.

Virginia McConnell Simmons, *The Upper Arkansas*, Pruett Publishing Company, Boulder, Colorado, 1990, pp. 152, 160-161, 280-281.

FUTURITY

Off the Beaten Path

- *Chaffee County, Cottonwood Creek drainage*
- *Accessible by graded dirt road; all on private property*
- *Town did not have a post office; original structures remain*

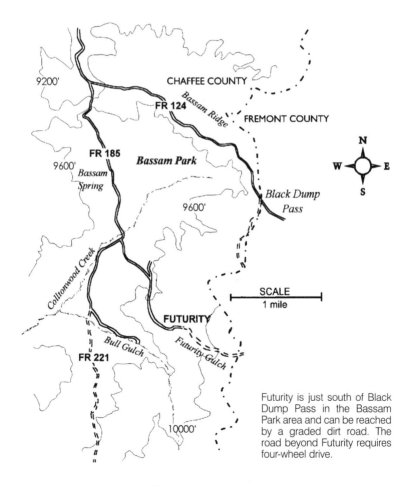

Futurity is just south of Black Dump Pass in the Bassam Park area and can be reached by a graded dirt road. The road beyond Futurity requires four-wheel drive.

Futurity's main street. The mine which supported the town is behind the photographer. *(Kenneth Jessen 103A4)*

Few historical accounts mention Futurity, and this mining camp is among the most obscure in the State of Colorado. It is located in the rolling hills between Turret to the south and Trout Creek Pass to the north. Its original structures remain standing, and most have been restored for seasonal use.

Miners living in Futurity had only to walk one hundred feet or so to work. The mine sits along the town's main street.

Futurity probably was founded after the turn of the century. It is located in the same geological formation as Turret and Whitehorn. Pockets of gold ore were found below the surface layer of granite.

The easiest way to reach Futurity is to head south on the Castle Park Road from Trout Creek Pass. At the fork in Bassam Park, stay to the right and take FR 185 south. After crossing Cottonwood Creek, stay left. This road is rough, but it is only a mile to the town.

GARFIELD

Was Junction City

- *Chaffee County, South Arkansas River drainage*
- *Accessible by paved road*
- *Town had a post office; occupied site; original structures unknown*

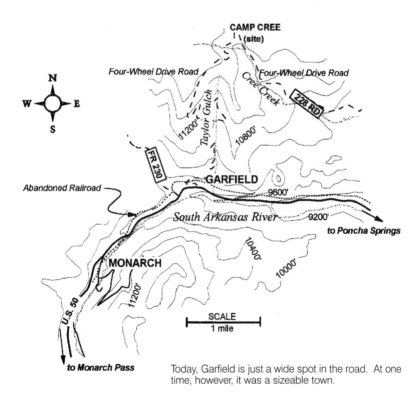

Today, Garfield is just a wide spot in the road. At one time, however, it was a sizeable town.

The town of Garfield, located on U. S. 50 between Salida and Monarch Pass, began as Junction City. Located at the junction of the south and middle forks of the South Arkansas River, its economic support was from area mines.

Virginia McConnell Simmons insists in her book, *The Upper Arkansas*, that Junction City and Garfield were two distinct places. She cites a Rand McNally source stating that mail delivery was made to both places during the same year. As compelling as this seems, George Crofutt in his 1885 grip-sack guide states very clearly that Garfield was called Junction City and lists its population at 250. This is supported by postal records that list only the Garfield post office that opened in 1880.

Businesses in Garfield included a dozen saloons, a dance hall and a hotel. There was also a doctor's office, assay office and a school. A stamp mill was possibly the town's largest employer. Garfield also had a croquet court, an unusual feature for a Colorado mining town.

Because Garfield was laid out on a steep hillside, its parallel main streets were offset vertically.

Originally called Junction City, this is a view of Garfield's main street in 1885. Unfortunately, fire destroyed much of the town and it was not rebuilt. *(Denver Public Library, Western History Department X-9621)*

In 1883, a fire started in one of the town's buildings and as it spread, a nearby store caught fire igniting 750 pounds of black powder. The explosion blew flaming kindling onto Garfield's remaining buildings, and the town was almost destroyed. Garfield was never rebuilt.

Among the area mines was the Lily at over 11,000 feet directly north of Garfield. It had an aerial tram 7,174 feet long to bring ore directly to a tipple at Garfield. Other mines were located up Kangaroo Gulch and Columbia Gulch, both north of Garfield.

The ore in the Garfield area was complex lead-galena carbonates containing some gold and silver. When the Sherman Purchase Act was repealed by Congress in 1893, the price of silver fell to nearly one half of its former level. This had a devastating effect on Garfield's economy as the mines closed. For a while, a marble quarry just east of Taylor Gulch provided limited employment. A large limestone quarry southwest of Garfield at Monarch, operated by Colorado Fuel & Iron, also provided employment.

The Denver & Rio Grande constructed a narrow gauge railroad up to the mine at Monarch. Completed in 1883, steep grades, sharp curves, and a switchback were required to reach the mine. Garfield was known to rail fans since this was the location of one of the switchbacks.

Today, a service station and maintenance garage for the Colorado Highway Department mark the Garfield site. There are several contemporary homes on the site, and it is not known if any of Garfield's original structures survive. Access to the site is restricted by private property.

Of note, north of Garfield was Camp Cree near the headwaters of Cree Creek. This camp consisted of a number of cabins scattered about at timberline near the mines. In recent years, decorative rock has been quarried at the site. Camp Cree is accessible via a steep, graded road which requires a vehicle with low gearing. Finding the correct road is not as easy as it looks, however. Taylor Gulch is narrow and steep. A more practical route is to use 228 RD from U.S. 50. There is a four-wheel drive only road to the right, following the power lines and a mountain property development to the left. The correct road continues climbing and is wide, steep and surfaced with crushed gravel.

There were two other mining camps to the northwest of Garfield along the Middle Fork of the South Arkansas River. Babcock was the highest, and little is known about its size or exact location. Only a mile and a half from the mouth of the Middle Fork was Columbus. By 1881, a stamp mill was operating at this camp. Columbus was owned by the Columbus Milling and Mining Company and gained its own post office in 1882. The post office closed in 1884, and a snow slide eventually destroyed the town.

Camp Cree is located at timberline at the head of Cree Creek. It was not a town as such since the remaining cabins are spread out in two shallow valleys. A decorative rock quarry is situated above this old cabin. *(Kenneth Jessen 009D12)*

George A. Crofutt, *Crofutt's Grip-Sack Guide of Colorado*, 1885 Edition, Johnson Books, Boulder, Colorado, reprint 1981, pp. 94-95.

History of the Arkansas Valley, Colorado, O. L. Baskin & Co., Chicago, Illinois, 1881, p. 499.

Russ Collman, "Narrow Gauge Operations on the Monarch Branch," *Trails Among the Columbine, 1993/1994*, Sundance Publications, Denver, 1994, pp. 87, 92.

Virginia McConnell Simmons, *The Upper Arkansas*, Pruett Publishing Company, Boulder, Colorado, 1990, pp. 131-132.

William H. Bauer, James L. Ozment and John H. Willard, *Colorado Post Offices*, Colorado Railroad Museum, Golden, Colorado 1990, p. 59.

GRANITE
Built on a Solid Foundation

- *Chaffee County, Arkansas River drainage*
- *Accessible by paved road*
- *Town has a post office; occupied town; a number of original structures still standing*

Granite was a rough place during its early years. It was the site of the assassination of Judge Dyer during the Lake County War. A horse-drawn sleigh is in the center of this winter photograph. *(Denver Public Library, Western History Department X-8756)*

Up and down the banks of the upper Arkansas River from Salida to Leadville prospectors, mined a variety of placer deposits during the early 1860s. Along with mining, several camps began to appear. Some, like Granite, grew into trade centers while others did not survive. Granite was established in 1867 and has never been abandoned. Just a year after Granite was established, it got its own post office.

The first industry in Granite was a small, two-stamp mill built by W. L. Millard and S. B. Kellogg. Soon a much larger mill was constructed by Lewis Hayden. Hayden built his mill for his Amizette Mine, and over $75,000 in gold (at today's prices) was recovered during its first month of operation. A third stamp mill was constructed for ore from the Yankee Blade Mine.

Granite gained a great deal of importance in 1868 when it became the Lake County Seat, having taken that position away from Dayton by popular vote. The citizens of Granite contributed $500 to have the county courthouse at Dayton moved on skids. (Dayton, incidentally, became the town of Twin Lakes. See "Dayton Becomes Twin Lakes" in Area 9 for more details.)

Having become the county seat, Granite had difficulty holding on to this title when Leadville began its unprecedented growth during the late 1870s. In 1878, Leadville's population alone exceeded that of Lake County's entire population the previous year. It became obvious that a new county had to be formed, and in February, 1879, the State Legislature created Carbonate County. This encompassed roughly the upper one third of the old Lake County with Leadville at its approximate center. Just two days later, the State Legislature changed the name of Lake County to Chaffee County and Carbonate County to Lake County. Granite now became the Chaffee County Seat, but its tenure was short-lived. In 1880, Buena Vista was declared the new county seat by popular vote.

Originally, placer miners along the Arkansas River near Granite used sluice boxes and Long Toms (an elongated form of a sluice box). Eventually this form of placer mining was replaced by hydraulic mining using high-pressure nozzles to wash the gravel down from the ancient streambeds and glacial moraines. Once this very destructive form of mining ended, gold dredges came into play. As the placer deposits were exhausted of gold, hard rock mining began. For many years, these forms of gold mining supported Granite's economy. There was, however, a period of stagnation for Granite. As the mines got deeper, refractory ore was encountered. No longer could simple stamp mills, followed by amalgamation with mercury, be used to extract the gold. Such complex ore required smelting.

When the Leadville boom began in 1879, Granite became a stage stop for the heavily traveled road along the Arkansas River. The Denver & Rio Grande constructed its narrow gauge railroad through Granite in 1880.

Granite, at one time, did have a neighbor in the form of Hawkinsville, located about a mile to the east. Although contemporary maps do not show Hawkinsville, it was located south of the trail over Low Pass. Hawkinsville, like Granite, had hotels, stores and saloons, but Granite was in a far better location with its abundant water supply next to the Arkansas River. Hawkinsville was abandoned when the mines ran into refractory ore which required smelting.

Granite is historic and worth a visit. The town sits just east and below U.S. 24. The schoolhouse still stands, overlooking the valley, and there are several old abandoned stores along Granite's main street. Granite also has a number of log structures and many are occupied by permanent residents.

The Granite Schoolhouse sits up on the hillside above the town, and it is now a private residence. *(Kenneth Jessen 103B8)*

History of the Arkansas Valley, Colorado, O. L. Baskin & Co., Chicago, Illinois, 1881, pp. 477, 483, 487.

Muriel Sibell Wolle, *Stampede to Timberline*, Sage Books, Chicago, 1949, p. 144.

Virginia McConnell Simmons, *The Upper Arkansas*, Pruett Publishing Company, Boulder, Colorado, 1990, pp. 58-59.

William H. Bauer, James L. Ozment and John H. Willard, *Colorado Post Offices*, Colorado Railroad Museum, Golden, Colorado 1990, p. 65.

HANCOCK

Supports Railroad

- *Chaffee County, Clear Creek drainage*
- *Accessible via graded dirt road*
- *Town had a post office; no standing structures remain*

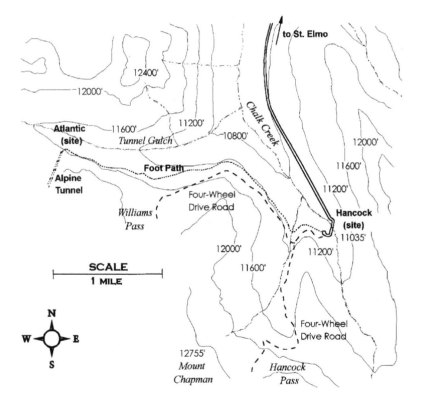

Hancock is located beyond St. Elmo in Chalk Creek Canyon at the end of a graded dirt road. A footpath leads to the Alpine Tunnel.

During the 1880s, Hancock's main street was lined with cabins and false-front stores. By the 1940s, when Muriel Sibell Wolle was writing *Stampede to Timberline*, she visited the Hancock site and reported, "There were a few widely scattered cabins in various stages of dilapidation." The red water tank, used to replenish the water in locomotive tenders, still stood. She returned in 1950 and photographed a substantial, two-story log home set off in the trees. In 1963, Robert L. Brown, a contemporary ghost town historian, found only one building standing. Today, Hancock hasn't any standing structures. This illustrates the rapid deterioration of wooden structures exposed to the harsh elements in the high country.

Hancock was first located in 1880 by prospectors moving up Chalk Creek. It really didn't grow until the following year, when the Denver, South Park & Pacific Railway laid its track parallel to the town's main street. A town company was formed at this time to sell lots, but Hancock was never incorporated.

Pioneer photographer Joseph Collier took this photograph of Hancock during its glory days with a Denver, South Park & Pacific train, pulled by two locomotives, headed toward the Alpine Tunnel. Note the row of buildings in the background along Hancock's main street. None of these structures remain today. *(Denver Public Library, Western History Department C-112)*

The economic support for Hancock came from area mines, such as the Iron Chest high above the town, and the Allie Bell and Flora Bell, located along the railroad. Hancock, however, was more of a railroad town. The ambitious 1,800 foot Alpine Tunnel was started in 1880, and the tunnel headings met in July of the following year. This was the first tunnel under the Continental Divide in North America. In 1882, trains began running up Chalk Creek Canyon, through Hancock, to Gunnison.

A small construction camp, called Atlantic, was set up below the east portal to house the tunnel workers. It is likely, however, that many of them elected to live in Hancock.

The Hancock site itself is above 11,000 feet, and heavy winter snows produce frequent avalanches. This forced the railroad to keep many section workers in Hancock to keep the line open. Up to 100 men would shovel snow to clear the tracks.

The railroad constructed a combination depot and telegraph office at Hancock with its own living quarters. There was also a two-story section house. Hancock had a coal bin and long passing track as well as the water tank. The town sat along one long main street. There were five stores, a hotel, several saloons, some dining halls, two sawmills and a number of cabins. A former resident, F. C. Buell, stated that the town contained about fifteen houses and that a 1902 snow slide leveled all but four. Another resident related that the railroad depot burned to the ground during the early 1890s and was not replaced. The peak population of Hancock was about 200.

Hancock's post office opened in 1880, the year the town was founded. Hancock's growth was short-lived and the last lot sold five years later. The post office remained open until 1887. The Alpine Tunnel closed in 1890 and was not reopened until 1895. A spurt in mining caused the Hancock post office to reopen briefly in 1903. The tunnel was abandoned for good in 1910, and Hancock was abandoned.

Hancock's last standing structure collapsed during the early 1990s from the weight of heavy winter snow. As for the railroad facilities, only the four supports for the water tank remain, half hidden in a willow thicket. There are bits of glass and pieces of wood scattered about, plus what was once an outhouse. The open meadow where the busy town of Hancock was located is now overgrown with aspen and spruce trees. The Forest Service has added a parking lot just beyond the town site for visitors wishing to walk or ride a bicycle to the Alpine Tunnel, two miles away. The rough four-wheel drive road over Hancock Pass takes off a hundred yards or so beyond the town site.

This partially collapsed cabin was the last structure to yield to the elements at the ghost town of Hancock located near the head of Chalk Creek Canyon. This photograph was taken in July, 1990. *(Kenneth Jessen 008D4)*

Dow Helmers, *Historic Alpine Tunnel*, Swallow Press, Chicago, 1963, pp. 23-24, 27, 34.

Mac Poor, *Denver South Park & Pacific*, Rocky Mountain Railroad Club, Denver, 1976, p. 431.

Muriel Sibell Wolle, *Stampede to Timberline*, Sage Books, Chicago, 1949, pp. 155-158.

Robert L. Brown, *Jeep Trails to Colorado Ghost Towns*, Caxton Printers, Caldwell, Idaho, 1963, pp. 108-109.

William H. Bauer, James L. Ozment and John H. Willard, *Colorado Post Offices*, Colorado Railroad Museum, Golden, Colorado 1990, p. 68.

HARVARD CITY

- *Chaffee County, Cottonwood Creek drainage*
- *Accessible via paved road; private property limits access*
- *Town did not have a post office; several original structures remain*

At the junction of South and Middle Cottonwood creeks, placer deposits were discovered during the late 1860s. Harvard City was laid out by the placer miners, and when the road over Cottonwood Pass to Taylor Park opened, it became a stage station. It was here that teamsters changed their horses for the hard pull over the pass. For the entertainment of passengers, Harvard City had a dance hall and a saloon. There was also a general store and several homes.

Harvard City gained enough population to become an election precinct. Although several historians claim that the town also had a post office, no record of one could be found.

As lode mining replaced placer mining, the stagecoach and wagon traffic through Harvard City kept the place alive. Cottonwood Pass lasted as the primary pass over the mountains until 1882. At this time, a toll road over Independence Pass was opened to provide a shorter route to the silver mines around Aspen, and Harvard City was abandoned. During this century, modern homes have been constructed on the site.

Harvard City, at one time, had enough population to become an election precinct. This is one of the few original remaining structures. The town site is at the junction of South and Middle Cottonwood creeks on the Cottonwood Pass road. *(Kenneth Jessen 105C11)*

A History of Chaffee County, edited by June Shaputis and Suzanne Kelly, Buena Vista Heritage, Buena Vista, Colorado, 1982, p. 18.

Don and Jean Griswold, *Colorado's Century of "Cities,"* self-published, 1958, pp. 131-132.

Muriel Sibell Wolle, *Stampede to Timberline*, Sage Books, Chicago, 1949, p. 144.

Virginia McConnell Simmons, *The Upper Arkansas*, Pruett Publishing Company, Boulder, Colorado, 1990, p. 124.

HORTENSE
At the Base of Chalk Cliffs

- *Chaffee County, Chalk Creek drainage*
- *Accessible by paved road; private property*
- *Town had a post office: original structures remaining unknown*

At the base of Chalk Cliffs near the mouth of Chalk Creek Canyon were several hot springs. Native Americans were well aware of their therapeutic value. Father John Dyer, known as the "snow-shoe itinerant," climbed one of the high peaks in the area during the summer of 1877. He ended up descending to one of the springs near the point where it flowed into Chalk Creek. Dyer was exhausted from the climb and reasoned that where the steaming water from the spring met the ice cold water in the creek, the temperature for bathing would be perfect. Instead, the hot spring water flowed side by side with the ice cold creek and didn't mix for some distance. His statement was, "...while the hot water did not quite blister, the cold water did not quite freeze." In any event, he filed a claim on one of the springs and constructed a cabin. At the time, claims were held by possession, and Rev. Dyer was called by his church to move to New Mexico. A claim jumper took over the property. Later, however, Dyer was able to get back his property.

The spring was originally named Hortense, and it became the Hortense Station on the Denver, South Park & Pacific narrow gauge railroad. A water tank, two-story combination depot/section house, telegraph office and a coal loading facility were constructed at Hortense. For ore shipments, Hortense also had a siding for the Hortense Mine high on the side of Mount Princeton. A post office opened in 1877 under the Hortense name, but in 1884,

429

the name was changed to Heywood. It remained closed from
1888 to 1901, then reopened for another six years.

There has been considerable confusion over the spelling of
Heywood. Robert L. Brown in his book, *Colorado Ghost Towns,
Past and Present,* insists that it was spelled Haywood. The name
came from a government surveyor, D. H. Heywood. The surveyor
ended up purchasing the spring from Rev. Dyer and had title to
820 acres surrounding the spring. The railroad was forced to pay
him $3,000 for the right of way through his property. Historic
photographs verify the spelling as Heywood, in fact, the sign over
the hotel's entrance reads, "Heywood Hot Springs House."

Hortense or Heywood Hot Springs was not really a town in
the sense that it had a main street, stores and homes. Instead, it
was a resort and railroad stop. In 1881, its population was listed
as fifty. A new lodging facility, called the Antero Hotel, was completed in 1891. This hotel was large and spectacular. It even had
towers at opposite ends, with one tower reaching 100 feet in
height. This four-story hotel had 100 rooms with initial rates of
$10 per week. Eventually, it was incorporated, and its name
became Mt. Princeton Hot Springs. The structure sat abandoned
for years after rail service ended and public interest died. In 1949,
the hotel was razed and part of it was reassembled in Texas.

Today, a modern bathhouse sits on the site of the old hotel
and a number of homes have been constructed on the site. The
site is west of the intersection of 321 RD and the Chalk Creek
Road, 162 RD.

George A. Crofutt, *Crofutt's Grip-Sack Guide of Colorado,* 1885 Edition, Johnson Books, Boulder, Colorado, reprint 1981, p. 103.

Judy Hassell, "Hortense," *A History of Chaffee County,* edited by June Shaputis and Suzanne Kelly, Buena Vista Heritage, Buena Vista, Colorado, 1982, p. 129.

Mac Poor, *Denver South Park & Pacific,* Rocky Mountain Railroad Club, Denver, 1976, p. 427.

Rev. John L. Dyer, *The Snow-Shoe Itinerant,* Cranston & Stowe, Cincinnati, Ohio, 1890, pp. 356-358.

Robert L. Brown, *Colorado Ghost Towns, Past and Present,* Caxton Printers, Caldwell, Idaho, 1977, pp. 124-127.

William H. Bauer, James L. Ozment and John H. Willard, *Colorado Post Offices,* Colorado Railroad Museum, Golden, Colorado 1990, pp. 73-74.

KELLEY'S BAR and
GEORGIA BAR

- *Lake County, Arkansas River drainage*
- *Sites near paved road*
- *No structures remain*

A. G. Kelley spent most of his time in Auraria organizing a party of prospectors. They set out for the mountains in February, 1860. The twenty-four men traveled well beyond where others had gone the year before along the Arkansas River. By looking at the gravel deposits and testing the sand as they went, they found placer gold near the confluence of Pine Creek and the Arkansas River. The prospectors immediately named the place in honor of their leader, and it was known as Kelley's Bar. It was one of the earliest settlements in this area. Prospectors were removing $2 to $5 per day in gold, and soon the place was overrun. Kelley's Bar was located approximately four miles south of Granite.

In early April, 1860, prospectors discovered gold in the sand near the mouth of Cache Creek. Sluice boxes were constructed of whipsawed lumber and placer mining began. This location was not named.

Another placer deposit, approximately two miles south of Granite opposite the mouth of Clear Creek, was discovered by a party from Georgia. It became Georgia Bar. Father Dyer, an itinerant Methodist minister who traveled extensively throughout Colorado's mining districts, preached a sermon in Georgia Bar and also conducted funeral services during the same visit.

At Georgia Bar, miners had to deal with too much water

from Clear Creek so that the sand in the riverbed could not be effectively mined. In 1861, a company was formed to construct a dam on Clear Creek to reduce the flow and allow the miners to sluice the streambed. The dam soon failed and this ended operations at Georgia Bar.

Activity by individual prospectors lasted only a year or two, when a far richer discovery was made to the north in California Gulch. Kelley's Bar and Georgia Bar were, to some extent, depleted of the "easy" gold which could be removed by primitive means. These sites were abandoned as the prospectors moved north and formed the town of Oro City in California Gulch. Later, large scale hydraulic mining was used for gold recovery at Kelley's Bar and Georgia Bar.

Don and Jean Griswold, *History of Leadville and Lake County*, Colorado Historical Society, Denver, 1996, pp. 40, 49, 51.

History of the Arkansas Valley, Colorado, O. L. Baskin & Co., Chicago, Illinois, 1881, pp. 478-479.

Muriel Sibell Wolle, *Stampede to Timberline*, Sage Books, Chicago, 1949, p. 144.

MAYSVILLE

- *Chaffee County, South Arkansas River drainage*
- *Accessible via paved road; access limited by private property*
- *Town had a post office; several original structures remain*

As shown in this photograph taken between 1877 and 1882, Maysville was a substantial town. Note the false-front dry goods store located along its main street. *(Denver Public Library, Western History Department X-12313)*

Originally known as Feather Ranch, Maysville was founded in 1879 as a tent camp. Adjacent to Maysville was another place called Crazy Camp, and the two camps merged. The name Maysville came from the Kentucky hometown of General William Marshall. It was General Marshall who is credited with the discovery of Marshall Pass to the south.

By 1882, Maysville was Chaffee County's largest town and had several hotels, a bank, lumberyard, stores and a number of homes. It also had two newspapers, the *South Arkansas Miner* and the *Maysville Chronicle.* The latter boasted of one thousand readers. The town got its own post office in 1879, and it remained open until 1893.

A toll road was constructed through Maysville in 1879 over Monarch Pass to the Gunnison area. A second toll road originated in Maysville and served Shavano ten miles away up the North Fork of the South Arkansas River.

One of the stories associated with Maysville had to do with a shoot-out that took place in 1879 between drunk miners. During the conflict, four men were shot and two died immediately. One wounded survivor, a man named Flynch, was recovering in his bed when his assailant hunted him down and shot him again to make sure he died. After this incident, the city fathers may have over-reacted by hiring a justice of the peace, a constable and a deputy sheriff.

A fire spread through the town in 1880 and destroyed five buildings before a bucket brigade could get the blaze under control.

Maysville enjoyed prosperity until the silver crash of 1893 when the United States abandoned the silver standard. Without the U. S. Government's required purchase of silver, the price dropped to almost half of its previous value. Maysville was nearly abandoned.

Today, Maysville can be reached on U.S. 50 west of Poncha Springs. There are a number of contemporary homes, but the old schoolhouse has been restored and sits below the highway.

This is the Maysville schoolhouse today located below U.S. 50. It was constructed in 1882 and remained in use until 1939 as indicated by the sign. Contemporary homes surround the structure. *(Kenneth Jessen 100A6)*

Judy Hassell, "Maysville," *A History of Chaffee County*, edited by June Shaputis and Suzanne Kelly, Buena Vista Heritage, Buena Vista, Colorado, 1982, pp. 143-144.

Muriel Sibell Wolle, *Stampede to Timberline*, Sage Books, Chicago, 1949, pp. 161-162.

Muriel Sibell Wolle, *Timberline Tailings*, Sage Books, Chicago, Illinois, 1977, pp. 130-131, 135-137.

William H. Bauer, James L. Ozment and John H. Willard, *Colorado Post Offices*, Colorado Railroad Museum, Golden, Colorado 1990, p. 96.

MINNEAPOLIS
But Not In Minnesota

- *Chaffee County, Cat Gulch drainage*
- *Accessible by graded dirt road*
- *Town did not have a post office; no structures remain*

Music was the order of the day at this log home in Minneapolis, a small mining community was located a mile to the southeast of Turret. Nothing remains at the site today. *(Denver Public Library, Western History Department X-12330)*

Nothing remains today at the Minneapolis site except depressions where buildings once stood, bits of glass and what was once a root cellar. Visitors to the area drive by on their way to Turret without realizing that a town once existed on this site. Minneapolis could be regarded as a suburb of Turret since it was located only a mile to the southeast.

Started in 1897, prospectors first lived in tents and later built permanent structures. As lumber came from a sawmill in Whitehorn, the tents yielded to frame buildings. Its occupants originally named the place Klondike hoping for impressive gold strikes.

In 1901, residents recognized their close ties with Turret and began to call their town South Turret. The Klondike Hotel changed its name to the South Turret Hotel.

Several of the mines in the area were owned by the Twin Cities Mining Company. The town's second hotel was called The Twin Cities Hotel and was constructed in 1902 by the Twin Cities Development Company of Minneapolis-St. Paul, Minnesota to house dignitaries visiting the mines. Presumably, the development company was associated with the mining company. Unfortunately, the Twin Cities Hotel burned to the ground just weeks after it was completed.

The town settled on its final name Minneapolis. The former Klondike Hotel, then called the South Turret Hotel, also changed its name to the Minneapolis Hotel. The town of Minneapolis had fourteen structures not counting outhouses. A survey was made of the town, but never filed. A town hall was constructed in 1902, but the town was never incorporated and had no municipal offices. Instead, the town hall was used for social occasions including dances. A schoolhouse was built in 1902 halfway between Turret and Minneapolis to serve both communities.

By 1907, Minneapolis began to deteriorate. The mines yielded little in the way of valuable ore, and many residents moved away, probably to Turret. Even the town hall was moved to Turret to become an addition to a hotel. Other buildings were dismantled, and some were moved to the marble quarry on the road to Calumet. Fire destroyed other structures until soon, nothing remained.

For a map showing Minneapolis, see "Calumet."

Dick Dixon, "Cat Gulch - 1880-1902," *Trails Among the Columbine 1995/1996*, Sundance, Denver, 1996, pp. 116-128.

MONARCH

Began as Chaffee City

- *Chaffee County; South Arkansas River drainage*
- *Site near paved road*
- *Town had a post office; no original structures remain*

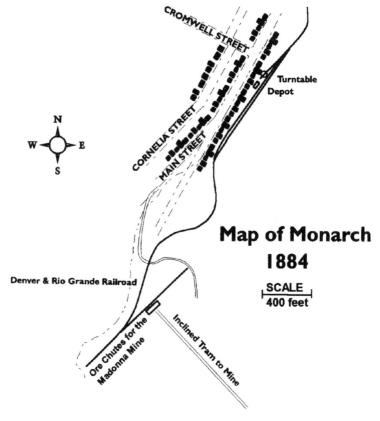

Monarch's businesses were situated along one long main street making it sort of a strip city. Homes occupied a parallel street. As underground mining was replaced by a limestone quarry operation, the town was abandoned and the site partially buried.

L ocated two miles above Garfield along the South Arkansas
River was the town of Chaffee City. The name was only fitting
since Jerome B. Chaffee had done so much to promote mining in
Colorado, and he became a United States Senator.

Ore, as lead-silver carbonates, was discovered in 1878. One
of the prospectors who made the discovery at Monarch was N. C.
Creede. He later discovered the Holy Moses and started the rush
to the town of Creede. Chaffee City got its own post office the
year following the discovery. The population of the area soon
swelled to several thousand.

In 1883, the name was changed to Monarch, and the post
office remained in operation until 1903. Historians later speculated
that too much confusion resulted from having a town and a county
with the same name. The owners of the Monarch Mine, directly
above the town, may have also prompted the name change.

The Madonna Mine came to dominate the activity at

As this 1884 photograph shows, Monarch was a substantial town. Other views of the
town show it had nearly ninety structures along its two parallel streets. Among its businesses were the Miner's Exchange, the Palace of Pleasure and the Eureka Dance Hall.
(Denver Public Library, Western History Department X-12361)

Monarch and employed 300 men. The upper level of this mine was serviced by a spectacular funicular tramway. The tramway used two sets of mine cars. As one set moved downward, loaded with ore, the other set of empty cars was pulled upward to the top. The speed was controlled by a brake. In the middle of the tramway, the rails parted, allowing the sets of three cars to pass each other. The tram had grades up to 77%. Ore was dumped directly into bins at the bottom of the tram.

The Denver & Rio Grande constructed a narrow gauge railroad from Salida up the South Arkansas River to the ore bins at the Madonna Mine in 1883. As many as thirty carloads of ore were shipped each day. Local attempts were made to smelt the complex ore. Eventually, the ore was hauled to the Colorado Fuel & Iron steel mill at Pueblo where smelting was done free of charge. Embedded in limestone, the ore made excellent flux for the steel making process. The Pueblo steel maker eventually purchased the Madonna Mine and operated it as an open pit limestone quarry rather than as an underground mine. The precious metal content became incidental to the quarry's output.

Historical accounts of Monarch state that the town had one hundred to one hundred and twenty-five houses. An early photograph taken from the top of the tramway shows that Monarch had at least eighty-five structures excluding outhouses.

Monarch also had three saloons, three stores and three hotels. Among its more colorful businesses were the Miner's Exchange, the Palace of Pleasure and the Eureka Dance Hall. Its businesses were situated along its long main street, making Monarch sort of a strip city. Homes occupied a parallel street. By 1936, Monarch was abandoned since operation of the limestone quarry required little labor. Only a dozen or so structures show up in historic photographs taken at this time. By 1950, there were even fewer buildings as the waste rock from the quarry began to bury the site. Quarry operations continued into the 1980s, then in 1984, the quarry was closed and the rails removed. Today, nothing in the way of original structures remain at the site.

As an incidental piece of history, Muriel Sibell Wolle states that another town was located one and a half miles below Monarch. It was called Hartville, but no information could be found on its size or exact location. She received a letter in 1966 from a woman who had camped at the site and mentioned a cemetery with a dozen or so graves. The location is approximately four miles below the summit of Monarch Pass on its eastern side.

Monarch's Main Street (*drawing by Julia McMillan*)

George G. Everett and Dr. Wendell F. Hutchinson, *Under the Angle of Shavano*, Golden Bell Press, Denver, 1963, p. 171.

History of the Arkansas Valley, Colorado, O. L. Baskin & Co., Chicago, Illinois, 1881, p. 499.

Muriel Sibell Wolle, *Stampede to Timberline*, Sage Books, Chicago, 1949, pp. 166-167.

Muriel Sibell Wolle, *Timberline Tailings*, Sage Books, Chicago, Illinois, 1977, p. 139.

Russ Collman, "Narrow Gauge Operations on the Monarch Branch," *Trails Among the Columbine, 1993/1994*, Sundance Publications, Denver, 1994, pp. 116-117, 123, 144, 152.

William H. Bauer, James L. Ozment and John H. Willard, *Colorado Post Offices*, Colorado Railroad Museum, Golden, Colorado 1990, p. 32.

NATHROP and SCHWANDERS

- *Chaffee County; Arkansas River drainage*
- *Nathrop accessible via paved road; Schwanders on private property*
- *Nathrop has a post office; several original structures remain at Nathrop and none at Schwanders*

Charles Nachtrieb opened a store in California Gulch near Oro City in 1868. Living in a mining town did not agree with him, and he decided to become a rancher. Nachtrieb moved south along the Arkansas River to its confluence with Chalk Creek where he constructed the area's first flour mill. Water from Chalk Creek was used via a millrace to power the mill. Located eight miles south of Buena Vista, settlers began to join Nachtrieb and a small community developed. In 1879, a post office under the name of Chalk Creek was established, but the name was changed to Nathrop the following year.

Nathrop was incorporated in 1880 and became a railroad center with the arrival of both the Denver & Rio Grande and the Denver, South Park & Pacific. The town did not grow much beyond 200 people, however. The D. & R. G. continued construction north to Leadville, then west over Tennessee Pass with a second line over Fremont Pass. The D. S. P. & P. constructed west up Chalk Creek to the St. Elmo mining area, then through the Alpine Tunnel to Gunnison. The two railroads jointly constructed a large stone depot at Nathrop.

Seeing the opportunities brought by the railroads, Nachtrieb built a large, two-story hotel within walking distance of the depot. He called the place the Nachtrieb Hotel, and it attracted

passengers wishing for a place to stay after the long train ride
from Denver. The hotel had six rooms in the basement, five
rooms on the first floor and thirteen rooms on the second floor.
Drinking water was piped to the hotel from Chalk Creek.

Charles Nachtrieb was a leader when it came to improving
the roads in the area. He petitioned the county commissioners
for a road south over Poncha Pass in 1871 and was involved in the
construction of a road to the west up Chalk Creek Canyon.

Nachtrieb built his home in 1876 near his flour mill. He was
also a vigilante leader during the Lake County War in 1874-1875.
(For more information, see *The Lake County War* in the
Introduction.)

Over a dispute involving just twenty-five cents in wages, Bert
Remington shot Nachtrieb to death in his store on October 3, 1881.

As the mines to the west began to decrease in output, the
town of Nathrop began to die. No longer were there numerous
stagecoaches coming into Nathrop. The D. S. P. & P. was dismantled in 1926, and Nathrop's one remaining store was moved up

Nathrop's schoolhouse, constructed in 1881, was restored by the Gas Creek
Homemakers Club. *(Kenneth Jessen 103B4)*

from the river bottom to the present-day highway.

Nathrop, however, is anything but a ghost town today. New homes have been built and the schoolhouse has been restored.

Slightly over four miles to the north of Nathrop was a railroad facility called Schwanders. Even though not a town in the true sense of the word, several families called it home. The men were employed by the Denver, South Park & Pacific to care for the coal chutes and the water tank located at the site.

Benjamin Schwanders settled in this location in 1864. He had ventured down the Arkansas Valley looking for good farm land and picked the area near the mouth of Box Canyon where Trout Creek flowed out across an alluvial fill to the Arkansas River.

The railroad constructed its line through Box Canyon in 1884, then turned south through Nathrop. The railroad also built an extension north to connect with its other line. Near the switch where the two rail lines separated was Benjamin Schwanders' ranch. It was logical for the railroad to call the place Schwanders.

As the hills above Trout Creek were denuded of timber, floods began coming down Trout Creek carrying tons of silt. Much of the farmland in the area was ruined. The lower portion of Box Canyon was buried in silt. After having its track buried several times, the Denver, South Park & Pacific gave up on its line through Box Canyon in 1908 and used its connection to the north.

In 1924, all rail service on the D. S. P. & P. was discontinued, and the line was abandoned. Along with it, Schwanders and other small railroad dependent towns were also abandoned. By this time, successive silt deposits had buried one home and much of the land. Not a trace of the old right of way at Schwanders can be seen today.

Mac Poor, *Denver South Park & Pacific*, Rocky Mountain Railroad Club, Denver, 1976, pp. 178, 426-427.

Peggy Scanga, "Nathrop," *A History of Chaffee County*, edited by June Shaputis and Suzanne Kelly, *Buena Vista Heritage*, Buena Vista, Colorado, 1982, pp. 145-146.

William H. Bauer, James L. Ozment and John H. Willard, *Colorado Post Offices*, Colorado Railroad Museum, Golden, Colorado 1990, pp. 32, 103.

ROMLEY

And the Mary Murphy Mine

- *Chaffee County, Chalk Creek drainage*
- *Accessible by graded dirt road; town had a post office*
- *Several structures remain*

As shown in this photograph taken between 1915 and 1925, Romley was more of a collection of buildings related to the mining industry than it was a town. *(Denver Public Library, Western History Department X-13199)*

Romley was a mining and smelter town located three miles up Chalk Creek from St. Elmo. Its economy was based almost exclusively on the Mary Murphy Mine to the south in Pomeroy Gulch. The Mary Murphy Lode was discovered by Dr. A. E. Wright and John Royal during the mid-1870s. The name, Mary Murphy, was that of a Denver nurse who cared for John Royal. He remembered her kindness and bestowed her name to the mine.

After its original owners developed the Mary Murphy, they sold it to a Kansas company. The new owners constructed a smelter at Alpine to process the lead-silver ore, but the smelter was a failure. The mine was sold again. This time, milling and smelting facilities were constructed at Romley.

Ore was brought down from the mine's No. 4 level high on Chrysolite Mountain by an aerial tramway. The Mary Murphy Mine became the biggest producing mine in the Chalk Creek district.

An English syndicate was the next owner of the mine and milling complex in 1909. Shipments increased and employment rose to 250 men. By 1917, the ore reserves were depleted and the mine closed. From that point on, mining was sporadic, and exploration work was done on the mine as late as 1981 in hopes of finding new ore deposits.

In 1881, the Denver, South Park & Pacific constructed a narrow gauge main line up Chalk Creek Canyon, past Romley, to the Alpine Tunnel. Trains ran from Denver to Gunnison via this route. A small depot was constructed at Romley, and a spur track was used to handle cars. In 1915, a turntable was installed for trains running up Chalk Creek just to Romley.

There are few records about life in Romley. It had a post office, opened in 1886, and a boarding house. Other structures included a mine office, several large mill and smelter structures, and of course, the railroad depot. It is not known if there were any homes at Romley.

The post office closed in 1893, then reopened in 1914 when mining activity resumed. The post office closed again in 1919, then opened the following year and closed for good in 1924. So little traffic was handled by the railroad that the line was abandoned and the rails removed in 1926.

During the 1940s, the mill burned, leaving the aerial tramway and its lower unloading station. The boarding house, railroad depot, mine office and several other structures were still standing at that time. All were painted red with white window trim. Today, there are plenty of ruins to look at and the lower

terminal for the tramway remains standing above the road. Up
Pomeroy Gulch are quite a few other structures, some in relatively
good condition. Of note is a picturesque cabin sitting on the
opposite side of the creek from the access road to the mine. Also
standing is the mine office with its outhouse still intact. The partially collapsed remains of an ore loading bin sit by the road and
other buildings still stand near the mine.

The lower tram station still stands complete with all of its machinery. It is located above
the road near the Romley site. *(Kenneth Jessen 009D20)*

Dennis Bailey, "Romley," *A History of Chaffee County*, edited by June Shaputis and Suzanne Kelly,
    Buena Vista Heritage, Buena Vista, Colorado, 1982, pp. 150-151.

Mac Poor, *Denver South Park & Pacific*, Rocky Mountain Railroad Club, Denver, 1976, p. 431.

Muriel Sibell Wolle, *Stampede to Timberline*, Sage Books, Chicago, 1949, pp. 149-155.

William H. Bauer, James L. Ozment and John H. Willard, *Colorado Post Offices*, Colorado
    Railroad Museum, Golden, Colorado 1990, p. 124.

SHAVANO

At the Base of Mt. Shavano

- *Chaffee County, North Fork of the South Arkansas drainage*
- *Accessible via rough graded road*
- *The town had a post office; remains of one cabin*

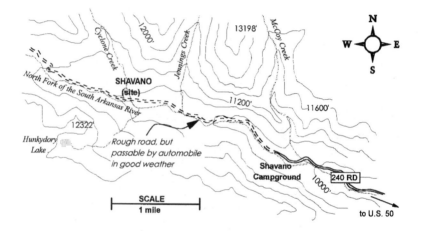

Shavano is located on a rough dirt road beyond the Shavano Campground. As its one remaining structure deteriorates, the site will become increasing difficult to locate.

Located on the North Fork of the South Arkansas River, Shavano was an isolated mining camp. At an elevation of 11,000 feet, life must have been difficult and possibly mining was done on a seasonal basis. The original name for this camp was Clifton, and it got its start in 1879. The name was soon changed to Shavano for the chief of the Uncompahgre Utes and the name of the high mountain, in excess of 14,000 feet, towering immedi-

All that remains of the isolated mining camp of Shavano. The site is located on the North Fork of the South Arkansas River. *(Kenneth Jessen 107A1)*

ately above the camp.

A toll road was built from Maysville to serve the town. Shavano promoters offered a free lot, firewood and water to any settler who would grade the street in front of his or her property. Shavano grew to about 100 people and had three general stores, a saloon, a sawmill and a small smelter. All were log structures. After only three years, Shavano was a ghost town. The ore was low grade.

A short distance west of Maysville on U. S. 50, FR 240 heads northwest and follows the North Fork of the South Arkansas River. The road is dirt but graded to the campground. Beyond the campground, the road becomes rough for the remaining distance to Shavano. The site is marked only by a partially collapsed cabin on the north side of the road where Cyclone Creek joins the North Fork. It will not be long before the site can no longer be identified. FR 240 continues past Shavano to a high basin containing a number of mines including "The Pride of the West" with its spectacular concrete collar.

June Shaputis, "Shavano," *A History of Chaffee County*, edited by June Shaputis and Suzanne Kelly, Buena Vista Heritage, Buena Vista, Colorado, 1982, p. 160.

Muriel Sibell Wolle, *Timberline Tailings*, Sage Books, Chicago, Illinois, 1977, pp. 135-136.

William H. Bauer, James L. Ozment and John H. Willard, *Colorado Post Offices*, Colorado Railroad Museum, Golden, Colorado 1990, p. 131.

ST. ELMO

Is Well Preserved

- *Chaffee County, Chalk Creek drainage*
- *Accessible via a graded dirt road*
- *Town had a post office; partially occupied site; numerous original structures*

Taken between 1880 and 1890, this was St. Elmo during its boom years. Some of these structures remain standing today in what is one of Colorado's best-preserved ghost towns. *(Denver Public Library, Western History Department X-13484)*

Out of all the mining towns in Chalk Creek Canyon, the one that had the longest life was St. Elmo. It is also one of the best-preserved ghost towns in the state. Its row of abandoned buildings form a backdrop for the high mountains. One can walk down its main street and ponder what it must have been like during its glory days. The old town can be reached over a well-graded dirt road which runs west from Nathrop. Because of its accessibility, St. Elmo receives many visitors, and a store operates during the summer months. It is not totally abandoned, however, and there are cabins which have been restored for seasonal use.

The early history of St. Elmo is coupled with the life of Dr. Abner Ellis Wright. After graduating from medical school in New York, he worked his way West doing a variety of jobs. This included store keeper, sawmill operator and cowboy. He spent a number of years in Iowa, and then Wright joined the 1849 rush to California. It was here that he began to practice medicine in one of the mining camps and do some prospecting on the side.

During his life in California, Dr. Wright had a close call with a grizzly bear. The bear charged him as he fired several shots at the advancing animal. The bullet wounds simply made the bear angry. The bear grabbed him by his shoulder and shook him like a rag doll. The rest of his hunting party rushed to his aid and opened fire at the bear. Every one of their shots missed, but four of their bullets struck Wright. A slug also hit his powder horn which exploded. The flash and loud noise caused the bear to release its grip and run away, but Wright was badly burned. He survived his rescue and later allowed his hair to grow long to cover a missing ear. He also lost part of a rib which left a deep scar in his chest. Later in life, he related the bear story in a humorous manner, concluding that he had been blown up, torn up and shot up all at once.

After returning to Iowa, he became interested in Colorado's mineral wealth. In 1871, he was prospecting in Chalk Creek Canyon and camped at the future site of St. Elmo. Wright teamed up with a prospector named John Royal, and together, the two men were able to cover a lot of ground. Royal had something in common with the doctor; he too had been attacked by a grizzly bear. Royal also wore his hair long to cover an ear lost in the struggle with the bear.

In 1875, the pair discovered a rich vein of gold and silver ore high on Chrysolite Mountain. Sometime during his past, Royal

had been cared for by a Denver nurse named Mary Murphy. This
is the name he selected for the claim.

Dr. Wright sold his part of the Mary Murphy for $75,000,
which in today's dollars, would be worth over three-quarters of a
million. He moved to Buena Vista in 1878 and apparently was
never tempted to go prospecting again. Dr. Wright settled into the
practice of medicine for the next twenty years. It is not known
what became of his partner, John Royal.

Captain William W. Cambell located a ranch on the future
site of St. Elmo in 1878. As the town developed at the site, he constructed one of its first homes. Because of its dense stand of trees,
the town was originally called Forest City. The Forest City name,
however, was duplicated in California, and the post office insisted
town residents come up with a new name. A committee came up
with the title of a novel, *St. Elmo*, by Augusta J. Evans. The St.
Elmo post office opened in 1880 and remained active until 1952.

The first newspaper was the *St. Elmo Rustler*, and after only

When Dow Helmers was doing his research on the Alpine Tunnel during the 1940s, he
took this photograph of the buildings along St. Elmo's main street. The building with
the bell tower is the St. Elmo Fire Co. and City Hall. The only residents at the time were
the brother and sister, Tony and Annabelle Stark. *(Denver Public Library, Western History
Department X-13465)*

one issue in 1880, the name was changed to *The St. Elmo Mountaineer.* Area ranchers may have objected to the use of "rustler" in the newspaper's name. The paper lasted only five years.

The Mary Murphy mine was extensively developed during the 1880s and was the largest producing mine in Chalk Creek Canyon. There were, however, approximately fifty other mines in and above Chalk Creek Canyon, but by 1887, only a couple of mines were still in operation.

To bring ore down from the mine high on Chrysolite Mountain, a gravity tram nearly a mile long was constructed. The ore was delivered to Romley, four miles above St. Elmo, by a tram supported by fifty towers. Each of its ninety-six buckets could handle two hundred pounds of ore. During the course of a day, the tram could deliver 128 tons of ore. Once two mills in St. Elmo processed the ore from the Mary Murphy, but they were later replaced by a more modern mill at Romley.

St. Elmo's economy was not entirely based on mining. The town was situated at the junction of several major toll roads to other mining areas. Freighting was a big business. There was the Maysville and Chalk Creek Toll Road over to the next valley and the Altman Pass road to Pitkin. Service to Tin Cup was provided over the Chalk Creek and Elk Mountain Toll Road. Stages ran daily through St. Elmo and down Chalk Creek Canyon to Buena Vista.

In 1880, the rails of the Denver, South Park & Pacific reached St. Elmo. The following year, the line was extended through Hancock, and on to Gunnison via the Alpine Tunnel. Depots were constructed at both Romley and St. Elmo. The railroad started running trains from Denver to Gunnison through St. Elmo in 1882. The Alpine Tunnel, by the way, was built at an elevation of 11,608 feet and was the first tunnel drilled under the Continental Divide. After mining began to dwindle, the last train pulled out of St. Elmo in 1926, long after the Alpine Tunnel had been closed.

During its boom years, St. Elmo had numerous businesses, including three hotels, five restaurants, a general store, a grocery store, a butcher shop, a shoe store, a livery stable, a feed and grain

Dow Helmers went inside the Stark Brothers Mercantile store in St. Elmo. The store was still operating when he took this photograph during the late 1940s. Note the well-stocked shelves of oil lamps, clocks, hats, flour sifters, medicines and canned foods. *(Denver Public Library, Western History Department X-13473)*

store, a drug store, a billiards hall, several sawmills and two ore processing mills. Professional services included an attorney at law, a watchmaker, a surveyor and an assayer. St. Elmo supported a grade school and had a small cemetery one-mile below town near Iron City. The city government had an elected mayor and board of trustees. Taxes were collected for street repairs, cemetery maintenance, police and waterworks. In 1891, the board of trustees established an official town seal which featured an eagle with outspread wings.

The south side of St. Elmo was partially destroyed by fire in 1890, never to be rebuilt. The post office, butcher shop, one of the hotels, a bakery, a shoe store, and a warehouse were lost in the fire. A high stone wall, which still stands today, prevented the fire from spreading. Today, all that remains of this portion of St. Elmo is a row of fire hydrants.

One of St. Elmo's colorful "watering holes" was Pat Hurley's saloon. Miners squandered their paychecks and lived it up a bit. It provided relief from their otherwise bleak lives. Still standing, Hurley's saloon is located on the right side of the main street near the entrance to the town.

Schooners of beer sold for five cents, and miners could get a free lunch consisting of roast beef, ham, pickled tripe, pigs feet, pretzels, crackers and hard-boiled eggs. The general idea Pat

Hurley had was to keep the miners in his establishment by providing a reasonable lunch. Within the bar were poker tables, and the walls were decorated with pictures of nude women, common to many Colorado bars. The back of the bar had a diamond dust mirror with the long line of whiskey bottles reflecting in the mirror. A glass case at the end of the bar contained tobacco products.

Beer came from a keg, and miners could purchase a bucket to take home. Grease applied to the inside of the bucket prevented foaming, thus increasing its capacity. A ten-pound pail of beer was only a quarter.

Nights are cold in St. Elmo even during the summer. A pot-bellied stove kept Hurley's customers warm. A container filled with water was kept on top of the stove for washing glasses, mugs and dishes. A coal scuttle, shovel and poker rounded out the items near the stove. Illumination was provided by kerosene lamps. Typical of most bars, Hurley's floor was covered with sawdust. Patrons during those days often chewed tobacco and spit on the floor.

Charlotte Merrifield, in her book *Memories of St. Elmo*, wrote that her father had the propensity to drink and gamble away his paycheck at Pat Hurley's saloon. A family member sent to find him could usually talk him into leaving for home. One payday, however, Charlotte's mother had had just about enough after waiting two hours for father to return. Unable to control her anger, she walked down St. Elmo's main street and picked an apron full of rocks as she went. She stormed into the predominantly male establishment and spied father drinking and playing poker. She began immediately to throw rocks. The missiles shattered the diamond dust mirror, and many whiskey bottles were broken. Pat Hurley had previously been asked to help the family by sending father home. He had difficulty upholding the request to evict a loyal customer, and now his establishment was being demolished! From that day on, Charlotte Merrifield's father brought home his paycheck and walked by Pat Hurley's saloon.

The history of St. Elmo is closely coupled to the Stark family, beginning in 1860 when St. Elmo's population was just 160 residents. The Starks became St. Elmo's most prominent family and eventually operated the Home Comfort Hotel, the Stark Store and the post office. Anton Stark was born to Russian immigrants in Hayes, Kansas and later married Anna Griffith. They and their children, Annabelle, Tony and Roy, had a profound influence on St. Elmo spanning five decades.

Anna convinced her husband to move to Chalk Creek and settle in Hancock. Hancock was a railroad town and provided the labor necessary to keep the Alpine Tunnel open. Anton became a section boss for the railroad while Mrs. Stark ran a boarding house. Eventually, the Starks moved down the canyon to St. Elmo and purchased the two-story Home Comfort Hotel. In newspaper

The abandoned Stark home, store and hotel located along Main Street in St. Elmo. The Stark family ran the local store and hotel for a span of five decades and became the town's most prominent family. *(Kenneth Jessen 011D6)*

ads, the Starks boasted that all the comforts of home could be found at the Home Comfort Hotel by traveling "commercial" men and that the best meals in St. Elmo were served at the hotel. The hotel also had telephone and telegraph service. On the first floor, the Starks ran their store and guests stayed on the second floor.

Anna Stark was tough as nails despite her petite size. She had an unyielding, stern face and never cracked a smile, believing that having fun was foolish. She kept her hair combed straight back and tied in a tight bun on the back of her head. Her store, the hotel and her home were kept spotless.

Anna faced a dilemma when she was raising a young calf. As with any mountain town, wild animals prowled the night and often a young domestic animal fell prey. Anna solved this problem by bringing the calf into her home every night and tying it to the kitchen table. In order to keep her house spotless, she put newspapers down on the kitchen floor.

Anna worked her children constantly, leaving them no time for play. Annabelle, her beautiful daughter, got to the age where she wanted to date boys and go to dances. Down the street was Pat Hurley's saloon. Every Saturday night at the saloon there was a respectable dance patrolled by the police to insure no drunks got inside. Married couples felt comfortable enough to bring their children to the dance.

Annabelle could have had her choice of any of the eligible bachelors in town and longed to go to the dance, but her mother would not let her out. A miner who lived at the hotel felt sorry for the young lady, and after some fast-talking, he convinced Anna to let him escort her daughter to a dance. Annabelle became so excited during the evening that she forgot about her mother's 11:00 p.m. curfew. Mrs. Stark marched down to the dance shortly after 11:00 p.m. and made Annabelle leave at once. That was the first and the last dance the young woman was allowed to attend until she got out from under her mother's iron grip and took a job in Salida.

Not much is written about Anton Stark. Anna eventually

locked him out of his own house for drunkenness, and Anton moved to Buena Vista. Only on occasion did he get to see his family. After he was badly injured, he was placed in the Salida Railroad Hospital. Annabelle visited her father often and sent telegraph messages about his condition back to the family. Eventually gangrene set into Anton's injured leg and it had to be amputated. A short time later, he died.

Once Annabelle was out on her own, however, she met a man named Ward and went with him to California. They were married in 1921, a fact which Annabelle informed her mother of by telegram.

Apparently, Annabelle was not happy in California and longed for the mountains and her family. With her husband, she returned to St. Elmo and moved into the family home. Trying to live with her domineering mother proved impossible for the couple. Anna never approved of the marriage and showed her hatred every moment she could toward Annabelle's husband. Eventually the Wards had their fill of Annabelle's mother and moved back east. After Mr. Ward passed away, Annabelle returned to St. Elmo to help run the store and post office. By this time, Anna Stark had passed away leaving Tony in charge. However, Annabelle could not stand to live with her brother any more than she could live with her mother. Tony constructed a lean-to next to the hotel for Annabelle.

The hotel closed many years before Annabelle moved back to St. Elmo. In fact, by 1926, there were only six residents in a town which once supported a population of over 500. Gradually, Tony and Annabelle filled the hotel with all sorts of junk they collected. After the post office closed in 1952, the county stopped plowing the road during the winter, and the Starks were completely isolated. By this time, the Starks were the only residents of St. Elmo, and it had become a ghost town. Eventually, the brother and sister became too old to care for themselves and were taken away. Tony died in 1958 and Annabelle passed away in a nursing home two years later, ending the era of the Stark family in St. Elmo.

At the time Muriel Sibell Wolle wrote her book *Stampede to*

On the east end of St. Elmo's main street are the ramshackle remains of the old Pawnee Mill livery stable and barn where horses and carriages could be rented. Since this photograph was taken, these buildings have had new roofs installed to preserve the structures. *(Kenneth Jessen 009D16)*

Timberline during the late 1940s, Annabelle Stark and her brother were still operating the general store and post office in St. Elmo. The Starks joked with the tourists by telling them to watch out for streetcars. Wolle wrote an article for *Ford Times* about the ghost town of St. Elmo. Annabelle Stark took exception to St. Elmo being referred to as a ghost town and claimed that it hurt her business. She said people would be afraid to visit any place called a "ghost town." She claimed that if they believed the place to be uninhabited, they would not make the long drive up Chalk Creek Canyon to patronize her store. Muriel Wolle meant no harm and illustrated her article with a beautiful watercolor of St. Elmo which showed its dilapidated, abandoned buildings and uneven board sidewalks. The run-down look further upset Annabelle Stark and caused a feud between her and the Colorado historian.

Iron City, as mentioned before, was the site of St. Elmo's cemetery and was located just three-quarters of a mile away. It was also a small mining camp. A smelter was constructed there in 1880 to process silver ore from area mines. The camp didn't last long and was later known as Morley's Mill. All that remains today is a campground and the ruins of the smelter.

Williams Building, St. Elmo *(drawing by Julia McMillan)*

Charlotte Merrifield and Suzy Kelly, *Memories of St. Elmo*, self-published, 1993, pp. 1-5, 7-8, 30-34.
Peter Anderson, *From Gold to Ghosts*, B & B Printers, Gunnison, Colorado, 1983, pp. 1-9, 84-86.
Muriel Sibell Wolle, *Stampede to Timberline*, Sage Books, Chicago, 1949, pp. 150-154.

TURRET

In Cat Gulch

- *Chaffee County, Cat Gulch drainage*
- *Accessible via graded dirt road; some private property*
- *Town had a post office; numerous original structures remain*

This 1902 photograph of Turret was taken during the town's boom years as a mining center for the area. As the gold ore was exhausted, the town was slowly abandoned. *(Denver Public Library, Western History Department X-13897)*

Turret is located in a scenic valley surrounded by large, rounded granite boulders. The area looks like a movie set. The most famous rock in the vicinity is "Swinging Rock" which became the town's informal symbol. Many photographs were taken of this rock with both adults and children on its top.

Unlike the high mountains to the west, Turret has more of a desert-like setting. The gold ore was overlooked by the first

461

prospectors since easy to see surface ore was relatively rare among the granite outcroppings. Turret's mineral wealth was not obvious, and this explained why the rush to Turret came considerably later than for other Arkansas Valley mining towns.

In 1879, prospectors George Smith and Nicholas Creede passed through Cat Gulch. Placer gold deposits were discovered below Turret at the base of Cat Gulch. Smith returned with David Austin. It is Austin who was credited with the discovery of gold ore at what became the Gold Bug and Anaconda mines in 1885.

In 1881, the Denver & Rio Grande laid a steep track up Railroad Gulch, passing south of Turret to reach rich iron ore deposits at Calumet.

According to contemporary historian Dick Dixon, an expert on Turret's history, pioneer David Austin did not come into the Turret area originally to prospect. The charcoal business flourished along the Denver & Rio Grande's main line. The charcoal was shipped to Leadville for its smelters. By 1884, the hills near the railroad were stripped of timber. This prompted Austin and his family to move up Cat Gulch to access uncut stands of timber.

By the time ghost town historian Muriel Sibell Wolle visited Turret to take this photograph, it was almost a ghost town. This photograph was taken in the late 1940s. *(Denver Public Library, Western History Department X-5589)*

Austin constructed three small cabins for his family. Later he constructed a large frame home. Tree cutters were hired and moved into the cabins, and the resulting lumber camp was called Camp Austin. The wood was hauled down to the charcoal kilns at Nathrop via the primitive Austin Trail.

More gold ore was discovered during 1886 and 1887 which brought prospectors to Camp Austin. Sometime between the late 1880s and 1895, the name was changed to Turret or Turret City for Turret Mountain, located to the north.

The Austin's little girl, Louisa, was accidentally struck in the head by her six year old brother with a pick. Louisa, just three years old, lingered for several weeks before her death. She was buried on a small knoll overlooking Turret. This grave is marked today by a picket fence. At least four others were interred in the small Turret cemetery.

David Austin, by the way, continued to live in this home well after the mining and lumber industries had vanished. He was still in his home in 1937 and was among the few residents in the nearly abandoned town of Turret.

By 1897, Turret had one hundred residents. Many lived in tents. The Gold Bug Mine had a fifty-foot shaft and contained 300 feet of tunnels. Other mines in the area had also developed by this time and many were making regular ore shipments. Turret began to take on the appearance of a permanent town with a meat market opened by Cole and Larkin from Whitehorn. A well was dug by willing hands in hopes of striking rich ore in the process.

A great deal of the early success of Turret was due to town promoter Pete Schlosser. He formed a miner's protective association, improved the Austin Trail, got the well started and ended up being the town's notary public. Schlosser filed a survey for the town, however, Turret was never incorporated.

In 1898, Turret got its own post office. It remained active until 1939 when the town was practically abandoned.

J. J. Noonan began regular stagecoach service from Salida.

He was plagued by accidents and advertised that he would upgrade to Concord coaches. These coaches were too expensive and Noonan had to be content with surreys, buckboards and wagons.

A telephone line was run from Salida to Turret, and enough trees remained to string the wires between them. A cross arm was simply nailed to a point near the top of the tree. Turret's single telephone was placed in the town center near the flagpole. Typical of most early telephone systems, it consisted of two wires. Subscribers were added by connecting to the wires. This allowed subscribers to listen to the conversations of others. In March, 1899, subscribers could use this feature to listen to a concert performed in Salida by the Denver & Rio Grande band at the opera house. This same year, the *Turret Gold Belt* began publication. Up to this time, the *Whitehorn News* acted as the voice of Turret.

By 1901, the town had two hotels, the Hotel Turret and The Gregory Hotel. The latter was made of logs and stood two stories high. The Gregory family lived on the ground level and guests stayed on the second story level. Later they constructed a home of their own, allowing them to use all of the hotel for guests. There was a saloon run by E. G. Holman, but Emil Becker's Sample Room Saloon was probably the most popular watering hole. Oscar Chambers ran a meat market and Charles Roberts operated the Pioneer Store. The drug store was run by Dr. A. B. Phillips, the town doctor. The town also had a dry goods store, bakery, tin shop and a barbershop. Turret probably had a population of about 200 at this time.

An early town plat shows that Turret could have become a sizable town. Most of the lots were never occupied, however. The town had impressive street names such as Turret Avenue, State Street, Russell Street, Dauphine Avenue, Highland Avenue and so on.

Another look at life in Turret is provided by Dick Dixon with the story of the feud between William Record and Andrew Cyrus Dore. The two men were at one time friends and lived together in Whitehorn. After Record brought his wife and child to Whitehorn,

Dore continued to live in their home. Dore had a daughter who lived with an aunt, but no one seemed to know anything about Dore's wife. One day, Dore showed up with a woman. He wanted her to move in with him. Record asked Dore to leave, saying that such an arrangement was not a good influence on his family. To that, Dore bragged that he would kill Record, and it became only a matter of time until their feud resulted in violence.

On March 11, 1903, each man followed the other from saloon to saloon in Turret. They taunted each other and got drunk in the process. Dore needed a place to rest and asked saloon owner Emil Becker if he could lie down in his small cabin. As Dore was resting, Record came to the door of the cabin with a gun in his hand. Dore told him to leave, but Record raised his gun and fired at Dore. Dore fired back and jumped out of bed. Record

This structure was Turret's last schoolhouse. School was still taught in this building during the 1930s. *(Kenneth Jessen 103A10)*

was hit and fell over backward, with his heels resting on the door-sill. He raised his body up enough to fire a second shot into the cabin. He then collapsed and died. Dore was uninjured.

The Coroner's Jury declared that Andrew Cyrus Dore had fired in self-defense. Record became the only man killed in Turret in a gunfight. Ironically, Dore was killed years later in a gunfight in Creede.

Turret's peak year was 1905, and the town had an estimated population of 600. Photographs show over seventy structures not counting outhouses. Residents had been working and investing for years in area mines. None of the mines produced any great amount of wealth, however, although some mines had three shifts. Gold came in pockets.

In 1910, the once optimistic editor of the *Turret Gold Belt* gave up and moved his paper to Salida. Transportation costs ate up any profits from mining. Efforts were made to get the Austin Trail improved, but Chaffee County could not see any economic reason. The railroad to Calumet was damaged beyond repair in 1901, but mining promoters tried to get the money to rebuild the line. The cost of hand shoveling ore from wagons to railroad cars at Helca Junction was great. Attempts at concentrating the ore at Turret to reduce the amount of material shipped failed.

As time passed, residents moved away. The process was gradual and by the 1930s, Turret was all but abandoned. By 1934, less than twenty people lived in the town. When postmaster Pete Schlosser passed away in 1939, the post office was closed permanently.

When Muriel Sibell Wolle, Colorado ghost town historian, visited Turret in the late 1940s, many of its buildings were still standing. Time, weather, vandals and fires have reduced Turret today to a few structures. Some are still standing, while others have collapsed. Nevertheless, a visitor can get a good feel for the size of the town by walking its streets and admiring the beautiful rock formations intermingled with the abandoned structures and foundations. At least two of the houses are still occupied seasonally. Private property restricts full exploration of the old town. All of the mines are privately owned, and most are posted.

From Salida, FR 175 follows The Ute Trail route into the Turret area. By staying on FR 175 and not turning to the right on 182 RD, the visitor will pass Long Gulch. FR 175 continues northeast up Calumet Mountain to Whitehorn, while FR 185 heads northwest to Turret. Just past where FR 185 crosses Railroad Gulch, another road, FR 184, takes off to the left and begins its climb up to Turret. At the top of the grade, the road descends past the Minneapolis site to Turret. To the right, FR 155 runs past the water-filled marble quarry and on to the Calumet site. In dry weather, passenger cars can make the climb to Turret, but it is a steep gravel road laid out on a rock ledge. There is a second road up to Turret, leaving FR 155 just beyond Railroad Gulch. This road is also quite steep, but not quite as exposed.

For a map showing Turret, see "Calumet, Camp Jeffery and Hematite."

Dick Dixon, "Cat Gulch - 1880-1902" and "Turret - 1903-1907" *Trails Among the Columbine* 1995/1996, Sundance, Denver, 1996, pp. 77-91, 129, 132, 161, 319.

Muriel Sibell Wolle, *Stampede to Timberline*, Sage Books, Chicago, 1949, pp. 158-159.

William H. Bauer, James L. Ozment and John H. Willard, *Colorado Post Offices*, Colorado Railroad Museum, Golden, Colorado 1990, 9. 144.

WHITEHORN and BADGER

- *Fremont County, Willow and Badger Creek drainages*
- *Access limited by private property; graded dirt road to sites*
- *Towns did have post offices; several structures remain at Whitehorn*

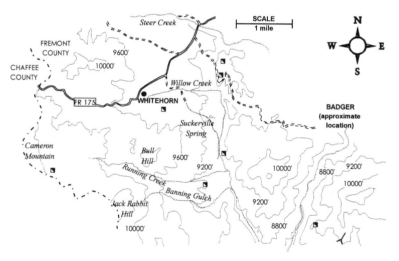

Whitehorn was originally located in Chaffee County, but a subsequent change in the county line location placed it in Fremont County. It is located just west of a shallow pass separating the counties.

NOTE: *Although Whitehorn and Badger are both in Fremont County today, they were originally within Chaffee County and are included in Area 11.*

Mineralization in the form of gold ore was discovered in 1896, and the camp was started in March, 1897, by a couple of prospectors, James H. Day and James Moore. They had a grub-stake consisting of food and supplies in exchange for a share in any discovery they might make. This particular winter was harsh with cold weather and heavy snow. Looking for minerals under such conditions was very difficult, and the two men joked about being suckers for even trying. They called their camp "Suckerville," and at the end of a hard day, they returned to dry their boots and wet clothing.

The name Suckerville was used for some months, and today, this is the name of the spring near the town site. Arthur L. Whitehorn was appointed a mineral surveyor for the area and set up a tent on Willow Creek not far from the Day and Moore "Suckerville" camp. Whitehorn was very generous with his time and was willing to grubstake a prospector or provide his expert opinion on the quality of an ore sample brought in for an assay. Because of Whitehorn's generosity, the camp once called Suckerville was renamed Whitehorn. A survey was made, and the meadow was divided into forty lots. The right to purchase a lot was done by a drawing.

As news spread about the prospects of gold in the region, Whitehorn gained population. A general store was constructed, and by June, 1897, Whitehorn had twenty structures plus a number of tents. Several eating establishments opened, and the population was estimated at around two hundred. The following month, Whitehorn got its own post office. The Whitehorn Mining District was started, overlapping an earlier mining district, the Cameron Mining District.

Whitehorn was the first among the small mining camps in the area to start its own newspaper. The first issue of the *Whitehorn Whim* came out on June 15, 1897. It was replaced by the *Whitehorn News* which lasted for many years.

The families in Whitehorn wanted their own school. Since the town was located almost on the line between Fremont and

Chaffee, they applied to both counties to establish a school district. They were turned down and a private subscription raised the necessary money to start a school. As a side note, Whitehorn eventually ended up in Fremont County, following a county line dispute.

The ability to predict an outcome had its advantages. Before the United States had actually won the Spanish-American War, Whitehorn residents celebrated by setting off several explosions using blasting powder. A few days later, official news reached Whitehorn that the war was won. Residents realized they had jumped the gun and to correct their mistake, they held a second celebration!

The Denver Times reported that by December, 1898, Whitehorn had 800 residents. The town had grown to cover ten blocks. The streets were graded and lined on both sides with boardwalks. The business district had three general stores and a saloon. By the turn of the century, however, the population was listed at only 100 and six businesses survived. A fire in 1902 destroyed half of Whitehorn's structures, and the town was never rebuilt. Citizens used a bucket brigade from the town well in a futile effort to put out the flames.

An economic surge in 1905 increased the number of businesses, and then the town began a steady decline. The mines were not nearly as profitable as the prospectors hoped, and the ore body was not extensive. The *Whitehorn News* closed in 1911, and by the following year, Whitehorn's only general store closed. By 1914, the population had dwindled to just forty, and in 1916, the post office closed. Some of Whitehorn's structures were moved.

Today, there are many foundations in the meadow where Whitehorn was once located. One of the foundations is a large concrete pad. There are also the remains of several standing structures; however, access to the site is limited by private property.

Badger did not last as long as Whitehorn nor did it become as large. Badger was located along Badger Creek in Gribbles Park. It was founded by prospectors from the Cripple Creek area in

1896. As that winter approached, snow began to limit their activity. It somehow made sense to build a town in the meadow where they had selected to camp.

In January of the following year, news leaked out that gold had been found in the Badger Creek area. This brought in more prospectors and soon, a 320-acre town site was laid out. Mining centered around a twelve-foot hole called the Octopus. The first business was a sawmill to produce lumber for Badger's buildings. A restaurant opened in a tent, and meals were provided at fifteen cents each. In the meantime, carefully selected ore samples were placed on display in Salida.

All was not peaceful in Badger and some moved two miles to the east to found Badger City. Nothing ever came of this second settlement. American City was laid out four miles upstream on Badger Creek, but all this amounted to were mine buildings.

This is the one remaining structure at the Whitehorn site which could potentially date back to the town's origins. Located a short distance from this structure was the town center with its streets faintly outlined in the meadow. *(Kenneth Jessen 103A5)*

Badger continued to grow and reached 200 residents. It got its own general store, and the Badger Hotel was constructed. The largest structure was Henry Schencke's 30-foot by 50-foot saloon. A local barbershop was located in the corner of this structure. Several applications were made for a post office, and finally, in February, Badger got a post office under the name of Skinner. (The Badger name had already been used for a post office in another part of the state. Postal officials often refused to let two postal locations within the same state have the same name.)

By March, 1897, Badger had an estimated population of 500 with seventy to eighty buildings along with thirty to forty tents. By this time, there were several general stores, a couple of grocery stores and six saloons. A hardware store was combined with a bank. After the passage of several months, over 500 lots had been sold, and the town grew to one hundred structures.

No ore in any great quantity nor of any great value came out of the mines in the area. The Turret area to the west seemed more promising to most, and Badger's population began to decline. Some of the wooden structures were moved away. By 1899, Badger was on its way to becoming a ghost town, and the post office closed. Nothing remains at the site today.

Dick Dixon, "Badger," *A History of Chaffee County*, edited by June Shaputis and Suzanne Kelly, Buena Vista Heritage, Buena Vista, Colorado, 1982, pp. 120-121.

Dick Dixon, "Whitehorn," *A History of Chaffee County*, edited by June Shaputis and Suzanne Kelly, Buena Vista Heritage, Buena Vista, Colorado, 1982, pp. 167-168.

Muriel Sibell Wolle, *Stampede to Timberline*, Sage Books, Chicago, 1949, pp. 159-160.

William H. Bauer, James L. Ozment and John H. Willard, *Colorado Post Offices*, Colorado Railroad Museum, Golden, Colorado 1990, pp. 132, 151.

Virginia McConnell Simmons, *The Upper Arkansas*, Pruett Publishing Company, Boulder, Colorado, 1990, pp. 147-148.

AREA TWELVE · 12

Gunnison County

continued

AREA 12: Gunnison County
Selected Towns

Introduction to Gunnison County

The county could be divided in half with the Gunnison River forming the dividing line. To the northwest is a vast coal deposit, and here, a number of coal mining towns were established. Most prominent is Crested Butte, a viable town today based on the recreational industry. There are the abandoned towns of Anthracite, Floresta, Baldwin, Castleton and Kubler.

To the northeast are high mountains, crystal clear streams and alpine meadows. Within this region, prospectors found gold, silver, copper, zinc and lead. Numerous mining camps were founded, and most were abandoned after the mineral resources were exhausted. Only a few survive today as summer retreats including Tincup, Whitepine, Ohio City, and Abbeyville. Abandoned towns dot this part of the county, including Bowerman, Bowman, Dorchester, Elko, Hillerton, North Star, Schofield, and many more.

South of the Gunnison River is a vast arid area of rolling hills. Trees are found only in isolated pockets primarily in creek beds. Most of the area is covered with sagebrush. This was the Gold Belt where widespread deposits of gold-bearing quartz were discovered. A number of mining towns were established, and when the gold ore was exhausted, the towns were abandoned. They didn't have the appeal of the towns to the north and were not located in lush high mountain meadows. Included among the Gold Belt towns were Chance, Cochetopa, Iris, Morris, Sillsville, Spencer and many more.

Supply towns, with railroad facilities, also played an important part in the development of the county. Thousands of tons of ore were shipped from places like Sargents and Iola. The Denver, South Park & Pacific is also of note as the first railroad in North America to construct a tunnel under the Continental Divide at Alpine Tunnel.

The most unusual part of Gunnison County is near its northern border. Marble deposits were discovered above Yule Creek leading to a substantial marble industry and the town of Marble.

The history of Gunnison County's ghost towns is varied and complex as the stories of these towns indicates.

ALPINE TUNNEL,
SHERROD and WOODSTOCK

- *Gunnison County, Middle Quartz Creek drainage*
- *Accessible by graded dirt road*
- *One structure remains standing at Alpine Tunnel*

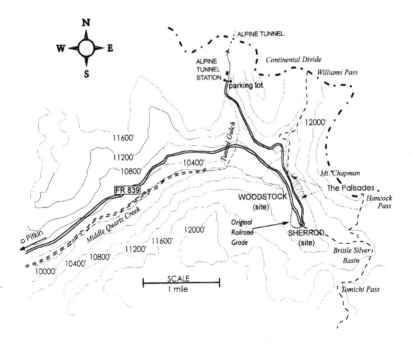

After the long climb above Middle Quartz Creek, the Denver, South Park & Pacific made a reverse loop at Sherrod. From that point for another mile, an artificial shelf was constructed across the Palisades.

Alpine Tunnel was strictly a railroad facility for the Denver, South Park & Pacific and not a town. A number of railroad workers lived at Alpine Tunnel, however, in a large boarding house located near the west portal. At an elevation of approximately 11,500 feet, winters were severe and summers were short. The work force also had the duty of shoveling out the track to keep the railroad operating. At times, snowfall was so heavy that the railroad was blocked for days.

The following is a list of structures as of 1886:

Stone section house	29 ½ by 56 feet
Addition to section house	16 by 25 ½ feet
Engine house (with turntable)	54 by 153 feet
Stone boarding house	14 by 16 ½ feet
Store house	10 by 16 feet
Wash house	10 by 18 feet
Water tank, coal chute and turntable	

The small storehouse was converted into a combination depot and telegraph office. In 1906, a fire swept through Alpine Tunnel, and all but the small depot was destroyed. In 1907, a new two-story frame boarding house was built. In 1910, the tunnel closed for good and the site was abandoned. Today, the Forest Service has a display at Alpine Tunnel. Volunteers man the small depot to tell visitors about the site's history. A short section of track, using original rail, runs in front of the depot to give visitors a feel for what it must have looked like.

To reach Alpine Tunnel from Pitkin, the railroad made a long climb along the north side of Middle Quartz Creek on a shelf high above the valley floor. This is now FR 839. Part way up is the Woodstock Tank, which remains standing today. At the head of the creek, a large reverse loop was built on a fill to allow the line to change directions for its final climb to the tunnel. This was called the Sherrod Curve or Sherrod Loop. The grade went along the base of a spectacular cliff called The Palisades. The railroad was obligated to construct a shelf built of large granite blocks, hand fitted without mortar. All but a few of these blocks remain in place today. The Alpine Tunnel is located a mile or so beyond The Palisades. All of the grade, with the exception of the Sherrod Curve, can be driven by an automobile during the summer.

Along the lower leg of the railroad grade and directly below the Palisades was a small mining camp called Woodstock. Established in 1881, it was located along the Alpine & South Park Toll Road (now called the Williams Pass road). The trees above this point were harvested by the railroad and cut into ties. This laid bare a dangerous avalanche path and set the stage for one of Gunnison County's worst disasters.

The economy of Woodstock was supported by the mines in Brittle Silver Basin at the base of Tomichi Pass. The railroad set up a construction camp at Woodstock for its push down Middle Quartz Creek. Stonecutters stayed at Woodstock during the construction of the roadbed along The Palisades. The first train to Gunnison passed through Woodstock in June, 1882.

Businesses at Woodstock included the Delmonica Restaurant, a saloon and a store. The railroad added a combination boarding house and telegraph office. The railroad also built a

A number of rail fans ventured up to the west portal of the Alpine Tunnel during the 1960s. The station was in poor condition, and the boarding house was about to collapse. *(Neal Miller)*

water tank and laid a 500-foot siding. Miner's cabins rounded out the structures. A post office opened in Woodstock in 1882, and at the time, the population was about 200.

The boarding house, owned by the railroad, was run by an Irish widow, Mrs. Marcella Doyle. Her husband had passed away leaving her to raise six children. The boys helped the railroad workers, and the girls helped their mother prepare meals.

After a heavy snowfall in March, 1884, an enormous avalanche came down from the west-facing slope of Mt. Chapman. This was where the railroad had denuded the slope of its trees for railroad ties. The avalanche struck with its full force when it reached the upper level of track taking with it heavy timbers left for the construction of a show shed. The snow was mixed with rock and other debris when it smashed into Woodstock. People were killed where they stood, and in all, thirteen perished. This included all six of Mrs. Doyle's children.

A train, pulled by two locomotives, had just taken on

The abandoned Denver, South Park & Pacific grade stretches from the Alpine Tunnel to the collapsed portal of the Alpine Tunnel. This photograph was taken during the 1960s, and today, the ties have been replaced by a footpath. *(Neal Miller)*

passengers at Woodstock and was making its way around the
Sherrod Curve when the avalanche struck. Several passengers wit-
nessed this white death and saw Woodstock buried. Among them
was Eugene Teets, who later related that the air became filled with
snow so fine and so dense that it formed a fog. Teets also told of the
crashing sound of the avalanche and how Woodstock was buried.

It was a long time before help arrived. The Denver, South
Park & Pacific telegraph system went down, and it took quite a
while for someone to trudge through heavy snow to Pitkin. It
wasn't until 4:00 p.m. the following day before the first rescue
party arrived. Work continued until 2:00 a.m. More men arrived
as the news spread until fifty were at work. It took twelve hours to
rescue Mrs. Doyle and fifteen hours to free Miss Celia Dillon.
After two full days of digging, rescuers recovered ten of the thirteen bodies, and the remaining three were left until the spring
thaw. Probably in June or early July, their rotting remains, tangled
in the debris, were brought down for proper burial.

Mrs. Doyle later sued the railroad claiming they had intentionally built their boarding house directly in an avalanche path.
She certainly had a point since the railroad planned to construct a
snow shed directly above the town to protect the tracks. Since she
was a widow, her sole means of support was the operation of the
boarding house. Her children were a part of her livelihood, and
she sued for future lost wages. The final result is unknown.

Woodstock was never rebuilt although the railroad later
constructed a small two-room bunkhouse at the site. Scattered
timbers are all that remain at the site today. It is marked by a
Forest Service sign along the right of way.

At the reverse loop, the mining camp of Sherrod was founded in 1903, because of renewed activity in Brittle Silver Basin. The
camp was started by three prospectors who failed to find riches at
Bowerman and came up Quartz Creek, looking for rich silver ore.
One of the men was W. H. Sherrod, for whom the town was
named. By the end of the following year, town lots were for sale at
$75 to $150, and the town's population stood at around 200. The

town had two hotels and two mercantile stores. The railroad built a small waiting room, and Sherrod also had a short siding for ore shipments. Several log homes added to the structures, but most of Sherrod's residents lived in tents.

Sherrod got its own post office in 1904, but by 1905, prospectors had determined that the ore was low grade. Prospectors began to leave, and in 1906, the post office closed. Sherrod's population soon stood at just seven men who hung on to the hope of riches. By 1908, Sherrod was a ghost town. A Forest Service sign marks the site today, and the remains of one cabin can be seen below the railroad grade.

One remaining cabin at Sherrod. The Sherrod Loop railroad grade can be seen in the background. *(Kenneth Jessen 105B10)*

Duane Vandenbusche, *The Gunnison Country*, B & B Printers, Gunnison, Colorado, 1980, pp. 194-196.

Mac Poor, *Denver South Park & Pacific*, Rocky Mountain Railroad Club, Denver, 1976, pp. 220-221, 440.

William H. Bauer, James L. Ozment and John H. Willard, *Colorado Post Offices*, Colorado Railroad Museum, Golden, Colorado, 1990, pp. 130, 154.

ANTHRACITE
Located at Smith Hill

- *Gunnison County, Slate River drainage*
- *Accessible via graded dirt road*
- *Town had a post office; several structures remain*

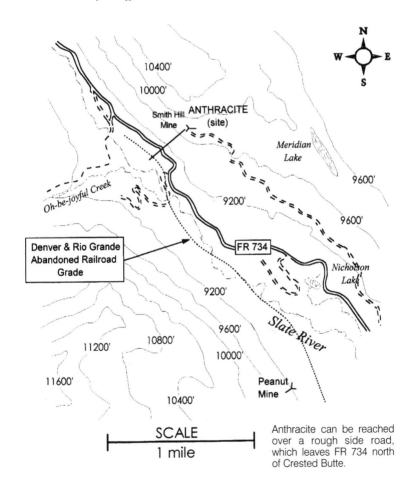

Anthracite can be reached over a rough side road, which leaves FR 734 north of Crested Butte.

The Crested Butte area produced large quantities of coal, and this was its primary industry for many years. Smith Hill was the second largest mine and was located four miles north of Crested Butte above the Slate River on Anthracite Mesa. Howard Smith, known as "the father of Crested Butte," developed this mine. Smith and two partners purchased the coal deposit in 1879, and they opened the mine on top of the mesa. The coal was transported down the mountain by a tram 1,628 feet in length. Coal production began in the spring of 1882. Within several months, the Denver & Rio Grande constructed a narrow gauge spur from Crested Butte to the breaker and tipple at the base of the hill. The breaker, incidentally, was the largest of its type west of Pennsylvania.

Most coal mining towns were located at the base of the mountain, but not the town of Anthracite. It was on the mesa near the entrance to the Smith Hill Mine. Its high altitude location, overlooking the valley, explains why it was originally named Cloud City.

Unlike most coal mining towns, Anthracite was at the top of a mesa and its buildings were primarily of log construction. This photograph was taken around 1901 or 1902. *(Author's collection CP045)*

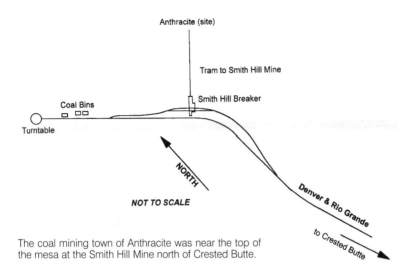

The coal mining town of Anthracite was near the top of the mesa at the Smith Hill Mine north of Crested Butte.

The coal company owned the community of Anthracite and provided a number of homes, a library, school and several boarding houses. Over 200 people lived at the site. In January, 1883, an avalanche plowed into the boarding house near the mine entrance, killing six men. Despite the avalanche danger, Anthracite grew, and in 1884, the town got a post office. Coal production reached a level where ten to twenty railroad cars a day were filled.

Through leases, Colorado Fuel & Iron got the rights to the Smith Hill Mine. The coal contained a high percentage of carbon, excellent for use in the steel making process after its conversion to coke. In 1903, Colorado Fuel & Iron failed to renew the lease since quality coal mines were developed closer to Colorado Fuel & Iron's steel mill at Pueblo.

Smith Hill was mined sporadically, and in 1906, the post office closed. The mine closed in 1908, but was reopened in 1913. The original coal breaker burned to the ground and was rebuilt only to burn again. Anthracite managed to survive through World War I and into the 1930s. Natural gas became more popular for heating in Colorado than coal. As the demand for coal fell, the mine was closed for the last time and the town abandoned. The

The Smith Hill cable tram used to bring coal down from the mine entrance to the coal breaker. *(Author's collection CP082)*

tracks of the Denver & Rio Grande remained in place until 1947 to allow haulage of the Smith Hill Mine dump. This discarded material proved excellent for flux in the steel making process at the C.F.&I. Pueblo plant.

When Muriel Sibell Wolle visited Anthracite during the 1940s, about fifteen cabins, although roofless, were still standing. The coal breaker and the railroad tracks were also in place. Today, there are several collapsed log structures at Anthracite. The road into the site is rough and may not be suitable for an automobile.

Duane Vandenbusche, *The Gunnison Country*, B & B Printers, Gunnison, Colorado, 1980, pp. 216-218.

Muriel Sibell Wolle, *Stampede to Timberline*, Sage Books, Chicago, 1949, p. 206.

William H. Bauer, James L. Ozment and John H. Willard, *Colorado Post Offices, Colorado* Railroad Museum, Golden, Colorado, 1990, p. 12.

BOWERMAN

Its Life and Death

- *Gunnison County, Hot Springs Creek drainage*
- *Accessible via graded dirt road*
- *Town had a post office; No standing structures remain*

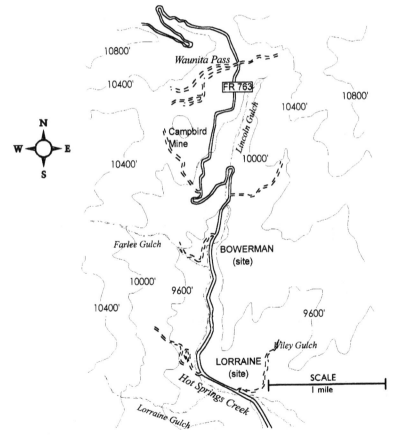

The town sites of Bowerman and Lorraine are located along FR 763 just south of Waunita Pass.

J. C. Bowerman's wife slaved, away working odd jobs and taking in wash. This gave her husband the luxury of prospecting, which he did for a quarter of a century over a wide area including the San Juans, Cripple Creek and the Blue River Valley. Using a grubstake provided by Stephen Dunn, the Denver & Rio Grande's Chief Dispatcher, Bowerman prospected in the Hot Springs Creek area above Waunita Hot Springs. In 1903, he claimed to have found rich gold ore including nuggets. He said he could pan $300 a day in gold flakes from the stream.

What started a gold rush into the area was an article in the *Gunnison News Chronicle* on July 17, 1903. The headline covering J. C. Bowerman's discovery read, "GOLD FIND UNPARALLELED." The article began its story with, "A gold find which staggers the imagination..." Clearly designed to fuel the reader's imagination, it talked of wire gold in a nugget and of an assay showing the ore to be worth over $70,000 a ton. Soon a flood of eager prospectors, numbering one-thousand or more, came into the area. A mining camp named Nugget City was formed consisting of over 100 tents. The camp's first hotel was a large tent named the Bowerman House. The Gold Nugget Restaurant could be identified among the other tents by a wash basin in front of its entrance. The *Bowerman Herald* was published without the benefit of a printing press by having the work done in Denver.

After staking out numerous claims, among them the Independent, Bowerman sent for his wife. She lived in their Pitkin home, but was in the middle of doing other peoples laundry. Since her husband had made wild claims before, she was skeptical. She finally moved the family to the new mining camp.

In late July, a meeting was held, and the mining camp of Nugget City was surveyed. An application for a post office was filed, but when it came time to name the post office, Bowerman was selected. It was also called Camp Bowerman. The name Nugget had already been used for a small mining camp in Gilpin County. Mail delivery to Bowerman began in October, 1903.

One curious fact was that none of the thousand or so

prospectors could find any ore resembling that claimed by J. C. Bowerman. No pans were filled with nuggets, and no wire gold specimens were discovered. Dunn quite his job with the Denver & Rio Grande and joined Bowerman to guard the mine. The mine was fenced and no one was allowed to enter. Bowerman failed to ship any ore from the Independent claiming that he was still doing development work. Pressured, he said he would show his mine after a mine office was completed, but he reneged on his promise. Again pressured, he said he would show the mine after the election of a deputy sheriff, but again he didn't keep his word.

In late July, Bowerman said he would open the doors to his mine after the town's first church service. On the door of the Gold Nugget Restaurant was tacked a notice of a church service to be held the afternoon of August 2. A tent saloon was to be used for the service, but so many people showed up that the service had to be moved. There was a combination saloon and dance hall under construction at the time. The floor joists were in place, but only a quarter of floor boards had been laid. Chairs were placed up to the edge of the flooring, and the rest of the congregation stood on the joists or sat on logs.

Reverend T. J. Mackay from Leadville officiated from a pulpit made from a rough board. On the pulpit was a tin cup of water and several rocks to hold down the sermon. The saloon across the street remained open, but when it came time to sing a hymn, its patrons joined in. When the hymn ended, the saloon patrons con-

One of several collapsed cabins in the valley where Bowerman and Lorraine were located. *(Kenneth Jessen 117D11)*

tinued to sing and had to be quieted by the Reverend. The collection netted only $8.70, and one man asked for change for a dollar so he could contribute a dime. Once the service ended, Bowerman broke his promise to show his mine.

Mrs. Phillips, a widow, arrived in the new camp during the summer of 1903 with a tent and a sheet-iron stove. She began baking bread and pies clearing $2.25 her first day. She teamed up with another widow, Mrs. McMurtry, the two women sold forty to fifty loaves of bread per day at a dime a loaf. They posted daily specials on a board tacked to the peak of their tent. Their tent bakery was so small that only one woman could work at a time.

Mrs. Sherwood, a baker, heard of the new camp and baked thirty-three loaves. She lived in Pitkin and packed up her household possessions. When she arrived in Bowerman, she sold all her bread at fifteen cents a loaf before dismounting from her wagon. She pitched her tent and opened the camp's second bakery.

The town's only laundry operator was a black woman named Oney Coombs. She maintained pick-up points throughout the camp and would go around and gather up the wash for the day. She then carried them to Pitkin where they were washed and ironed. For a formal shirt with a collar, she charged a quarter, while regular flannel shirts were washed for half that amount.

In April, 1904, the Camp Bird Mine did prepare a single wagonload of ore. Citizens helped construct a primitive road down from the mine. The town of Bowerman turned out in number to celebrate. A large American flag was flown from one of the buildings. After the ore reached a Pueblo smelter, it was confiscated by a tunnel company for an unpaid debt. Not a single penny in profit resulted.

It seems that J. C. Bowerman's find was a hoax. In 1904, the *Colorado Business Directory* listed the town as having 500 residents. It had two bakeries, four grocery stores, four saloons, two drug stores, a general merchandise store, the post office, two hotels and the *Bowerman Herald*. By the end of the following year, the town had lost many of its businesses and was down to one grocery store and two saloons. The two hotels remained open. The town was stable in size for another year, but by the end of 1907, it had no saloons, only one hotel, and the newspaper had apparently gone out of business. It did have a general merchandise store and its post office. By 1910, Bowerman had only a bakery and the offices of several mining companies. The post office was moved to Waunita Hot Springs. No businesses were listed for 1911, and Bowerman became a ghost town.

Today, the meadow where Bowerman was located is littered with the remains of many cabins. All are in an advanced state of deterioration.

Duane Vandenbusche, in his book *The Gunnison Country*, writes of two other mining camps located near Bowerman and not covered in other ghost town sources. Camp Sterling was north of J. C. Bowerman's Independent Mine. The camp was named for its founder, K. C. Sterling. It had no more than five log structures, and its population was probably fifty or less. By 1904, Camp Sterling had been abandoned.

Another small camp was Lorraine. Located a mile south of Bowerman along Hot Springs Creek, it started as a tent camp in 1903. By the end of the year, over ten permanent structures had been built. The small camp survived until 1906.

Neither Camp Sterling nor Lorraine had a post office.

Duane Vandenbusche, *The Gunnison Country*, B & B Printers, Gunnison, Colorado, 1980, pp. 196-198.

Francis B. Rizzari, "Full Stop for Bowerman," *1949 Brand Book*, Denver Posse of The Westerners, Denver, 1950, pp. 69-92.

William H. Bauer, James L. Ozment and John H. Willard, *Colorado Post Offices,* Colorado Railroad Museum, Golden, Colorado, 1990, p. 22.

CAMP WILLARD and SILLSVILLE

Cochetopa Creek Towns

- *Gunnison County, Cochetopa Creek drainage*
- *Accessible via paved road*
- *One town had a post office; structures remain at Sillsville*

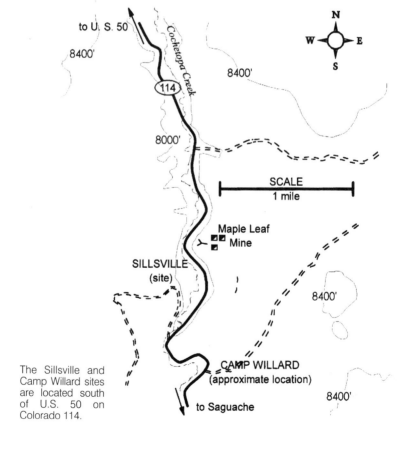

The Sillsville and Camp Willard sites are located south of U.S. 50 on Colorado 114.

492

Prospectors Willard Frances and H. C. Nicholas rode north out of the mountains to Gunnison with samples of gold-bearing quartz they had found along Cochetopa Creek. They had the samples assayed, and the results projected a yield better than $2,000 a ton. This news created a gold rush into the region and was the beginning of defining what became the Gold Belt.

Camp Willard was established along Cochetopa Creek in 1880, along what is now Colorado 114. Camp Willard soon had hundreds of prospectors living in tents, and by the fall of 1880, several permanent structures had been built. The first business to open was a saloon, illustrating the priorities at the time!

The *Gunnison Review* reported that many of the prospectors came from Ruby City and Irwin. By October, Camp Willard had a barber shop, five grocery stores, a meat market and four saloons. When winter arrived, most of the prospectors left. The area's gold ore turned out to be elusive and low grade. A few returned to Camp Willard the following spring, and only two of the cabins were occupied. Soon, the camp was deserted.

This fine old log cabin is located near the Sillsville site. *(Kenneth Jessen 100A2)*

North of Camp Willard another mining camp was established many years later in 1904. It was called Sillsville and was located only a short distance north of Camp Willard. One of its frame stores still stands on the west side of Cochetopa Creek visible from Colorado 114. Its post office was opened in 1903, closed in 1907, and reopened in 1908, only to close for good in 1910. The town consisted of fifteen to twenty buildings and had a population of seventy-five to one hundred residents. The Maple Leaf Mine, located across from Sillsville on the east side of Colorado 114, supported the town. The Sillsville site is occupied by a ranch today.

The Maple Leaf Mine also had a resident population. There was a bunkhouse, a boarding house and a large stamp mill on the site. Ore was shipped by wagon north to the Denver & Rio Grande narrow gauge railroad for shipment to a smelter. The Maple Leaf Mine closed in 1907.

Duane Vandenbusche, *The Gunnison Country*, B & B Printers, Gunnison, Colorado, 1980, pp. 288-289, 300-301.

William H. Bauer, James L. Ozment and John H. Willard, *Colorado Post Offices*, Colorado Railroad Museum, Golden, Colorado, 1990, pp. 35, 132.

CASTLETON, MOUNT CARBON, BALDWIN and KUBLER

- *Gunnison County, Ohio Creek drainage*
- *Accessible via paved or graded dirt roads*
- *Towns had a post office; a number of structures remain at Baldwin*

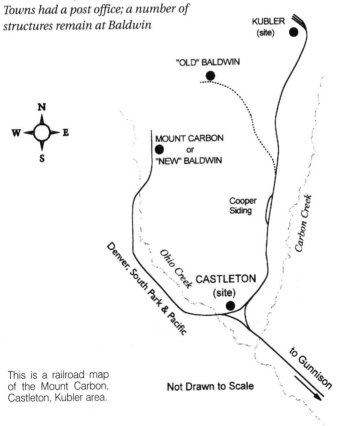

This is a railroad map of the Mount Carbon, Castleton, Kubler area.

Not Drawn to Scale

In the area near the junction of Carbon Creek and Ohio Creek north of Gunnison, vast coal deposits were discovered during the 1870s. At the confluence of the two drainages, the coal mining town of Castleton was founded. The arrival of the Denver, South Park & Pacific in 1883 made it practical to develop the mines. A railroad station named Baldwin was established at this location while the rails were laid another three miles north along Ohio Creek. Grading was partially completed almost to Ohio Pass. A second rail line was constructed up Carbon Creek to serve what became known as the "Old" Baldwin Mine. Later, the rails were extended to the Kubler Mine.

There is a great deal of confusion over town names in this area. The name, Baldwin, was applied over the years to three distinct locations, all within a few miles of each other. When the Denver, South Park & Pacific first issued a timetable in 1882, it showed its proposed extension up Ohio Creek and listed a place called Richardson in the Ohio Creek Valley. The place was named for Sylvester Richardson, who had opened up the first coal mine on Mount Carbon. When the railroad actually reached the conflu-

The Alpine Mine at "New" Baldwin operated until 1946. *(Denver Public Library, Western History Department X-11000174)*

ence of Ohio Creek and Carbon Creek, it named the place Baldwin. The town was Castleton, and eventually, the railroad changed its station name to Castleton. At the end of the track, which followed Ohio Creek, was the Mount Carbon Mine. The coal mining camp at the mine became Mount Carbon. This camp was later renamed Baldwin, and the name of the mine was changed to the Alpine Mine.

Confused? At the end of the railroad spur up Carbon Creek was the Baldwin Mine. The mining camp at the mine was naturally called Baldwin, and when the camp was deserted, it was generally known as "Old" Baldwin. Since "Old" Baldwin was abandoned, the town of Mount Carbon took the name Baldwin. It was generally known as "New" Baldwin.

After the Baldwin Mine (at "Old" Baldwin) was exhausted of its coal, the track was moved a short distance and laid north to the Kubler Mine. Fortunately for historians, this particular mining camp was always called Kubler.

Postal history adds to the information. Castleton got its own post office in 1882, and it remained in operation for a dozen years. Mount Carbon's post office opened in 1884, and in 1891, was moved to "Old" Baldwin. It remained open under the name Baldwin until 1909 when that site was abandoned. In the meantime, "Old" Baldwin did have its own post office, which opened when the mining camp was first founded in 1883. In 1909, the Mount Carbon post office became Baldwin, and remained active until 1948.

"Old" Baldwin was a company town owned by the Rocky Mountain Fuel Company. Rows of identical frame houses can be seen in a historic photograph of the town. A boarding house and a false-front store were also located at this site, which was home to 100 people.

According to research done by contemporary historian Duane Vandenbusche for his book, *The Gunnison Country*, "Old" Baldwin was the first town in the county to hold a football game. They played a team from Crested Butte.

Kubler was founded in 1881 and was supported entirely by the Kubler Mine. The mine operated almost continuously for the next three decades. A gravity tram was used to lower the loaded mine cars from the adit to the tipple. The Denver, South Park & Pacific laid a spur tack to the mine in 1896, a distance of 1.8 miles. Kubler grew to become a town of 200 residents. Historical photographs show a number of identical company houses and several mine structures. It also had a boarding house, approximately two-dozen homes and a saloon. Kubler did not have a post office.

The mine at Kubler closed in 1913 and was reopened in 1936. It closed for good in 1946 and the railroad tracks were taken up. It is not known what structures remain at the site today.

Mount Carbon was started by William Hinds, and his original idea was to use the coal for coke. This derivative of coal was in great demand in the precious metal smelting industry and in the steel industry. The Ohio Creek Anthracite Coal Company was formed by Hinds in 1884, and this was when the town of Mount Carbon was established. After the construction of some structures and laying foundations for coke ovens, Hinds made the unpleasant discovery that the coal was not suitable for conversion to coke. Coal mining continued at the mine, however.

In 1893, the *Gunnison Review* indicated that Mount Carbon had been abandoned. It explained that the post office remained open even though for the last three years the town had but one resident. Mount Carbon was destroyed by fire.

The old mine was purchased and reopened as the Alpine Mine after the turn of the century. The coal company constructed twenty houses for its miners at the site. The small town was still called Mount Carbon, but was also known locally as Alpine. As has been mentioned previously, after the mine at "Old" Baldwin closed, Mount Carbon (or Alpine) took the name Baldwin. At the new town of Baldwin, population fluctuated from 100 to 250 depending on the level of mining activity. Aside from its post office, there was also a company store, saloon and dance hall, hotel, schoolhouse and over forty homes.

There are several structures still standing at "New" Baldwin, a ghost town north of Gunnison located along the Ohio Creek Road (730 RD). The site is fenced in and posted no trespassing. *(Kenneth Jessen 095D11)*

"New" Baldwin had an active baseball team, and they played other towns including Crested Butte, Jack's Cabin and Gunnison. Adding to its social life, the town also had a jazz band. An occasional prizefight took place, and after one particular fight, a union man and a non-union man got into their own fight. One man died of a knife wound, and while awaiting trial, the winner of the conflict committed suicide.

In 1946, the Alpine Fuel Company was faced with a miner's strike. Since most of the coal reserves had been removed, the mine at "New" Baldwin was closed for good. The post office, as mentioned, remained open until 1949.

The "New" Baldwin site sits on the east side of the Ohio Creek Road (730 RD), and contains a number of original structures. The site is completely fenced in and posted no trespassing thus limiting exploration.

Duane Vandenbusche, *The Gunnison Country*, B & B Printers, Gunnison, Colorado, 1980, pp. 349-351.

Robert W. Richardson, "Colorado & Southern: An Operations Baedeker," *The South Park Line, Colorado Rail Annual No. 12.*, Colorado Railroad Museum, Golden, Colorado, 1974, pp. 150-151.

Tiv Wilkins, *Colorado Railroads*, Pruett Publishing Company, Boulder, Colorado, 1974, pp. 51, 113, 241.

William H. Bauer, James L. Ozment and John H. Willard, *Colorado Post Offices*, Colorado Railroad Museum, Golden, Colorado, 1990, pp. 16, 31, 98, 102.

CIMARRON

A Denver & Rio Grande Town

- *Montrose County, Cimarron Creek drainage*
- *Accessible via paved road*
- *Town has a post office; remaining original structures unknown*

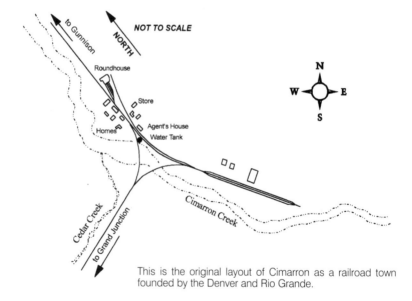

This is the original layout of Cimarron as a railroad town founded by the Denver and Rio Grande.

In 1881 and 1882, General Palmer pushed the narrow gauge tracks of the Denver & Rio Grande through the upper part of the Black Canyon from Gunnison. When his surveyors reported that in the lower part of the canyon construction of a railroad would be impossible, the decision was made to exit at Cimarron River. It would be many years before the lower portion of the Black Canyon would be fully explored.

The new town of Cimarron was founded about a mile from

the confluence of the Cimarron River and the Gunnison River.
It was also at the base of the steep climb over Cerro Summit to
Montrose.

The land was originally owned by Captain W. M. Cline, and
the location was known as Cline's Ranch. Part of the ranch was
sold to the railroad, and in 1881, the location was renamed
Cimarron. Although early Cimarron was nothing but a tent city,
it soon gained a general store, several restaurants, one dance hall
and an astounding eleven saloons. In August, 1882, it became a
rough and rowdy end of track town filled with surveyors, track
gangs and laborers. Most slept in a string of twenty-seven railroad
cars converted into sleeping accommodations and parked on a
siding.

The following month, Cimarron was quiet as the laborers
moved on toward Cerro Summit and Montrose. Soon, regular
train service started, and both east and westbound trains stopped

The Denver & Rio Grande engine house is in the foreground with several of Cimarron's homes sitting along the track in the center of the photograph. *(Denver Public Library, Western History Department X-11486)*

at Cimarron to take on water. For the passenger trains, the passengers were allowed to get off and get a meal.

A post office was opened in 1883 and remains open to this day. The railroad constructed extensive railroad facilities at Cimarron including a repair shop, roundhouse, depot, water tank and a section house. The town soon attracted settlers and several homes were constructed.

Today, Cimarron is the site of the National Park Service visitor's center for the Morrow Point Dam. A display of narrow gauge freight cars sits just outside the visitor's center. In the canyon, an entire train, locomotive and all, sits on the original bridge over the Gunnison River. None of the original buildings constructed by the Denver & Rio Grande survive. It is unknown if any of the homes at Cimarron date back to the town's early days. The town site is not abandoned and there are two service stations at Cimarron.

An entire narrow gauge train, with one of the Denver & Rio Grande's original locomotives, sits on the original bridge over the Gunnison River leading to Cimarron. *(Kenneth Jessen 082D1)*

Duane Vandenbusche, *The Gunnison Country*, B & B Printers, Gunnison, Colorado, 1980, pp. 97, 171-172.

William H. Bauer, James L. Ozment and John H. Willard, *Colorado Post Offices*, Colorado Railroad Museum, Golden, Colorado, 1990, p. 34.

CRESTED BUTTE

Coal Mining to Skiing

- *Gunnison County, Slate River drainage*
- *Accessible via paved road*
- *Occupied town with post office; many original structures remain*

This is an early view of Crested Butte's business district taken in the 1890s. *(Denver Public Library, Western History Department F5480)*

It is relatively rare that a mining town can make the transition to a recreation driven economy. Although gold was found in the river bottoms in the Crested Butte area, it wasn't precious metals that made this town a lasting success, it was coal. The Slate River Valley is rich in coal, and early miners used the abundant supply to heat their cabins.

Although coal was mined on a limited scale for a number of years, it took Howard F. Smith to make coal the dominant resource of the area. He was a partner in the Iowa Smelting Company and had heard of the vast bituminous coal deposits in the Elk Mountains. After a brief survey, Smith immediately purchased most of the coal land in the Crested Butte area in 1878. During that summer, he laid out the town taking its name from nearby Crested Butte Mountain. Smith, along with his partners, organized the Crested Butte Town Company. In July, 1880, they formally incorporated the town. Soon, Smith's smelting company constructed a twenty-five ton per day smelter in Crested Butte to process ore from area mines.

Mine owners not only needed a smelter for their ore, they also needed an abundant supply of milled lumber for the construction of homes, mine buildings and timbering within the mines. Smith opened up a sawmill, and soon, three sawmills were in operation along with the smelter. A boarding house was constructed for the workers. To supply the growing town, a store opened for business. Crested Butte's first bar was a felled tree,

The City Hall was damaged during a blast to create a firebreak during 1893. The firemen used fifty pounds of powder to level a building across the street to save the town. The Crested Butte City Hall, constructed in 1883, remains standing today and is used for city offices. *(Denver Public Library, Western History Department X-7662)*

split in half and laid across a couple of barrels. A drink sold for a quarter in a day when wages were $2.00 a day for a laborer and $3.00 for a skilled miner.

Several thousand miners were living in small camps and in the canyons in the general area. Satellite towns such as Gothic, Ruby City, Irwin, Elkton, Pittsburg and others sprang up. Crested Butte became the supply point for these scattered mining camps.

In today's dollars, Howard Smith had invested millions in the smelter and coal deposits. What was badly needed for continued growth was cheap rail transportation to outside markets. To promote the construction of a railroad into town, he sold off part of his holdings to the Denver & Rio Grande. The railroad constructed its narrow gauge line from Gunnison, through Almont, and reached Crested Butte in 1881. The railroad's arrival was of such importance that the exact time it reached Crested Butte was recorded: 11:59 a.m. on November 21, 1881.

Outside investors were attracted to Crested Butte. The most notable was Horace Tabor, one of the richest men in Colorado. He started the Bank of Crested Butte in 1881 and served as its absentee president.

Converting coal to coke became a major part of Crested Butte's economy. Coke is produced when coal is burned in a reduced atmosphere such that the volatile matter is driven off leaving behind carbon. For this, numerous coke ovens were constructed on the edge of town. Coke is an important ingredient for making steel and in reducing certain precious metal ores.

Colorado Fuel & Iron operated a large steel mill in Pueblo and needed a reliable supply of both coal and coke. In 1881, Smith sold 320 acres of his coal deposit at the Coal Creek Mine to Colorado Fuel & Iron. C. F. & I. also operated other coal mines in the Crested Butte area.

At a point four miles north of Crested Butte along the Slate River, Smith discovered a deposit of anthracite coal. The railroad was encouraged to construct a branch up to the deposit. It was named Smith Hill and the mining camp above the river valley at the mine entrance was called Anthracite. (The ghost town of Anthracite is covered in this chapter as a separate story.)

After all of the contributions Howard Smith made to Crested Butte, it was not a surprise that he became the town's first mayor. During the early 1880s, the town grew to a population of 400, but there were an estimated 1,000 or more in the general area living in tents and scattered cabins. At this time, Crested Butte had fifty structures including a hotel.

The *Crested Butte Republican* began business and boasted about the area's resources. The first issue read more like an advertisement than a newspaper. It lasted until 1883 when it was sold to a couple of democrats. They immediately changed the name to the *Crested Butte Gazette*. In 1886, competition from the town's second newspaper, the *Elk Mountain Pilot*, forced the *Crested Butte Gazette* to close. The *Elk Mountain Pilot* continued publication until 1949.

By the mid-1880s, the town had come into its own with roughly a thousand residents and all types of businesses. A water company built a reservoir on Coal Creek to bring piped water under pressure into the town. A telephone line was brought twenty-eight miles up from Gunnison. Crested Butte constructed a city hall in 1883, which remains standing today and still serves its original purpose. Hotels played an important role in the town's development, and the Elk Mountain House was considered among the finest in Colorado. A massive three-story structure, it was constructed in 1881. Crested Butte also got several schools and churches.

It was a melting pot for miners from various part of Europe. There were Slavs, Italians, and people from Cornwall, Wales, Scotland and Ireland. Teaching English to Crested Butte schoolchildren was a major task for the teachers.

Life in Crested Butte was not especially pleasant during the winter months. The weather is extremely cold with many days below zero. Deep snow made travel difficult. The most unpleasant aspect of life in this town was the pollution created by the numerous coke ovens. They operated throughout the year, day and night, releasing tons of foul-smelling, sulphur-laden gases. On still days, a constant haze hung over the town, and sometimes, the smog was so thick it obscured visibility.

Virtually every tree in and around Crested Butte had been felled by local sawmills leaving the landscape barren. Streams were polluted with human waste combined with the chemical byproducts from mining. The water could not be used for domestic purposes. This was the price paid by residents for progress.

Eventually the coal deposits were exhausted. Labor troubles made life difficult for mine owners. The Big Mine, owned and operated by C. F. & I., closed in 1952. The railroad was dismantled. The Keystone Mine continued operation until the late 1960s, but it was clear that Crested Butte was at the end of an era.

The best thing to do with long winters and heavy snow is to construct a ski area. Back in the 1800s, skiing had become popular among the miners as a means of getting around. The first gondola was installed for the 1962-1963 ski season, and skiing became Crested Butte's primary industry. Fortunately, Mount Crested Butte is located above and north of the original town. This allowed lodges, ski lifts and modern condos to be constructed without the destruction of the many historic buildings in Crested Butte proper. Nearly every original structure has been restored, making Crested Butte a wonderful place to visit.

Duane Vandenbusche, *The Gunnison Country*, B & B Printers, Gunnison, Colorado, 1980, pp. 202-210.

CRYSTAL

And Its Picturesque Power Plant

- *Gunnison County, Crystal River drainage*
- *Accessible via four-wheel drive road*
- *Town had a post office; a number of original structures remain*

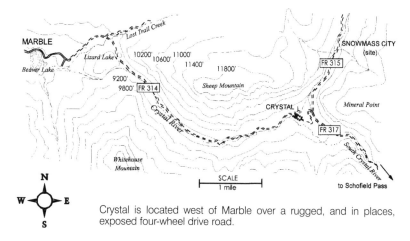

Crystal is located west of Marble over a rugged, and in places, exposed four-wheel drive road.

The old power plant below Crystal is among the most photographed mining structures in Colorado. Only the vertical log structure for the waterwheel and the log power house itself remain. The large Sheep Mountain Mill, which once stood by the powerhouse, collapsed many years ago. The builders took advantage of a natural ledge, where construction of a small dam was relatively easy. Water was diverted into a flume which, in turn, flowed into the vertical, wooden shaft and over the water wheel. In the process, ninety horsepower was generated to drive the air compressor for the Sheep Mountain Tunnel.

Crystal is located in a magnificent, narrow valley surrounded by high mountains. It was founded in 1880, based on the discovery of silver ore. Hundreds of prospectors entered the area, many arriving over the hazardous Schofield Pass to the south. The town of Crystal was established in the only sizable flat area in the canyon where the north and south forks of the Crystal River join. Due to the prodigious amount of snow and its isolation, Crystal was a seasonal town for several years. Eventually, substantial log cabins were constructed, and miners could then endure the long winter months.

By 1881, less than two-dozen cabins had been constructed at Crystal. In 1883, a wagon road over Schofield Pass was constructed, and the population climbed to around 600. This was Crystal at its height and from that point on, its population varied from 200 to 400.

Crystal got its own post office in 1882. It remained open until 1909. Crystal had a number of saloons, two general stores, a pool hall and over seventy homes. For men only, the Crystal Club acted as the town's social center.

In this photograph taken in 1937, the Sheep Mountain Mill can be seen to the right of the powerhouse. Note the flume that provided water to the vertical water wheel. (Denver Public Library, Western History Department X-7580)

Norwegian snowshoes were the forerunners of modern skis. The original ones were designed for cross-country travel and were around fifteen feet long. Those interested in skiing as a sport joined the Crystal Snowshoe Club. A more serious use was by Albert and Fred Johnson, who came to Crystal in 1880. They used Norwegian snowshoes to carry the mail to and from Crested Butte. The run was called the Snowshoe Express.

Albert Johnson was the editor and publisher of the *Crystal River Current*, the town's newspaper. His paper began publication in 1886 and lasted half-a-dozen years. He also became the post-

Often referred to as a mill, this is actually the power plant which served the Sheep Mountain Mill. The mill collapsed many years ago and sat to the right of the power plant. This, by the way, is among the most photographed mining structures in Colorado. *(Kenneth Jessen 085B11)*

master and operated the general store.

The year 1893 was significant for Crystal. This was the year the United States abandoned the silver standard, and the U. S. Government was no longer obligated to purchase a fixed amount of silver as backing its currency. As a result, the price of silver dropped nearly to half of its previous price, and most silver mines in Colorado closed. Although Crystal never recovered, its rich mines kept producing. By 1899, the only remaining business was a general merchandise store.

Isolation and lack of a good wagon road hurt Crystal's chances of survival. By 1917, the mines around Crystal were nearly exhausted of their ore. The population slipped to just eight individuals. Crystal eventually stood empty until it was discovered as a summer paradise. A number of individuals purchased its old cabins and restored them. This explains why so many original structures remain standing today.

When ghost town historian Muriel Sibell Wolle visited Crystal during the 1940s, she noted that the town had a dozen houses, some two-stories high. Most were in good condition. Crystal had residents at the time and some of the mines were still producing limited amounts of ore. By the 1960s, historian Robert L. Brown noted that ten structures remained at the town site.

Duane Vandenbusche, *The Gunnison Country*, B & B Printers, Gunnison, Colorado, 1980, pp. 245-246.

Muriel Sibell Wolle, *Stampede to Timberline*, Sage Books, Chicago, 1949, pp. 220-223.

Robert L. Brown, *Ghost Towns of the Colorado Rockies*, Caxton Printers, Caldwell, Idaho, 1977, pp. 110-114.

William H. Bauer, James L. Ozment and John H. Willard, *Colorado Post Offices*, Colorado Railroad Museum, Golden, Colorado, 1990, p. 41.

DUBOIS and TALIAFARO

Goose Creek Towns

- *Gunnison County, Goose Creek drainage*
- *Accessible by dirt road or by foot*
- *Dubois had a post office; remaining structures unknown*

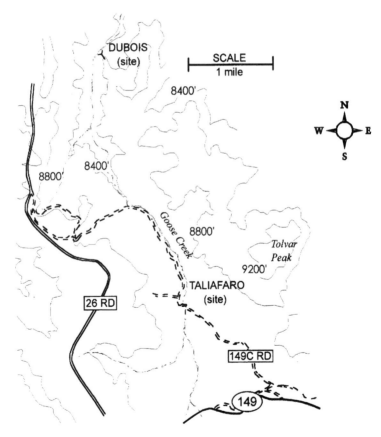

No road is shown to the Dubois site on contemporary topographic maps, however, Taliafaro can be reached on 149C RD.

On Goose Creek, located northwest of Powderhorn, was the gold mining town of Dubois. The site is a mile and a half south of the confluence of Goose Creek and Cebolla Creek. At one time, Dubois was on the main wagon road running south to Lake City, but on today's maps, not even a four-wheel drive trail is indicated to the site.

A Leadville prospector located the "Pride of Denver" in 1892. Near the mine and along the creek, the mining camp of Goose Creek was formed. The name was changed to Dubois in honor of Idaho Senator Fred Dubois. Typical of other mining heroes, Dubois fought for unlimited "free" coinage of silver, which would have kept silver prices high. The repeal of the Sherman Silver Purchase Act in 1893 caused the price of silver to drop to nearly half of its previous price and ended large scale silver mining in the West. It was this event that drove many prospectors to seek areas like Dubois where gold ore hopefully could be discovered.

By 1893, Dubois had over fifty structures including a number of businesses. There was an assay office, stores, saloons, a livery stable and probably a hotel or two. The population was around 250. There were two stage lines operating into Dubois daily: one made round trips to Sapinero and the other came from Gateway. Both of these towns were located on the Denver & Rio Grande. The first issue of the *Dubois Pick and Drill* appeared in December, 1893. The paper was printed in Gunnison and transported to Dubois for distribution. It lasted a year.

Another newspaper, the *Dubois Chronicle*, began publication in April, 1894. It carried an article that read, "We have no telegraph and mail service is not the best, hence, outside news may not be of the latest, but we are here to stay." A marriage license could be obtained at the newspaper office.

Dubois grew to a town of well over 100 cabins by some estimates and was incorporated in 1894. A post office opened this same year. A poor quality photograph verifies that the town had at least fifteen structures sitting in the creek bed.

The Dubois Tunnel reached 1,800 feet in length, and after

the expenditure of a great deal of money, the project was abandoned. The vein of ore, discovered on the surface at the Denver City lode, could not be found below the surface. Only small pockets of ore were encountered during the drilling process. Dubois was almost deserted by 1896, but the post office remained in operation until 1910 serving area ranchers. It is not known if any original structures remain.

Between the Lake Fork of the Gunnison River and Cebolla Creek, the town of Nugget City was started on Goose Creek. It was located west of Tolvar Peak where gold ore had been discovered. By the fall of 1895, the town had a hotel and general store. The name, Nugget City, was unacceptable to the U. S. Postal Service because of a town named Nugget in Gilpin County. The name was changed to Taliafaro for one of its founders. (Postal records, however, fail to indicate a post office at Taliafaro.)

Taliafaro's population reached 300 by 1896, and the town built its own school. The Nugget City Gold Mining and Milling Company, along with two other companies, raised the capital necessary to develop the area mines. After three years, veins that initially looked rich on the surface failed to produce paying quantities of ore. Taliafaro was abandoned.

It is not known what remains at the Taliafaro town site, but it can be reached by a dirt road that leaves Colorado 149 a little over a mile west of the Powderhorn post office.

Duane Vandenbusche, *The Gunnison Country*, B & B Printers, Gunnison, Colorado, 1980, pp. 290-296.

Muriel Sibell Wolle, *Stampede to Timberline*, Sage Books, Chicago, 1949, p. 192.

William H. Bauer, James L. Ozment and John H. Willard, *Colorado Post Offices*, Colorado Railroad Museum, Golden, Colorado, 1990, pp. 27, 47, 134.

ELKTON, HIDALGO, OH-BE-JOYFUL and PITTSBURGH

- *Gunnison County, East Creek, Washington Gulch, and Slate River drainages*
- *Accessible via graded dirt roads or by four-wheel drive road*
- *Some towns had a post office; Elkton has several original structures*

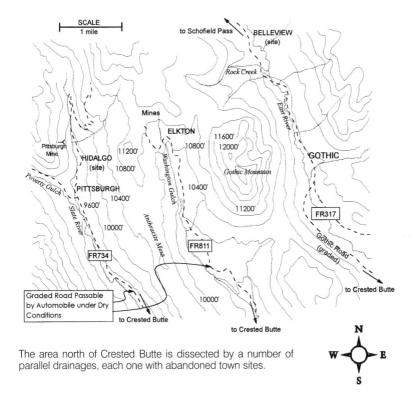

The area north of Crested Butte is dissected by a number of parallel drainages, each one with abandoned town sites.

On the east side of Anthracite Mesa below the Painter Boy Mine in Washington Gulch, was the small mining camp called Minersville, dating back to 1861 and founded by placer miners. Washington Gulch produced over a million dollars in gold before the discovery of silver ore two decades later.

Long after Minersville was abandoned, M. J. Gray and Joseph McCay discovered silver ore at the head of Washington Gulch. Not far below their mine, they laid out the town of Elkton. It was named for the Elk Mountains and owned by the Elk Mountain Consolidated Mining Company. Unusual for a Colorado mining town, no gambling or saloons were allowed within the city limits. Elkton had several boarding houses, a two-story store and about a dozen cabins. The town got its own post office in 1881, but it closed the following year. The population of Elkton was estimated at about eighty. Hard hit by the demonetization of silver by the U. S. Government, the town was probably abandoned in 1893. Fire destroyed most of Elkton's buildings.

It is difficult to say if Elkton superseded Minersville. Elkton is located on a small flat area on the ridge well above Washington Gulch. Minersville was down at the creek. Nothing remains to mark Minersville, however. Elkton has several standing restored structures and is privately owned. Log homes, occupied during the summer, make Elkton easy to find. The log home closest to the road appears to date back to the early years of the town.

Oh-Be-Joyful consisted of eight or nine cabins constructed near the headwaters of Oh-Be-Joyful Creek below Democrat Basin. It was started in 1880, and it didn't last more than two years before being abandoned. It never gained enough population to merit a post office. In that short time span, its name was changed to Tucson. The good things that were predicted about Oh-Be-Joyful never came to pass. Heavy winter snow and the lack of a good road isolated the small camp. Ore could not be mined, hauled out and processed economically. Nothing remains at the site today.

Located near the confluence of the Slate River and the creek coming out of Poverty Gulch was the mining town of Pittsburgh. Silver mines in the area supported its development. Founded in the spring of 1881, Pittsburgh got its name from its proximity to vast coal deposits.

The Pittsburgh post office opened in the summer of 1881,

What few structures remained at Elkton after its abandonment have been restored for seasonal use. *(Kenneth Jessen 109B6)*

and apparently the town's population remained sufficient until its closure in 1896. Pittsburgh, at first, had just four cabins, a store, an assay office and a number of tents. Permanent structures replaced the tents, and its population grew to an estimated 200.

The mines above Pittsburgh were in rugged country and at altitudes near or over 10,000 feet. The Augusta Mine, near the 12,559-foot summit of Augusta Mountain, was probably the most well known mine in the area. So hazardous was getting in and out of this mine during the winter that the miners remained at the property. An attempt was made to construct a tram to the mine, but it was soon wiped out by an avalanche.

On the side of Cascade Mountain was the Black Queen Mine, and the Excelsior Mine was located at the head of Poverty Gulch. The silver ore was quite rich and the mines remained operating for many years despite the lack of good transportation.

Avalanches added to the hazards of mining, and in 1886, three men perished at the Excelsior Mine. In 1904, six miners died near the Augusta Mine while trying to escape from a severe blizzard.

Pittsburgh reached its peak in 1886, and had grown to twenty-five cabins, several saloons, two boarding houses, two stores and a sawmill. The town also enjoyed daily stagecoach service from Crested Butte. Pittsburgh weathered the 1893 repeal of the Sherman Silver Purchase Act and was not abandoned until after 1896.

Renewed mining activity brought miners back to Pittsburgh in 1903. Below the Augusta Mine, a new compressor plant was constructed to pipe compressed air up to the mine. Pneumatic drills were put to use to increase productivity. New tunnels were drilled, and a tram was constructed in 1908 despite the fact that an earlier tram was carried away by an avalanche. A mill was built at the base of the tram to process ore. Mining continued until 1909 when an avalanche destroyed many of the buildings and part of the tram.

Pittsburgh has been repopulated in recent years, and modern homes mark the site today. No trespassing signs limit exploration, but from the road, Pittsburgh does not appear to have any of its original structures.

Just a half mile north of Pittsburgh was another mining camp called Hidalgo. The Hidalgo Town and Mining Company started the town in 1881 and owned the site. Superintendent Thomas Hookey was the town promoter. Many of the miners came from the Silver Cliff area, and Hidalgo was sometimes referred to as Silver Cliff. There were only a couple of log cabins constructed, and most of the miners lived in tents. Hidalgo never gained enough population for a post office. Nothing remains at the site today.

Duane Vandenbusche, *The Gunnison Country*, B & B Printers, Gunnison, Colorado, 1980, pp. 282-283.

William H. Bauer, James L. Ozment and John H. Willard, *Colorado Post Offices*, Colorado Railroad Museum, Golden, Colorado, 1990, p. 50.

Muriel Sibell Wolle, *Stampede to Timberline*, Sage Books, Chicago, 1949, p. 209.

FLORESTA

A Colorado Fuel & Iron Coal Town

- *Gunnison County, Anthracite Creek drainage*
- *Accessible by foot*
- *Town had a post office; no standing structures remain*

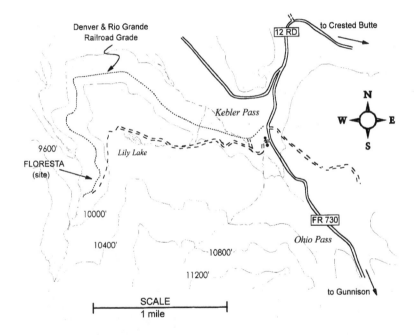

The old wagon road leading to the Floresta site is the shortest route to this ghost town. Rail fans, however, prefer the longer route over the old Denver & Rio Grande grade. Either way requires walking.

West of Ohio Pass was the substantial coal mining town of Floresta. It was located in the Anthracite Creek drainage and was founded in 1880 as Ruby-Anthracite. The Osage Coal and Mining Company originally owned the claim to the vast coal deposits in the area. This area is remote and with no railroad transportation from the deposit, little work was done to develop the mine. What little coal was mined was sold locally to the surrounding mining camps.

J. A. Kebler, representing the Colorado Fuel Company in Pueblo, purchased the deposit at Ruby-Anthracite. This company became Colorado Fuel & Iron, the largest single industry in the state.

With Colorado Fuel & Iron ownership, the Denver & Rio Grande became interested in constructing a narrow gauge branch from Crested Butte to the deposit. Grading was completed up Coal Creek, over Kebler Pass and down Anthracite Creek. The new railroad to Ruby-Anthracite was opened in September, 1893. A substantial railroad yard was constructed at the coal breaker.

This same year, C. F. & I. established the company town of

This large coal breaker once stood at Floresta. The town can be seen below. *(U.S.G.S. W. T. Lee 466)*

Ruby-Anthracite. A few privately owned log cabins had been constructed previously, and C. F. & I. added a half-dozen or so precut homes for its employees. A boarding house, capable of housing ninety men, was also constructed. A Colorado Company Supply Store, owned by C.F. & I., was opened and offered various types of merchandise. The town also had a school and was connected to Crested Butte by telegraph. The town site was located below the railroad grade near the small creek that flows through the valley.

The Ruby-Anthracite Mine proved difficult to work efficiently and was closed in 1899. A mine called the Floresta began production and proved more practical. C. F. & I. had a tradition of keeping the name of the town and the name of the mine the same. As a result, the town of Ruby-Anthracite became Floresta in 1901.

Since the arrival of the railroad in 1893, a post office operated under the name Ruby. Not many miles to the northeast was the town of Ruby City near Irwin. Its post office was also called Ruby. Fortunately, the Ruby City post office had closed by the time the Ruby-Anthracite office opened, otherwise mail delivery could have been quite confusing. The Ruby post office changed its name to Floresta in 1897 and remained open for another twenty-two years.

Floresta grew to 250 with 100 men working directly for C. F. & I. The company found it difficult to retain its workers due to Floresta's isolation, severe winter weather and poor working conditions. The company paid premium wages of $4.25 a day at a time when $3.00 a day for a coal miner was considered good. Despite the higher wages and company housing, only a dozen families remained during the winter. The Denver & Rio Grande was often unable to keep its track clear during mid-winter thus forcing closure of the mine. Coal production became seasonal.

Despite the obvious disadvantages of coal mining at Floresta, the largest coal breaker west of Pennsylvania was constructed in 1898. This seven story high structure could handle 2,000 tons of coal a day, which proved overkill. Because of the difficulties encountered in the mine itself, including concentrations

A couple of ladies appear in the left of this photograph with the company cooks in the center. This was taken at the Floresta boarding house in 1901. *(Author's collection CP049)*

of toxic gas, the typical output was no more than 300 tons a day.

The coal seam at Floresta dipped at a steep angle. This meant that several adits or crosscuts were necessary at various levels to bring out the coal. The coal was lowered from the upper levels by steel lined chutes to mining cars. The mining cars were then taken to the upper portion of the coal breaker where the coal was dumped. From there, the coal was sent through a rotary screen and automatically sorted by size.

The cost of mining at Floresta led to the decision to close the mine in December, 1918. The town was abandoned at this time. The tailings pile was sold for use as flux, and the railroad continued to operate until 1929 hauling out the material.

Today, the Floresta site is accessible only by foot. It is approximately three miles to the site through rugged country. The old wagon road is the easiest route, but it is possible to walk the railroad grade. The grade requires detours around missing trestles.

Broken lumber marks the remains of the coal breaker. The cinder-covered railroad grade is plainly visible and the foundations of other structures can be found among the trees.

There is another ghost town site along the abandoned railroad grade between Floresta and Crested Butte. It was a lumber camp called Telco, founded in 1917 by Harry Endner. The name stood for The Endner Lumber Company. A logging road was built to the south up Splains Gulch to service a vast timbered area.

The lumber company employed thirty men at its sawmill next to the railroad, while others worked up on the hillside cutting timber. Telco had a boarding house, blacksmith shop and several cabins. The railroad added a siding to allow cars to be loaded with milled lumber. A million board feet was shipped each year. Telco was abandoned in 1929 when the Denver & Rio Grande ceased operation over the branch line.

Telco was not the only lumber camp in the area. Its predecessor was Kebler, located near the foot of Kebler Pass on the Ohio Pass Road. This town was also owned by the same company. There were living quarters for its workers including a boarding house. The sawmill at Kebler closed in 1917, the same time the sawmill at Telco began operation. The cabins at Kebler were moved to Telco. Nothing remains at either site.

Duane Vandenbusche, *The Gunnison Country*, B & B Printers, Gunnison, Colorado, 1980, pp. 276-277.

Tiv Wilkins, *Colorado Railroads*, Pruett Publishing Company, Boulder, Colorado, 1974, p. 93.

William H. Bauer, James L. Ozment and John H. Willard, *Colorado Post Offices*, Colorado Railroad Museum, Golden, Colorado, 1990, pp. 54, 125.

Muriel Sibell Wolle, *Stampede to Timberline*, Sage Books, Chicago, 1949, pp. 206-208.

GATEVIEW
A Place with Many Names

- *Gunnison County, Lake Fork Creek drainage*
- *Accessible by paved road*
- *Town had a post office; remaining original structures unknown*

A stage coach stop at the confluence of Indian Creek and the Lake Fork of the Gunnison River was established in 1876, coincident with the opening of a post office. The place was named Barnum, and its buildings were of log construction. Barnum was not a town as such, but acted as a stopping place for passengers traveling from Gunnison to Lake City.

In 1881, Benjamin Allen purchased the ranch where Barnum was located and changed its name to Allen. He petitioned the post office to also change its name to Allen. Benjamin Allen became Allen's postmaster, and when he moved from the area in 1892, the post office moved to Gateview. Gateview was a short distance away where there is a natural "V" opening in the mountains carved by the Lake Fork of the Gunnison.

After the Denver & Rio Grande constructed its narrow gauge railroad south from a point near Sapinero in 1889, the stage station was abandoned. The Gateview post office was closed in 1895 to be superseded by the Dayton post office. Dayton was located south of Gateview along the river. The Denver & Rio Grande made daily stops to drop off and pick up mail. Except for a brief period of time, the Dayton post office remained open until 1911. Today, there are a number of privately owned ranches in the vicinity of these old sites.

Duane Vandenbusche, *The Gunnison Country*, B & B Printers, Gunnison, Colorado, 1980, pp.164-165.
William H. Bauer, James L. Ozment and John H. Willard, *Colorado Post Offices*, Colorado Railroad Museum, Golden, Colorado, 1990, pp. 11, 17.

GOTHIC

Saved by One Man

- *Gunnison County, East River drainage*
- *Accessible via graded dirt road*
- *Town had a post office; several original structures remain*

Well past its prime, this photograph shows how Gothic looked before it was purchased in 1928 for the Rocky Mountain Biological Laboratory. *(Denver Public Library, Western History Department X-9768)*

Gothic, located along the East River north of Crested Butte, is old mining town that survives today. Named for nearby Gothic Mountain, it gained its position as the supply point for other mining camps to the north. The town was also supported by the silver mines in the area.

Brothers John and David Jennings were responsible for the discovery of the first major silver lode in the Gothic area. The ore contained rare wire silver, so rich that it assayed at $15,000 a ton. Obediah Sands, a hotel owner from Chicago, grubstaked the two men. Overwork had ruined Obediah's health, and he came to Colorado to recover or die. After the Jennings brothers discovered the Sylvanite Lode, it can be presumed that Sands shared in their wealth. The lode, incidentally, was located about four miles from Gothic at the head of Copper Creek.

Gothic grew out of shanties thrown up by prospectors entering the area. The miners took turns getting the mail from Crested Butte. The designated mail carrier for the day would stand on a box in the center of town and call out the name on each letter. By August, 1879, the place had enough population to open a post office. The post office remained open until 1896.

Gothic was incorporated in 1879. Area sawmills tried to keep up with the demand for milled lumber, while many prospectors elected to construct log cabins. During this single year, Gothic rose out of an empty meadow to a town with 200 buildings. The business district was on both sides of the main road, while cabins were spread out in the surrounding area. Gothic, combined with the surrounding area, had a population of around 1,000. When the winter of 1879-1880 came, the population dropped dramatically. Winters in this area are hard with snow accumulation in the hundreds of inches. During that winter, only twenty-six families remained in Gothic. Mail was brought from Crested Butte by a mail carrier on skis.

By June, 1880, the hordes of prospectors returned to dig up practically every square inch in the area. The population of the Gothic area again swelled to 1,000 or more. A large, long frame hotel was constructed, and Gothic gained a number of stores. It also had the usual complement of saloons. To litigate conflicting mining claims, Gothic also had five law firms.

On Sundays, the town had horse races. On warm evenings, an orchestra might play. A big bonfire was another Gothic tradition giving residents a time to socialize after a hard day of work. Even though half of the residents carried guns, shootings were rare.

The Elk Mountain Bonanza began publication in June, 1880, financed by Leadville millionaire Horace Tabor. Despite his backing, its last issue was in March, 1881. Under new ownership, the newspaper was reborn as the Gothic Miner. It lasted four months until much of Gothic's population left for a warmer climate. The *Silver Record* was Gothic's last experiment in newspapers, with its first issue in 1882 and its last issue four years later.

Former United States President Grant visited Gothic in 1880 and was welcomed by the sounds of a brass band. Blasting powder and gunfire enhanced his arrival. A reception and ball was held for Grant at the Olds Hotel. Grant also got to tour some of the area mines before heading north over Schofield Pass.

Typical of the more practical approach to politics, the Gothic mayor was elected by the roll of the dice. Lew Wait, editor of the *Silver Record*, became the town's first "elected" official.

What kept Gothic going were the roads radiating over various passes including Schofield to the north, East Maroon to the northeast and a road which ran to Tin Cup. Hundreds of pack animals crowded Gothic's main street. The teamster using East Maroon Pass to connect Gothic and Aspen owned upholstered sleighs to haul passengers during the winter. Lap robes were included as part of the fare.

Even with a network of roads, transportation costs for getting the ore to smelters were high. This limited mining along the East River to lodes containing only the richest ore. As the ore was exhausted, Gothic began to lose its population. The town was nearly deserted by 1893 but its post office remained open. After a brief mining boom from 1907 to 1914, Gothic became a ghost town except for Garwood H. Judd. Judd lived in Gothic for approximately fifty years. A movie was made about him in 1928, and he was the subject of several articles.

In 1928, Dr. John C. Johnson, a professor at Western State College in Gunnison, established the Rocky Mountain Biological Laboratory in Gothic. The entire town was purchased, some buildings were razed and those in better condition were restored for use as classrooms or dormitories. Johnson changed Gothic, but saved it from falling into ruin and vanishing like other towns in the area. Today, students can be seen walking to and from their summer classes.

There was another mining camp about two miles north of Gothic called Belleview. It got started in 1880, but never had sufficient population to support a post office. It survived only for a year, and nothing remains at the site today.

Gothic   *(drawing by Julia McMillan)*

Duane Vandenbusche, *The Gunnison Country*, B & B Printers, Gunnison, Colorado, 1980, pp. 253-255.

Helen Hunt Jackson, "Oh-Be-Joyful Creek and Poverty Gulch," *Atlantic Monthly*, LII, December, 1883.

Muriel Sibell Wolle, *Stampede to Timberline*, Sage Books, Chicago, 1949, pp. 199-202.

William H. Bauer, James L. Ozment and John H. Willard, *Colorado Post Offices*, Colorado Railroad Museum, Golden, Colorado, 1990, p. 64.

HILLERTON,
ABBEYVILLE and GARFIELD

- *Gunnison County, Willow Creek drainage*
- *Accessible via graded dirt road; limited by private property*
- *Hillerton and Abbeyville had a post office*

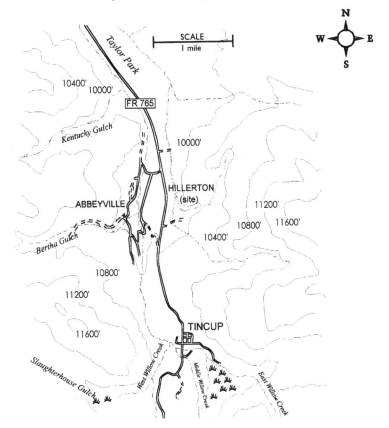

The town sites for Hillerton and Abbeyville are two miles north of Tincup. Abbeyville is fenced in and is on private property, while FR 765 passes through the Hillerton site.

529

Edwin H. Hiller, a Denver banker, visited the Willow Creek area in 1878 and selected a site for a future town based on the mines in the area. When he returned the following year, he discovered that a group of prospectors had laid out a town in the very same spot. It was called Virginia City, later renamed Tin Cup. This prompted Hiller to establish his town two miles to the north.

Hiller organized the Hillerton Town & Improvement Company in May, 1879 to develop the site he selected. The town was laid out east of Willow Creek in a beautiful valley surrounded by sagebrush-covered hills in Taylor Park. A copy of the town plat shows fourteen cross streets and four north and south primary streets. A business district was defined, and in May, a post office opened. The first bank in Gunnison County opened its doors in Hillerton.

A newspaper called *The Occident* came out on June 23, 1879 making it the first such publication in Gunnison County. Its publisher and editor was Henry C. Olney, owner of Lake City's *Silver World.* He had a great deal of difficulty getting his printing press, type and other equipment to the site. There weren't any good graded roads into the area, and during the course of the trip, his wagon turned over twice. What greeted him was a newspaper "office" void of windows, doors or a roof.

With over one hundred miners arriving each day, the future looked bright for Hillerton. By the end of 1879, the town had fifty log cabins plus a few frame structures. A shaft was dug down in the loose gravel and a ditch was completed to supply water for placer mining. Even with its cabins, most of the residents lived in tents.

By the following year, Hillerton grew to 160 homes with six grocery stores, a sawmill, two dry goods stores, a saloon and its newspaper and bank. Population estimates for Hillerton and the surrounding area ran as high as 3,000.

Within a short distance, but on the west side of Willow Creek, a smelter was constructed. It was located at the mouth of Bertha Gulch, and shipped the first bullion produced in Gunnison County. By the summer of 1880, over $1,000 was being shipped from the smelter every day. Most of the ore came from the Doctor Mine in the Spring Creek area or from the Star Mine near the headwaters of Italian Creek. Associated with the smelter was a mining camp called Abbeyville, founded in 1880 by C. F. Abbey. Its population grew to around 300. As Hillerton began to lose population, its post office was moved over to Abbeyville.

Hillerton could not compete with Virginia City. Hillerton was too far from the mines, and Virginia City was also located at the base of Tin Cup Pass, the area's major supply route. As Hillerton began to decline, some residents skidded their cabins over to Abbeyville or south to Tin Cup. Edwin Hiller, however, remained at his town. The *Denver Republican* said that, "Mr. Hiller officiates as chief mourner and gives the place about the only sign of life it possesses…" By the turn of the century not one structure remained, and today, the site is so overgrown that it is difficult to locate. FR 765 passes through the town site.

Abbeyville did not do any better as a mining camp. Although the town peaked at 300, it declined very fast and by 1884, its post office closed. The smelter was not efficient and mine owners began to ship their ore to other smelters. The same year the town lost its post office it also lost its founder, C. F. Abbey.

This is a drawing of the gold dredge that operated near Hillerton.

He died from a fall down an elevator shaft in New York City.

The last mining done in the Hillerton-Abbeyville area was by the Columbine Gold Dredging Company between 1908 and 1912.

Abbeyville has since been developed as a mountain property resort and is completely fenced in. From the public road, it does not appear to have any of its original structures. To the west and within sight of the road are the remains of the gold dredge.

One other mining camp of note, Garfield, was at the head of West Willow Creek, four miles south of Tin Cup and just below Cumberland Pass. The town was supported by area mines. Joe Cotter started the small camp, and at first, it was named Cotterville. It never gained enough population to merit a post office.

In November, 1880, James Garfield was elected United States President and the name of this small, remote mining camp was changed to Garfield. Production from the area mines looked promising, and the *Garfield Banner* began publication with its first issue in September, 1881. The newspaper was printed in Tin Cup and delivered to its subscribers. The following year, it became the *Tin Cup Banner*. In 1883, just when Garfield looked like it might survive, a fire destroyed the business district.

Joe Cotter was a great politician and was elected to the position of Gunnison County Treasurer. He was well liked and trusted. During the summer of 1882, Joe Cotter vanished along with all of the county funds.

The Garfield site itself is void of structures, however, there is a small cabin on the road below Cumberland Pass near the old town site.

Conrad F. Schader, *Colorado's Alluring Tin Cup*, Regio Alta Publications, Golden, Colorado, 1992, pp. 44-53.

Duane Vandenbusche, *The Gunnison Country*, B & B Printers, Gunnison, Colorado, 1980, pp. 364-366.

Muriel Sibell Wolle, *Stampede to Timberline*, Sage Books, Chicago, 1949, p. 186.

William H. Bauer, James L. Ozment and John H. Willard, *Colorado Post Offices*, Colorado Railroad Museum, Golden, Colorado, 1990, pp. 9, 73.

IOLA

And Other Towns along the Gunnison River

- *Gunnison County, Gunnison River drainage*
- *Original sites are under the Blue Mesa Reservoir*
- *All towns had a post office; no structures at original site locations*

This is the Iola Hotel and Fishing Resort, located near the Gunnison River. Today, this site is below the waters of the Blue Mesa Reservoir. *(Denver Public Library, Western History Department X-9536)*

About the only reminder of Iola is its name on a campground sign near the site. Iola was located along the Denver & Rio Grande's main line on the banks of the Gunnison River, and the site today is below the Blue Mesa Reservoir. The story of Iola begins with another settlement a short distance to the west called Kezar. Kezar was founded by the Kezar Town and Land Company in 1881, and it got its own post office that same year. The post office was initially named Stevens and its name was changed to Kezar in 1882.

The *Gunnison Review* predicted that Kezar would become a great resort town. It was located in a grove of trees close to the Gunnison River. By 1882, the town had four general stores, two boarding houses, a number of homes and five saloons. It was also a temporary end of track town as the Denver & Rio Grande constructed its narrow gauge railroad along the Gunnison River.

Unusual in Colorado small town history, Kezar was moved a short distance to the west in 1896 to create Iola. This included some of its buildings and its post office.

At Iola, a schoolhouse was constructed, and aside from the post office, the town had a general store. The population grew to around one hundred. Iola became the resort town that Kezar was predicted to become. Places to stay included the Wilt Hotel, the Zeigler Hotel, the Rio Vista Resort and the Iola Hotel. The attraction was fishing in the Gunnison River.

Iola's biggest event was when storekeeper L. E. Champlin, from Powderhorn, shot his boss, Mat Cavanaugh. A few days before this incident, Cavanaugh broke a rifle stock over Champlin's head. Champlin hunted down Cavanaugh and finally met him in front of the Iola post office. Without any warning, Champlin fired three shots in rapid succession mortally wounding Cavanaugh. It was cold-blooded murder, but the incident was dismissed as self-defense.

Another town site, also below the Blue Mesa Reservoir, is Sapinero. It was located near the confluence of the Lake Fork and the Gunnison River. Supported by tourism, the railroad and ranching, Sapinero had two substantial hotels. It was founded in 1881, but wasn't formally laid out as a town until 1888. At first, Sapinero was called Soap Creek and was an end of track construction camp for the railroad. In November, 1882, its name was changed to Sapinero coincident with the opening of its post office. The name came from a Ute Chief and brother-in-law of Chief Ouray. Sapinero was at the hub of several roads radiating out to Barnum, Powderhorn and other locations to the south. It had two hotels, a general store and its own schoolhouse.

The post office remained open until the 1960s when the reservoir was constructed. Sapinero was moved to a point above the water line, and its post office remained in operation until 1986.

Between Sapinero, located at the far west end of the Blue Mesa Reservoir, and Iola, at the east end, was yet another small community called Cebolla. Like the other towns, it was dependent on fishermen and hunters. J. J. Carpenter founded Cebolla when the Denver & Rio Grande built through the valley and he could see the tourist potential of the area. In 1888, Carpenter constructed the Sportsman's Lodge to cater to just such a business. The original lodge burned to the ground in 1902, but was quickly rebuilt. Cebolla got its own post office in 1894, and it remained open until 1935. The town site is under the Blue Mesa Reservoir.

Duane Vandenbusche, *The Gunnison Country*, B & B Printers, Gunnison, Colorado, 1980, p. 165.
Muriel Sibell Wolle, *Stampede to Timberline*, Sage Books, Chicago, 1949, p. 191.
William H. Bauer, James L. Ozment and John H. Willard, *Colorado Post Offices*, Colorado Railroad Museum, Golden, Colorado, 1990, pp. 37, 78, 128.

IRIS and CHANCE

Gold Basin Towns

- *Gunnison and Saguache counties, Gold Basin Creek drainage*
- *Not accessible*
- *Both towns had a post office; several structures remain at Iris*

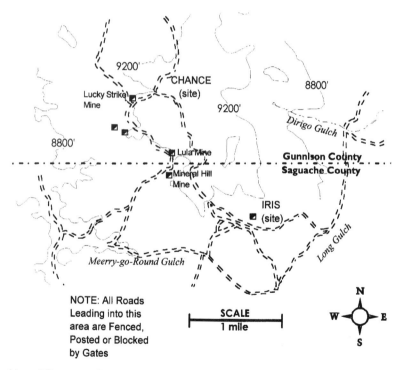

NOTE: All Roads
Leading into this
area are Fenced,
Posted or Blocked
by Gates

Iris and Chance are in a remote region of Colorado along the Gunnison and Saguache county line. The area shown on this map is east of 38 RD and west of Colorado 114.

The land north of U.S. 50 in Gunnison County has high mountains, lush meadows, clear streams and dense forests. The area receives a prodigious amount of snow. The opposite is true for the land south of U.S. 50. This area is barren, and most of it is covered with sagebrush. Stands of trees survive only in creek beds and on the higher mountains.

Gold ore was discovered in this arid region in 1880, but a mining industry wasn't fully developed until a decade later. The Grant brothers opened the Denver City Mine fourteen miles south of Gunnison and shipped some gold ore in paying quantities. One of the Grant brothers located the Dirigo Lode and showed the ore in Gunnison. This started a gold rush into the region, and over 1,000 prospectors poured into the area. The towns of Iris and Chance were established in 1894, and were located just two miles from each other near Green Mountain.

Iris was originally called Union Hill, but the name was rejected by the Postmaster General. The name was then changed to Iris for the daughter of the county land office registrar, J. I. Heiner. The Iris post office opened in 1894, closed briefly the following year, and then remained open until 1902. The Chance post office opened at the same time, but closed in 1901.

Iris grew into a town of twenty structures, and as more people arrived, Iris continued to grow. By 1895, Iris had telephone service to Gunnison, and two stamp mills were kept busy processing the gold-bearing quartz produced by area mines. This same year, the *Cochetopa Gold Belt* came out with its first issue. By 1896, Iris had a couple more grocery stores, a meat market and three more homes. The ore started to run out in 1897, and by 1903, the town had but three residents. Soon after, Iris was a ghost town.

Chance reached its peak at the same time as Iris. There were twenty to thirty log structures built at Chance. It was a smaller town, but it did have several stores and its own school. Mine owners had a sense of humor and played on the name of the town. One of the nearby mines was named The Last Chance and another mine was called The Only Chance.

Anne Ellis wrote of her life in Chance in a book titled *The Life of an Ordinary Woman.* She described Chance as having, "...many new log houses, a few store buildings, of course, saloons and a schoolhouse." She also told of several young bachelors living in a cabin. Some worked in the mines and others were teamsters. They drank a good deal to pass the time, and whenever they celebrated, they called it a birthday. One of the young men had a birthday every payday!

Anne Ellis also wrote about the stamp mill near Chance. It was built along a small creek to allow the stamps to be powered by a water wheel. It had five stamps, which were raised by cams on a common shaft. When the shoulder on the rod connected to one of the heavy stamps was lifted more than a foot and a half, it would reach the end of the cam and fall onto the ore, crushing it. After several blows, the ore was beaten into a fine powder. Water carried the pulverized ore over copper plates wetted with mercury. The fine particles of gold in the ore were trapped by the mercury as an amalgam. The worthless rock was carried away by the water.

Periodically, the stamp mill would be shut down. The mercury-gold amalgam would be scraped off of the copper plates and fresh mercury added to the plate. The amalgam was placed in a chamois skin and forced through. The gold was left in the skin as a "button" the size of a hen's egg. It would then be heated to drive off the remaining mercury leaving behind nearly pure gold. Ellis commented that the egg size lumps were few and far between from the mines near Chance. The mill was a marginal operation and eventually burned to the ground.

One Christmas, Anne was just one of two women in Chance. It was a sad time for the lonely men. By nightfall, every man was either crying or singing drunk. She described a street filled with men, including those who had worked all day, staggering around, stumbling and fighting.

In today's dollars, over a million was spent on mining in the area, and it is doubtful that anywhere near that amount was recovered. The veins of ore narrowed or "pinched out" as the mines got deeper. The mines closed, and by 1901, Chance was almost deserted.

In 1942, Muriel Sibell Wolle visited both town sites and found a dozen cabins still standing at Iris. Some of the cabins even contained furniture. Her only comment about Chance was that the cabins were more scattered.

Neither the Iris nor the Chance town sites can be reached by public roads. All approaches are blocked by fences or locked gates. Using a four-wheel drive trail from Sillsville, it is possible to get within sight of Iris. There appears to be two or three log structures still standing. Since private property prevents exploration, it is not known if any structures survive at Chance. There are, however, a number of mine buildings on Mineral Hill which can be seen from a ridge east of Chance. The closest approach to these town sites is via the Gold Basin Creek Road (38 RD), which runs south from the Gunnison Airport.

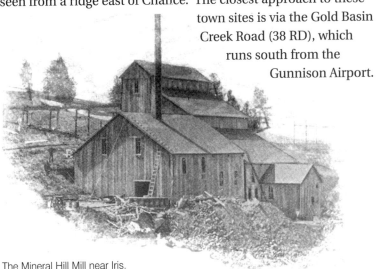

The Mineral Hill Mill near Iris.

Anne Ellis, *The Life of an Ordinary Woman*, Houghton Mifflin, Boston, 1957 (reprint), pp. 190-191, 195.

Duane Vandenbusche, *The Gunnison Country*, B & B Printers, Gunnison, Colorado, 1980, pp. 289-291.

Muriel Sibell Wolle, *Stampede to Timberline*, Sage Books, Chicago, 1949, pp. 193-194.

William H. Bauer, James L. Ozment and John H. Willard, *Colorado Post Offices*, Colorado Railroad Museum, Golden, Colorado, 1990, pp. 32, 78.

IRWIN

And Its Neighbor, Ruby City

- *Gunnison County, Ruby Gulch drainage*
- *Accessible via graded dirt road*
- *Towns had a post office; one original structure remains*

An overview of Irwin taken in 1882. The Presbyterian Church stands out on the right side. Of note are frame structures as high as four stories. The town contained approximately seventy-five buildings, and none of them remain today. *(Denver Public Library, Western History Department X-9554)*

In 1879 and after having prospected in the Gothic area and finding nothing of value, A. T. Gilkerson was broke. He had spent a dozen years of his life in the West looking for his fortune. He and his family loaded their wagon in preparation for heading out of Colorado and across the plains to farming country where he felt he could make a living. When he went to get his mules, he found one animal dead. He lacked the money to purchase another mule. He left his family in Gothic to look for a temporary job in one of the area mines. Gilkerson and a friend, R. A. Duncan, were on their way up Coal Creek toward Kebler Pass when they sat down to have lunch. They were at the mouth of Ruby Gulch and their horses kicked off some of the soil revealing mineralization. Gilkerson took a sample and had an assay made. It showed that it contained ruby and pure wire silver. Gilkerson filed a claim, which he soon sold for $50,000. This would amount in today's dollars to well over half-million. This lode became the Lead Chief.

Less than a week later, a tenderfoot named William Fisher became mired in the mud near Ruby Gulch. O. P. Mace used his draft animals to pull Fisher's wagon free. For his help, Fisher promised Mace half interest in any valuable lode he discovered. The following morning, Fisher found two exposed veins of ore containing wire silver. He named them the Forest Queen and the Ruby King. Mace got the Ruby King, which he sold for $100,000, while Fisher sold the Forest Queen for $40,000. Other discoveries followed by prospectors coming into the area, and selling claims made many rich men.

During 1879, a few cabins were constructed in Ruby Gulch, but the majority of prospectors lived in tents. The small settlement was inside the Ute Indian Reservation and, technically, off limits to prospecting and land acquisition. For their own protection, the prospectors constructed a large log cabin surrounded by a stockade. The Meeker Massacre scared many into leaving, and one prospector later wrote that 450 out of 500 packed up and left.

Captain Curtis, a former Indian scout, volunteered to lead a band of miners against the Utes. He even sent a telegram to Colorado's governor offering the services of his "Ruby Scouts." Fortunately, the governor did not accept the offer since there were no Ruby Scouts. Since the mining camps were inside the Ute Reservation, they were technically outside the United States. Residents refused to pay Gunnison County taxes as a result. They could not, however, legally own any of the land.

It began snowing in November and snowed for forty days without stopping. By spring, over forty feet of snow covered the area. Only fifty stayed in Ruby Gulch during this time. Since there were not enough provisions, several of the men were forced to ski over Ohio Pass and into the valley below to purchase supplies.

When spring arrived, a number of camps were established in Ruby Gulch. Duane Vandenbusche in his book, *The Gunnison Country,* recited the names of the various camps beginning at the mouth of Ruby Gulch with White Cloud, then Ruby City, then Irwin, then Silver Gate and finally, Hopewell. The only camps to survive were Ruby City and Irwin. The two camps were separated by only a quarter of a mile and were known for years as Ruby-Irwin. Eventually Irwin absorbed Ruby City.

Charlie Christopher was responsible for founding Ruby City. He platted the town and began selling lots. He promised the town would have a hotel, grocery store and an office building. He also talked about building a theater. A newspaper began publication in Irwin as the *Elk Mountain Pilot.* Christopher tried to get its publisher to leave Irwin and move the quarter of a mile to Ruby City. Making money selling lots was what motivated Christopher. After he sold a number of lots, he vanished.

Irwin was founded by two mining engineers in November, 1879 and was officially platted in February of the following year. The town was named for Dick Irwin, who was one of the famous Pony Express riders and had served in the Colorado Legislature. He owned shares in the Ruby Chief and Forest Queen mines. He was well respected by his fellow prospectors.

In the early spring, 1880, hundreds of miners camped on the south side of Ohio Pass waiting for the snow to melt so they could get to Ruby-Irwin. Freighters were hired to carry supplies on their backs using snowshoes. The snow was so deep in the camps that the cabins were completely covered. This forced those that had endured the winter to dig vertical shafts from their front door. As the snow melted, the Ohio Pass road became a sea of mud, compounding the difficulties in reaching the area.

By summer, Irwin's population had risen from fifty to five thousand. By the fall of 1880, it was reported that the town had over 500 houses, but this does not agree with historic photographs. Irwin had a mile-long main street lined with false-front stores and homes. In 1879, town lots sold for practically nothing, and the following year, some choice lots sold for $5,000.

There weren't any dairies in the area, and fresh milk and butter had to be brought in by wagon over a rough road from Crested Butte. After the ten mile ride, the milkman discovered that if the cream was left floating on the milk, it would become butter by the end of the trip. In this way, he was able to satisfy the demand for both products.

Taken in 1880 shortly after the town was founded, Irwin's main street, lined with false-front stores, is shown on the left. Men can be seen standing on a walkway on the roof of the building in the foreground. *(Denver Public Library, Western History Department X-9550)*

The town of Irwin was named for this man, Dick Irwin. He was well respected by his fellow prospectors. *(Author's collection CP105)*

Irwin was a wide-open town and had nearly two-dozen saloons, seven dance halls and a number of brothels. A post office opened under the name Ruby in 1879, but was moved to Irwin the following year. The Irwin post office remained active until the turn of the century.

By 1885, Irwin's permanent population stabilized to about 450 residents. The town now had a bank, one stamp mill, three churches, one theater and several hotels.

George Crofutt, in his 1885 edition of the *Grip-Sack Guide of Colorado*, revealed the potential of Irwin and the surrounding camps. Mining, lumbering, mercantile and mineral springs with "...rare medicinal properties" were among the area's virtues according to Crofutt. As for its people, Crofutt commented that they are, "...enterprising people – a people that are self-reliant, honest and industrious."

The *Elk Mountain Pilot* was the creation of John Phillips. His experience was running a print shop in Rosita. He moved to Irwin when he heard of the rich wire silver ore. He ordered a Washington hand press with the intention of starting a newspaper. His press and other equipment were hauled to the foot of Ohio Pass in May, 1880. He envisioned multitudes of subscribers just waiting for the arrival of his newspaper. He had to settle for the fact that the road was under many feet of snow, and that the only way to get his equipment to Irwin was to employ "snowshoe freighters." They carried the lead type, the type cases, pieces of the press, ink and paper over the pass. The ascent was made, and

Irwin was reached when the town was still buried under snow. The only sign of the town was holes in the snow, some with smoke rising upward from a stove far below. As the snow melted, he found that his newspaper office was a log cabin lacking windows, a floor and a door. Nevertheless, the first issue came out on June 17, 1880.

Prices in Irwin were high, even for a Colorado mining town. Canned goods sold for a dollar each and flour sold for twenty dollars per hundred pound sack. This attracted freighters with hundreds of pack animals. The streets of Irwin were filled with stagecoaches and freight wagons.

Edward Travers was Irwin's first mayor. He was known for drinking whisky and for gambling. Travers was tall and wiry, and his facial features were sharp and angular. Normally gentle, he could turn into a demon when drunk. He had no fear of any man and kept the lawless element in line.

When the Fourth of July, 1880, approached, the patriotic Mayor Travers issued a proclamation that all should celebrate this event to suit themselves. This included the discharge of firearms within the city limits since there were no fireworks on hand for the celebration. The town's ordinances were suspended for the day. Irwin survived the Fourth of July with one fatality: a horse killed by a stray bullet.

When drunk, Travers was found in a saloon practicing his skill with a revolver. The saloonkeeper placed his hand against the wall, fingers spread. Travers would then attempt to put a bullet between each of the separated fingers. The two men switched roles after a cylinder full of cartridges had been discharged. Neither man was injured, and those who were a little wiser put a stop to the gunplay.

After leaving office in Irwin, Travers headed south to Hillsboro, New Mexico. He rode into a saloon and began shooting. The owner, a man named Blum, returned fire from behind the bar. Travers rode out into the street only to return later. When Blum saw him, he made a lucky shot, and Travers fell dead.

In Irwin, prostitution was allowed. The prostitutes, who

frequented the dance halls, had colorful names such as "Ham Bone Jane," "Shorty" and "Cock Eye." One of the girls had a receding hairline and was named "Timberline."

These women would approach a male patron in a dance hall, and after dancing, they would escort their man to the bar for a round of drinks. A commission from the bar owner was customary, and this was part of the compensation the girls enjoyed. As put by one of the journalists, they "...drank down glasses of the foulest liquor that ever was distilled outside of some place which savored of Hades." Depending on the "business arrangement," the ladies of the evening might lead their gentlemen friend to their crib for more entertainment.

Irwin's saloons offered gambling as another way of bolstering income. Games of chance included keno, roulette, craps, poker and faro. The town also had a theater with a seating capacity of around 600. There were nightly performances and sometimes, matinees.

The Irwin Club was the only place where men could meet, have a drink and socialize outside of a saloon. It gained 100 members and some were married. The ladies had their suspicions about the Irwin Club and its real agenda. The members tried to dispel rumors about wholesale gambling and drinking by holding a ball open to the ladies. As Irwin dwindled in size, membership fell, and by the end of 1883, only five were left. Editor John Philips was put in charge of liquidating the club's assets and paying all of its debts. With this done, all that remained of the Irwin Club was nine dollars.

The Ruby-Irwin area did not turn out to be another Leadville in magnitude. By 1883, many of the mines closed. No ore was shipped that year, and people began to leave. John Phillips moved his *Elk Mountain Pilot* to Crested Butte in 1884. At the time, only the Forest Queen, Bullion King and Ruby Chief mines remained in operation. The ore was found in knife blade width seams and as the mines got deeper, ground water forced mine owners to add large pumps. This added to the cost and limited mine depth.

The Bank of Irwin remained open as well as a saloon, hotel and one store. The Windsor Hotel burned to the ground in 1885, and many of the structures around the Forest Queen also were consumed by flames. A geologist named Arthur Lakes visited the town in 1885 and let his horse stay inside one of the many deserted stores. He fed the horse off the store counter. Irwin was a ghost town by 1890.

When Muriel Sibell Wolle first visited the Irwin site, she found no trace of the town except for its fire hydrants. All of Irwin's false-front buildings and its homes were piles of rotting lumber. In June, 1946, she returned, and only when she drove up the hill above the town did she appreciate how large Irwin was. As she looked down, she could see where the streets had been.

Not far from the turnoff from the Coal Creek Road onto FR 826, there is a less traveled dirt road to the right. It follows the creek bed. This road leads directly to the Irwin town site although the other road loops around Lake Irwin to the same spot. The old town site is resplendent with no trespassing signs, which are located about every fifty feet or so along the road. This makes Irwin the most heavily posted mining town in Colorado! There is one original miner's shack and the remains of the buildings at the Forest Queen Mine. The mine is on the hillside above the town site and is also closed to visitors. Numerous mountain homes dot the valley.

Duane Vandenbusche, *The Gunnison Country*, B & B Printers, Gunnison, Colorado, 1980, pp. 262-264.

George A. Crofutt, *Crofutt's Grip-Sack Guide of Colorado*, 1885 Edition, Johnson Books, Boulder, Colorado, reprint 1981, pp. 108-109.

Muriel Sibell Wolle, *Stampede to Timberline*, Sage Books, Chicago, 1949, pp. 210-217.

"Reminiscences of Irwin or Ruby Camp," *Camp and Plant, Vol. IV.*, January 9, 1904, No. 26, pp. 605-611.

William H. Bauer, James L. Ozment and John H. Willard, *Colorado Post Offices*, Colorado Railroad Museum, Golden, Colorado, 1990, pp. 78, 125.

MARBLE

The City of Stone

- *Gunnison County, Crystal River drainage*
- *Accessible via paved road*
- *Town has a post office; occupied town; a number of original structures remain*

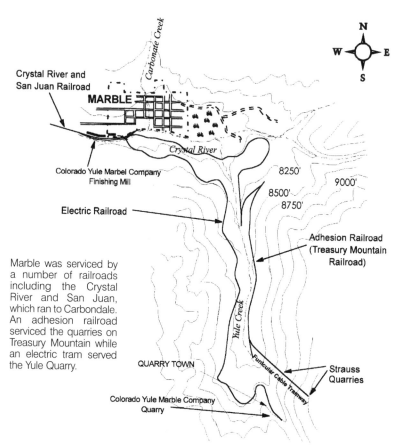

Marble was serviced by a number of railroads including the Crystal River and San Juan, which ran to Carbondale. An adhesion railroad serviced the quarries on Treasury Mountain while an electric tram served the Yule Quarry.

The first prospector to take note of the economic potential of the marble deposits in the Yule Creek drainage was Sylvester Richardson in 1873. He predicted that the deposits would support a great stone industry. Richardson was also the future founder of Gunnison. George Yule, for whom Yule Creek is named, noted the deposits the following year. An unknown individual took samples of the Yule marble down from the mountain, had them polished and then put them on display in Denver. Despite the discovery of marble, attention focused on silver-bearing galena found in the upper Crystal River Valley. The mining boom spawned the towns of Crystal and Schofield on the Crystal River. The boom lasted as long as the United States Government was required to purchase a certain amount of silver every year. When the U. S. went off of the silver standard in 1893, the mines closed.

John Mobley, his wife and two children came over the rugged and dangerous Schofield Pass from Crested Butte in 1880. Their meager supplies included flour, a bar of soap, a box of matches, but no salt. On East Lost Trail Creek, the donkey carrying their children ran off. A miner named William Woods rescued the children. Winter was fast approaching, and Mobley constructed a cabin at the west edge of Beaver Lake near where the future town of Marble would be located.

In the spring of the following year, the Mobley children walked up Carbonate Creek to the cabin of William Parry and G. D. Griffith, a couple of prospectors working a silver claim. The children begged for some salt, much to the surprise of the prospectors living in this virtually unpopulated part of Colorado. As it became known that silver ore was found in the region, other prospectors came into the area over Schofield Pass. William Woods and William Parry laid out the town of Marble, and at the same time, John Mobley and William Mason founded the town of Clarence. The town sites were close together near the confluence of Rock Creek and Carbonate Creek. Later, Rock Creek was renamed the Crystal River. Other town sites were also established, but never flourished including Stonington and Maurice.

A Mr. Howell opened the first known marble quarry near Crystal in 1884. It was a continuation of the deposit along Yule Creek. The white stone had received a lot of publicity, but the lack of rail transportation precluded any large-scale development. Howell was able to ship limited amounts of marble, however.

A number of claims were filed in 1885 and 1886 on the deposit along Yule Creek including The London, New Discovery, Blue Marble and White Marble. These formed the center for future marble quarry operations.

In 1885, G. D. Griffith started blasting marble from the cliff along Yule Creek. Griffith, incidentally, was a former marble worker from Wales and owned one of the claims. John B. Osgood, founder of Redstone, was one of the financial backers for this operation. Osgood owned the Yule Creek White Marble Company and at great expense, cut a block of marble from his quarry, had it finished and put it on display at the World Colombian Exposition in 1893.

This was the receiving area where the quarried blocks of marble were unloaded from the electric tram for finishing. Note the overhead crane. *(Denver Public Library, Western History Department MCC-1993)*

The Elk Mountain Railroad was organized and started construction along the Crystal River from Carbondale. The attempt was abandoned, and the grade can still be seen running parallel to the Crystal River Railroad grade.

Marble did not have the population to merit a post office until 1890. After only two years, the post office was moved to Clarence. It became the Marble post office that same year when the two towns merged. At this time, an electric tram was surveyed from Pittsburgh at the head of the Slate River. This rail line would have run from the head of the Slate River, over rugged Yule Pass and down to Marble. Although some grading was done, the route was not practical.

In an interesting turn of events, Yule Creek marble was selected for the State Capitol in 1894. A contract was let the following year for 140,000 square feet to be used for the interior of the structure. Transportation problems again plagued the full development of marble quarries in the area. To meet the contract, heavy slabs had to be skidded down Yule Creek during the winter nearly four miles to Marble. From there, the marble was transported by wagon thirty miles to the closest railroad at Carbondale. During 1897, $100,000 was shipped to complete the order.

The story of how Marble finally got rail transportation is complex. In 1892 using the abandoned Aspen & Western narrow gauge line south of Carbondale, the Crystal River Railroad began operating. This railroad converted the track to standard gauge. The portion of the Aspen & Western running into Thompson Canyon was dismantled, and the Crystal River continued construction to the south. By the end of 1892, it had six miles in operation. Construction continued the following year adding nearly eight miles of track. It wasn't until 1898 that more construction took place, and Redstone was reached to service the Colorado Fuel & Iron's coke ovens. In 1899, another 3.4 miles was constructed ending at Placita south of Redstone. In 1906, the Crystal River & San Juan was organized and continued construction. It built 7.3 miles of track to Marble finally giving the quarry town its long awaited rail connection. The Crystal River & San Juan eventually leased and operated the entire Crystal River line to Carbondale.

At the quarries, four openings were made in the steep marble cliff above Yule Creek. The marble was cut from the interior of the cliff, forming vaults. A channeling machine, mounted on rails, was used to cut vertical slots deep into the rock around a block. Wire saws, using diamond dust, cut the block free from the deposit. A derrick was used to lift the blocks out of the quarry, and then the blocks were transferred either to a funicular tram or to a cable tram. The blocks were lowered to the grade, which ran down Yule Creek to the finishing mill. The upper funicular tram, called the Pea Vine, was constructed on a curving trestle supported by bents, which clung to the steep side of the cliff. It provided a means of moving blocks from the Number 2 quarry opening. A second funicular tram allowed blocks to be lowered farther to the grade. The cableway stretched across the canyon, anchored into solid rock on both sides.

Up until 1907, the heavy blocks of marble were brought down by teamsters. In 1908, a Best steam tractor was used to handle up to seven wagonloads of marble on wagons connected together like a train. The road to the quarry was widened and in 1910, an electric tramway was built. The 3.9-mile line had grades from six to fourteen percent, extremely steep for a standard gauge adhesion railroad. It worked only because all of the weight was hauled downhill, and when the electric powered cars went uphill, they were empty. Due to primitive brakes and heavy loads, this rail line had a number of serious accidents. Despite its limitations, the electric railroad operated up until the quarries were closed in 1941. At that time, the line was dismantled.

The electric railroad used powered flat cars, with small wooden cabs at either end, to transport marble directly to the mill. A typical "train" consisted of a non-powered flat car with powered cars at either end.

At this point, it might be well to mention that many quarry workers preferred to live at the quarry rather than commute to and from Marble. An informal camp, called Quarry Town, sat on the lip of the cliff above the electric tram grade and below the quarry openings. Access from below was by a series of long wooden staircases perched on the steep slope. From the quarries, however, a narrow trail was cut directly across the hillside to Quarry Town. To bring workers to the quarry, a funicular tram flatcar was fitted with benches. The buildings in Quarry Town were of frame construction, and seventeen structures appear in historic photographs. The slope was so steep that the backs of the homes (or shacks) were supported by stilts a full story high while the front entrances were at ground level. On the uphill side of the trail through Quarry Town, staircases were used to gain access to the structures. These structures were dug into the hillside. This was no place for a person with a fear of heights. Winters were severe, and Quarry Town was sometimes buried roof high in snow. Tunnels had to be dug to each dwelling. It is not known how many lived in Quarry Town, but a good guess would be around fifty to seventy. There were still several remaining structures in Quarry Town in the 1970s, but today, nothing remains. The lack of the wooden staircase restricts access to the site.

In an effort to reach its quarry on Treasury Mountain, the Treasury Mountain Railroad constructed a steep four-mile long

Today, all that remains of the mill at Marble are the support columns plus a few outbuildings. Sandra Dallas, noted historian, took this photograph in 1966. *(Denver Public Library, Western History Department X-12294)*

standard gauge railroad in 1910 from Marble to the Strauss Quarry. A switchback, where the train had to reverse directions, was required. The line used a geared locomotive, and was abandoned four years later.

Colonel Channing F. Meek was the energy behind getting the quarries to a commercial operating level. As president of the Colorado Yule Marble Company, he invested over three million dollars. During his tenure, the quarries supplied marble for over 100 structures all across the United States. In addition, under his direction, the largest marble finishing mill in the world was built at the south edge of town, and it eventually measured 1,700 feet in length. During its boom years, Marble became the third largest marble producer in the United States.

On an electric tram excursion, outfitted for passengers, a serious accident occurred. It happened on a warm August day in 1912, and among the passengers was Colonel Channing F. Meek. The tram had a set of new brakes, and on the steep grade, the brakes had to be applied for the entire trip from the quarry to the bottom at the finishing mill. The brakes failed on a steep section, and the tram accelerated suddenly. Jumping for their lives, two quarry workers tumbled to the ground. Meek instructed the other passengers to jump on the inside of an approaching curve. Colonel Channing F. Meek jumped and landed such that he was thrown forward and was unable to get up. The passengers that stayed with the tram were uninjured. The brakes somehow started working and brought the cars to a safe stop. Meek died four days after the accident.

The town of Marble was not effected by the silver crash in 1893 and continued to grow. It was, for all purposes, a company town owned and controlled by the Colorado Yule Marble Company. Freedom of the press was suppressed and its citizens were even told how to vote. At first, Marble was a town of scattered homes, then as business grew, the Colorado Yule Marble Company constructed rows of identical houses. The supervisors lived in company owned cottages considerably larger than the homes of the workers. Despite the somewhat rigid nature of Marble, those that lived and worked at the quarries had a far better life than others did in a typical Colorado mining town.

Sylvia Smith had left a fiery trail across part of Colorado before she arrived in Marble. She worked in Lake City, was a schoolteacher at Jack's Cabin and ran a millinery shop in Crested Butte. She began the *Weekly Citizen* in Crested Butte in 1900 and was quick to criticize any large corporation. She stood for freedom of the press and women's rights. During her stay in Crested Butte, she attacked the high-handed tactics of Colorado Fuel & Iron and the Denver & Rio Grande.

In 1908, when Sylvia Smith arrived in Marble, she became the owner and editor of the *Marble City Times.* This gave her a voice to criticize anyone or anything she wanted, especially the controlling influence of the Colorado Yule Marble Company.

After an avalanche damaged the finishing mill in March, 1912, Sylvia Smith wrote of how the company's stock had "carried desolation into many homes and written despair over many lives." Investors became skeptical about the company, and Smith's editorials threatened jobs. A large number of Marble's citizens gathered in the Masonic Hall and signed a petition to rid Marble of this red-haired editor. After refusing to leave, Smith was placed in jail. She was then put on a Crystal River & San Juan train and banished from the town. Smith later retaliated by hiring a Denver lawyer to file damages against the town, the railroad and the marble company. She collected over ten thousand dollars, and never returned to Marble.

The peak years for Marble were between 1910 and 1914 when the quarries and finishing mill were running at capacity. The town's population approached the 2,000 mark.

After the death of Colonel Channing Meek in 1912, his successor could not handle the complexities of the Meek marble empire. The largest contract in the history of the company, however, was signed in 1913 for the Lincoln Memorial. The mill had to be enlarged just to fill the contract. The statistics of this order

Marble suffered from devastating floods in 1941 and again in 1945 from Carbonate Creek. Somehow, the bell tower survived both floods. *(Kenneth Jessen 020B11)*

were staggering. For starters, the building required thirty-six columns, each one seven feet in diameter. The columns were built in segments, and when each segment was stacked, the full height of forty-six feet was obtained. The quarry had to supply 1,800 slabs up to thirty tons each. It took over 600 railroads cars during the course of three years to get the marble to Washington D. C to build the monument.

A fire in 1925 damaged the finishing mill, and the Vermont Marble Company took over the Colorado Yule Marble Company in 1928. The company then received a contract for the largest single block of marble every quarried. Unfinished, it weighed 124 tons and required a custom-built derrick to hoist it to the surface. The 3.9 mile trip down the steep electric tram grade took four days. The large block was sent across the United States in February, 1931. It was to become the Tomb of the Unknown Soldier at the Arlington National Cemetery outside of Washington D. C.

During the Great Depression, where once 1,000 worked, only 55 men were required to meet the demand for marble. The town fell from its population of nearly 2,000 to just 150. Floods down the Crystal River Valley in 1941 and in 1945 destroyed many of Marble's buildings. The quarries closed in 1941, and the great mill was dismantled. Only the marble support columns for the overhead crane remain today. All of the rail lines were abandoned and the rails removed. Its isolation and high production costs, not the amount of marble remaining in the quarries, put a temporary end to this industry.

A partial list of buildings and monuments constructed from Yule marble: The Tomb of the Unknown soldier, Arlington National Cemetery, Arlington, Virginia; The Lincoln Memorial, Washington, D. C.; Colorado State Museum, Denver (original one); The Colorado National Bank, Denver; Federal Building, Denver; Public Service Company of Colorado, Denver; The Symes Building, Denver; The Empire Building, Denver; The Federal Courthouse, Denver; The Cheesman Park Memorial, Denver; and The New Customs House, Denver.

In 1990, work started to get the quarries back into production. Not one piece of machinery had been left from the old days. Even some of the piles of waste rock had been removed and converted into marble powder.

The old drainage tunnel was expanded to handle haulage trucks, and the floor of the quarries were pumped dry of water. Debris was removed, and modern channel machines were brought in. The first block of commercial marble was brought down the old railroad grade by truck to the town in September, 1990.

Dell McCoy and Russ Collman, *The Crystal River Pictorial*, Sundance, Denver, Colorado, 1972, pp. 169-174.

Duane Vandenbusche, *The Gunnison Country*, B & B Printers, Gunnison, Colorado, 1980, pp. 206-207, 234-239, 242-244.

Duane Vandenbusche and Rex Myers, *Marble Colorado, City of Stone*, Gold Bell Press, Denver, Colorado, 1970, pp. 8-12, 19, 43-47, 58-59.

Marble City Times, March 22, 1912.

Oscar McCollum Jr. Marble, *A Town Built on Dreams*, Volume II, Sundance, Denver, Colorado, 1993, pp. 253-348.

Tiv Wilkins, *Colorado Railroads*, Pruett Publishing Company, Boulder, Colorado, 1974, pp. 95, 123, 163, 181, 193.

William H. Bauer, James L. Ozment and John H. Willard, *Colorado Post Offices*, Colorado Railroad Museum, Golden, Colorado, 1990, p. 95.

OHIO CITY
And Nearby Gold Creek Mining Camps

- *Gunnison County, Quartz Creek and Gold Creek drainages*
- *Accessible by paved or graded dirt roads*
- *One town had a post office; many original structures remain*

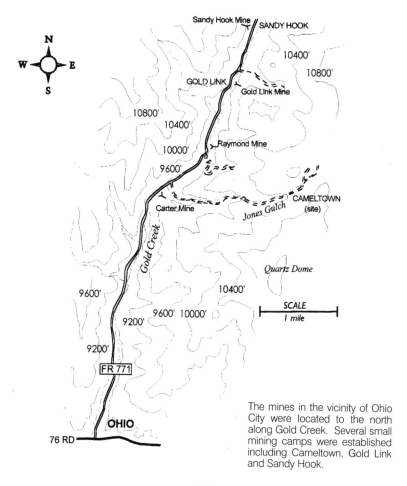

The mines in the vicinity of Ohio City were located to the north along Gold Creek. Several small mining camps were established including Cameltown, Gold Link and Sandy Hook.

Ohio City was founded in 1880 at the confluence of Gold and Quartz creeks. It got its own post office this same year, and this post office remained open until 1972. Rich ore was discovered in the area. The small camp was named Eagle City, but since so many of the early arrivals came from Ohio, the town's name was changed. Soon, Ohio City had thirty or more log structures mixed with many tents. As sawmills began producing milled lumber, Ohio City took on a more permanent look.

Most of the better claims were located north along Gold Creek. The primary precious metal was gold, but the mines also produced some silver.

In his excellent book, *The Gunnison Country*, contemporary historian Duane Vandenbusche tells of Ohio City's first gun battle. In May, 1880, a Leadville prospector, James Edward, came to the tent of James Reid. Reid was also from Leadville and may have known Edward from some previous time. Asleep on his cot, Reid woke when Edward yelled at a boy to get out of the way. Apparently expecting trouble, Reid came out of his tent with his gun blazing. Both men were found dead, each with a bullet through the heart.

As the mines began steady production, Ohio City grew. It got a boost in 1882 when the narrow gauge Denver, South Park & Pacific constructed its line through the Alpine Tunnel, down Quartz Creek, through Pitkin and into town. The railroad continued to Gunnison thus placing Ohio City on its main line.

Ohio City grew to a population of around 300. It had a fine hotel, the Arlington House. Just under 100 stamps pounded the gold-bearing quartz into powder at the mills around the town. The ore was easy to process by simple amalgamation with mercury.

Ohio City stagnated for a time, but during the 1890s, new mines were opened and two newspapers were started, the *Gold Brick* and the *Ohio City Times*. A new schoolhouse was constructed in 1904, shared by the town of Parlin to the south.

The Carter Mine, a few miles north of Ohio City, drove a tunnel a mile and a half into the mountain to undercut older veins, which had untapped ore bodies. The Raymond Mine, a mile north of the Carter Mine, produced enough ore to merit construction of its own mill. It closed in 1917 after having yielded over seven million dollars.

Ohio City's prosperity lasted much later than other mining towns in the general area. This was due to the steady output from the mines along Gold Creek. Ranching, lumber and tourists added to the economy. The Alpine Tunnel closed in 1910, ending Ohio City's position on the main line of a railroad. As the ore in the mines was exhausted and only the Carter Mine was left in operation, much of Ohio City was abandoned. By 1940, only seventy-eight residents remained, and a decade later, only fifty called

This may have been an old boarding house. It is located at the mining camp of Gold Link, north of Ohio City along Gold Creek. *(Kenneth Jessen 117D9)*

Ohio City home. Today the town is seasonally occupied as a summer retreat.

There were several satellite mining camps near Ohio City. Gold Link was located a mile farther north of the Raymond Mine. The ruins of what could have been a boarding house plus one frame home still stand at the site. As many as ninety men worked at the mine and its stamp mill. Many probably lived at Gold Link. The mine and mill closed in 1913.

Sandy Hook, located farther north along Gold Creek, still has one log home and one two-story frame boarding house. Both have been restored for seasonal use. There were probably other homes and cabins in the general area for miners who wished to live near where they worked.

Up Jones Gulch was the mining camp of Cameltown, also called Campbellville. It was laid out in 1881 about two miles east of the Carter Mine on Gold Creek. Cameltown had about thirty-five residents working in the mines. As reported in the *Pitkin Independent,* Cameltown had a good supply of water, but this also applied to its supply of snow during the winter. However, it did say residents were happy and contented with their lot in life. Al Campbell was one of the town's founders, and he played his banjo in the evening for the entertainment of the other residents. Pieces he selected included plantation songs from the South. As the Carter Mine expanded, Cameltown was destroyed.

Duane Vandenbusche, *The Gunnison Country*, B & B Printers, Gunnison, Colorado, 1980, pp. 190-191.

Muriel Sibell Wolle, *Stampede to Timberline*, Sage Books, Chicago, 1949, pp. 188-190.

William H. Bauer, James L. Ozment and John H. Willard, *Colorado Post Offices*, Colorado Railroad Museum, Golden, Colorado, 1990, p. 106.

PIEPLANT

And Other Towns in the Taylor River Drainage

- *Gunnison County, Taylor River drainage*
- *Access either by graded dirt road or by foot*
- *Several towns had a post office; Pieplant has several structures and Dorchester one*

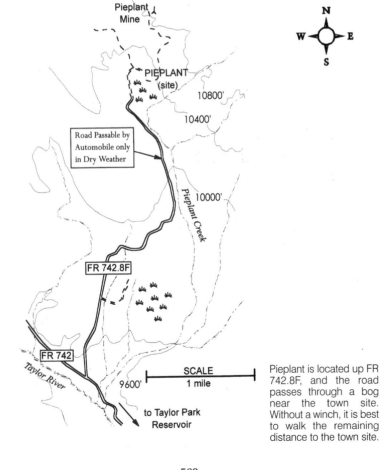

Pieplant is located up FR 742.8F, and the road passes through a bog near the town site. Without a winch, it is best to walk the remaining distance to the town site.

Getting to Pieplant (also spelled Pie Plant) in the spring requires a certain amount of courage and may demand that the owner have a good winch. The bogs are virtually impassable without the right equipment, and it is best to walk the remaining mile to this small camp. At Pieplant, several log cabins remain standing, and the impressive stone foundation of the mill sits to one side of the meadow where this small town was located.

In 1896, after it seemed like every valley and mountain had been explored, James Jenkins and John Lynch discovered some promising ore up Pieplant Creek. After an exploratory tunnel was drilled, the two men decided to develop the mine. In 1903, a large cyanide-processing mill was constructed less than a mile below the mine. A small sawmill provided the lumber for the mill.

The mining community of Pieplant grew up near the mill and reached a peak population of about 100. The name came from the abundant wild rhubarb, which grows in the surrounding marsh. Around fifty men worked at the mill and another forty or so worked at the mine. Besides a number of cabins, the town had a boarding house. The local saloon was located down Pieplant Creek below the town. The Pieplant post office opened in 1904, but closed after only two years of operation.

Disputes over the development of the ore body forced the closure of the mine and the mill in 1910. Soon, Pieplant was just another Colorado ghost town.

Up Trail Creek and west of the Taylor Park road was the mining camp of Forest Hill. Founded in 1880, it was originally called Camp Harbert for one of its founders, Marion Harbert. It was renamed Forest Hill for the mountain to the southwest. Forest Hill was a company town owned by the Forest Hill Mining Company. The mining camp never became large enough to merit a post office and consisted of a dozen cabins, a boarding house and a number of tents. The population peaked at 125 in 1882. Other major mines in the area included the Bonanza King and St. Crispen.

Forest Hill was abandoned in 1885 as the ore bodies in the

area mines failed to produce. A new mining company took over the claims ten years later and began mining not only for gold, but also for copper, iron, lead and silver. A mill was constructed a mile and a half below the mine along Trail Creek. After the ore was concentrated in the mill, it was shipped to a smelter in St. Elmo over Tin Cup Pass or south to Almont to the railroad. The camp died after the turn of the century although a new mill was constructed to replace the old mill around 1913. The mine operated intermittently from then until 1920. It is not known if any of the original structures remain at Forest Hill, but a historic photograph shows the camp, consisting of a half-dozen cabins, sitting in a broad meadow.

Dorchester is easy to find and is identified by a neat log guard station. The town was located in a large meadow next to the present-day guard station. None of its original structures remain standing.

Dorchester was originally called Taylor City and was established in 1896 by a town company. The mines were at some distance from the town, however. The Star Mine is located several miles up Italian Creek and the Enterprise Mine is located up a steep trail at 11,400 feet.

In 1900, Taylor City was renamed Dorchester, a name provided by the new postmaster for a town in Massachusetts. The post office remained open for a dozen years.

This town enjoyed a relatively long life as a supply center. It was a stopover for travelers going to and from the Aspen area over Taylor Pass. By 1901, Dorchester had a store, saloon, hotel, livery barn and a number of cabins. The Dorchester Hotel was a large two-story structure made of hand-hewn logs. The cabins, which constituted the remainder of the town, were located close to the hotel. Typical of most mining camps, a single proprietor wore many hats. In the case of Alex Malmgren, he was the postmaster and also owned and ran the saloon, the general store and the hotel.

By 1910, Dorchester had grown to a town of two saloons, two stores and even a restaurant. It also had a barbershop. Many of the miners from the surrounding area came to town for a hot meal, a bath and some saloon-style entertainment.

As mining in the area declined and railroads took over as a means of getting passengers and freight into and out of the area, the importance of Dorchester diminished. By 1920, the town was deserted.

The major employer in the Dorchester area was the Enterprise Mine. Ore was carried from the mine entrance by an aerial tram to a mill located 800 feet below. After the turn of the century, the mine and mill were electrified. The Enterprise Mine continued operation up until 1950 and was one of the more successful mines in Gunnison County. The road to the mine, with its many switchbacks, is visible from the Taylor River Valley.

The stone foundation of the Pieplant Mill is an impressive ruin. *(Kenneth Jessen 098B11)*

Also of importance to the area was the Star Mine near the headwaters of Italian Creek. A small community formed around this isolated mine, and several of the original cabins remain standing. The Star Mine has been operated in recent years on a seasonal basis.

The Bowman site is located near the headwaters of Taylor Creek in a small meadow. It was preceded by a place called Grandville. John Bowman purchased the site and built facilities for travelers passing through the area.

Bowman became an important way station for teamsters coming and going over Taylor Pass. It was situated where the long climb began. Taylor Pass, especially the Taylor Park side, is a rough, dangerous and difficult road in good weather. On the Aspen side, the upper part is a narrow exposed shelf road. During

Pieplant is located in a lush flower-covered meadow. This is one of several standing structures. *(Kenneth Jessen 098B12)*

periods of storms, the freighters would wisely wait at Bowman until the road was passable. As many as forty outfitters came and went through Bowman on a regular basis.

A large barn was constructed for changing horses. By 1881, Bowman had grown to include the Taylor Park Hotel, three stores, a blacksmith shop, and a number of cabins. Population estimates place Bowman at around 100 people. One type of business notable by its absence was a saloon. Bowman's post office opened in 1880, but lasted only two years.

What ended Bowman was the arrival of the narrow gauge Denver & Rio Grande into Aspen in 1887. The following year, the standard gauge Colorado Midland arrived in Aspen. On the Gunnison side, the Denver, South Park & Pacific as well as the Denver & Rio Grande served the area. It was no longer necessary to use the treacherous Taylor Pass and traffic declined. Mining continued to support the town until 1915 when Bowman was abandoned. The site is located where Bowman Creek flows into the Taylor River at the end of the graded dirt road through Taylor Park (FR 742). Nothing remains at the site today except for some stone foundations. There is also a ditch once used to carry water from Bowman Creek to placer deposits to the south.

One of the most obscure mining camps in Gunnison County was Tellurium. It was located somewhere near the head of Tellurium Creek and was occupied from 1880 to 1883. According to Duane Vandenbusche in his book, *The Gunnison Country*, the only way it was known to exist was by a report filed by geologist John Hallowell. He visited the small camp in 1882 and reported its population at 125.

Duane Vandenbusche, *The Gunnison Country*, B & B Printers, Gunnison, Colorado, 1980, pp. 378-381, 383.

Conrad F. Schader, *Colorado's Alluring Tin Cup*, Regio Alta Publications, Golden, Colorado, 1992, pp. 236-238, 240-243.

Muriel Sibell Wolle, *Stampede to Timberline*, Sage Books, Chicago, 1949, pp. 186-188.

William H. Bauer, James L. Ozment and John H. Willard, *Colorado Post Offices*, Colorado Railroad Museum, Golden, Colorado, 1990, p. 22, p. 112.

Tiv Wilkins, *Colorado Railroads*, Pruett Publishing Company, Boulder, Colorado, 1974, p. 61.

PITKIN

The Largest Town on Quartz Creek

- *Gunnison County, Quartz Creek drainage*
- *Accessible by paved road*
- *Town has a post office; many original structures remain*

Pitkin was a substantial town. A large mill, served by a railroad spur, is on the left. The center of town is in the middle of this photograph and the railroad facilities are on the far distant right. *(Denver Public Library, Western History Department MCC2019)*

The story of how rich silver ore was found in the Quartz Creek area varies. One account tells of two discouraged prospectors who had spent two years combing the area and found nothing. While they were eating lunch on a large rock, one lamented on how there wasn't anything of value along Quartz Creek. He struck the rock they were sitting on with his hammer as he spoke. His second blow dislodged a chunk, but it didn't fall to the ground. It hung suspended by strands of pure wire silver. The men quickly staked a claim, and the ore ran eighty percent solid silver. It became the Fairview Mine.

This planted the seed for a mining camp named Quartzville. The name was soon changed to Pitkin in honor of Colorado Governor Frederick W. Pitkin. Its first buildings were log cabins with ridgepole, sod-covered roofs. The town's only hotel was a large tent with sawdust covering its dirt floor. Bunks were arranged in rows in one large room, and the bedding was loose hay gathered from the surrounding meadow. A stove heated the canvas structure, but there wasn't any furniture. Guests were provided with a thin gray blanket and had to use their clothing as a pillow. For all of this "comfort," it cost fifty cents a night.

Pitkin became the center of activity for mining in and around Quartz Creek. So rapid was its growth, its post office was established in 1879 when few permanent structures had been completed. A toll road was constructed to the south amplifying the migration into the region.

By the spring of 1880, the town of Pitkin was well established in a long, flat meadow. There was plenty of good water and numerous places to build. At this time, most of Pitkin's residents lived in tents. The demand for lumber was so high that a number of sawmills were kept operating at capacity. Pitkin grew to include fifteen hotels and restaurants. The town could accommodate over 1,000 people. Prospectors arrived at the rate of seventy-five a day.

By the summer of 1880, population estimates topped 1,000, and the town could boast of nearly 200 structures. Daily stagecoach service was initiated from Gunnison and a bank opened in Pitkin. A dozen saloons and eight restaurants were in operation at the time. Among the miners and their families were fifty-five children. For them, the town established a school with classes in the town hall.

The *Pitkin Independent* opened with the publication of its first issue in July, 1880. It carried colorful columns under headings such as "Mining Matters" and "Pitkin Pellets." Frank Sheafor was its editor and publisher. A wide sombrero, long black hair, sinister mustache turned up at the ends and beady black eyes made Frank easy to recognize. One of Frank's "accessories" was the large revolver he wore on his hip. Frank sold his paper and promised its new owner not to start a rival newspaper in Pitkin. Sheafor broke his promise immediately with the publication of the *Pitkin Mining News.*

Sheafor was noted for his outrageous behavior that culminated when he raided the Lady Gay Dance Hall. It was located just outside the Pitkin city limits. Crimes were committed in the establishment against innocent miners who just stopped by for a drink. After one particular miner was beaten and robbed, Sheafor called his friends together for action. During the raid, the bartender reached for his gun and was shot twice for his efforts. The prostitutes fled through a back door while Sheafor and his comrades set the place on fire.

When the winter of 1880-1881 arrived, Pitkin was practically abandoned due to the lack of enough permanent heated structures. When the miners returned the following spring, Pitkin's population was estimated to have reached 4,000. This included those camped in the area. All of its hotels, restaurants, and saloons were booked to capacity.

The cost of living was staggering relative to prices elsewhere. The demand for merchandise was so high that merchants did not have to worry about placing items on their shelves. Everything could be sold from the pile left by the freighter in the street.

In addition to the gold found along Quartz Creek, silver ore was discovered in the nearby mountains. Pitkin's future looked bright, and in July, 1882, the narrow gauge Denver, South Park & Pacific reached the town. Its route was up Chalk Creek Canyon on the east side of the Continental Divide, through the Alpine Tunnel and down Middle Quartz Creek to Pitkin. The arrival of the railroad prompted the *Pitkin Independent* to comment that other towns, including Tincup and Gothic, were just temporary camps.

As it turned out, the silver ore at the surface was rich and assayed values were high, but as mining began, the vein vanished. By 1883, half of Pitkin's population had moved on, and the following year, this once bustling town had but 500 residents. A few mines, however, did have substantial amounts of ore and continued operation providing economic support for the town. In 1893, the U. S. Government abandoned the silver standard for currency. The Government was no longer required to purchase a given amount of silver every

The Pitkin City Hall sits back from the main street, and has been beautifully restored *(Kenneth Jessen 098C11)*

year. The price of silver fell to nearly half of its previous value, and the silver mines throughout Colorado closed. This was a crushing blow to Pitkin and its hopes for the future.

Many of Pitkin's buildings were destroyed in an 1898 fire. In 1903, fire again swept through the town, taking even more structures. The town was never rebuilt.

The Alpine Tunnel was closed in 1910 due to the expense of keeping the line to the tunnel open during the winter months. In addition, the tunnel was subject to cave-ins due to the geology of its location. The Denver, South Park & Pacific gave up its Western Slope operations to rival Denver & Rio Grande. Pitkin became a branch line, and its economy shifted to lumber. Its main customers were the coal mines in the Crested Butte area. When these mines closed in the 1950s, Pitkin was left with tourism and seasonal residents as its economic base.

Today, Pitkin has a grocery store, a cafe and a museum. A

beautiful community church sits at one end of the town. The scenery in and around Pitkin is exquisite with high snow-capped mountains and lush meadows. The town is filled with historic buildings and is well worth the visit.

In addition to Pitkin, Duane Vandenbusche, author of *The Gunnison Country,* mentions a ghost town called Camp Crescent. It was located near the headwaters of South Quartz Creek at the foot of Granite Mountain. This was a high altitude camp, near 12,000 feet, and was seasonally occupied. It was founded in 1881, and about twenty hardy souls lived in Camp Crescent. The camp lasted only a year. It is not known what structures were built at the site.

Today, Pitkin is a delightful place to visit with a summertime population. These old stone stores sit along its main street. *(Kenneth Jessen 098C10)*

Duane Vandenbusche, *The Gunnison Country,* B & B Printers, Gunnison, Colorado, 1980, pp. 179, 180-181.

William H. Bauer, James L. Ozment and John H. Willard, *Colorado Post Offices,* Colorado Railroad Museum, Golden, Colorado, 1990, p. 114.

POWDERHORN

And Other Towns in the Cebolla Creek Drainage

- *Gunnison County, Cebolla Creek drainage*
- *Accessible via paved or dirt roads*
- *Powderhorn has a post office; original structures remain at Powderhorn*

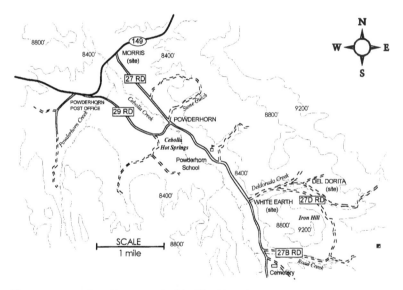

There were a number of towns south of the Blue Mesa Reservoir in the Cebolla Creek valley as shown on this map. Powderhorn is the only one of these towns shown on modern maps.

White Earth was located southeast where Deldorado Creek joins Cebolla Creek. It was established as a trade center dependent on the ranching and agriculture in the general area. It was also a stage stop for traffic coming and going to Lake City. White Earth's post office opened in 1876 and closed in 1880. At this time, the town of Powderhorn began to grow and to replace

White Earth as the economic center of the area. The post office was moved from White Earth to Cebolla Hot Springs into a combination store and blacksmith shop not far from Powderhorn. The stage stop was also relocated to Powderhorn. In the early 1880s, stagecoach and freight traffic averaged thirty-five teams a day.

White Earth was abandoned by 1881, and Powderhorn was growing. It constructed its own school, and attendance grew to the point where the original schoolhouse had to be replaced by a larger one eight years later. This second schoolhouse lasted over sixty years. A number of cabins for sportsmen were constructed in and around Powderhorn and some of those that remain today are built of hand-hewn logs.

A. J. Store developed Cebolla Hot Springs and constructed a hotel at the site. Bathhouses were built, and the spring drew customers from the surrounding area. After having passed through a number of owners over the years, there are still cabins for rent.

Del Dorita was a small mining camp located near spring-fed Deldorado Creek about one mile east of its confluence with Cebolla Creek. The town was started in 1882, after White Earth

This cabin is of modern vintage and sits next to the Powderhorn post office. Many log structures in this same area are in excellent condition and some possibly date back to the founding of Powderhorn in 1880. *(Kenneth Jessen 109B3)*

had been abandoned. The Bay State Mining and Milling Company owned half of the town site and held title to most of the mining claims in the area. Lots in Del Dorita were priced from $25 to $300 with choice locations going for as much as $1,000.

The surface deposits of quartzite revealed the presence of gold. Shafts were sunk in anticipation of finding more gold, but instead, the veins narrowed. Duane Vandenbusche speculated in his book, *The Gunnison Country,* that it is quite doubtful that any ore was shipped from the area for processing. Del Dorita was a ghost town only a year after it was founded. The houses constructed at the site crumbled with time.

Not far away where Powderhorn Creek empties into Cebolla Creek was yet another small mining camp named Morris. A couple of prospectors, Horne and Mallette, sank a twenty-foot shaft near the Morris town site in 1886. They called the mine the Old Lot. Horne was a large man and a bully, while Mallette was small. Horne, in a fit of anger, threatened Mallette, but as Horne began to climb out of the shaft, Mallette hit him in the head with a rock. This rendered Horne temporarily unconscious. Frightened by the incident and possible retaliation, Mallette fled. Horne recovered sufficiently to chase after Mallette. Using his rifle, Horne fired at his partner, but every round missed. Horne returned to the Old Lot, sent for a doctor, but died later of an infection caused by the blow to the head. Mallette was never charged with any crime.

A Michigan mining company eventually purchased the Old Lot, and Morris was picked for the site of a stamp mill. Morris got its own post office in 1896 under the name Tucker. The town site was abandoned by the end of the following year after it was discovered that no extensive gold ore deposit was found. The boarding house constructed by the mining company was moved to the mine. The Old Lot, unlike other area mines, did make limited ore shipments for a number of years. It was still in operation in 1935 although it had been sold four times for back taxes.

To the south was yet another mining camp. Copperville was located at the mouth of Rudolph Gulch along Cebolla Creek. It

was founded in 1897 on the hopes that the copper ore in the area would prove rich. Copperville had a hotel, saloon and nine or ten homes. The closest mine was the Cashier, about a mile to the west up Rudolph Gulch. Early assays showed the presence of copper ore as well as gold and other minerals. High quality ore, however, was never discovered, and by the turn of the century, Copperville was deserted. Its buildings were razed and nothing remains at the site today.

The Powderhorn post office has been moved in recent years to a building near Colorado 149. The old Powderhorn town site remains occupied by a handful of residents. Within the valley where the town sits are numerous log cabins. Many were constructed to accommodate visitors and it is difficult to determine if any date back to the town's early days.

Duane Vandenbusche, *The Gunnison Country*, B & B Printers, Gunnison, Colorado, 1980, pp. 151, 154.

William H. Bauer, James L. Ozment and John H. Willard, *Colorado Post Offices*, Colorado Railroad Museum, Golden, Colorado, 1990, pp. 116, 143, 151.

William Brown, *History of the Cebolla-Powderhorn County*, Master's Thesis, Western State College, 1935.

QUARTZ
Nothing but a Meadow Remains

- *Gunnison County, Quartz Creek drainage*
- *Accessible by graded dirt road*
- *Town did have a post office; no structures remain*

Only a sign placed by the Forest Service remains at the town site of Quartz, yet this was once a vibrant town with hopes for the future. The site is located in a wide meadow east of Pitkin near the confluence of North and Middle Quartz Creek. This was where the narrow gauge Denver, South Park & Pacific left this drainage for its long climb up to the Alpine Tunnel.

Started in 1879, Quartz was a stopover for travelers into the region. During the summer of 1882, the railroad arrived, and at this time, the Quartz Town Company was formed to sell lots. A post office was also established. A small mill was located at Quartz along with the cabins of several miners, a log hotel, two stores and several saloons. The railroad added to the structures at Quartz with an eight-room combination depot and telegraph office. The structure has living quarters for the agent. Ore from as far away as Tincup was shipped by wagon to Quartz to be loaded on railroad cars. Logs and milled lumber also made up shipments from this camp. In 1882, the population of Quartz was more than 100 with three times that many camping in the surrounding area.

Quartz did have a hanging of sorts. A trio of miners swapped some rich ore from a mine near Tincup and replaced it with some low-grade ore from a mine near Quartz. They were arrested because of an informant named Smith. After the miners were released, they hunted down Smith and hanged him from a tree limb. On the point of suffocation, they lowered Smith and tried to get him to promise to leave the area forever. He refused and was promptly hauled off the ground by the neck again. This time he nearly died. Smith then saw the reality of the situation and decided it might be good for his health if he did leave the area. After Smith was released, he immediately went to the local authorities and reported the incident. The final outcome is unknown.

Quartz began to lose population as the ore in the area turned out not to be as rich as originally thought. In 1886, the post office closed. Silver made up much of the precious metal recovered in the mines, and when the U. S. abandoned the silver standard in 1893, the mines closed. Shipments of ore from Quartz came to a halt, and the siding for the railroad was converted into a passing track. Nevertheless, up to 800 carloads of lumber were shipped each year from Quartz. When the railroad was abandoned in 1934, Quartz was also abandoned. Apparently the buildings were either moved or deteriorated since nothing remains at the site today.

Duane Vandenbusche, *The Gunnison Country*, B & B Printers, Gunnison, Colorado, 1980, p. 191.

Mac Poor, *Denver South Park & Pacific*, Rocky Mountain Railroad Club, Denver, 1976, p. 440.

William H. Bauer, James L. Ozment and John H. Willard, *Colorado Post Offices*, Colorado Railroad Museum, Golden, Colorado, 1990, p. 117.

SARGENTS
And Other Railroad Towns

- *Saguache County, Marshall Creek drainage*
- *Accessible via paved road*
- *Town had a post office; a number of original structures remain*

There are a number of railroad stops located between the base of Marshall Pass and Gunnison. These places acted as freight transfer points and many began as stagecoach stations. Agricultural products as well as ore from area mines made up much of the outbound freight.

Starting at the base of Marshall Pass was Sargents, then to the west was Elko, Crookston and Haig clustered in the same area. Doyleville, Bonita and Parlin made up the other towns between Sargents and Gunnison.

Sargents was among the most important of these places during the development of Gunnison County's natural resources. It began when Joseph Sargent settled at the foot of Marshall Pass along Marshall Creek. He laid out Marshalltown in 1880 in anticipation of the coming of the Denver & Rio Grande from Salida. Marshalltown got its own post office this same year, but in 1882, the name was changed to Sargents for its founder. The railroad arrived in July 1881, and Sargents became an end-of-track transfer point for Gunnison-bound freight. It was also, at least for a few weeks, a construction town of over 1,000.

The *Gunnison Review* commented that of the first fourteen buildings in the town, eight were saloons. A half dozen freight companies operated out of Sargents, and most prominent was the Barlow and Sanderson stagecoach line.

The Denver & Rio Grande maintained extensive facilities at

Sargents. For eastbound trains, there was a staging area where an extra (or helper) locomotive was coupled ahead of the lead engine to help the train over the pass. As a result, the Denver & Rio Grande constructed a six-stall roundhouse for its helper locomotives. It also had a coaling dock and a water tank. The railroad also maintained a depot, restaurant, and section house for railroad employees. After the Denver & Rio Grande construction crew moved on to Gunnison, Sargents matured with three saloons, a couple of restaurants, two stores, two hotels, several lumber mills and a barber shop. The steady population was around 100 people, most employed by the railroad.

The ore from the mines along Tomichi Creek to the north was shipped from Sargents. This included the North Star and the May-Mazeppa mines. After mining faded, the Trinchera Lumber Company, with 400 to 500 employees shipped from Sargents for many years.

Like so many Colorado towns, fire destroyed most of the structures at Sargents. In 1909, a fire leveled nearly the entire town except for some of the railroad structures and a few cabins. It is not known how much of the town was rebuilt.

In 1955, the rails of the Denver & Rio Grande were removed. The population of Sargents fell to approximately fifteen. All but one business closed, and when U.S. 50 was rebuilt, it bypassed the town.

Today, a number of the original Denver & Rio Grande railroad structures can be seen to the south of U.S. 50. This includes the depot, tool house, section house and water tank. In addition, there are a number of frame homes and trailers in Sargents. Private property limits exploration in Sargents, and vicious dogs make photography somewhat hazardous.

Other points along the main line of the Denver & Rio Grande have been mentioned. Here is a little more detail on these places:

Elko: This place had a siding for loading hay and lumber. Its post office lasted from 1881 to 1884.

Haig: This place had a siding used by the Trinchera Lumber Company.

Crookston (also called Crooksville): This was originally a stage station established by Cyrus Crooks in 1877 and was used as a transfer point after the arrival of the railroad. It had a siding and loading pens. The railroad constructed a water tank and section house. It also had a school and post office. The post office was first opened in 1878 and closed in 1885. It reopened in 1904 and closed for good in 1906.

Bonita: This was a railroad siding.

Doyleville: Homesteaded in 1876 by Henry Doyle, this was originally a stage station for the Barlow and Sanderson line. Its post office was established in 1881. In 1882, the name was changed to Gilman. The following year, it was changed back to Doyleville. The post office remained active until 1969. The small town had a school, depot, and railroad siding. It once had a population of over 100, and a few people still live at the town site today.

Parlin: Established in 1877 by John Parlin, this small community had a hotel, several stores, a saloon and a blacksmith shop. Originally named Tumichi (not Tomichi), its post office opened in 1879. The name was changed to Parlin the following year.

It was a stage station and transfer point for the railroad.

The old Denver & Rio Grande section house at Sargents. *(Kenneth Jessen 075A19)*

Both the Denver, South Park & Pacific as well as the Denver & Rio Grande narrow gauge railroads passed through Parlin on parallel tracks. Both railroads constructed facilities at Parlin including a depot, water tank and wye. The Denver, South Park & Pacific had a six-room section house plus a two-room bunkhouse.

When it came time for the Denver & Rio Grande to acquire the right of way through John Parlin's ranch, John struck a deal. He gave the railroad the right of way in return for a depot. He required that passenger trains stop long enough for him to sell a glass of milk to anyone interested. Today there is a combination store and post office at Parlin plus a frame home.

Duane Vandenbusche, *The Gunnison Country*, B & B Printers, Gunnison, Colorado, 1980, pp. 409-411.

Mac Poor, *Denver South Park & Pacific*, Rocky Mountain Railroad Club, Denver, 1976, p. 441.

Tiv Wilkins, *Colorado Railroads*, Pruett Publishing Company, Boulder, Colorado, 1974, pp. 264-265.

William H. Bauer, James L. Ozment and John H. Willard, *Colorado Post Offices*, Colorado Railroad Museum, Golden, Colorado, 1990, pp. 47, 50, 95, 111, 128, 143.

SCHOFIELD

And Other Crystal River Towns

- *Gunnison County, Crystal River drainage*
- *Accessible by four-wheel drive roads*
- *Some towns had a post office; several structures remain*

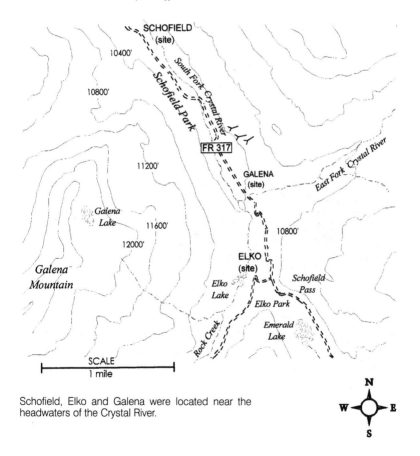

Schofield, Elko and Galena were located near the headwaters of the Crystal River.

Schofield was located above Crystal on the Crystal River north of Schofield Pass. The town was situated in a long meadow through which the South Fork of the Crystal River flows. Although silver ore was discovered in the early 1870s, no mining was done until 1879. Schofield was platted at this time by a small party of prospectors led by B. F. Schofield. By the summer of the following year, the town had thirty buildings. The demand for milled lumber was satisfied by a couple of sawmills. In anticipation of processing local ore, a smelter was constructed in 1880. The following year, the *Gunnison Daily News-Democrat* reported that Schofield had fifty structures including two stores, two restaurants, four saloons, a shoe store and a livery stable. The massive three-story Elk Mountain Hotel opened in Schofield in 1882. The town's population was estimated at about 300.

The mill that once processed silver ore at Schofield sat in the middle of Schofield Park and was powered by a vertical water wheel. *(Author's collection CP088)*

After Schofield's jail was complete, ironically, the first inmate was the town sheriff. It was a practical joke played by some of the men. They first got the sheriff drunk, then locked him up!

Under the name "Scofield," the town got its own post office in 1880. It remained active for six years until the town's population fell below the required level for such service.

Most mine owners, in order to boost the price of the stock,

wanted a famous person listed among the stockholders. When former United States President Grant visited Schofield in 1880, the mine owners got him into a poker game. During the game, they served Grant as much whiskey as he would drink, then tried to lose the title to a mine to the former president. After this scheme failed, they tried to give him stock in the property. Grant survived his visit to Schofield and left unencumbered with any mining stock.

On the edge of Schofield Park at the end of a side road sits the town's one remaining structure.

Elko was a small mining camp located near Elko Lake in a broad meadow south of the confluence of the East and South forks of the Crystal River. The site is noted as Elko Park on contemporary maps.

Willis McGlothlen prospected in the area in 1869. He discovered silver ore and returned three years later with a party of thirty men. He selected Elko Park as the ideal location for a camp. The first cabin was constructed in 1874. A plat was filed for the town of Elko in 1881. Some resident prospectors tried to rename the place Golconda since the original thirty men worked for the Golconda Placer Mining Company.

A sawmill was erected in Elko. A mining company invested in a concentrator in 1881 as Elko's population grew to about 200. Elko had a general store, a saloon and several cabins. A post office opened in 1881 and remained open for three years. Area mines had such colorful names as Slim Jim, Duke of Wellington, Hard Cash and Pride of Cinnamon.

After 1893, when the price of silver fell, Elko was abandoned. In 1901, there was renewed interest in the area and a 3,000-foot tunnel was bored under Galena Mountain. Elko was repopulated. A mill was constructed to process the complex silver ore, however, the project was soon abandoned. The mine owners had failed to understand the complex nature of the ore nor had they taken into account the cost of transporting the concentrate to the nearest railroad for shipment to a smelter.

One cabin remains standing at the site, which is located

near Schofield Pass.

Duane Vandenbusche in his book, *The Gunnison Country*, provides information on two other obscure mining camps in the general area. At the south end of Elko Park was a little camp called Galena. Platted by a group of prospectors in 1880, it was named for the silver-bearing mineral in the area. The camp was located about three-quarters of a mile north of Schofield Pass where the East Fork of the Crystal River meets the main stream. Its mines were located on Galena Mountain. The town hardly lasted a year and never supported a large enough population to merit a post office. Nothing remains at the site today.

Snowmass City was one and a half miles north of Crystal. It was also called Silver Center or Sheep Mountain. Founded in 1880, its reason for existence was the mines in nearby Lead King Basin. The mines had names such as the Gray Copper, the Elk Mountain Bonanza and the Grand Republic. Physical features above Snowmass City reflected the rugged nature of the area. About four miles away to the east was Frigid Air Pass and a mile and a half north was the Devil's Rock Pile. Snowmass City was named for the dominant peak in the area, Snowmass Mountain, elevation 14,092 feet.

Snowmass City did gain enough population to get its own post office in 1882, but it closed the following year. The small camp was abandoned in 1886. The ore in the area was not rich enough to be mined economically. Isolation and transportation costs plus the severe winter conditions spelled an end to the town. Nothing remains at the site today.

Duane Vandenbusche, *The Gunnison Country*, B & B Printers, Gunnison, Colorado, 1980, pp. 249, 251-252.

Muriel Sibell Wolle, *Stampede to Timberline*, Sage Books, Chicago, 1949, p. 204.

Robert L. Brown, *Colorado Ghost Towns*, Past and Present, Caxton Printers, Caldwell, Idaho, 1977, pp. 97-100.

Ron Ruhoff, "Adventure Trails of Northern Gunnison County," *Trails Among the Columbine*, 1990, Sundance Books, Denver, 1990, p. 176.

William H. Bauer, James L. Ozment and John H. Willard, *Colorado Post Offices*, Colorado Railroad Museum, Golden, Colorado, 1990, pp. 130, 133.

SPENCER, MIDWAY
and VULCAN

- *Gunnison County, Wildcat Gulch, Willow Creek and Camp Creek drainages*
- *Accessible by dirt roads; access to Midway limited by private property*
- *Two of the towns had a post office; several remaining structures at Vulcan*

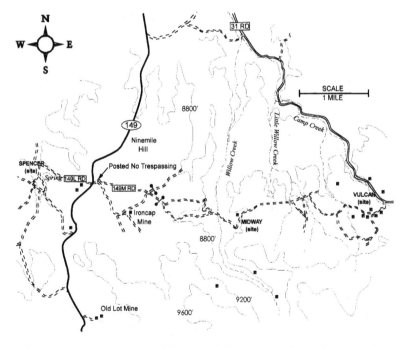

This map shows three of the ghost towns located south of the Blue Mesa Reservoir.

At the head of Wildcat Gulch and located a mile west of Colorado 149 was the town of Spencer. In 1946, Muriel Sibell Wolle visited the Spencer site and found one log cabin. It was occupied by a rancher. Today, the site is void of structures, but the imprints of foundations are still visible in the small meadow. Spencer was started in 1893 and was first named Cameron. It was named for one of many politicians who fought for the free coinage of silver, Senator Don Cameron of Pennsylvania. Prospectors flocked into the area driven by geology similar to Cripple Creek.

When the small mining camp applied for a post office the following year, the name Cameron was rejected. There was a town named Cameron near Cripple Creek. The town was renamed Spencer for the Gunnison County Clerk, and the post office opened in 1894. By the end of this year, Spencer had about fifty structures. Merchants from Creede established branch stores at Spencer including a hardware store, a furniture store, a saloon and a freight service. Located two miles to the east of Spencer, the Iron Cap Mine was one of the major producers. Many of the buildings at the Iron Cap are still standing.

The Lake City Branch of the Denver & Rio Grande ran through Gateview. Those wishing to travel to Spencer would get off at Gateview and take a stagecoach.

An experienced newspaperman, C. A. Frederick, began publication of the *Spencer Times* in 1894. It published local and area news for four years. The *Spencer Pick and Drill* also began publication in 1894, but did not last a year. At the time, Spencer had a population of 300 with twice that many prospectors camping in the surrounding sagebrush-covered hills.

A four-month term school opened in Spencer in 1894. After using several structures, a new schoolhouse was constructed in 1902.

As was the case for all other Gold Belt towns south of Gunnison, the ore in the mines near Spencer was soon exhausted. Spencer's population fell to fifty-two residents by the turn of the century. For a while, copper ore was mined in the region. This caused a resurgence in Spencer's population. The Copper King was the area's largest producer. Just like the gold, ore was hauled by freight wagon down Ninemile Hill to Iola for shipment to a smelter. Lack of direct rail service limited the copper mining. In 1907, Spencer's post office closed, and by 1920, the mines had closed. The empty town site sits at the junction of three dirt roads.

Midway was another Gold Belt camp. It was located on Willow Creek about midway between Spencer and Vulcan. The road into Midway from Colorado 149 has been blocked by a private property owner, and what structures remain are unknown. Unlike other Gold Belt towns, Midway had a good water supply. A water-powered stamp mill was constructed. Population estimates place the town at twenty men working at the stamp mill and probably an equal number working in the nearby mines. Midway lasted from 1894 to 1902.

The largest Gold Belt town was Vulcan, located on Camp Creek. Like the other towns, it got its start in 1894. Vulcan occupied a shallow valley and had a distinct main street with several side streets.

Spencer was located in a shallow valley west of modern-day Colorado 149. This 1912 photograph shows one structure under construction. Nothing but the meadow remains today. *(U.S.G.S. J. F. Hunter 112)*

When Muriel Sibell Wolle visited the deserted town during the mid-1940s, she found a number of cabins, a store and a schoolhouse. The mine buildings above the town were also standing. Inside one of the cabins, crude benches and some furniture remained. Today, there are seven full or partially standing structures and one appears to be occupied at times. The large tailing pile from the Good Hope Mine overlooks the town site.

The site is ten miles south of U. S. 50 on 31 RD. After a rain or snowfall, this road requires four-wheel drive because Camp Creek overflows onto the road creating a quagmire. Near Vulcan, the road can have deep ruts.

Vulcan was first called Fulton and then became Camp Creek. The name Vulcan was finally selected for the Vulcan Crest volcanic formation near the town.

The Vulcan Lode was discovered in 1894 and was twenty-two feet wide consisting of gold-bearing glassy quartz. When first discovered, however, it didn't appear to be all that rich. Assays, however, proved its value at $600 a ton or better. The Vulcan, Mammoth Chimney and Good Hope mines all tapped this same vein producing endless litigation over mining rights.

A post office opened in Vulcan in 1895 and remained open through several phases of mining in the area. It closed in 1912. The town reached a population of 500 and had a hotel and several stores. Teams of horses were in constant use hauling wagonloads of ore north to Iola on the road along Camp Creek. David Moffat, in association with a mining syndicate, purchased the Vulcan Mine in 1895 bringing in new capital.

Vulcan also had several newspapers. The first one was printed in Gunnison and brought to Vulcan for distribution. It was called the *Gold Belt Enterprise* and lasted from 1896 to 1899. In 1901, the *Vulcan Enterprise* made its appearance, but it was closed by the end of the following year.

The Vulcan Mine was closed in 1897 by a sulphur fire. It burned itself out after two weeks. In 1899, the Vulcan Mine was taken over by force. Union miners from the Western Federation of

Miners engaged in a labor dispute with mine owners. The strike escalated into violence, resulting in the injury of several non-union men. The union leaders were brought to trial resulting in a hung jury. In a second trail, the union leaders were acquitted.

By 1906, the gold ore deposits were exhausted. What had plagued all of the mines in the area was sulphur. What saved these mines was sulphur. Thousands of tons of sulphur were shipped each year to the Dupont Company. A refinery was built in 1909 with the capacity to process ten tons of sulphur per day. After its success as a sulphur mine, the Vulcan was struck by lighting. This ignited twenty tons of sulphur stored at the mine. The resulting fire destroyed all of the buildings.

The final phase of mining in the Vulcan area was copper. The increased demand during World War I kept the mines operating. After the end of the war, the mines closed, and Vulcan was abandoned.

As a side note, there was a small unnamed mining camp two miles north of Vulcan on Camp Creek. Today, two cabins still mark the site, and there are signs of mining to the east of the site.

The Good Hope Mine at Vulcan was of considerable size as indicated in this 1912 photograph. The town was located in a shallow valley below the mine. *(U.S.G.S. J.F. Hunter 119)*

Duane Vandenbusche, *The Gunnison Country*, B & B Printers, Gunnison, Colorado, 1980, pp. 296-299.

Muriel Sibell Wolle, *Stampede to Timberline*, Sage Books, Chicago, 1949, pp. 192, 194-195.

William H. Bauer, James L. Ozment and John H. Willard, *Colorado Post Offices*, Colorado Railroad Museum, Golden, Colorado, 1990, pp. 27, 134, 147.

SPRING CREEK CITY
and MOSCOW

- *Gunnison County, Spring Creek drainage*
- *Accessible via graded dirt road;*
- *Both camps had a post office; remaining structures at these sites unknown*

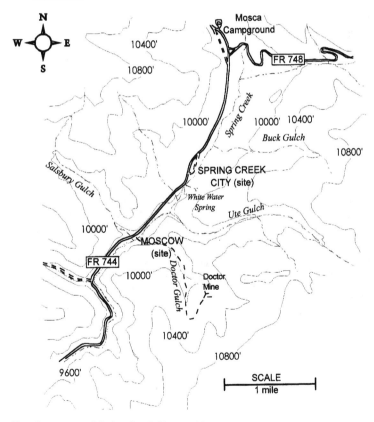

The ghost towns of Spring Creek City and Moscow are located along FR 744, which follows Spring Creek.

Leadville prospectors, led by Martin Brennan, discovered some lead-silver ore high above Spring Creek Canyon and north of the Taylor River. Severe winter conditions drove them out of the high country in 1879, but they did return in the spring of 1880. The result of the discovery was the Doctor Mine, located at 10,200 feet.

Prospectors founded two mining camps along Spring Creek. One became known as Spring Creek City, but at times, it was called Rood City or Petersburg. The camp was located just a mile above the confluence of the creek in Doctor Gulch and Spring Creek. The second camp was at the mouth of Doctor Gulch and was called Moscow.

Until a wagon road was constructed up Spring Creek, the trail into the area was quite hazardous. It came east from Cement Creek to Deadman Gulch.

Spring Creek City soon had a couple of stores and three log cabins plus many tents. Other cabins were under construction during the summer of 1880. By that fall, the small camp also had a hotel and two saloons.

Although other lead-silver lodes were discovered in Gunnison County, the Doctor Mine became the greatest producer. A solid vein of lead carbonate ore, similar to that found in the Leadville area, was uncovered. It was eight feet wide and four to ten feet thick with up to 276 ounces of silver per ton. The ore was packed down a steep trail in Doctor Gulch, then hauled out to a smelter at Abbeyville near Tin Cup.

Under the name Spring, Spring Creek City got its own post office in the spring of 1881, only to have it close the following year when the town was abandoned for the winter.

Moscow was incorporated in May, 1881, and it continued to grow. A dairy was established to satisfy the demand for milk. The local assayer complained that he could not keep up with the flow of ore samples brought in for analysis. Moscow got its own post office in the fall of 1881. It opened under the name Turner for some unknown reason, but as is often the case, the first postmaster probably named the office for himself.

At first, Spring Creek City seemed to grow faster than Moscow, but the close proximity to the Doctor Mine caused Moscow to become the largest of the two towns. Some time during the 1890s, however, the miners decided rather than make the long arduous trip up to the Doctor Mine, they would live by the mine. Moscow was at a far more comfortable altitude of 9,500 feet while the Doctor Mine was at well over 10,000 feet.

Even after the price of silver dropped in 1893, the Doctor Mine continued operation. More development work was done in 1910, and the mine was worked continuously through World War I for its lead and zinc. Mining continued off and on until 1952, and by then, over one million dollars in metals had been removed.

Both sites can be reached on FR 744, a graded dirt road. It is not known what structures remain.

As a side note, a small way station for teamsters to stay overnight was located south of Moscow in Spring Creek Canyon. It was about equal distance between Moscow and the railroad at Almont. The station was called Bogan's Camp, and it had a number of log structures including a livery barn.

Duane Vandenbusche, *The Gunnison Country*, B & B Printers, Gunnison, Colorado, 1980, pp. 324-329.

William H. Bauer, James L. Ozment and John H. Willard, *Colorado Post Offices*, Colorado Railroad Museum, Golden, Colorado, 1990, pp. 135, 144.

TINCUP

And Its Most Hazardous Job

- *Gunnison County, Willow Creek drainage*
- *Accessible via graded dirt road*
- *Town had a post office; many original structures remain*

Virginia City grew to become the largest, most successful mining town in the Willow Creek area. It outlasted all the other nearby camps. It was started in 1879 and was laid out in a large meadow where three branches of Willow Creek converge. Virginia City was on the major supply route over 12,156-foot Tincup Pass from St. Elmo into the Gunnison region. The population of other unsuccessful camps combined with the steady influx of prospectors created an instant town.

By the end of its first year, Virginia City had nearly 1,000 living in and around the town. When the winter of 1879-1880 came, however, nearly all of its residents left for a warmer climate. Of the 120 that stayed, twelve were women and eight were children.

An even bigger rush came as the snow melted in 1880, and a census report showed that the town had 1,500 residents with another 2,000 living in tents in the general area. It was this year that Virginia City was incorporated.

Residents could not agree on the name of the town. Both Nevada and Montana had prominent mining towns called Virginia City. Postal officials knew that this would certainly lead to mail delivery problems. Although a post office had been established in 1879, the following year postal officials changed the name to Tin Cup. This was the name of the mining district. Resistant to change, it took two years of debate for residents to incorporate the town under its new name. The town remained Tin Cup until 1895 when the spelling was changed to a single word, Tincup. This remains the official spelling in use today although many historians prefer the older spelling. The post office lasted until 1918.

Guns were used in Tincup to settle arguments. William Woll arrived in 1879 and decided to pitch his tent next to a saloon. One night, gunfire erupted outside the saloon, and Woll stayed low in his tent. When he got up the next morning, he counted eight bullet holes in the canvas.

The town marshal was Tincup's most hazardous job, and few survived a full term in office. F. B. Willis was elected Tincup's first marshal in 1880. The town's criminal element told him that the first man arrested would be his last. He was to give the appearance of law and order so that robberies could continue

Tincup's town hall, constructed in 1903, now serves as a community church. *(Kenneth Jessen 098C6)*

unimpeded. To this, he carried out his instructions.

Apparently, the residents had had enough. Tom Leahy took over and knew how to shoot. He carried out his duties fearlessly and upheld the law. At one point in time, he marched off angry mob members at gunpoint to jail. This was his way of showing contempt for the lawless element in Tincup.

Frank Emerson became marshal next, but was not liked by his predecessor. In 1882, the two ex-marshals were drunk, and Emerson made a sudden move as if to go for his gun. Leahy drew and fired, killing Emerson with bullets through the neck and the heart. Emerson was unarmed. Leahy was acquitted since the shooting was ruled an accident.

Harry Rivers became the new town marshal and turned up the heat on the disorderly crowds at the saloons. He arrested so many so fast that the jail was soon full, and a night court was necessary to fine those brought in by Rivers. Jack Ward was among the worst thugs in Tincup and struck terror in the mind of anyone he confronted. Ward was involved in a shootout on the streets where over one hundred shots were fired. Rivers intervened, and after an exchange of gunfire, arrested Ward. Ward spent time in jail, and much to everyone's surprise, became a reformed man. He eventually occupied the pulpit in Glenwood Springs.

The next violent encounter in March, 1882, cost Rivers his life. He was called upon to arrest saloonkeeper Charles LaTourette. The *Tin Cup Record* published an account of the incident. LaTourette had threatened to kill a particular fellow, and to stop such an event, Rivers arrested LaTourette on a minor charge. The police magistrate waved any testimony until the following morning. After returning home, LaTourette headed back to his place of business, The Bullion Exchange. He suddenly met Rivers face to face. According to the newspaper account, Rivers drew his gun, cocked it, pulled the trigger and snapped the hammer. He did this several times, but the gun failed to fire. Not wishing to test his luck, LaTourette drew and fired at Rivers. He put three rounds into the marshal's head, dropping Rivers where he stood. LaTourette

598 _____ *Area 12:* TINCUP

was arrested. The case against him was dismissed on the grounds of self-defense.

Tincup's next marshal was Sam Mickey. He reluctantly accepted the post. The constant threats against his life forced him to resign after only seven months. He ended up in an insane asylum and died within a few weeks.

The tin star was put on next by Andy Jameson in 1883. One day, Jameson was in the process of beating a fellow. A friend of the victim, Will Taylor, put an end to the beating and to Jameson's life. Taylor was convicted of murder and served a prison sentence.

The position of town marshal remained unfilled for some time. Finally, to fight fire with fire, a man with a bad reputation was put into the town marshal's position. His name was Dave Corsant. He became the first town marshal to survive a full term in office!

Tincup peaked at around 3,000 residents living in the town or in the immediate area. In 1882, the town had a staggering twenty-six saloons. There were five grocery stores, two butcher shops, a bakery, two banks, two drug stores, a dry goods store, four hotels, a lumber yard and a livery stable. The town also built a schoolhouse, but during its early years, Tincup was void of a church. Hotels included the Grand Central, the Pacific Hotel and Aunt Kate Fisher's Hotel. Similar to the cemetery above Central City, Tincup's place of rest was divided into Catholic, Protestant, Jewish and a "boot hill" section.

What led to Tincup's downfall was the lack of good transportation, severe winter weather and complex ore. The ore was composed of sulfides, carbonates and chlorides containing silver, gold, lead and copper. Had the ore been in a single chemical family, local smelters probably could have been successful.

Miners and prospectors owed little in the way of loyalty to a town. They began leaving for other areas, and by 1886, Tincup had only 400 residents. Just two years later, 300 remained. Since most of the revenue came from silver, the demonetization of silver by the United States in 1893 closed the mines. The price of silver

This photograph dates back to the early part of this century. Fires have destroyed many of the buildings especially in the business district. *(Kenneth Jessen collection)*

fell to nearly half of its former value. Until a second mining boom in 1904, Tincup was nearly deserted. A considerable amount of development work was done between 1904 and 1910 by large mining companies. No great pockets of rich ore were discovered. The area's best mine, Gold Cup, continued to operate until 1917.

The last large-scale mining was gold dredging along Willow Creek north of Tincup near Abbeyville. The Columbine Dredge operated from 1908 until 1912 and lost money every year. It recovered 20,000 ounces of gold, however. The Tin Cup Gold Mining and Dredging Company took over in 1913. A giant 300-ton dredge was constructed with the machinery brought from the railhead at St. Elmo over Tin Cup Pass. To do this, the mining company had to first spend money improving the pass. Since there was no local source of electric power, a power line was laid over the Continental Divide from St. Elmo to the dredge. The dredge dug its way to bedrock and began processing the river gravel. It left behind a 300-foot wide swath of sterile rock. It did no better economically, and operations were discontinued in 1917.

Today, Tincup's buildings are scattered about the town site. There are numerous vacant lots between structures. Much of the town was destroyed in two major fires, one in 1906 and the other in 1913. Even with water supplied from a reservoir and fire hydrants at strategic locations, the town's fire department could not control the flames.

Radio personality Pete Smythe kept the Tincup name alive with his homespun broadcast from a Denver radio station. The broadcast presumably originated from the fictitious mining town of East Tincup.

Tincup is a delightful place to visit during the summer. It has a number of seasonal residents who have restored many of the cabins. In addition, there is a general store and gas station. Tincup also has a fine restaurant just across from the store. Take mosquito repellent, however.

Original Remaining Structures in Tincup

On Grand Avenue:

Beckley Brothers house 1880s
Hillerton Building 1880s
Tincup Store 1900s
Town Hall 1903
John Phillip Korn House 1893
Lowry Englebright House 1880s
Jules Hunsinger cabin 1880s
Lawrence Winsheimer cabin 1890s

On Main Street:

Samuel Gollagher House 1890s
David McWherter House 1880s
William Mitchell House .... circa 1905
Charles LaTourette House .... circa 1900

Don and Jean Griswold, *Colorado's Century of "Cities,"* self-published, 1958, pp. 210-213.

Duane Vandenbusche, *The Gunnison Country*, B & B Printers, Gunnison, Colorado, 1980, pp. 367-373.

Eleanor Perry, *I Remember Tin Cup*, self-published, 1986, p. 11.

George A. Crofutt, *Crofutt's Grip-Sack Guide of Colorado*, 1885 Edition, Johnson Books, Boulder, Colorado, reprint 1981, p. 151.

Monta Hill, *A Place History of Tincup*, (map), 1992

Nolie Mumey, *History of Tin Cup, Colorado*, Johnson Publishing Company, Boulder, Colorado, 1963, pp. 111-116.

William H. Bauer, James L. Ozment and John H. Willard, *Colorado Post Offices*, Colorado Railroad Museum, Golden, Colorado, 1990, pp. 141, 147.

WHITEPINE
And Other Tomichi Creek Towns

- Gunnison County, Tomichi Creek drainage
- Accessible by graded dirt road
- Towns had post offices; several original structures remain at Whitepine

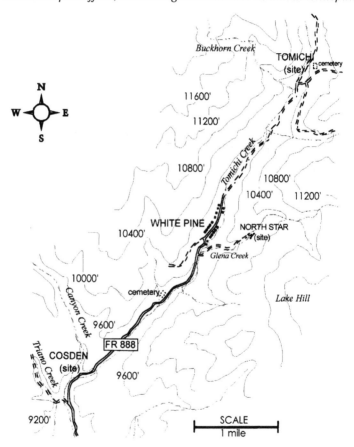

This map shows the principal towns along Tomichi Creek. Whitepine is the only town with population, and it is seasonally occupied.

In May, 1879, five prospectors made their way across the Continental Divide via Old Monarch Pass and descended into Tomichi Valley. They soon discovered lead-silver ore in the Whitepine region and marked out claims. Others followed, and in August, the miners organized the Tomichi Mining District to define the size of claims, formally register claims and to bring some organization to the area.

As the winter of 1879-1880 approached, most left the area and returned over the Continental Divide due to the uncertainty of getting supplies. Most returned the following spring and resumed their work prospecting and developing mines. A toll road over Monarch Pass helped reduce the isolation and improved the flow of provisions. During the winter of 1880-1881, ten to fifteen stayed at the new mining camp of Whitepine.

In 1880, there was sufficient population for Whitepine (earlier spelling was White Pine) to get its own post office. Postal service continued uninterrupted for the next forty-eight years. In 1949, the post office was reopened and remained open until 1954.

The Denver & Rio Grande constructed its narrow gauge railroad over Marshall Pass in 1881. Sargents, located south of Whitepine, became one of the major supply points in the region. Daily stage service began up Tomichi Creek, and soon, a second stagecoach line opened. Other routes to Whitepine included Black Sage and Tomichi passes.

In 1881, the *White Pine Journal* made its first appearance. The newspaper was printed in Maysville east of the Continental Divide and carried by foot to Whitepine. It was the only newspaper carried over the Continental Divide, and it lasted two years. A second newspaper was started in April, 1883 called the *White Pine Cone* and was owned by publisher George Irwin. The first office for the *White Pine Cone* lacked a door, windows and even a floor. Irwin and his assistant stayed in a primitive cabin on Whitepine's only street. He published it for the next nine years and was known for his wit and sarcastic comments. One particular article read, "White Pine suffered an agonizing famine this week. For two whole days, there was not a drop of whiskey in town. Nothing but a liberal supply of peach brandy and bottled beer prevented panic."

Mountain rats are a typical problem, especially in the primitive cabins so typical of a mining town. In the case of Irwin and his assistant, the rats ran under the floor during the night. In desperation, Irwin fired his .44 caliber carbine at the floor at the sound of the rat. It was a lucky shot, and he killed the rat. After lifting the floorboard, the two men found silverware, necklaces and other possessions that had mysteriously vanished. It was a mountain pack rat!

By 1884, Whitepine had five stores, a couple of livery stables, meat market, barbershop and three hotels including the two-story, frame White Pine Hotel. There were three saloons and a small sawmill located near town. About fifty structures lined both sides of Whitepine's main street. Population estimates showed 1,000 either living in Whitepine or in the general vicinity.

The terrain for a town was not ideal. The canyon where Whitepine is located is narrow. On the west side of the main street, structures are quite a bit higher than street level and many had staircases for access. The opposite was true on the east side where the land drops off sharply into Tomichi Creek.

Festivities at the 1885 Fourth of July celebration opened with a thirteen-gun salute. No details survive as to what kinds of guns were used. The salute was followed by the reading of the Declaration of Independence. Contests, such as foot races and sack races, were held in the afternoon. The most spectacular contest was between miners to see who could drill the deepest hole in a piece of granite in fifteen minutes. Fireworks were set off after sunset culminating with the launch of an illuminated balloon.

The town raised the money for a new schoolhouse in 1889. It came largely from generous donations by unmarried men. At its completion, a drama was presented using Whitepine's local talent.

Prosperity did not last, and one of the area's largest mines closed in 1892. The following year, the U. S. abandoned the silver standard, and the price of silver fell to nearly half of its original value. Most of Colorado's silver mines closed, never to reopen. Soon, Whitepine was nearly deserted.

An interesting story appeared in the *Gunnison News-Champion.* So vital was the outcome to the vote by the U. S. Senate on the issue of demonetizing the currency that a large crowd gathered at the telegraph office at Sargents. Loaded ore wagons were waiting in line to be unloaded of their silver ore destined for shipment to a smelter.

The telegraph agent alerted the crowd that a message was coming over the wire. It was not good news; the Senate passed the bill to remove silver as a backing for U. S. currency. A second message came in from railroad officials not to ship any more silver ore, and the final message, also from railroad officials, was to not accept any ore at Sargents.

The courier, who was assisting the telegraph agent, mounted his horse and dashed off toward Whitepine. As he passed loaded ore wagon after ore wagon, he shouted, "unload; turn in." He had a fresh horse waiting at the halfway point in the trip so he could deliver the message to Whitepine residents as quickly as

Tomichi's Main Street *(drawing by Julia McMillan)*

possible. Many discouraged freighters dumped their load and returned home.

Henry Lake and two other prospectors crossed the Continental Divide in the spring of 1879 searching for precious metals. They struck a rich vein of silver in June at the base of Lake Hill. After digging out several tons of ore, they hid their find under tree branches. Several other miners came by to find out how they had done. The three men sat on the pile of branches and stated firmly that they had found nothing. After the curious miners left, Lake and his companions staked their claim, which they called the North Star.

Originally, the mining camp of North Star was called Lake's Camp. It was born out of necessity by eliminating the commute from Whitepine. In 1886, the town had grown to twenty privately owned homes and was incorporated. It also had two hotels and two boarding houses. There was one grocery store and one saloon.

In 1889, Lake's Camp got its own post office, and in 1900, the name was changed to North Star. The post office remained open until 1903. The town reached a population of about 100 and

This old structure in Whitepine probably dates back to its early days as a mining camp. Modern mountain homes are interspersed among Whitepine's older buildings. *(Kenneth Jessen 095D12)*

eventually, the Bon Ton Restaurant was added to its businesses as well as a second saloon.

The nearby May-Mazeppa Mine produced so much ore there were times when teamsters couldn't handle the volume. The May-Mazeppa kept as many as eleven teams hauling ore continuously. The output from the North Star Mine almost matched that of the May-Mazeppa Mine. The Denver & Rio Grande considered building a branch line north from Sargents up Tomichi Creek to serve the area. Both mines, however, went bankrupt in 1892, and the town of North Star was abandoned.

At the turn of the century, mining resumed in the Whitepine area. Zinc yielded the most profit and silver became a byproduct.

North Star is less than a mile up Glena Gulch east of Whitepine. The road requires four-wheel drive and is full of large river gravel. It follows a streambed, and it is like driving in a trench. The road leaves the graded dirt road just south of Whitepine at the extensive mill tailings pile. There is a locked gate at the bridge over Glena Creek. The town site has been fenced off in recent years and is posted no trespassing. A modern structure sits in the small flat area where once the town of North Star was located. There are a few crumbling frame cabins at the site.

Over the years, North Star has been a favorite haunt for ghost town historians. The Colorado Division of Commerce and Development sent a photographer into the area probably during the 1930s. This photograph of North Star shows several log structures, but a substantial number of clapboard frame buildings.

Muriel Sibell Wolle visited North Star in 1941 when working on *Stampede to Timberline*. She discovered ten standing structures including the office of the Morning Star Mine, a false-front white boarding house and a two-story building made of hand-hewn logs. The boarding house was called the Leadville House, and the log structure once served as the town's post office. The buildings were still furnished, and a pile of schoolbooks was found in the mining office dating back to 1914. No one lived at North Star at the time.

When Robert Brown visited North Star during the 1960s, a false-front store was still standing beside the large hand-hewn log structure. Both were in relatively good condition. Sandra Dallas visited North Star while working on her book, *Colorado Ghost Towns and Mining Camps*, two decades later. Photographs taken by her daughter, Kendal Atchison, show the log structure leaning a little, but the false-front store had partially collapsed. Today, neither structure remains.

Near the headwaters of Tomichi Creek, the small mining town of Tomichi was founded. Laid out in a meadow, it was located between two high peaks. Silver ore was discovered in 1876 by a number of prospectors. The first mining camp was called Glenwood, and it was a half-mile above Tomichi. Glenwood was deserted and in 1884, was destroyed by an avalanche.

Tomichi was laid out in the spring of 1880 and was initially called Argenta. It got its own post office in July, and the following month, the town and the post office became Tomichi. The population of Tomichi peaked at about 500, but a total of 1,000 lived in the general area. In 1882, the *Tomichi Herald* began publication. So strapped for funds, the newspaper used wrapping paper to save money. The paper discontinued publishing in 1885, and the *White Pine Cone* took over as the voice of the region.

Tomichi had a bank, established in 1882, plus a number of stores, several saloons, hotels and a concentration mill to save shipping costs. Historic photographs show Tomichi's main street with false-front stores on either side. The town had at least thirty structures of various types. The Bank of Tomichi shared its space with a supply store. The Cummings House was a story-and-a-half log, half frame structure. The largest mine in the area was the Magna Carta Tunnel. Its entrance was on the edge of town.

The Magna Carta Tunnel was started in 1881, and it eventually reached nearly a mile in length. It undercut several lodes of silver ore. As timber was cut from the mountains above the mine, the avalanche danger increased on the denuded slopes. In 1884, after two weeks of constant snowfall, an avalanche smashed into the blacksmith shop, nearly killing two workers. Just after the rescue party left the area, a larger slide destroyed the mine's surface structures, piling snow 100 feet deep on the valley floor.

The concentrator at Tomichi was destroyed by fire in 1883 and was not rebuilt. This meant that only the highest-grade ore was economical to mine. Transportation costs were too high for most mines to continue operation. Severe weather made mining a seasonal proposition, and the Magna Carta Tunnel survived as the only significant mining operation near Tomichi.

The 1884 avalanche that destroyed the Magna Carta buildings was just a warning. The winter of 1898-1899 was quite severe throughout the Colorado mountains. In March, Tomichi was smashed to splinters by a massive slide, and in the process, four residents died. Those that were trapped and survived in the debris waited for many hours before being rescued. This was the end of the town, and the few remaining residents moved to Whitepine. All that remains at the site today is the small cemetery.

Where Canyon Creek and Tomichi Creek join was a stage station called Cosden. Originally named Wagon Town, its name was changed to Healsburg, but it was also called El Tinjos or Redwood. It was founded in 1880, and originally, it was the farthest point up Tomichi Creek that wagons could pass. Prospectors going into the Whitepine-Tomichi area would leave their wagon and begin packing their supplies on their backs. After a decent wagon road was constructed, it became the place where teamsters could stop, rest their horses and get something to eat. In 1883, residents settled on Cosden as the name of the town. Aside from a few cabins, Cosden had a stage station combination restaurant and saloon. It also had a livery barn. It was an active lumber camp during the early 1880s and supplied ties to the Denver & Rio Grande.

Cosden's importance grew when a sampling works was constructed to treat ore from the smaller mines. In 1901, a smelter was constructed at the site. It employed twenty-five men.

A post office opened in 1883 and lasted two years. Cosden, by this time, had a grocery store, hotel, boarding house, a number of cabins and of course, the stage station. With a population of 100, a city hall was constructed in 1884. When the area mines closed after the silver crash in 1893, Cosden lost most of its population. The ruins of the smelter are all that are left at the Cosden site.

Duane Vandenbusche, *The Gunnison Country*, B & B Printers, Gunnison, Colorado, 1980, pp. 392-401.

George A. Crofutt, *Crofutt's Grip-Sack Guide of Colorado*, 1885 Edition, Johnson Books, Boulder, Colorado, reprint 1981, p. 151.

Muriel Sibell Wolle, *Stampede to Timberline*, Sage Books, Chicago, 1949, pp. 169-176.

Robert L. Brown, *Jeep Trails to Colorado Ghost Towns*, Caxton Printers, Caldwell, Idaho, 1963, pp. 152-154.

Sandra Dallas, *Colorado Ghost Towns and Mining Camps*, University of Oklahoma Press, Norman, Oklahoma, 1985, pp. 142-143.

William H. Bauer, James L. Ozment and John H. Willard, *Colorado Post Offices*, Colorado Railroad Museum, Golden, Colorado, 1990, pp. 13, 142, 106, 151.

INDEX